NON-LEAGUE FOOTBALL TABLES OF THE WEST MIDLANDS OF ENGLAND 1889-2019

EDITOR
Michael Robinson

FOREWORD

Following the success of our 'Non-League Football Tables' series of books, the first of which was published in 2002, we long considered introducing a number of regionalised titles about various football leagues both past and present.

The first book in the eventual series, 'Non-League Football Tables of South West England 1892-2015' was published in 2015 and 'Non-League Football Tables of North West England 1889-2016', 'Non-League Football Tables of South East England 1894-2017' and 'Non-League Football Tables of North East England 1889-2018' were published in subsequent years. All of these books are available for purchase at our address shown below, each priced £11.99.

This fifth book, of a planned series of six, covers eight football leagues from the West Midlands region of England. The earliest of these commenced in 1889 and still continues to operate to this day.

The Leagues which currently form the apex of the 'Non-League Pyramid', namely the National League (formerly the Football Conference) and its three feeder leagues (Northern Premier, Southern Premier & Isthmian) continue to be covered by our yearly National League and Non-League Football Tables books.

As always, we are indebted to Mick Blakeman for providing tables for the various Leagues included in this book.

British Library Cataloguing in Publication Data
A catalogue record for this book is available from the British Library

ISBN: 978-1-86223-414-7

Copyright © 2019 Soccer Books Limited, 72 St. Peters Avenue, Cleethorpes, DN35 8HU, United Kingdom (01472 696226)

All rights are reserved. No part of this publication may be reproduced, stored into a retrieval system or transmitted, in any form or by any means, electronic, mechanical, photocopying, recording, or otherwise, without the prior written permission of Soccer Books Limited.

Printed in the UK by 4edge Ltd.

CONTENTS

West Midlands (Regional) League 1889-2019 .... Pages 4-47
    (Formerly the Birmingham & District League)

Shropshire & District League 1890-1900 .... Pages 48-50

Birmingham Combination 1892-1954 .... Pages 50-62
    (Formerly the Birmingham & District Junior League)

Staffordshire County League (South) 1892-1996 .... Pages 62-82
    (Also including the Walsall & District Junior League, Walsall & District League and Walsall Senior League)

Midland Combination 1927-2014 .... Pages 82-116
    (Formerly the Worcestershire Combination)

Warwickshire Combination 1953-1967 .... Pages 117-121
    (Formerly the South Warwickshire League)

Midland Football Alliance 1994-2014 .... Pages 121-126

Midland League 2014-2019 .... Pages 126-130

WEST MIDLANDS (REGIONAL) LEAGUE 1889-2019
(Formerly the Birmingham & District League)

The formation of the Football League in 1888 was highly successful and the following year several more leagues were formed in areas where there were already a significant number of established clubs. In the Birmingham district, 3 of its major clubs – Aston Villa, West Bromwich Albion and Wolverhampton Wanderers – had been founder members of the Football League and 3 more – Birmingham St. Georges, Walsall Town Swifts (later just Walsall) and Small Heath (later Birmingham City) – became founder members of the second tier Football Alliance in 1889.

There were still many more established clubs in the West Midlands and so a meeting was called at the Grand Hotel in Birmingham on 31st May 1889 to form the Birmingham & District League. Of the 17 clubs who were invited, 13 sent representatives but it was decided to start with a 12-team league.

The 12 clubs selected were: Aston Victoria, Great Bridge Unity, Hednesford Town, Ironbridge, Kidderminster Harriers, Kidderminster Olympic, Langley Green Victoria, Oldbury Town, Smethwick Carriage Works, Unity Gas Department, Wellington St. Georges and Willenhall Pickwick. The 13th club who attended the meeting but were not admitted to the league was Worcester Rovers.

BIRMINGHAM & DISTRICT LEAGUE

1889-90

Kidderminster Olympic	21	19	2	0	84	9	40
Kidderminster Harriers	21	13	2	6	75	38	28
Oldbury Town	21	11	4	6	43	33	26
Smethwick Carriage Works	21	11	3	7	72	46	25
Langley Green Victoria	21	9	7	5	52	40	25
Hednesford Town	19	7	3	9	50	72	17
Wellington St. Georges	21	6	5	10	41	61	17
Aston Victoria	20	7	1	12	53	64	15
Unity Gas Department	21	5	5	11	37	68	15
Willenhall Pickwick	21	5	4	12	44	78	14
Ironbridge	22	5	3	14	46	65	13
Great Bridge Unity	19	6	1	12	41	64	13

8 games were not played so no champions were officially declared.

Kidderminster Olympic and Kidderminster Harriers merged and moved to the Midland League as Kidderminster, entering their reserves in the Birmingham League as Kidderminster Rovers. Aston Victoria changed their name to County Victoria and moved to the Warwickshire County Cricket Ground at Edgbaston following the demise of Warwick County who had been playing there, having links with the county cricket club. Ironbridge and Wellington St. Georges both left and joined the newly formed Shropshire & District League and Great Bridge Unity, Unity Gas Department and Willenhall Pickwick also left. Brierley Hill Alliance, Burton Alma, Stourbridge and Wednesbury Old Athletic joined but the league was reduced to 10 clubs.

1890-91

Brierley Hill Alliance	17	9	5	3	41	23	23
Oldbury Town	15	8	2	5	31	35	18
Hednesford Town	13	8	1	4	46	15	17
Stourbridge	15	8	1	6	30	33	17
Langley Green Victoria	13	6	3	4	32	24	15
Wednesbury Old Athletic	11	6	1	4	37	22	13
Smethwick Carriage Works	16	6	1	9	35	47	13
Burton Alma	15	4	2	9	21	37	10
County Victoria	15	4	1	10	26	41	9
Kidderminster Rovers	12	3	1	8	13	35	7

19 games were not played so no champions were officially declared. Kidderminster disbanded in March 1891 and their reserves, Kidderminster Rovers, withdrew from the league but their record was not deleted. Kidderminster Harriers and Kidderminster Olympic both reformed and joined the league for the 1891-92 season but Olympic folded before the start of the season. County Victoria changed their name back to Aston Victoria. Wednesbury Old Athletic moved to the Midland League and Burton Alma and Hednesford Town also left. Great Bridge Unity and Redditch Town joined but only 9 clubs competed in the league.

1891-92

Brierley Hill Alliance	15	12	2	1	56	8	26
Stourbridge	15	10	2	3	39	17	22
Aston Victoria	16	9	3	4	47	22	21
Smethwick Carriage Works	16	5	5	6	27	29	15
Kidderminster Harriers	15	5	4	6	25	30	14
Redditch Town	13	5	2	6	21	31	12
Langley Green Victoria	15	3	3	9	27	42	9
Oldbury Town	13	1	5	7	8	37	7
Great Bridge Unity	12	1	2	9	10	44	4

9 games were not played so no champions were officially declared.

West Midlands (Regional) League 1892-1898

Great Bridge Unity and Oldbury Town both disbanded during the season and were unable to complete their fixtures but their records were not deleted. Aston Victoria disbanded at the end of the season and Langley Green Victoria also left the league. Wolverhampton Wanderers Reserves joined from the Shropshire & District League and Aston Villa Reserves, Halesowen, Old Hill Wanderers and West Bromwich Albion Reserves also joined, increasing the league to 10 clubs.

1892-93

Wolverhampton Wanderers Reserves	18	15	1	2	66	12	31
Aston Villa Reserves	18	15	1	2	81	18	31
Brierley Hill Alliance	18	11	1	6	38	23	23
West Bromwich Albion Reserves	18	8	5	5	33	25	21
Stourbridge	18	9	2	7	42	36	20
Old Hill Wanderers	18	7	4	7	34	43	18
Kidderminster Harriers	18	5	6	7	33	41	16
Redditch Town	18	4	2	12	23	53	10
Smethwick Carriage Works	18	3	2	13	20	69	8
Halesowen	18	0	2	16	14	64	2

Stafford Rangers joined from the Shropshire & District League and Berwick Rangers, Small Heath Reserves and Worcester Rovers also joined, increasing the league to 14 clubs.

1893-94

Old Hill Wanderers	26	19	2	5	70	30	40
Aston Villa Reserves	26	16	5	5	76	46	37
Wolverhampton Wanderers Reserves	26	14	5	7	66	39	33
Stourbridge	26	13	6	7	46	36	32
Halesowen	26	12	6	8	63	48	30
Brierley Hill Alliance	26	12	5	9	67	42	29
Small Heath Reserves	26	13	3	10	65	55	29
West Bromwich Albion Reserves	26	10	6	10	53	43	26
Worcester Rovers	26	10	4	12	53	61	24
Berwick Rangers	26	9	3	14	43	76	21
Smethwick Carriage Works	26	7	5	14	38	55	19
Stafford Rangers	26	5	6	15	38	70	16
Redditch Town	26	4	7	15	37	68	15
Kidderminster Harriers	26	6	1	19	36	82	13

Oldbury Town joined from the Birmingham Junior League and Singers (Coventry) also joined. Smethwick Carriage Works changed their name to Smethwick.
The League was increased to 16 clubs.

1894-95

Aston Villa Reserves	30	26	3	1	133	35	55
West Bromwich Albion Reserves	30	23	4	3	100	49	50
Stourbridge	30	21	3	6	93	44	45
Wolverhampton Wanderers Reserves	30	20	4	6	106	46	44
Berwick Rangers	30	14	9	7	51	41	37
Small Heath Reserves	30	16	4	10	118	65	36
Oldbury Town	30	13	3	14	64	64	29
Worcester Rovers	30	11	5	14	72	72	27
Brierley Hill Alliance	30	12	3	15	53	65	27
Old Hill Wanderers	30	11	5	14	44	65	27
Kidderminster Harriers	30	10	6	14	64	74	26
Redditch Town	30	12	0	18	64	96	24
Singers (Coventry)	30	7	5	18	46	91	19
Halesowen	30	4	5	21	45	102	13
Stafford Rangers	30	5	2	23	45	106	12
Smethwick	30	3	3	24	26	109	9

Old Hill Wanderers disbanded and Smethwick left the league.
Hereford Thistle joined from the Western League and Shrewsbury Town joined from the Shropshire & District League.

1895-96

Aston Villa Reserves	30	21	6	3	84	29	48
Small Heath Reserves	30	21	5	4	100	35	47
Wolverhampton Wanderers Reserves	30	20	4	6	98	35	44
West Bromwich Albion Reserves	30	18	5	7	100	46	41
Stourbridge	30	15	6	9	50	30	36
Berwick Rangers	30	15	3	12	57	51	33
Hereford Thistle	30	15	3	12	61	62	33
Kidderminster Harriers	30	11	7	12	44	41	29
Halesowen	30	13	3	14	64	80	29
Worcester Rovers	30	12	4	14	51	55	28
Brierley Hill Alliance	30	9	5	16	40	59	23
Shrewsbury Town	30	8	5	17	46	98	21
Singers (Coventry)	30	9	2	19	36	68	20
Redditch Town	30	7	5	18	45	90	19
Oldbury Town	30	6	6	18	41	86	18
Stafford Rangers	30	5	1	24	35	87	11

Stafford Rangers moved to the North Staffordshire League and Hereford Town joined from the Shropshire League.

1896-97

Hereford Thistle	30	23	3	4	82	25	49
Wolverhampton Wanderers Reserves	30	20	4	6	77	29	44
Small Heath Reserves	30	15	8	7	76	43	38
Berwick Rangers	30	14	6	10	51	41	34
Hereford Town	30	14	5	11	60	47	33
Brierley Hill Alliance	30	14	5	11	53	52	33
Aston Villa Reserves	30	12	8	10	49	40	32
Worcester Rovers	30	10	10	10	56	65	30
Stourbridge	30	10	9	11	63	52	29
Kidderminster Harriers	30	10	8	12	52	45	28
West Bromwich Albion Reserves	30	11	4	15	56	68	26
Shrewsbury Town	30	11	3	16	58	67	25
Singers (Coventry)	30	10	5	15	45	63	25
Halesowen	30	11	3	16	49	91	25
Oldbury Town	30	6	7	17	34	60	19
Redditch Town	30	3	4	23	49	122	10

Oldbury Town moved to the Walsall & District League and Redditch Town moved to the Studley League. Bristol Eastville Rovers and Bristol St. Georges joined while continuing to play in the Western League.

1897-98

Wolverhampton Wanderers Reserves	30	21	8	1	93	16	50
Aston Villa Reserves	30	19	6	5	107	36	44
Bristol Eastville Rovers	30	20	4	6	84	34	44
Worcester Rovers	30	20	2	8	64	43	42
Small Heath Reserves	30	17	7	6	83	49	41
Bristol St. Georges	30	12	6	12	50	45	30
Singers (Coventry)	30	13	3	14	50	59	29
Hereford Thistle	30	11	5	14	55	62	27
Stourbridge	30	11	5	14	45	65	27
Berwick Rangers	30	11	3	16	53	63	25
Shrewsbury Town	30	10	3	17	44	65	23
West Bromwich Albion Reserves	30	11	1	18	56	88	23
Hereford Town	30	9	5	16	33	64	23
Halesowen	30	8	6	16	58	81	22
Brierley Hill Alliance	30	6	4	20	43	83	16
Kidderminster Harriers	30	6	2	22	31	96	14

Dudley St. James of the West Midlands League were elected but in the event, a newly formed professional club called Dudley took their place.
Wellington Town joined from the Shropshire & District League and Singers (Coventry) changed their name to Coventry City.
The League was increased to 18 clubs.

West Midlands (Regional) League 1898-1904

1898-99

Team	P	W	D	L	F	A	Pts
Wolverhampton Wanderers Reserves	34	29	2	3	118	19	60
Aston Villa Reserves	34	26	5	3	142	45	57
Stourbridge	34	21	5	8	85	54	47
Bristol Eastville Rovers	34	20	5	9	132	49	45
Small Heath Reserves	34	18	5	11	88	64	41
Bristol St. Georges	34	17	5	12	87	69	39
Coventry City	34	13	7	14	57	63	33
West Bromwich Albion Reserves	34	14	5	15	65	81	33
Brierley Hill Alliance	34	14	4	16	57	82	32
Halesowen	34	13	2	19	70	84	28
Wellington Town	34	11	6	17	44	82	28
Hereford Town	34	10	7	17	41	63	27
Shrewsbury Town	34	10	6	18	65	90	26
Dudley	34	10	6	18	51	88	26
Kidderminster Harriers	34	11	4	19	45	85	26
Hereford Thistle	34	10	5	19	49	94	25
Worcester Rovers	34	8	5	21	48	89	21
Berwick Rangers	34	7	4	23	52	95	18

Bristol Eastville Rovers moved to the Southern League and were replaced by their reserves. Bristol St. Georges and Hereford Thistle both disbanded. Wellington St. Georges and Walsall Reserves both joined from the Shropshire & District League.

1899-1900

Team	P	W	D	L	F	A	Pts
Aston Villa Reserves	30	21	7	2	93	37	49
Wolverhampton Wanderers Reserves	30	20	3	7	73	30	43
Dudley	30	19	4	7	93	43	42
Small Heath Reserves	30	16	4	10	63	49	36
West Bromwich Albion Reserves	30	14	4	12	69	57	32
Hereford Town	30	12	8	10	47	42	32
Stourbridge	30	11	9	10	73	59	31
Wellington Town	30	11	7	12	59	50	29
Bristol Rovers Reserves	30	11	6	13	50	63	28
Kidderminster Harriers	30	11	6	13	47	74	28
Halesowen	30	11	5	14	69	59	27
Brierley Hill Alliance	30	10	6	14	50	66	26
Walsall Reserves	30	9	6	15	51	81	24
Shrewsbury Town	30	9	3	18	40	73	21
Berwick Rangers	30	7	3	20	41	82	17
Coventry City	30	6	3	21	47	100	15

Worcester Rovers resigned in mid-January and their record was deleted when it stood as follows: 17 3 1 13 20 65 7
Wellington St. Georges disbanded in early February and their record was deleted when it stood as: 19 1 3 15 17 41 5
Bristol Rovers Reserves and Walsall Reserves also left the league.
Stafford Rangers and Stoke Reserves both joined from the North Staffordshire & District League, Ironbridge joined from the Shropshire & District League and Ruabon Druids joined from The Combination.

1900-01

Team	P	W	D	L	F	A	Pts
Wolverhampton Wanderers Reserves	34	29	3	2	107	18	61
Aston Villa Reserves	34	23	6	5	116	37	52
Stourbridge	34	17	8	9	68	52	42
Stoke Reserves	34	17	5	12	80	51	39
West Bromwich Albion Reserves	34	16	6	12	83	62	38
Stafford Rangers	34	16	6	12	57	49	38
Halesowen	34	16	6	12	82	71	38
Dudley	34	17	2	15	71	65	36
Small Heath Reserves	34	12	9	13	73	57	33
Brierley Hill Alliance	34	12	8	14	64	80	32
Hereford Town	34	13	6	15	46	61	32
Ruabon Druids	34	11	9	14	61	62	31
Berwick Rangers	34	12	6	16	48	53	30
Coventry City	34	10	6	18	63	102	26
Ironbridge	34	10	4	20	58	85	24
Wellington Town	34	9	5	20	50	89	23
Kidderminster Harriers	34	9	2	23	44	110	20
Shrewsbury Town	34	7	3	24	29	96	17

Wellington Town moved to The Combination.
Crewe Alexandra joined from the Lancashire League.

1901-02

Team	P	W	D	L	F	A	Pts
West Bromwich Albion Reserves	34	26	2	6	126	32	54
Stourbridge	34	21	4	9	77	46	46
Crewe Alexandra	34	20	4	10	93	54	44
Aston Villa Reserves	34	18	6	10	91	49	42
Small Heath Reserves	34	19	4	11	79	45	42
Dudley	34	20	2	12	76	76	42
Wolverhampton Wanderers Reserves	34	17	6	11	74	50	40
Stafford Rangers	34	18	2	14	85	68	38
Stoke Reserves	34	15	6	13	50	45	36
Ironbridge	34	15	3	16	61	67	33
Shrewsbury Town	34	14	4	16	57	80	32
Brierley Hill Alliance	34	13	4	17	75	82	30
Ruabon Druids	34	12	4	18	54	82	28
Halesowen	34	11	5	18	54	94	27
Berwick Rangers	34	11	4	19	59	71	26
Coventry City	34	7	6	21	42	97	20
Hereford Town	34	6	6	22	31	75	18
Kidderminster Harriers	34	5	4	25	38	109	14

Hereford Town ceased playing altogether.
Wellington Town joined from The Combination.

1902-03

Team	P	W	D	L	F	A	Pts
Aston Villa Reserves	34	21	9	4	96	30	51
Crewe Alexandra	34	22	2	10	92	51	46
West Bromwich Albion Reserves	34	19	7	8	68	37	45
Stourbridge	34	18	5	11	81	49	41
Wolverhampton Wanderers Reserves	34	17	6	11	81	61	40
Shrewsbury Town	34	13	11	10	60	44	37
Coventry City	34	15	6	13	75	67	36
Small Heath Reserves	34	14	8	12	67	61	36
Stafford Rangers	34	16	3	15	67	62	35
Stoke Reserves	34	14	6	14	63	45	34
Ruabon Druids	34	13	5	16	48	58	31
Dudley	34	13	5	16	56	77	31
Kidderminster Harriers	34	12	6	16	70	68	30
Halesowen	34	11	7	16	52	72	29
* Worcester City	34	12	2	20	40	67	26
Wellington Town	34	10	5	19	66	101	25
Brierley Hill Alliance	34	10	4	20	51	75	24
Ironbridge	34	4	7	23	35	143	15

* Berwick Rangers started the season but was liquidated as a limited company in mid-September 1902. A new club, Worcester City, was formed which took over Berwicks record and completed their remaining fixtures. This record stood as follows: 2 1 0 1 3 3 2
Ironbridge disbanded at the end of the season and were replaced by Walsall who joined from the Midland League.

1903-04

Team	P	W	D	L	F	A	Pts
Aston Villa Reserves	34	24	4	6	117	33	52
Stoke Reserves	34	21	6	7	89	55	48
Wellington Town	34	18	7	9	75	57	43
Crewe Alexandra	34	17	7	10	57	57	41
Small Heath Reserves	34	17	6	11	82	59	40
West Bromwich Albion Reserves	34	15	7	12	73	50	37
Wolverhampton Wanderers Reserves	34	16	5	13	71	69	37
Stourbridge	34	13	10	11	80	58	36
Stafford Rangers	34	13	9	12	65	59	35
Shrewsbury Town	34	14	6	14	51	48	34
Coventry City	34	12	7	15	53	58	31
Kidderminster Harriers	34	12	6	16	57	66	30
Walsall	34	11	7	16	45	65	29
Halesowen	34	9	7	18	45	81	25
Worcester City	34	7	11	16	39	91	25
Ruabon Druids	34	10	4	20	63	78	24
Brierley Hill Alliance	34	7	10	17	47	77	24
Dudley	34	7	7	20	39	87	21

Ruabon Druids moved to The Combination. Burslem Port Vale Reserves joined from the North Staffordshire & District League.

West Midlands (Regional) League 1904-1910

1904-05

Team	P	W	D	L	F	A	Pts
Aston Villa Reserves	34	23	4	7	109	34	50
Stoke Reserves	34	20	5	9	68	33	45
Kidderminster Harriers	34	17	10	7	54	32	44
Wolverhampton Wanderers Reserves	34	17	9	8	66	39	43
Small Heath Reserves	34	19	4	11	75	59	42
Crewe Alexandra	34	16	9	9	53	44	41
Stafford Rangers	34	15	6	13	49	49	36
Brierley Hill Alliance	34	15	4	15	59	53	34
Worcester City	34	15	4	15	44	53	34
Dudley	34	13	6	15	55	62	32
Wellington Town	34	13	5	16	51	59	31
Burslem Port Vale Reserves	34	9	12	13	57	62	30
Stourbridge	34	13	3	18	43	56	29
Walsall	34	11	6	17	44	77	28
West Bromwich Albion Reserves	34	11	5	18	48	79	27
Shrewsbury Town	34	10	4	20	42	63	24
Coventry City	34	9	4	21	51	82	22
Halesowen	34	7	6	21	45	77	20

Halesowen moved to the Walsall & District League, Wrexham joined from The Combination and Small Heath changed their name to Birmingham.

1905-06

Team	P	W	D	L	F	A	Pts
Aston Villa Reserves	34	24	5	5	121	46	53
Wolverhampton Wanderers Reserves	34	22	5	7	81	43	49
West Bromwich Albion Reserves	34	21	6	7	106	51	48
Crewe Alexandra	34	16	12	6	58	39	44
Birmingham Reserves	34	16	7	11	91	58	39
Wrexham	34	17	5	12	72	55	39
Stourbridge	34	15	6	13	68	49	36
Stoke Reserves	34	14	7	13	71	60	35
Brierley Hill Alliance	34	15	5	14	74	70	35
Shrewsbury Town	34	15	3	16	57	84	33
Coventry City	34	13	6	15	64	61	32
Dudley	34	11	10	13	53	56	32
Kidderminster Harriers	34	12	6	16	42	51	30
Stafford Rangers	34	10	8	16	44	52	28
Worcester City	34	7	7	20	53	91	21
Walsall	34	7	6	21	42	89	20
Wellington Town	34	9	2	23	47	134	20
Burslem Port Vale Reserves	34	8	2	24	47	102	18

Wellington Town moved to the Walsall & District League swapping places with Halesowen who moved in the opposite direction.

1906-07

Team	P	W	D	L	F	A	Pts
Aston Villa Reserves	34	23	4	7	102	44	50
Birmingham Reserves	34	19	5	10	84	47	43
Kidderminster Harriers	34	18	7	9	69	44	43
West Bromwich Albion Reserves	34	18	6	10	78	50	42
Wolverhampton Wanderers Reserves	34	16	7	11	55	48	39
Brierley Hill Alliance	34	17	3	14	66	61	37
Coventry City	34	16	4	14	70	58	36
Crewe Alexandra	34	15	4	15	58	56	34
Stoke Reserves	34	13	8	13	62	64	34
Wrexham	34	14	6	14	68	76	34
Stourbridge	34	13	6	15	60	63	32
Halesowen	34	14	4	16	63	72	32
Walsall	34	14	4	16	58	79	32
Worcester City	34	12	5	17	69	75	29
Dudley	34	10	6	18	58	75	26
Stafford Rangers	34	10	6	18	56	89	26
Burslem Port Vale Reserves	34	8	8	18	53	83	24
Shrewsbury Town	34	7	5	22	61	106	19

Burslem Port Vale disbanded.
Burton United joined from the Football League – Division Two.

1907-08

Team	P	W	D	L	F	A	Pts
Aston Villa Reserves	34	23	5	6	92	36	51
Crewe Alexandra	34	20	7	7	80	41	47
West Bromwich Albion Reserves	34	19	5	10	86	54	43
Coventry City	34	18	3	13	97	64	39
Shrewsbury Town	34	16	7	11	67	65	39
Wrexham	34	14	9	11	51	56	37
Kidderminster Harriers	34	16	5	13	55	64	37
Worcester City	34	17	2	15	76	56	36
Stafford Rangers	34	16	3	15	57	68	35
Walsall	34	15	3	16	67	72	33
Stoke Reserves	34	12	9	13	53	57	33
Dudley	34	14	4	16	57	68	32
Burton United	34	14	3	17	51	50	31
Birmingham Reserves	34	12	7	15	54	63	31
Halesowen	34	14	2	18	55	62	30
Brierley Hill Alliance	34	7	9	18	43	81	23
Wolverhampton Wanderers Reserves	34	8	6	20	53	76	22
Stourbridge	34	5	3	26	31	92	13

Coventry City moved to the Southern League.
Stoke dropped out of the Football League and placed their first team in the Birmingham League instead of their reserves.
Wellington Town joined from the Walsall & District League.

1908-09

Team	P	W	D	L	F	A	Pts
Aston Villa Reserves	34	24	6	4	118	36	54
Crewe Alexandra	34	23	4	6	99	42	52
Wolverhampton Wanderers Reserves	34	21	6	7	71	46	48
West Bromwich Albion Reserves	34	18	6	10	85	43	42
Brierley Hill Alliance	34	14	8	12	57	54	36
Shrewsbury Town	34	11	13	10	51	48	35
Kidderminster Harriers	34	13	6	15	58	85	32
Stoke	34	13	5	16	71	64	31
Worcester City	34	14	3	17	71	70	31
Stafford Rangers	34	11	9	14	51	63	31
Wrexham	34	14	3	17	60	76	31
Birmingham Reserves	34	11	7	16	53	73	29
Burton United	34	13	3	18	48	75	29
Stourbridge	34	9	10	15	49	57	28
Walsall	34	10	8	16	47	56	28
Wellington Town	34	11	5	18	60	86	27
Halesowen	34	11	4	19	42	83	26
Dudley	34	10	2	22	55	89	22

1909-10

Team	P	W	D	L	F	A	Pts
Aston Villa Reserves	34	25	4	5	98	36	54
Crewe Alexandra	34	23	3	8	117	56	49
Wolverhampton Wanderers Reserves	34	22	5	7	74	46	49
Brierley Hill Alliance	34	19	8	7	79	49	46
Walsall	34	18	7	9	66	44	43
Birmingham Reserves	34	17	7	10	73	60	41
Stoke	34	15	7	12	82	52	37
West Bromwich Albion Reserves	34	16	5	13	76	65	37
Stourbridge	34	15	3	16	78	74	33
Wrexham	34	13	7	14	61	62	33
Shrewsbury Town	34	13	5	16	48	63	31
Worcester City	34	10	9	15	65	66	29
Wellington Town	34	10	7	17	48	76	27
Kidderminster Harriers	34	9	6	19	52	83	24
Dudley	34	9	5	20	65	87	23
Stafford Rangers	34	9	5	20	48	80	23
Halesowen	34	8	3	23	44	90	19
Burton United	34	6	2	26	36	121	14

Burton United disbanded.
Wednesbury Old Athletic joined from the Birmingham Combination.

1910-11

Stoke	34	24	2	8	95	48	50
Aston Villa Reserves	34	22	4	8	97	41	48
Walsall	34	20	6	8	60	44	46
Wrexham	34	17	7	10	74	52	41
Crewe Alexandra	34	16	8	10	85	61	40
Stourbridge	34	16	6	12	82	54	38
Worcester City	34	17	4	13	77	79	38
Wellington Town	34	15	7	12	65	62	37
West Bromwich Albion Reserves	34	13	8	13	54	58	34
Dudley	34	13	7	14	56	67	33
Shrewsbury Town	34	14	4	16	61	74	32
Wednesbury Old Athletic	34	14	2	18	61	82	30
Wolverhampton Wanderers Reserves	34	12	5	17	69	75	29
Brierley Hill Alliance	34	10	9	15	63	75	29
Birmingham Reserves	34	11	4	19	73	92	26
Stafford Rangers	34	11	4	19	45	73	26
Kidderminster Harriers	34	6	8	20	37	66	20
Halesowen	34	6	3	25	48	99	15

Crewe Alexandra moved to the Central League and Halesowen moved to the Birmingham Combination. Stoke withdrew their first team so that they could concentrate on their Southern League fixtures and placed their reserves in the Birmingham League. Darlaston and Willenhall Swifts both joined from the Birmingham Combination.

1911-12

Aston Villa Reserves	34	24	5	5	111	56	53
Darlaston	34	19	8	7	69	45	46
Worcester City	34	20	3	11	80	49	43
Walsall	34	17	7	10	56	34	41
West Bromwich Albion Reserves	34	17	6	11	75	55	40
Wrexham	34	15	10	9	62	52	40
Wolverhampton Wanderers Reserves	34	17	3	14	75	58	37
Kidderminster Harriers	34	15	6	13	55	53	36
Stoke Reserves	34	11	12	11	51	52	34
Dudley	34	14	5	15	66	62	33
Birmingham Reserves	34	13	6	15	60	68	32
Wednesbury Old Athletic	34	13	6	15	55	65	32
Brierley Hill Alliance	34	12	5	17	57	68	29
Willenhall Swifts	34	11	4	19	52	68	26
Wellington Town	34	8	10	16	43	60	26
Stourbridge	34	11	4	19	58	91	26
Shrewsbury Town	34	9	3	22	44	76	21
Stafford Rangers	34	7	3	24	38	95	17

Stafford Rangers moved to the Birmingham Combination.
Coventry City Reserves joined the league.

1912-13

West Bromwich Albion Reserves	34	21	5	8	86	32	47
Coventry City Reserves	34	19	6	9	62	41	44
Worcester City	34	20	3	11	64	53	43
Willenhall Swifts	34	19	4	11	71	58	42
Birmingham Reserves	34	16	9	9	99	60	41
Wrexham	34	16	4	14	58	48	36
Walsall	34	15	5	14	60	54	35
Wellington Town	34	15	5	14	74	74	35
Dudley	34	15	4	15	53	75	34
Shrewsbury Town	34	14	5	15	59	50	33
Brierley Hill Alliance	34	12	9	13	55	61	33
Aston Villa Reserves	34	15	2	17	62	72	32
Wednesbury Old Athletic	34	13	3	18	63	71	29
Stoke Reserves	34	13	3	18	58	75	29
Darlaston	34	12	4	18	57	72	28
Wolverhampton Wanderers Reserves	34	10	6	18	61	88	26
Kidderminster Harriers	34	9	5	20	39	63	23
Stourbridge	34	8	6	20	55	89	22

1913-14

Worcester City	34	20	8	6	93	33	48
Shrewsbury Town	34	21	5	8	76	48	47
Aston Villa Reserves	34	20	5	9	71	44	45
Stoke Reserves	34	17	7	10	73	46	41
Birmingham Reserves	34	18	3	13	79	51	39
Wolverhampton Wanderers Reserves	34	16	6	12	64	56	38
Wrexham	34	15	8	11	46	47	38
Dudley	34	15	5	14	66	70	35
Stourbridge	34	12	10	12	59	48	34
Walsall	34	13	8	13	48	61	34
West Bromwich Albion Reserves	34	11	11	12	67	46	33
Kidderminster Harriers	34	11	8	15	61	85	30
Brierley Hill Alliance	34	12	5	17	43	76	29
Wednesbury Old Athletic	34	11	5	18	43	56	27
Darlaston	34	9	8	17	47	64	26
Coventry City Reserves	34	9	7	18	56	83	25
Willenhall Swifts	34	10	4	20	51	80	24
Wellington Town	34	7	5	22	48	97	19

1914-15

Birmingham Reserves	34	26	1	7	160	39	53
West Bromwich Albion Reserves	34	23	5	6	88	39	51
Walsall	34	21	5	8	66	44	47
Darlaston	34	19	4	11	83	47	42
Wolverhampton Wanderers Reserves	34	19	3	12	84	73	41
Wrexham	34	16	8	10	63	49	40
Brierley Hill Alliance	34	16	8	10	55	52	40
Stoke Reserves	34	17	5	12	80	52	39
Aston Villa Reserves	34	15	8	11	96	65	38
Dudley	34	15	5	14	71	68	35
Stourbridge	34	12	9	13	68	65	33
Shrewsbury Town	34	12	6	16	62	69	30
Kidderminster Harriers	34	9	6	19	61	95	24
Worcester City	34	9	3	22	39	81	21
Wellington Town	34	9	3	22	44	98	21
Willenhall Swifts	34	6	9	19	37	88	21
Coventry City Reserves	34	8	4	22	52	115	20
Wednesbury Old Athletic	34	7	2	25	34	104	16

In 1915, Aston Villa Reserves moved to the Central League and Nuneaton Town joined from the Birmingham Combination. The league then closed down for the duration of the war.
Dudley disbanded during the war and in 1919, Hednesford Town joined from the Birmingham Combination to replace them. Meanwhile, Willenhall Swifts merged with Willenhall Pickwick of the Birmingham Combination to form a new club called Willenhall.

1919-20

West Bromwich Albion Reserves	34	18	9	7	61	45	45
Wellington Town	34	18	5	11	94	66	41
Wrexham	34	17	5	12	73	45	39
Coventry City Reserves	34	18	3	13	88	57	39
Hednesford Town	34	15	9	10	82	64	39
Birmingham Reserves	34	18	2	14	78	57	38
Stourbridge	34	16	5	13	77	78	37
Nuneaton Town	34	16	4	14	70	66	36
Wolverhampton Wanderers Reserves	34	16	4	14	74	85	36
Darlaston	34	15	4	15	63	55	34
Willenhall	34	14	5	15	86	84	33
Stoke Reserves	34	14	4	16	73	68	32
Worcester City	34	12	6	16	62	69	30
Shrewsbury Town	34	14	2	18	59	95	30
Kidderminster Harriers	34	11	7	16	55	76	29
Walsall	34	11	6	17	53	62	28
Wednesbury Old Athletic	34	11	5	18	42	72	27
Brierley Hill Alliance	34	7	5	22	42	88	19

West Midlands (Regional) League 1920-1926

1920-21

Wellington Town	34	26	1	7	84	25	53
Birmingham Reserves	34	24	5	5	91	35	53
Wrexham	34	22	5	7	77	32	49
Hednesford Town	34	18	9	7	74	53	45
Walsall	34	18	6	10	68	47	42
Shrewsbury Town	34	17	4	13	69	55	38
West Bromwich Albion Reserves	34	15	7	12	46	41	37
Willenhall	34	16	5	13	63	73	37
Coventry City Reserves	34	12	9	13	56	57	33
Stourbridge	34	12	7	15	61	61	31
Nuneaton Town	34	11	9	14	54	61	31
Stoke Reserves	34	11	6	17	46	62	28
Darlaston	34	8	9	17	38	61	25
Brierley Hill Alliance	34	10	5	19	38	65	25
Wolverhampton Wanderers Reserves	34	8	8	18	56	70	24
Kidderminster Harriers	34	8	7	19	46	67	23
Worcester City	34	8	4	22	44	93	20
Wednesbury Old Athletic	34	6	6	22	33	86	18

Walsall and Wrexham both moved to the new Northern Section of the Football League – Third Division while the reserves of Birmingham, Stoke, West Bromwich Albion and Wolverhampton Wanderers all moved to the Central League. Bilston United, Burton All Saints, Cannock Town, Redditch, Stafford Rangers and Tamworth Castle all joined from the Birmingham Combination.

1921-22

Willenhall	34	23	7	4	86	44	53
Wellington Town	34	22	5	7	102	34	49
Hednesford Town	34	20	5	9	89	39	45
Nuneaton Town	34	19	6	9	77	47	44
Shrewsbury Town	34	14	12	8	71	54	40
Bilston United	34	17	6	11	84	68	40
Darlaston	34	15	8	11	55	36	38
Worcester City	34	14	5	15	61	61	33
Burton All Saints	34	12	9	13	42	45	33
Cannock Town	34	14	4	16	67	71	32
Stourbridge	34	11	9	14	49	62	31
Brierley Hill Alliance	34	13	5	16	48	76	31
Stafford Rangers	34	12	6	16	74	66	30
Coventry City Reserves	34	10	10	14	54	61	30
Kidderminster Harriers	34	13	2	19	40	82	28
Tamworth Castle	34	5	10	19	28	66	20
Redditch	34	7	4	23	36	78	18
Wednesbury Old Athletic	34	6	5	23	32	105	17

Coventry City Reserves moved to the Southern League and Cradley Heath joined from the Birmingham Combination.

1922-23

Shrewsbury Town	34	23	4	7	82	41	50
Bilston United	34	22	3	9	100	46	47
Nuneaton Town	34	20	5	9	77	45	45
Worcester City	34	18	7	9	64	50	43
Willenhall	34	16	9	9	76	44	41
Stourbridge	34	18	5	11	66	46	41
Wellington Town	34	18	2	14	63	47	38
Darlaston	34	16	6	12	61	50	38
Cradley Heath	34	12	13	9	60	52	37
Burton All Saints	34	13	8	13	58	50	34
Redditch	34	15	3	16	59	65	33
Hednesford Town	34	11	9	14	55	63	31
Stafford Rangers	34	10	8	16	65	72	28
Brierley Hill Alliance	34	11	3	20	46	80	25
Cannock Town	34	7	9	18	42	79	23
Kidderminster Harriers	34	8	6	20	37	71	22
Wednesbury Old Athletic	34	7	6	21	41	94	20
Tamworth Castle	34	5	6	23	41	98	16

Tamworth Castle moved to the Birmingham Combination, swapping places with Oakengates Town who moved in the opposite direction.

1923-24

Stourbridge	34	22	8	4	70	21	52
Shrewsbury Town	34	21	3	10	78	43	45
Willenhall	34	20	4	10	77	47	44
Wellington Town	34	18	6	10	76	42	42
Worcester City	34	16	9	9	61	46	41
Burton All Saints	34	17	4	13	76	54	38
Cradley Heath	34	16	6	12	66	47	38
Redditch	34	16	3	15	56	57	35
Hednesford Town	34	15	5	14	60	67	35
Oakengates Town	34	13	6	15	64	71	32
Darlaston	34	11	10	13	47	64	32
Bilston United	34	13	5	16	55	63	31
Nuneaton Town	34	13	3	18	62	64	29
Cannock Town	34	11	7	16	57	73	29
Kidderminster Harriers	34	12	5	17	44	60	29
Stafford Rangers	34	11	5	18	48	71	27
Brierley Hill Alliance	34	8	7	19	38	81	23
Wednesbury Old Athletic	34	3	4	27	34	98	10

Nuneaton Town moved to the Southern League and Wednesbury Old Athletic moved to the Birmingham Combination. Oswestry Town joined from the Welsh National League and Wellington St. Georges joined from the Birmingham Combination. Burton All Saints changed their name to Burton Town.

1924-25

Worcester City	34	18	10	6	74	35	46
Kidderminster Harriers	34	21	4	9	71	37	46
Stourbridge	34	18	7	9	94	43	43
Cradley Heath	34	16	10	8	63	35	42
Wellington Town	34	16	9	9	72	44	41
Burton Town	34	17	6	11	79	46	40
Brierley Hill Alliance	34	18	4	12	53	52	40
Redditch	34	16	6	12	75	60	38
Shrewsbury Town	34	16	5	13	75	46	37
Oswestry Town	34	15	7	12	80	57	37
Wellington St. Georges	34	14	7	13	60	59	35
Willenhall	34	14	6	14	64	53	34
Stafford Rangers	34	12	8	14	52	65	32
Oakengates Town	34	9	11	14	50	69	29
Bilston United	34	9	6	19	49	79	24
Cannock Town	34	8	2	24	34	108	18
Darlaston	34	5	6	23	38	115	16
Hednesford Town	34	4	6	24	46	126	14

1925-26

Cradley Heath	34	24	5	5	100	38	53
Stourbridge	34	15	13	6	66	45	43
Wellington Town	34	17	7	10	86	44	41
Willenhall	34	18	5	11	70	60	41
Shrewsbury Town	34	17	4	13	76	59	38
Kidderminster Harriers	34	16	5	13	75	68	37
Oakengates Town	34	17	2	15	73	90	36
Brierley Hill Alliance	34	14	7	13	62	53	35
Bilston United	34	12	11	11	65	68	35
Oswestry Town	34	13	7	14	77	79	33
Worcester City	34	12	8	14	58	53	32
Burton Town	34	14	3	17	87	78	31
Darlaston	34	12	7	15	63	72	31
Wellington St. Georges	34	12	6	16	77	86	30
Stafford Rangers	34	12	5	17	79	91	29
Cannock Town	34	9	10	15	68	80	28
Redditch	34	11	5	18	72	97	27
Hednesford Town	34	5	2	27	47	140	12

West Midlands (Regional) League 1926-1932

1926-27

Team	P	W	D	L	F	A	Pts
Stafford Rangers	34	22	6	6	108	50	50
Burton Town	34	22	5	7	86	40	49
Kidderminster Harriers	34	19	7	8	79	49	45
Cradley Heath	34	17	9	8	79	42	43
Stourbridge	34	17	5	12	95	65	39
Brierley Hill Alliance	34	16	5	13	84	80	37
Wellington Town	34	16	4	14	76	65	36
Bilston United	34	16	4	14	64	73	36
Worcester City	34	14	6	14	68	67	34
Oakengates Town	34	13	6	15	58	70	32
Wellington St. Georges	34	14	4	16	67	90	32
Willenhall	34	13	5	16	77	72	31
Shrewsbury Town	34	13	4	17	73	79	30
Cannock Town	34	12	5	17	51	73	29
Redditch	34	10	6	18	69	75	26
Hednesford Town	34	11	3	20	73	103	25
Darlaston	34	9	3	22	62	112	21
Oswestry Town	34	5	7	22	68	132	17

1927-28

Team	P	W	D	L	F	A	Pts
Burton Town	34	25	3	6	107	40	53
Wellington Town	34	25	3	6	109	50	53
Stafford Rangers	34	24	2	8	127	71	50
Shrewsbury Town	34	20	4	10	119	71	44
Brierley Hill Alliance	34	20	1	13	90	81	41
Stourbridge	34	17	5	12	74	68	39
Willenhall	34	17	4	13	77	64	38
Cradley Heath	34	16	5	13	79	62	37
Oswestry Town	34	14	5	15	102	110	33
Kidderminster Harriers	34	10	11	13	57	74	31
Wellington St. Georges	34	13	4	17	77	85	30
Bilston United	34	10	8	16	59	85	28
Hednesford Town	34	11	5	18	80	116	27
Oakengates Town	34	10	5	19	74	86	25
Redditch	34	9	7	18	66	107	25
Worcester City	34	9	6	19	57	76	24
Cannock Town	34	8	8	18	55	87	24
Darlaston	34	4	2	28	43	119	10

Cannock Town and Darlaston both moved to the Birmingham Combination, swapping places with Hereford United and Walsall Reserves who both moved in the opposite direction.

1928-29

Team	P	W	D	L	F	A	Pts
Worcester City	34	25	1	8	102	48	51
Stafford Rangers	34	21	7	6	93	42	49
Oswestry Town	34	22	4	8	126	69	48
Wellington Town	34	16	11	7	92	44	43
Shrewsbury Town	34	19	3	12	97	69	41
Walsall Reserves	34	18	3	13	75	64	39
Cradley Heath	34	15	8	11	82	61	38
Willenhall	34	17	3	14	81	77	37
Burton Town	34	13	10	11	77	79	36
Bilston United	34	14	8	12	78	103	36
Hereford United	34	14	7	13	86	61	35
Kidderminster Harriers	34	12	10	12	78	76	34
Brierley Hill Alliance	34	10	10	14	56	69	30
Hednesford Town	34	12	4	18	69	88	28
Stourbridge	34	10	2	22	70	114	22
Oakengates Town	34	6	6	22	54	117	18
Redditch	34	5	6	23	54	113	16
Wellington St. Georges	34	2	7	25	42	118	11

Redditch moved to the Birmingham Combination. Kettering Town Reserves joined while continuing to play in the Northamptonshire League.

1929-30

Team	P	W	D	L	F	A	Pts
Worcester City	34	26	3	5	153	40	55
Stafford Rangers	34	22	3	9	100	61	47
Cradley Heath	34	20	2	12	105	49	42
Shrewsbury Town	34	19	4	11	78	55	42
Brierley Hill Alliance	34	19	4	11	82	65	42
Burton Town	34	19	2	13	90	59	40
Kidderminster Harriers	34	16	6	12	68	70	38
Oakengates Town	34	16	4	14	70	76	36
Oswestry Town	34	15	5	14	103	87	35
Kettering Town Reserves	34	14	7	13	63	58	35
Walsall Reserves	34	14	4	16	71	74	32
Wellington Town	34	12	6	16	63	74	30
Hereford United	34	11	7	16	79	83	29
Willenhall	34	12	4	18	70	110	28
Stourbridge	34	13	1	20	84	122	27
Hednesford Town	34	12	1	21	78	108	25
Bilston United	34	5	5	24	35	112	15
Wellington St. Georges	34	5	4	25	46	135	14

Willenhall disbanded. West Bromwich Albion "A" joined the league. Kettering Town joined from the Southern League taking the place of their reserves.

1930-31

Team	P	W	D	L	F	A	Pts
Cradley Heath	34	23	3	8	91	50	49
Oakengates Town	34	21	7	6	92	52	49
Stafford Rangers	34	18	11	5	114	56	47
Burton Town	34	18	6	10	112	61	42
Worcester City	34	18	5	11	106	59	41
Brierley Hill Alliance	34	17	7	10	81	54	41
Walsall Reserves	34	17	7	10	77	75	41
Wellington Town	34	18	3	13	82	76	39
Shrewsbury Town	34	14	5	15	76	79	33
Kidderminster Harriers	34	12	8	14	73	72	32
Kettering Town	34	11	8	15	72	83	30
Hereford United	34	11	8	15	55	75	30
Hednesford Town	34	11	5	18	71	92	27
Oswestry Town	34	12	3	19	83	111	27
Bilston United	34	10	4	20	59	84	24
Stourbridge	34	7	9	18	71	113	23
West Bromwich Albion "A"	34	6	7	21	47	97	19
Wellington St. Georges	34	7	4	23	60	133	18

Kettering Town moved to the Northamptonshire League, Wellington St. Georges moved to the Walsall & District League and West Bromwich Albion "A" also left. Colwyn Bay United, Rhyl Athletic and Wrexham Reserves all joined from the North Wales Combination.

1931-32

Team	P	W	D	L	F	A	Pts
Cradley Heath	34	21	5	8	93	46	47
Worcester City	34	21	5	8	118	62	47
Oakengates Town	34	19	5	10	83	61	43
Burton Town	34	18	5	11	94	69	41
Rhyl Athletic	34	18	2	14	94	79	38
Colwyn Bay United	34	16	5	13	79	78	37
Hereford United	34	16	4	14	75	70	36
Brierley Hill Alliance	34	15	5	14	65	71	35
Stafford Rangers	34	13	7	14	54	56	33
Shrewsbury Town	34	13	7	14	64	82	33
Stourbridge	34	11	9	14	59	69	31
Kidderminster Harriers	34	13	4	17	67	66	30
Wellington Town	34	12	6	16	67	80	30
Bilston United	34	12	6	16	48	89	30
Wrexham Reserves	34	11	5	18	60	70	27
Oswestry Town	34	12	3	19	71	91	27
Walsall Reserves	34	10	6	18	58	70	26
Hednesford Town	34	8	5	21	58	98	21

Bilston United disbanded but a replacement club called Bilston Borough was formed and joined the Walsall & District League.
Bangor City joined from the North Wales Combination.

West Midlands (Regional) League 1932-1937

1932-33

Wrexham Reserves	34	22	6	6	91	49	50
Worcester City	34	21	3	10	108	52	45
Wellington Town	34	19	6	9	85	53	44
Hereford United	34	18	7	9	78	58	43
Bangor City	34	15	7	12	76	59	37
Brierley Hill Alliance	34	14	9	11	82	71	37
Burton Town	34	16	4	14	92	64	36
Shrewsbury Town	34	15	6	13	70	62	36
Cradley Heath	34	14	8	12	78	71	36
Hednesford Town	34	16	3	15	90	76	35
Rhyl Athletic	34	16	3	15	68	72	35
Stourbridge	34	11	10	13	77	82	32
Colwyn Bay United	34	12	5	17	65	99	29
Kidderminster Harriers	34	10	5	19	65	87	25
Oswestry Town	34	10	5	19	64	101	25
Oakengates Town	34	10	5	19	47	93	25
Stafford Rangers	34	9	6	19	64	89	24
Walsall Reserves	34	7	4	23	48	110	18

Walsall Reserves moved to the Birmingham Combination.
Cannock Town and Nuneaton Town both joined from the Birmingham Combination and Port Vale Reserves joined from the Cheshire League.
The League was increased to 20 clubs.

1933-34

Wrexham Reserves	38	27	3	8	131	52	57
Worcester City	38	24	3	11	118	62	51
Kidderminster Harriers	38	23	5	10	115	75	51
Port Vale Reserves	38	22	7	9	91	67	51
Hereford United	38	23	4	11	97	61	50
Burton Town	38	22	5	11	103	51	49
Rhyl Athletic	37	20	6	11	82	61	46
Nuneaton Town	38	21	3	14	80	65	45
Bangor City	38	20	4	14	84	62	44
Shrewsbury Town	38	18	6	14	89	77	42
Hednesford Town	37	16	7	14	92	71	39
Brierley Hill Alliance	38	17	3	18	89	76	37
Wellington Town	38	15	5	18	88	106	35
Stourbridge	38	14	3	21	84	89	31
Stafford Rangers	38	9	8	21	65	118	26
Oswestry Town	38	11	3	24	79	117	25
Cannock Town	38	10	4	24	62	110	24
Colwyn Bay United	38	10	4	24	63	126	24
Cradley Heath	38	8	5	25	51	109	21
Oakengates Town	38	4	2	32	44	152	10

Hednesford Town vs Rhyl Athletic was not played.
Port Vale Reserves returned to the Cheshire League.
The League was reduced to 19 clubs.

1934-35

Wellington Town	36	26	4	6	131	51	56
Kidderminster Harriers	36	25	2	9	100	49	52
Nuneaton Town	36	23	6	7	85	44	52
Shrewsbury Town	36	21	6	9	81	43	48
Wrexham Reserves	36	23	1	12	117	68	47
Worcester City	36	20	7	9	90	60	47
Burton Town	36	19	4	13	102	59	42
Stourbridge	36	17	7	12	100	72	41
Hereford United	36	14	9	13	88	79	37
Cradley Heath	36	17	2	17	76	98	36
Hednesford Town	36	13	9	14	59	80	35
Colwyn Bay United	36	12	6	18	69	96	30
Oswestry Town	36	13	2	21	59	80	28
Bangor City	36	10	7	19	62	100	27
Stafford Rangers	36	8	6	22	58	90	22
Brierley Hill Alliance	36	9	4	23	49	83	22
Rhyl Athletic	36	8	6	22	59	115	22
Oakengates Town	36	8	5	23	60	112	21
Cannock Town	36	9	1	26	54	120	19

Burton Town moved to the Midland League. Cardiff City Reserves joined while continuing in the Western League and Dudley Town joined from the Birmingham Combination.
The League was increased to 20 clubs.

1935-36

Wellington Town	38	29	3	6	129	37	61
Brierley Hill Alliance	38	28	2	8	128	70	58
Shrewsbury Town	38	26	1	11	124	70	53
Kidderminster Harriers	38	24	5	9	104	66	53
Worcester City	38	19	11	8	104	68	49
Cardiff City Reserves	38	21	5	12	102	69	47
Wrexham Reserves	38	19	5	14	92	77	43
Dudley Town	38	17	7	14	91	72	41
Hednesford Town	38	17	4	17	80	82	38
Hereford United	38	15	4	19	77	81	34
Stafford Rangers	38	15	4	19	84	90	34
Bangor City	38	15	4	19	83	97	34
Stourbridge	38	15	3	20	110	111	33
Rhyl Athletic	38	10	11	17	80	81	31
Oswestry Town	38	13	5	20	71	97	31
Nuneaton Town	38	14	2	22	66	84	30
Cradley Heath	38	9	9	20	69	114	27
Oakengates Town	38	10	5	23	73	115	25
Cannock Town	38	8	4	26	56	161	20
Colwyn Bay United	38	6	6	26	52	133	18

Rhyl Athletic moved to the Cheshire League and Bristol Rovers Reserves joined while continuing in the Western League.

1936-37

Bristol Rovers Reserves	36	24	8	4	127	44	56
Shrewsbury Town	36	23	4	9	133	64	50
Brierley Hill Alliance	36	22	4	10	106	59	48
Wellington Town	36	20	7	9	114	55	47
Cardiff City Reserves	36	21	2	13	87	57	44
Stafford Rangers	35	19	3	13	68	65	41
Kidderminster Harriers	35	18	4	13	90	54	40
Bangor City	36	18	3	15	80	81	39
Dudley Town	36	16	6	14	63	61	38
Worcester City	36	15	6	15	70	66	36
Stourbridge	36	15	5	16	95	77	35
Hereford United	36	15	4	17	61	82	34
Wrexham Reserves	36	13	6	17	73	85	32
Cradley Heath	36	13	3	20	71	85	29
Oswestry Town	36	12	3	21	62	100	27
Hednesford Town	36	10	4	22	56	113	24
Nuneaton Town	36	9	5	22	65	115	23
Oakengates Town	36	10	1	25	62	148	21
Colwyn Bay United	36	7	4	25	51	123	18

The Stafford Rangers vs Kidderminster Harriers match on 24th April was abandoned 2 minutes from the end with Kidderminster leading 2-1 when many of the crowd invaded the pitch. The score was not included in the final table, nor was the game replayed. Staffords ground was closed for three weeks at the start of the next season as a result.
Cannock Town resigned from the league and disbanded in January 1937 and their record was deleted: 18   3   12   27   67   9
Shrewsbury Town moved to the Midland League, Nuneaton Town moved to the Central Amateur League, Bristol Rovers Reserves moved to the Southern League and Colwyn Bay United moved to the Welsh League (North).

The League was reduced to 15 clubs.

1937-38

	P	W	D	L	F	A	Pts
Kidderminster Harriers	26	17	9	0	60	22	43
Stourbridge	26	18	2	6	64	37	38
Brierley Hill Alliance	26	17	2	7	72	34	36
Oswestry Town	26	16	2	8	65	46	34
Wellington Town	26	12	6	8	55	41	30
Cardiff City Reserves	26	13	3	10	62	48	29
Worcester City	26	11	3	12	50	53	25
Bangor City	26	10	5	11	42	57	25
Hereford United	26	8	7	11	40	44	23
Oakengates Town	26	8	6	12	41	59	22
Dudley Town	26	8	2	16	44	66	18
Wrexham Reserves	26	6	6	14	38	64	18
Stafford Rangers	26	5	5	16	41	58	15
Cradley Heath	26	2	4	20	29	74	8

Hednesford Town resigned from the league on 16th February 1938 and their record was deleted: 13 5 0 8 24 25 10
Cardiff City Reserves and Worcester City both moved to the Southern League, Wellington Town and Wrexham Reserves both moved to the Cheshire League, Bangor City moved to the Lancashire Combination and Oakengates Town disbanded. Shrewsbury Town Reserves joined from the Midland Midweek League while Hednesford Town were re-formed as Hednesford and rejoined the league.
As the league had been reduced to 10 clubs, it was decided to split the season into two, with clubs competing for the Keys Cup up to the end of December and for the League Cup from the start of January.

1938-39

Keys Cup

	P	W	D	L	F	A	Pts
Kidderminster Harriers	18	16	1	1	70	14	33
Stourbridge	18	10	6	2	60	34	26
Oswestry Town	18	10	0	8	46	43	20
Brierley Hill Alliance / Revo Sports	18	8	1	9	42	40	17
Cradley Heath	18	7	3	8	34	41	17
Stafford Rangers	18	7	2	9	29	44	16
Dudley Town / Vono Sports	18	6	3	9	37	53	15
Shrewsbury Town Reserves	18	7	0	11	34	49	14
Hereford United	18	6	1	11	39	47	13
Hednesford	18	4	1	13	34	60	9

Brierley Hill Alliance resigned and disbanded in January 1939. Revo Sports of the Birmingham Works League took over their record (see below) and completed outstanding fixtures: 17 8 1 8 42 35 17
Dudley Town resigned and disbanded in mid-December 1938. Vono Sports of the Birmingham Works League took over their record (see below) and completed outstanding fixtures: 12 5 2 5 30 32 12
Both Revo Sports and Vono Sports also continued to play in the Birmingham Works League.

League Cup

	P	W	D	L	F	A	Pts
Kidderminster Harriers	18	14	2	2	57	18	30
Stourbridge	18	13	2	3	65	28	28
Oswestry Town	18	11	1	6	42	43	23
Shrewsbury Town Reserves	18	9	3	6	47	28	21
Hereford United	18	7	2	9	28	29	16
Vono Sports	18	6	4	8	38	40	16
Stafford Rangers	18	8	0	10	30	45	16
Cradley Heath	18	7	0	11	34	38	14
Hednesford	18	5	3	10	34	54	13
Revo Sports	18	1	1	16	13	65	3

Vono Sports left the league because of ground difficulties but continued to play in the Birmingham Works League. Kidderminster Harriers and Stourbridge both moved to the Birmingham Combination and Hereford United moved to the Southern League. Kidderminster and Hereford were replaced by their reserves. Burton Town Reserves, R.A.F. Cosford, R.A.F. Hednesford, Stoke City "A" and Worcester City Reserves joined. Revo Sports changed their name to Revo Electric.

The League was increased to 13 clubs.

1939-40

Peacetime Competition

	P	W	D	L	F	A	Pts
Burton Town Reserves	2	1	1	0	8	4	3
Hednesford	3	1	1	1	6	6	3
Revo Electric	1	1	0	0	2	0	2
Kidderminster Harriers Reserves	1	1	0	0	2	1	2
Hereford United Reserves	1	1	0	0	3	2	2
Stoke City "A"	2	1	0	1	5	5	2
Shrewsbury Town Reserves	2	1	0	1	7	9	2
Oswestry Town	1	0	1	0	2	2	1
R.A.F. Hednesford	1	0	1	0	1	1	1
Worcester City Reserves	1	0	0	1	3	5	0
R.A.F. Cosford	1	0	0	1	1	2	0
Stafford Rangers	2	0	0	2	2	5	0
Cradley Heath	0	0	0	0	0	0	0

The table shown is as at 3rd September 1939 when the competition was immediately abandoned after war was declared.
In early October, it was decided to set up an emergency wartime competition which consisted of 8 clubs, 5 of which – Hednesford, R.A.F. Cosford, R.A.F. Hednesford, Revo Electric and Stafford Rangers – were already members of the league. They were joined by the first teams of Burton Town, Kidderminster Harriers and Wellington Town.

Wartime Competition

	P	W	D	L	F	A	Pts
Wellington Town	13	10	3	0	67	29	23
Stafford Rangers	13	9	2	2	47	17	20
Revo Electric	14	9	2	3	62	36	20
Hednesford	14	7	4	3	62	20	18
Kidderminster Harriers	12	4	3	5	24	31	11
Burton Town	13	3	2	8	32	48	8
R.A.F. Hednesford	13	1	2	10	15	94	4
R.A.F. Cosford	14	0	2	12	24	58	2

It is believed that 3 games were not played: Wellington Town vs Stafford Rangers, Kidderminster Harriers vs Burton Town and R.A.F. Hednesford vs Kidderminster Harriers.
Burton Town, Kidderminster Harriers and Stafford Rangers left the league. Aston Villa, Birmingham Reserves, R.A.F. Bridgnorth, West Bromwich Albion Reserves and Worcester City also joined.

1940-41

	P	W	D	L	F	A	Pts
Hednesford	16	12	1	3	52	16	25
Wellington Town	16	11	1	4	54	32	23
R.A.F. Cosford	16	9	3	4	52	30	21
Worcester City	16	10	1	5	53	36	21
Revo Electric	16	6	3	7	56	60	15
West Bromwich Albion Reserves	16	7	1	8	45	54	15
Aston Villa	16	5	0	11	46	49	10
R.A.F. Bridgnorth	16	4	2	10	30	52	10
R.A.F. Hednesford	16	1	2	13	16	75	4

Birmingham withdrew from all football just before Christmas 1940 and their reserves record was deleted. R.A.F. Bridgnorth left the league and R.A.F. Lichfield and Wolverhampton Wanderers Reserves both joined.

1941-42

	P	W	D	L	F	A	Pts
Aston Villa	18	15	1	2	87	16	31
Revo Electric	18	13	1	4	72	37	27
Worcester City	18	11	2	5	63	41	24
Wellington Town	18	11	1	6	59	31	23
Hednesford	17	10	1	6	56	37	21
R.A.F. Cosford	17	7	2	8	31	35	16
West Bromwich Albion Reserves	18	6	2	10	35	44	14
Wolverhampton Wanderers Reserves	17	4	0	13	39	65	8
R.A.F. Hednesford	17	3	0	14	30	75	6
R.A.F. Lichfield	18	3	0	15	29	120	6

Because of transport difficulties, only Hednesford, Revo Electric, Wellington Town and Wolverhampton Wanderers Reserves were able to continue in the league for the 1942-43 season and so the league closed down.

West Midlands (Regional) League 1946-1952

The league was unable to resume until the 1946-47 season when there were 10 members – Aston Villa "A", Cheltenham Town Reserves, Gloucester City Reserves, Halesowen Town, Hereford United Reserves, Kettering Town, Oswestry Town, Shrewsbury Town Reserves, Walsall "A" and Wellington Town Reserves.

1946-47

Halesowen Town	18	12	4	2	56	27	28
Wellington Town Reserves	18	12	1	5	64	26	25
Aston Villa "A"	18	10	3	5	41	36	23
Shrewsbury Town Reserves	18	11	0	7	56	44	22
Kettering Town	18	10	1	7	58	42	21
Hereford United Reserves	18	7	5	6	45	44	19
Oswestry Town	18	7	2	9	48	51	16
Cheltenham Town Reserves	18	4	3	11	35	51	11
Walsall "A"	18	3	2	13	22	61	8
Gloucester City Reserves	18	2	3	13	31	74	7

Cheltenham Town Reserves left the league.
Cradley Heath joined having just been re-formed while Kidderminster Harriers and Worcester City Reserves joined from the Birmingham Combination, Lye Town joined from the Central Amateur League and Wolverhampton Wanderers "A" also joined.
The League was increased to 14 clubs.

1947-48

Kettering Town	26	20	1	5	83	33	41
Kidderminster Harriers	26	15	5	6	72	43	35
Oswestry Town	26	16	2	8	63	46	34
Halesowen Town	26	14	5	7	65	46	33
Wellington Town Reserves	26	12	5	9	74	51	29
Wolverhampton Wanderers "A"	26	14	1	11	52	53	29
Cradley Heath	26	13	2	11	58	62	28
Lye Town	26	10	5	11	56	57	25
Worcester City Reserves	26	10	3	13	49	49	23
Aston Villa "A"	26	8	6	12	46	53	22
Shrewsbury Town Reserves	26	9	3	14	55	65	21
Hereford United Reserves	26	9	2	15	60	70	20
Walsall "A"	26	7	2	17	39	74	16
Gloucester City Reserves	26	3	2	21	29	99	8

Kidderminster Harriers moved to the Southern League and were replaced by their reserves. Brierley Hill Alliance joined having just been re-formed, Brush Sports joined from the United Counties League while Leicester City "A" and Stoke City "A" also joined.
The League was increased to 18 clubs.

1948-49

Worcester City Reserves	34	23	6	5	85	38	52
Kettering Town	34	24	3	7	91	38	51
Brush Sports	34	23	5	6	111	50	51
Brierley Hill Alliance	34	22	5	7	84	53	49
Lye Town	34	20	3	11	96	69	43
Wellington Town Reserves	34	18	4	12	89	74	40
Halesowen Town	34	15	7	12	78	53	37
Shrewsbury Town Reserves	34	13	8	13	81	72	34
Cradley Heath	34	12	5	17	52	70	29
Oswestry Town	34	7	14	13	48	58	28
Kidderminster Harriers Reserves	34	12	4	18	55	76	28
Wolverhampton Wanderers "A"	34	10	7	17	59	62	27
Gloucester City Reserves	34	12	3	19	50	98	27
Hereford United Reserves	34	11	4	19	62	74	26
Stoke City "A"	34	11	3	20	45	83	25
Aston Villa "A"	34	8	9	17	57	68	25
Walsall "A"	34	7	10	17	47	87	24
Leicester City "A"	34	7	2	25	37	104	16

Leicester City "A" moved to the Leicestershire Senior League.
Boldmere St. Michaels and Whitwick Colliery both joined from the Central Amateur League while Whitwick had also been playing in the Central Alliance. The League was increased to 19 clubs.

1949-50

Hereford United Reserves	36	24	5	7	92	39	53
Brierley Hill Alliance	36	22	7	7	77	51	51
Brush Sports	36	20	9	7	93	53	49
Wolverhampton Wanderers "A"	36	20	8	8	66	53	48
Cradley Heath	36	19	9	8	81	49	47
Oswestry Town	36	17	9	10	86	58	43
Shrewsbury Town Reserves	36	16	6	14	75	68	38
Lye Town	36	15	8	13	86	79	38
Halesowen Town	36	15	7	14	66	58	37
Whitwick Colliery	36	17	2	17	76	72	36
Gloucester City Reserves	36	16	4	16	74	82	36
Aston Villa "A"	36	14	7	15	50	44	35
Kettering Town	36	15	4	17	84	70	34
Boldmere St. Michaels	36	12	8	16	36	63	32
Kidderminster Harriers Reserves	36	12	4	20	48	66	28
Worcester City Reserves	36	9	6	21	47	76	24
Wellington Town Reserves	36	8	5	23	41	86	21
Walsall "A"	36	7	4	25	40	101	18
Stoke City "A"	36	5	6	25	41	91	16

Kettering Town moved to the Southern League and Burton Albion joined as a newly formed club.

1950-51

Brierley Hill Alliance	36	28	3	5	129	49	59
Hereford United Reserves	36	24	3	9	91	31	51
Boldmere St. Michaels	36	19	11	6	75	47	49
Brush Sports	36	20	7	9	77	42	47
Shrewsbury Town Reserves	36	18	8	10	82	60	44
Cradley Heath	36	17	8	11	73	44	42
Oswestry Town	36	18	3	15	83	72	39
Halesowen Town	36	15	7	14	66	76	37
Aston Villa "A"	36	14	6	16	54	45	34
Whitwick Colliery	36	14	5	17	79	97	33
Wellington Town Reserves	36	14	3	19	81	84	31
Gloucester City Reserves	36	14	3	19	58	80	31
Stoke City "A"	36	12	7	17	46	71	31
Kidderminster Harriers Reserves	36	13	3	20	64	89	29
Walsall "A"	36	9	9	18	54	98	27
Burton Albion	36	10	6	20	63	97	26
Worcester City Reserves	36	11	4	21	51	99	26
Wolverhampton Wanderers "A"	36	9	6	21	75	86	24
Lye Town	36	9	6	21	57	91	24

Gloucester City Reserves moved to the Western League.
The League was reduced to 18 clubs.

1951-52

Brierley Hill Alliance	34	24	5	5	115	36	53
Hereford United Reserves	34	20	7	7	87	61	47
Oswestry Town	34	21	4	9	93	50	46
Lye Town	34	18	6	10	78	56	42
Burton Albion	34	17	7	10	81	62	41
Halesowen Town	34	18	2	14	70	60	38
Wolverhampton Wanderers "A"	34	14	8	12	75	67	36
Kidderminster Harriers Reserves	34	14	3	13	72	70	35
Boldmere St. Michaels	34	16	3	15	64	87	35
Worcester City Reserves	34	12	9	13	68	65	33
Aston Villa "A"	34	14	5	15	55	53	33
Brush Sports	34	12	8	14	65	68	32
Shrewsbury Town Reserves	34	14	3	17	62	61	31
Whitwick Colliery	34	11	4	19	77	100	26
Cradley Heath	34	8	9	17	63	85	25
Stoke City "A"	34	10	4	20	49	70	24
Wellington Town Reserves	34	9	6	19	47	79	24
Walsall "A"	34	4	3	27	37	128	11

Stoke City "A" left the league. Nuneaton Borough joined from the Birmingham Combination and Bloxwich Strollers joined from the Staffordshire County League (South).
The League was increased to 19 clubs.

1952-53

Oswestry Town	36	27	5	4	95	40	59
Kidderminster Harriers Reserves	36	24	3	9	91	45	51
Brierley Hill Alliance	36	21	7	8	117	53	49
Burton Albion	36	20	8	8	95	45	48
Nuneaton Borough	36	19	5	12	81	50	43
Hereford United Reserves	36	15	13	8	79	61	43
Brush Sports	36	19	5	12	76	62	43
Halesowen Town	36	18	6	12	97	74	42
Shrewsbury Town Reserves	36	17	7	12	89	73	41
Worcester City Reserves	36	17	4	15	93	87	38
Lye Town	36	14	8	14	79	90	36
Wolverhampton Wanderers "A"	36	13	6	17	69	73	32
Wellington Town Reserves	36	12	5	19	61	92	29
Bloxwich Strollers	36	10	6	20	51	96	26
Cradley Heath	36	9	7	20	63	94	25
Aston Villa "A"	36	10	5	21	60	93	25
Whitwick Colliery	36	8	6	22	86	126	22
Boldmere St. Michaels	36	8	1	27	47	123	17
Walsall "A"	36	5	5	26	43	95	15

Bromsgrove Rovers, Dudley Town, Hednesford, Redditch, Stourbridge and Walsall Reserves all joined from the Birmingham Combination.
Walsall "A" moved to the Staffordshire County League (South).

The League was increased to 24 clubs.

1953-54

Wolverhampton Wanderers "A"	46	33	5	8	158	57	71
Burton Albion	46	31	6	9	120	58	68
Brierley Hill Alliance	46	29	5	12	138	72	63
Nuneaton Borough	46	27	8	11	129	59	62
Kidderminster Harriers Reserves	46	27	8	11	100	73	62
Hednesford	46	25	7	14	122	81	57
Hereford United Reserves	46	23	10	13	124	74	56
Redditch	46	26	4	16	109	76	56
Oswestry Town	46	24	6	16	122	82	54
Bromsgrove Rovers	46	25	4	17	125	98	54
Stourbridge	46	25	3	18	89	68	53
Worcester City Reserves	46	22	5	19	116	119	49
Halesowen Town	46	19	8	19	99	104	46
Shrewsbury Town Reserves	46	17	11	18	98	86	45
Lye Town	46	17	9	20	89	96	43
Brush Sports	46	15	11	20	98	101	41
Aston Villa "A"	46	16	6	24	91	126	38
Walsall Reserves	46	14	7	25	66	112	35
Cradley Heath	46	10	11	25	64	114	31
Wellington Town Reserves	46	10	9	27	76	126	29
Whitwick Colliery	46	9	9	28	110	169	27
Bloxwich Strollers	46	8	11	27	58	138	27
Boldmere St. Michaels	46	5	9	32	70	194	19
Dudley Town	46	4	10	32	56	144	18

Atherstone Town, Banbury Spencer, Bedworth Town, Bilston, Birch Coppice, Darlaston, Gresley Rovers, Hinckley Athletic, Lockheed (Leamington), Moor Green, Rugby Town, Sutton Town and Tamworth all joined from the Birmingham Combination which then closed down.
Leek Town joined from the Manchester League, Symingtons joined from the United Counties League and Cheltenham Town Reserves also joined.

The League was increased to 40 clubs and separated into two divisions, Northern and Southern.

1954-55

Southern Division

Redditch	38	27	6	5	110	41	60
Lockheed (Leamington)	38	24	7	7	122	54	55
Brierley Hill Alliance	38	23	7	8	105	61	53
Banbury Spencer	38	20	11	7	84	42	51
Rugby Town	38	21	7	10	91	54	49
Worcester City Reserves	38	22	4	12	103	60	48
Stourbridge	38	21	6	11	86	56	48
Bromsgrove Rovers	38	18	8	12	77	56	44
Halesowen Town	38	20	4	14	100	84	44
Lye Town	38	18	4	16	76	72	40
Kidderminster Harriers Reserves	38	17	5	16	79	83	39
Cheltenham Town Reserves	38	17	3	18	67	87	37
Moor Green	38	15	4	19	74	78	34
Cradley Heath	38	9	9	20	70	83	27
Hereford United Reserves	38	11	5	22	73	97	27
Symingtons	38	11	5	22	64	97	27
Aston Villa "A"	38	8	5	25	56	108	21
Sutton Town	38	7	6	25	53	117	20
Dudley Town	38	6	7	25	54	125	19
Boldmere St. Michaels	38	5	7	26	41	130	17

Northern Division

Nuneaton Borough	38	26	7	5	112	43	59
Wolverhampton Wanderers "A"	38	24	2	12	106	65	50
Burton Albion	38	23	3	12	100	50	49
Shrewsbury Town Reserves	38	20	6	12	103	68	46
Brush Sports	38	19	7	12	90	57	45
Walsall Reserves	38	20	5	13	83	71	45
Bedworth Town	38	20	4	14	95	59	44
Bilston	38	17	10	11	86	65	44
Hinckley Athletic	38	18	7	13	89	77	43
Whitwick Colliery	38	18	6	14	95	70	42
Oswestry Town	38	17	6	15	84	72	40
Gresley Rovers	38	13	11	14	66	70	37
Hednesford	38	14	8	16	72	79	36
Atherstone Town	38	15	5	18	88	101	35
Tamworth	38	13	8	17	67	75	34
Leek Town	38	10	9	19	64	94	29
Darlaston	38	8	8	22	57	110	24
Wellington Town Reserves	38	8	5	25	59	123	21
Birch Coppice	38	6	8	24	47	99	20
Bloxwich Strollers	38	7	3	28	47	162	17

The top 10 clubs in each of the Northern and Southern Divisions (in bold type) moved into a new Division One and the remaining clubs moved into the new Division Two, with the exception of Birch Coppice who joined the Warwickshire Combination and Symingtons who disbanded. They were replaced by Evesham United from the Worcestershire Combination and West Bromwich Albion "A" from the Warwickshire Combination.

Promoted clubs are shown in bold type, relegated clubs in bold italics.

West Midlands (Regional) League 1955-1958

1955-56
Division One

Team	P	W	D	L	F	A	Pts
Nuneaton Borough	38	24	8	6	109	55	56
Stourbridge	38	24	5	9	85	48	53
Banbury Spencer	38	23	6	9	68	40	52
Lockheed (Leamington)	38	21	6	11	96	60	48
Burton Albion	38	20	7	11	82	48	47
Brierley Hill Alliance	38	18	8	12	91	81	44
Brush Sports	38	20	4	14	58	56	44
Bedworth Town	38	16	7	15	74	60	39
Wolverhampton Wanderers "A"	38	17	5	16	70	60	39
Bromsgrove Rovers	38	14	10	14	74	67	38
Halesowen Town	38	15	6	17	75	74	36
Walsall Reserves	38	13	9	16	66	68	35
Shrewsbury Town Reserves	38	13	7	18	84	87	33
Rugby Town	38	12	9	17	72	86	33
Worcester City Reserves	38	14	4	20	65	95	32
Whitwick Colliery	38	10	11	17	62	87	31
Bilston	*38*	*10*	*8*	*20*	*53*	*100*	*28*
Hinckley Athletic	*38*	*12*	*3*	*23*	*75*	*83*	*27*
Redditch	*38*	*7*	*10*	*21*	*50*	*101*	*24*
Lye Town	*38*	*7*	*7*	*24*	*50*	*103*	*21*

Division Two

Team	P	W	D	L	F	A	Pts
Tamworth	36	26	5	5	107	46	57
Atherstone Town	36	26	4	6	126	57	56
Aston Villa "A"	36	22	6	8	100	49	50
Oswestry Town	36	22	5	9	90	55	49
Gresley Rovers	36	21	5	10	78	50	47
Cradley Heath	36	18	8	10	75	47	44
West Bromwich Albion "A"	36	18	6	12	85	61	42
Hereford United Reserves	36	17	3	16	98	84	37
Evesham United	36	14	7	15	88	79	35
Hednesford	36	15	5	16	68	81	35
Cheltenham Town Reserves	36	15	4	17	82	71	34
Moor Green	36	15	3	18	78	96	33
Wellington Town Reserves	36	11	5	20	72	102	27
Darlaston	36	10	6	20	48	66	26
Kidderminster Harriers Reserves	36	11	4	21	79	112	26
Boldmere St. Michaels	36	11	2	23	66	100	24
Dudley Town	36	8	6	22	50	101	22
Leek Town	36	8	5	23	48	111	21
Sutton Town	36	7	5	24	56	126	19

Bloxwich Strollers resigned at the end of the first week of January 1956 and their record was deleted: 22 6 4 12 37 55 16
They replaced their reserve side in the Staffordshire County League (South) in 1956-57. Stoke City "A" joined the league.

1956-57
Division One

Team	P	W	D	L	F	A	Pts
Walsall Reserves	38	23	8	7	95	48	54
Bromsgrove Rovers	38	22	7	9	93	61	51
Tamworth	38	20	9	9	94	62	49
Burton Albion	38	17	11	10	98	74	45
Rugby Town	38	19	7	12	80	68	45
Lockheed (Leamington)	38	16	10	12	84	65	42
Banbury Spencer	38	17	7	14	87	71	41
Aston Villa "A"	38	17	7	14	93	79	41
Bedworth Town	38	16	8	14	85	75	40
Brierley Hill Alliance	38	18	3	17	62	77	39
Wolverhampton Wanderers "A"	38	16	6	16	84	79	38
Atherstone Town	38	16	5	17	100	99	37
Worcester City Reserves	38	14	7	17	82	107	35
Nuneaton Borough	38	14	6	18	76	75	34
Stourbridge	38	13	8	17	66	68	34
Shrewsbury Town Reserves	38	13	7	18	74	90	33
Oswestry Town	*38*	*12*	*8*	*18*	*71*	*86*	*32*
Halesowen Town	*38*	*10*	*9*	*19*	*74*	*96*	*29*
Brush Sports	*38*	*10*	*7*	*21*	*59*	*80*	*27*
Whitwick Colliery	38	6	2	30	42	139	14

Whitwick Colliery moved to the Leicestershire Senior League.

Division Two

Team	P	W	D	L	F	A	Pts
Bilston	36	27	7	2	103	30	61
Hereford United Reserves	36	24	3	9	96	52	51
Hinckley Athletic	36	21	6	9	97	53	48
Gresley Rovers	36	20	8	8	75	42	48
Evesham United	36	19	8	9	88	47	46
Cradley Heath	36	18	4	14	65	58	40
Redditch	36	15	9	12	68	60	39
West Bromwich Albion "A"	36	16	7	13	71	65	39
Lye Town	36	16	5	15	72	76	37
Darlaston	36	16	4	16	69	69	36
Hednesford	36	14	6	16	74	84	34
Stoke City "A"	36	13	7	16	55	63	33
Wellington Town Reserves	36	11	9	16	71	76	31
Boldmere St. Michaels	36	12	6	18	55	71	30
Moor Green	36	12	6	18	54	74	30
Cheltenham Town Reserves	36	11	6	19	74	77	28
Dudley Town	36	9	7	20	56	91	25
Kidderminster Harriers Reserves	36	7	4	25	43	106	18
Sutton Town	36	1	8	27	35	127	10

Leek Town resigned from the league in December 1956 and their record at the time was deleted: 17 4 3 10 21 45 11
They subsequently joined the Manchester League for the 1957-58 season.
Kidderminster Harriers Reserves moved to the Kidderminster League.
Stratford Town joined from the Worcestershire Combination and Birmingham City "A" and Coventry City "A" both joined from the Warwickshire Combination.

1957-58
Division One

Team	P	W	D	L	F	A	Pts
Wolverhampton Wanderers "A"	38	24	6	8	116	64	54
Walsall Reserves	38	24	4	10	83	60	52
Brierley Hill Alliance	38	22	6	10	82	61	50
Bilston	38	21	1	16	85	65	43
Bromsgrove Rovers	38	19	5	14	85	65	43
Stourbridge	38	17	9	12	67	63	43
Lockheed (Leamington)	38	17	7	14	73	52	41
Shrewsbury Town Reserves	38	17	7	14	85	71	41
Banbury Spencer	38	18	4	16	76	63	40
Hereford United Reserves	38	15	8	15	63	59	38
Burton Albion	38	14	8	16	60	65	36
Tamworth	38	14	7	17	57	57	35
Nuneaton Borough	38	13	7	18	68	79	33
Hinckley Athletic	38	14	5	19	69	81	33
Bedworth Town	38	12	9	17	61	78	33
Aston Villa "A"	38	13	7	18	68	92	33
Worcester City Reserves	*38*	*13*	*7*	*18*	*48*	*68*	*33*
Rugby Town	38	12	8	18	50	70	32
Gresley Rovers	*38*	*10*	*5*	*23*	*59*	*100*	*25*
Atherstone Town	*38*	*8*	*6*	*24*	*46*	*88*	*22*

Burton Albion, Nuneaton Borough and Rugby Town moved to the Southern League.

The Division was reduced to 18 clubs.

Division Two

Oswestry Town	38	28	5	5	134	43	61
Brush Sports	38	24	10	4	73	37	58
Halesowen Town	38	26	5	7	119	56	57
West Bromwich Albion "A"	38	23	4	11	107	56	50
Evesham United	38	22	6	10	92	51	50
Hednesford	38	20	8	10	106	73	48
Cradley Heath	38	21	5	12	90	56	47
Birmingham City "A"	38	18	7	13	84	69	43
Cheltenham Town Reserves	38	16	9	13	80	76	41
Lye Town	38	19	3	16	87	84	41
Wellington Town Reserves	38	15	9	14	64	65	39
Moor Green	38	14	10	14	63	71	38
Stoke City "A"	38	16	5	17	80	73	37
Sutton Town	38	14	7	17	65	74	35
Stratford Town	38	13	3	22	62	99	29
Darlaston	38	12	5	21	64	103	29
Boldmere St. Michaels	38	8	6	24	43	86	22
Coventry City "A"	38	5	3	30	45	116	13
Redditch	38	4	3	31	40	117	11
Dudley Town	38	5	1	32	45	138	11

Leicester City "A" joined from the Leicestershire Senior League.

1958-59

Division One

Wolverhampton Wanderers "A"	34	26	7	1	91	40	59
Oswestry Town	34	22	4	8	96	58	48
Brierley Hill Alliance	34	20	4	10	85	50	44
Bromsgrove Rovers	34	15	10	9	62	56	40
Tamworth	34	15	8	11	51	58	38
Lockheed (Leamington)	34	15	7	12	85	59	37
Banbury Spencer	34	15	6	13	59	55	36
Walsall Reserves	34	15	4	15	66	68	34
Brush Sports	34	14	6	14	54	61	34
Bilston	34	12	7	15	57	66	31
Hereford United Reserves	34	11	9	14	53	74	31
Bedworth Town	34	12	6	16	55	56	30
Shrewsbury Town Reserves	34	11	7	16	54	54	29
West Bromwich Albion "A"	34	11	6	17	77	75	28
Stourbridge	34	11	3	20	67	90	25
Halesowen Town	34	10	5	19	79	112	25
Aston Villa "A"	**34**	**9**	**6**	**19**	**63**	**86**	**24**
Hinckley Athletic	34	7	5	22	55	91	19

Hinckley Athletic moved to the Southern League, Oswestry Town moved to the Cheshire League and Shrewsbury Town Reserves moved to the Football Combination.

Division Two

Birmingham City "A"	38	31	3	4	114	35	65
Leicester City "A"	38	26	6	6	118	32	58
Atherstone Town	38	25	7	6	118	52	57
Stoke City "A"	38	25	7	6	102	51	57
Cheltenham Town Reserves	38	26	3	9	122	50	55
Evesham United	38	22	6	10	85	53	50
Sutton Town	38	17	8	13	74	76	42
Hednesford	38	18	4	16	72	73	40
Redditch	38	16	7	15	80	85	39
Worcester City Reserves	38	18	3	17	82	89	39
Cradley Heath	38	15	4	19	62	73	34
Lye Town	38	13	7	18	84	83	33
Moor Green	38	10	12	16	55	76	32
Wellington Town Reserves	38	11	9	18	66	106	31
Boldmere St. Michaels	38	10	6	22	61	96	26
Gresley Rovers	38	11	3	24	72	109	25
Stratford Town	38	9	5	24	51	103	23
Coventry City "A"	38	9	4	25	47	98	22
Darlaston	38	7	7	24	48	102	21
Dudley Town	38	2	7	29	46	117	11

Gresley Rovers moved to the Central Alliance.
The Division was reduced to 16 clubs.

1959-60

Division One

Bromsgrove Rovers	34	23	8	3	94	36	54
Birmingham City "A"	34	22	6	6	90	50	50
Wolverhampton Wanderers "A"	34	20	4	10	75	39	44
Bilston	34	17	6	11	82	77	40
Walsall Reserves	34	13	12	9	54	37	38
Brierley Hill Alliance	34	17	3	14	59	48	37
Leicester City "A"	34	15	6	13	75	70	36
Tamworth	34	15	4	15	55	52	34
Brush Sports	34	15	4	15	54	63	34
Atherstone Town	34	15	3	16	80	75	33
Lockheed (Leamington)	34	15	3	16	59	58	33
Hereford United Reserves	34	14	5	15	64	75	33
Halesowen Town	34	15	1	18	63	84	31
Banbury Spencer	34	10	7	17	60	71	27
West Bromwich Albion "A"	34	9	6	19	53	75	24
Stoke City "A"	34	7	8	19	48	76	22
Stourbridge	34	10	2	22	47	82	22
Bedworth Town	34	7	6	21	44	88	20

Brush Sports moved to the Central Alliance.

Division Two

Aston Villa "A"	30	21	3	6	104	52	45
Cheltenham Town Reserves	30	19	6	5	103	44	44
Sutton Town	30	17	3	10	61	47	37
Redditch	30	16	3	11	79	53	35
Worcester City Reserves	30	13	8	9	77	60	34
Evesham United	30	14	5	11	43	49	33
Stratford Town	30	14	4	12	55	40	32
Hednesford	30	14	4	12	64	60	32
Cradley Heath	30	12	6	12	66	63	30
Moor Green	30	12	4	14	52	53	28
Wellington Town Reserves	30	12	3	15	54	55	27
Lye Town	30	9	8	13	58	55	26
Boldmere St. Michaels	30	9	6	15	47	62	24
Coventry City "A"	30	11	2	17	53	83	24
Dudley Town	30	9	6	15	45	76	24
Darlaston	30	1	3	26	22	131	5

It was decided that membership would be restricted to clubs fielding their first teams. Aston Villa "A", Birmingham City "A", Coventry City "A", Leicester City "A", Stoke City "A", Walsall Reserves, West Bromwich Albion "A" and Wolverhampton Wanderers "A" therefore all left to become founder members of the Midland Intermediate League.

Cheltenham Town Reserves, Hereford United Reserves, Wellington Town Reserves and Worcester City Reserves moved to the Warwickshire Combination. Kidderminster Harriers joined from the Southern League.

The League was reduced to a single division of 22 clubs.

WEST MIDLANDS (REGIONAL) LEAGUE

1960-61

Bilston	42	33	5	4	149	51	71
Bromsgrove Rovers	42	30	7	5	140	48	67
Lockheed (Leamington)	42	29	4	9	125	46	62
Redditch	42	28	5	9	113	54	61
Brierley Hill Alliance	42	24	12	6	87	36	60
Kidderminster Harriers	42	23	7	12	99	58	53
Stourbridge	42	21	8	13	119	64	50
Atherstone Town	42	20	8	14	97	80	48
Tamworth	42	20	7	15	86	71	47
Banbury Spencer	42	21	5	16	108	92	47
Halesowen Town	42	20	6	16	106	90	46
Stratford Town	42	18	6	18	85	85	42
Sutton Town	42	19	1	22	88	82	39
Evesham United	42	16	3	23	76	89	35
Moor Green	42	14	6	22	76	99	34
Bedworth Town	42	14	5	23	78	96	33
Hednesford	42	13	5	24	73	123	31
Lye Town	42	11	7	24	65	112	29
Cradley Heath	42	8	9	25	73	143	25
Boldmere St. Michaels	42	7	5	30	49	118	19
Dudley Town	42	6	5	31	50	152	17
Darlaston	42	4	0	38	46	199	8

Cradley Heath disbanded.

The League was reduced to 21 clubs.

1961-62

Lockheed (Leamington)	40	31	5	4	124	37	67
Brierley Hill Alliance	40	27	8	5	96	37	62
Bromsgrove Rovers	40	27	5	8	117	56	59
Bilston	40	24	6	10	135	62	54
Kidderminster Harriers	40	24	6	10	102	58	54
Tamworth	40	21	7	12	91	63	49
Redditch	40	21	7	12	89	67	49
Sutton Town	40	21	7	12	104	79	49
Halesowen Town	40	21	6	13	97	75	48
Banbury Spencer	40	18	8	14	107	84	44
Stourbridge	40	18	6	16	84	70	42
Stratford Town	40	17	7	16	82	73	41
Darlaston	40	14	7	19	70	93	35
Moor Green	40	13	8	19	67	79	34
Atherstone Town	40	12	9	19	70	97	33
Bedworth Town	40	11	6	23	61	86	28
Lye Town	40	10	6	24	45	89	26
Evesham United	40	8	5	27	74	132	21
Boldmere St. Michaels	40	9	3	28	59	126	21
Hednesford	40	6	4	30	58	155	16
Dudley Town	40	3	2	35	45	159	8

Evesham United moved to the Warwickshire Combination.

The League's name was changed to the West Midlands (Regional) League and was reduced to 20 clubs.

1962-63

Lockheed (Leamington)	38	28	7	3	119	40	63
Stourbridge	38	26	6	6	98	38	58
Hednesford	38	22	7	9	97	62	51
Halesowen Town	38	23	3	12	97	53	49
Atherstone Town	38	23	3	12	95	57	49
Kidderminster Harriers	38	20	8	10	88	53	48
Bromsgrove Rovers	38	21	5	12	95	52	47
Brierley Hill Alliance	38	17	10	11	70	62	44
Dudley Town	38	19	6	13	72	71	44
Stratford Town	38	15	12	11	52	48	42
Tamworth	38	15	8	15	69	69	38
Darlaston	38	15	4	19	80	71	34
Banbury Spencer	38	15	4	19	86	86	34
Bilston	38	14	6	18	78	95	34
Moor Green	38	11	9	18	59	95	31
Lye Town	38	11	5	22	56	99	27
Bedworth Town	38	9	4	25	61	88	22
Redditch	38	6	9	23	44	95	21
Boldmere St. Michaels	38	4	5	29	39	133	13
Sutton Town	38	4	3	31	45	133	11

Boldmere St. Michaels moved to the Worcestershire Combination and Lockheed (Leamington) moved to the Midland League. Lower Gornal Athletic joined from the Worcestershire Combination.

The League was reduced to 19 clubs.

1963-64

Tamworth	36	29	2	5	88	35	60
Kidderminster Harriers	36	24	3	9	108	45	51
Halesowen Town	36	22	5	9	105	52	49
Bromsgrove Rovers	36	19	9	8	94	55	47
Dudley Town	36	19	7	10	90	63	45
Stourbridge	36	18	7	11	76	61	43
Hednesford	36	18	7	11	77	63	43
Bilston	36	14	11	11	70	60	39
Banbury Spencer	36	16	6	14	65	69	38
Atherstone Town	36	12	12	12	73	67	36
Brierley Hill Alliance	36	14	8	14	47	49	36
Lower Gornal Athletic	36	12	10	14	60	69	34
Lye Town	36	12	7	17	60	71	31
Darlaston	36	12	7	17	67	84	31
Stratford Town	36	11	7	18	48	78	29
Redditch	36	10	7	19	44	75	27
Moor Green	36	7	7	22	44	90	21
Bedworth Town	36	3	8	25	36	106	14
Sutton Town	36	2	6	28	41	101	10

Stratford Town changed their name to Stratford Town Amateurs and Sutton Town changed their name to Sutton Coldfield Town.
Walsall Reserves joined from the Midland Intermediate League.

The League was increased to 20 clubs.

1964-65

	P	W	D	L	F	A	Pts
Kidderminster Harriers	38	30	6	2	124	37	66
Halesowen Town	38	26	4	8	107	52	56
Dudley Town	38	27	1	10	103	42	55
Lower Gornal Athletic	38	23	6	9	74	50	52
Tamworth	38	24	4	10	101	69	52
Brierley Hill Alliance	38	23	4	11	87	58	50
Stourbridge	38	18	10	10	81	56	46
Bromsgrove Rovers	38	19	8	11	76	60	46
Walsall Reserves	38	21	4	13	75	61	46
Bilston	38	18	4	16	75	67	40
Hednesford	38	16	6	16	75	61	38
Redditch	38	13	8	17	55	56	34
Stratford Town Amateurs	38	10	9	19	68	80	29
Lye Town	38	11	4	23	64	104	26
Banbury Spencer	38	11	3	24	79	99	25
Darlaston	38	8	9	21	69	112	25
Atherstone Town	38	8	4	26	59	121	20
Bedworth Town	38	8	3	27	39	95	19
Moor Green	38	7	4	27	44	108	18
Sutton Coldfield Town	38	4	9	25	53	120	17

Banbury Spencer changed their name to Banbury United. Moor Green and Sutton Coldfield Town both moved to the Worcestershire Combination. Port Vale Reserves and Wolverhampton Wanderers "A" both joined from the Midland Intermediate League and Cinderford Town joined from the Warwickshire Combination, forming a new 21 club Premier Division.

A new Division One was formed of 11 clubs but with no automatic promotion and relegation. The 11 new clubs were Wrockwardine Wood who joined from the Shropshire County League and 10 reserve sides: Nuneaton Borough and Wellington Town from the Warwickshire Combination, Bilston, Dudley Town and Hednesford from the Staffordshire County League (South) and Kidderminster Harriers, Lower Gornal Athletic and Stourbridge from the Worcestershire Combination, plus Atherstone Town and Stafford Rangers.

1965-66
Premier Division

	P	W	D	L	F	A	Pts
Tamworth	40	29	7	4	123	51	65
Walsall Reserves	40	24	8	8	84	40	56
Banbury United	40	23	9	8	91	55	55
Kidderminster Harriers	40	22	8	10	85	54	52
Dudley Town	40	21	8	11	84	46	50
Hednesford	40	22	3	15	87	61	47
Bilston	40	19	9	12	71	60	47
Halesowen Town	40	21	4	15	97	76	46
Redditch	40	14	16	10	75	60	44
Port Vale Reserves	40	19	6	15	90	73	44
Stourbridge	40	16	9	15	73	69	41
Bromsgrove Rovers	40	16	8	16	73	76	40
Lower Gornal Athletic	40	15	9	16	76	73	39
Wolverhampton Wanderers "A"	40	13	10	17	77	73	36
Atherstone Town	40	13	10	17	82	97	36
Brierley Hill Alliance	40	13	10	17	75	91	36
Stratford Town Amateurs	40	12	6	22	58	88	30
Cinderford Town	40	10	5	25	54	81	25
Darlaston	40	6	6	28	58	123	18
Bedworth Town	40	6	6	28	41	126	18
Lye Town	40	6	3	31	53	134	15

Banbury United moved to the Southern League and Walsall Reserves moved to the Football Combination. Boston United joined from the United Counties League, Shrewsbury Town Reserves joined from the Football Combination and Coventry City "A" also joined.

The Division was increased to 22 clubs.

Division One

	P	W	D	L	F	A	Pts
Wrockwardine Wood	20	15	3	2	56	25	33
Hednesford Reserves	20	11	6	3	48	34	28
Nuneaton Borough Reserves	20	11	2	7	50	46	24
Kidderminster Harriers Reserves	20	9	4	7	38	30	22
Lower Gornal Athletic Reserves	20	9	4	7	49	45	22
Stourbridge Reserves	20	8	5	7	39	39	21
Wellington Town Reserves	20	6	4	10	45	51	16
Bilston Reserves	20	6	3	11	31	47	15
Stafford Rangers Reserves	20	6	2	12	38	47	14
Atherstone Town Reserves	20	5	3	12	42	60	13
Dudley Town Reserves	20	4	4	12	42	54	12

Atherstone Town, Dudley Town, Nuneaton Borough, Stafford Rangers and Wellington Town all left the league, having dispensed with their Saturday reserve teams. Instead, they introduced a first team squad system with fringe players taking part in mid-week games in various new Floodlit Leagues that were being formed. Sankey of Wellington joined from the Shropshire County League, Tividale joined from the Warwickshire and West Midland Alliance, Tamworth Reserves joined from the Staffordshire County League (South) and Darlaston Reserves also joined.

The Division was reduced to 10 clubs who played each other 4 times.

1966-67
Premier Division

	P	W	D	L	F	A	Pts
Boston United	42	32	6	4	139	42	70
Kidderminster Harriers	42	31	5	6	123	61	67
Darlaston	42	22	14	6	80	44	58
Stourbridge	42	24	8	10	97	62	56
Tamworth	42	22	9	11	90	59	53
Halesowen Town	42	22	8	12	94	66	52
Dudley Town	42	22	7	13	70	50	51
Bromsgrove Rovers	42	22	5	15	74	70	49
Bilston	42	20	7	15	88	94	47
Stratford Town Amateurs	42	17	12	13	70	69	46
Atherstone Town	42	17	7	18	75	82	41
Lower Gornal Athletic	42	17	6	19	73	66	40
Brierley Hill Alliance	42	15	8	19	66	75	38
Hednesford	42	14	7	21	65	87	35
Coventry City "A"	42	12	10	20	72	78	34
Port Vale Reserves	42	11	9	22	65	93	31
Cinderford Town	42	12	6	24	65	92	30
Redditch	42	9	10	23	36	81	28
Shrewsbury Town Reserves	42	11	5	26	66	98	27
Bedworth Town	42	10	7	25	50	95	27
Wolverhampton Wanderers "A"	42	6	13	23	38	74	25
Lye Town	42	7	5	30	48	106	19

Shrewsbury Town Reserves left the league and Hinckley Athletic joined from the Southern League.

Division One

	P	W	D	L	F	A	Pts
Tamworth Reserves	36	26	5	5	91	39	57
Sankey of Wellington	36	24	7	5	97	44	55
Wrockwardine Wood	36	22	6	8	99	53	50
Hednesford Reserves	36	20	9	7	83	60	49
Bilston Reserves	36	11	10	15	65	75	32
Stourbridge Reserves	36	11	8	17	62	79	30
Kidderminster Harriers Reserves	36	8	8	20	57	76	24
Tividale	36	7	9	20	72	102	23
Darlaston Reserves	36	7	7	22	55	103	21
Lower Gornal Athletic Reserves	36	6	7	23	39	89	19

Lower Gornal Athletic Reserves left the league. Baddesley Colliery and Stratford Town Amateurs Reserves joined from the Warwickshire and West Midlands Alliance, Bedworth Town Reserves, Coventry Amateurs, Hereford United Reserves and Warwick Saltisford Rovers (a merger of Saltisford Rovers and Warwick Town) all joined from the Warwickshire Combination, Tipton Town joined from the Wolverhampton Amateur League, Warley joined as a newly formed club and Stewarts & Lloyds and Dudley Town Reserves both also joined.

The Division was increased to 19 clubs.

West Midlands (Regional) League 1967-1969

1967-68

Premier Division

Boston United	42	24	14	4	91	44	62
Tamworth	42	25	11	6	101	44	61
Kidderminster Harriers	42	26	9	7	102	45	61
Dudley Town	42	22	10	10	73	48	54
Hednesford	42	22	8	12	101	63	52
Halesowen Town	42	22	6	14	93	65	50
Redditch	42	18	14	10	64	45	50
Bromsgrove Rovers	42	19	11	12	69	56	49
Atherstone Town	42	17	10	15	66	64	44
Bilston	42	15	14	13	60	59	44
Lye Town	42	17	9	16	61	76	43
Stratford Town Amateurs	42	15	10	17	58	59	40
Stourbridge	42	14	10	18	60	69	38
Cinderford Town	42	12	13	17	61	61	37
Darlaston	42	13	11	18	51	55	37
Lower Gornal Athletic	42	13	10	19	50	68	36
Brierley Hill Alliance	42	13	9	20	61	84	35
Bedworth Town	42	12	7	23	42	81	31
Coventry City "A"	42	10	10	22	46	77	30
Port Vale Reserves	42	9	9	24	52	99	27
Wolverhampton Wanderers "A"	42	11	5	26	39	82	27
Hinckley Athletic	42	4	8	30	25	82	16

Bedworth Town disbanded and were replaced by a newly formed club called Bedworth United. Boston United left to become founder members of the Northern Premier League while Coventry City "A" and Port Vale Reserves also left. Eastwood (Hanley) joined from the Manchester League.

The Division was reduced to 20 clubs.

Division One

Warley	36	27	5	4	120	29	59
Wrockwardine Wood	36	25	6	5	95	40	56
Kidderminster Harriers Reserves	36	20	6	10	78	48	46
Coventry Amateurs	36	19	7	10	86	44	45
Sankey of Wellington	36	20	5	11	85	50	45
Baddesley Colliery	36	16	8	12	86	73	40
Hereford United Reserves	36	13	11	12	74	76	37
Tipton Town	36	14	9	13	56	72	37
Warwick Saltisford Rovers	36	12	12	12	64	65	36
Dudley Town Reserves	36	10	14	12	58	69	34
Stewarts & Lloyds	36	13	7	16	63	81	33
Stourbridge Reserves	36	14	4	18	77	86	32
Darlaston Reserves	36	11	10	15	56	70	32
Tamworth Reserves	36	12	5	19	76	71	29
Tividale	36	11	7	18	64	74	29
Bilston Reserves	36	10	7	19	47	79	27
Hednesford Reserves	36	9	8	19	61	92	26
Stratford Town Amateurs Reserves	36	11	4	21	58	92	26
Bedworth Town Reserves	36	3	9	24	45	138	15

Sankey of Wellington changed their name to G.K.N. Sankey. Warley moved to the Midland League. Hednesford Reserves and Tamworth Reserves also both left. Brereton Social and Oxley both joined from the Staffordshire County League (South), Warley County Borough joined from the Birmingham A.F.A. and the reserves of Brierley Hill Alliance, Halesowen Town and Lye Town all joined from the Worcestershire Combination.

The Division was increased to 22 clubs.

1968-69

Premier Division

Kidderminster Harriers	38	32	4	2	123	25	68
Tamworth	38	27	5	6	109	41	59
Hednesford	38	26	7	5	98	43	59
Bromsgrove Rovers	38	24	5	9	90	46	53
Atherstone Town	38	22	6	10	76	53	50
Halesowen Town	38	20	8	10	88	53	48
Cinderford Town	38	18	7	13	81	74	43
Redditch	38	17	8	13	72	52	42
Stourbridge	38	16	9	13	67	68	41
Dudley Town	38	13	14	11	45	39	40
Eastwood (Hanley)	38	13	9	16	59	70	35
Lower Gornal Athletic	38	13	8	17	47	62	34
Brierley Hill Alliance	38	12	6	20	51	85	30
Bilston	38	10	9	19	51	79	29
Lye Town	38	9	8	21	56	83	26
Darlaston	38	10	4	24	42	70	24
Bedworth United	38	8	8	22	42	80	24
Stratford Town Amateurs	38	8	6	24	37	73	22
Wolverhampton Wanderers "A"	38	8	4	26	35	91	20
Hinckley Athletic	38	4	5	29	37	119	13

Cinderford Town moved to the Gloucestershire County League.

The Division was reduced to 19 clubs.

Division One

Wrockwardine Wood	42	29	10	3	111	35	68
Brereton Social	42	29	6	7	116	47	64
Warwick Saltisford Rovers	42	27	5	10	86	55	59
Tividale	42	23	11	8	95	52	57
Coventry Amateurs	42	25	6	11	100	53	56
Kidderminster Harriers Reserves	42	20	11	11	61	40	51
Oxley	42	20	11	11	100	66	51
Baddesley Colliery	42	21	8	13	85	61	50
G.K.N. Sankey	42	20	7	15	98	71	47
Stourbridge Reserves	42	17	10	15	74	61	44
Tipton Town	42	17	7	18	67	76	41
Stewarts & Lloyds	42	18	4	20	71	85	40
Halesowen Town Reserves	42	14	10	18	58	83	38
Brierley Hill Alliance Reserves	42	15	7	20	88	97	37
Lye Town Reserves	42	14	7	21	52	88	35
Bilston Reserves	42	12	8	22	83	94	32
Hereford United Reserves	42	10	12	20	62	78	32
Warley County Borough	42	11	8	23	56	90	30
Dudley Town Reserves	42	10	9	23	63	90	29
Darlaston Reserves	42	11	7	24	60	107	29
Bedworth United Reserves	42	7	5	30	46	116	19
Stratford Town Amateurs Reserves	42	4	7	31	44	131	15

Hereford United Reserves, Stourbridge Reserves and Stratford Town Amateurs Reserves all left the league.

The Division was reduced to 19 clubs.

1969-70

Premier Division

Kidderminster Harriers	36	26	7	3	115	34	59
Bromsgrove Rovers	36	27	2	7	105	32	56
Stourbridge	36	23	9	4	101	37	55
Tamworth	36	23	7	6	101	50	53
Hednesford	36	22	6	8	98	53	50
Atherstone Town	36	20	8	8	68	38	48
Redditch	36	15	9	12	53	60	39
Bedworth United	36	13	11	12	49	51	37
Halesowen Town	36	15	6	15	61	54	36
Bilston	36	12	11	13	53	56	35
Eastwood (Hanley)	36	13	8	15	62	78	34
Lower Gornal Athletic	36	13	7	16	50	65	33
Wolverhampton Wanderers "A"	36	11	8	17	43	63	30
Brierley Hill Alliance	36	8	12	16	37	59	28
Dudley Town	36	8	10	18	41	58	26
Lye Town	36	6	7	23	39	95	19
Darlaston	36	7	3	26	40	108	17
Stratford Town Amateurs	36	7	3	26	30	91	17
Hinckley Athletic	36	5	2	29	30	94	12

Stratford Town Amateurs moved to the Midland Combination.
Wellingborough Town joined from the Metropolitan League.
Redditch changed their name to Redditch United.

Division One

Warley County Borough	36	27	5	4	87	25	59
Coventry Amateurs	36	24	7	5	80	29	55
Wrockwardine Wood	36	20	13	3	67	33	53
Baddesley Colliery	36	22	8	6	83	35	52
G.K.N. Sankey	36	21	8	7	72	25	50
Brereton Social	36	18	8	10	78	51	44
Stewarts & Lloyds	36	17	9	10	53	52	43
Warwick Saltisford Rovers	36	17	7	12	88	47	41
Tividale	36	17	5	14	80	58	39
Tipton Town	36	13	8	15	70	67	34
Halesowen Town Reserves	36	14	6	16	79	80	34
Kidderminster Harriers Reserves	36	12	10	14	56	62	34
Bilston Reserves	36	12	9	15	60	57	33
Oxley	36	9	8	19	55	81	26
Lye Town Reserves	36	8	6	22	48	93	22
Bedworth United Reserves	36	6	9	21	34	71	21
Dudley Town Reserves	36	6	7	23	43	105	19
Brierley Hill Alliance Reserves	36	5	4	27	32	98	14
Darlaston Reserves	36	2	7	27	26	122	11

Stewarts & Lloyds changed their name to B.S.C. (Bilston) and Warwick Saltisford Rovers changed their name to Racing Football Club (Warwick). Wrockwardine Wood and the reserves of Bedworth United, Brierley Hill Alliance, Darlaston, Dudley Town, Lye Town and Kidderminster Harriers all left the league. Solihull Amateurs joined from the Midland Combination, Wellingborough Town Reserves joined from the United Counties League and Rowley United and the reserves of Atherstone Town, Burton Albion and Worcester City all also joined.

The Division was reduced to 18 clubs.

Promoted clubs are shown in bold type and relegated clubs are shown in bold italics in the following tables.

1970-71

Premier Division

Kidderminster Harriers	36	26	6	4	90	31	58
Bilston	36	23	8	5	62	17	54
Wellingborough Town	36	23	7	6	92	39	53
Tamworth	36	23	6	7	80	41	52
Bromsgrove Rovers	36	20	10	6	89	35	50
Stourbridge	36	22	4	10	79	40	48
Atherstone Town	36	18	10	8	68	34	46
Bedworth United	36	15	11	10	57	47	41
Eastwood (Hanley)	36	10	13	13	40	48	33
Hednesford	36	12	7	17	51	47	31
Halesowen Town	36	11	8	17	54	63	30
Dudley Town	36	10	9	17	37	49	29
Wolverhampton Wanderers "A"	36	9	8	19	39	66	26
Lye Town	36	7	12	17	31	57	26
Redditch United	36	8	9	19	43	70	25
Lower Gornal Athletic	36	9	7	20	33	72	25
Darlaston	36	10	4	22	37	91	24
Brierley Hill Alliance	36	5	12	19	29	56	22
Hinckley Athletic	36	4	3	29	22	130	11

Stourbridge and Wellingborough Town both moved to the Southern League and Warley joined from the Midland League.

Division One

Brereton Social	32	24	1	7	66	27	49
Warley County Borough	32	20	6	6	69	26	46
G.K.N. Sankey	32	20	6	6	72	32	46
Baddesley Colliery	32	19	8	5	70	36	46
Coventry Amateurs	32	16	8	8	65	36	40
Racing F.C. (Warwick)	32	19	2	11	62	36	40
Rowley United	32	15	7	10	58	48	37
Tipton Town	32	13	5	14	54	74	31
Worcester City Reserves	32	12	6	14	47	51	30
Tividale	32	12	5	15	44	53	29
Solihull Amateurs	32	11	6	15	41	58	28
Oxley	32	10	5	17	43	61	25
Bilston Reserves	32	8	9	15	40	58	25
Wellingborough Town Reserves	32	8	8	16	39	50	24
Burton Albion Reserves	32	9	4	19	43	58	22
B.S.C. Bilston	32	6	8	18	36	59	20
Halesowen Town Reserves	32	2	2	28	21	107	6

Atherstone Town Reserves withdrew during the season and their record was deleted. Wellingborough Town Reserves moved back to the United Counties League. Armitage joined from the Staffordshire County League (South) and B.S.C. (Bilston) changed their name to Springvale.
The Division was reduced to 16 clubs.

1971-72

Premier Division

Tamworth	36	25	7	4	81	38	57
Atherstone Town	36	24	7	5	74	32	55
Kidderminster Harriers	36	23	7	6	84	32	53
Bromsgrove Rovers	36	22	8	6	74	39	52
Bilston	36	16	9	11	63	37	41
Redditch United	36	17	6	13	75	59	40
Lye Town	36	14	10	12	52	46	38
Hednesford	36	16	6	14	65	59	38
Dudley Town	36	13	12	11	37	36	38
Bedworth United	36	14	8	14	72	64	36
Eastwood (Hanley)	36	13	9	14	51	58	35
Lower Gornal Athletic	36	13	6	17	47	60	32
G.K.N. Sankey	36	10	10	16	38	63	30
Warley	36	13	3	20	56	75	29
Brierley Hill Alliance	36	11	6	19	47	58	28
Wolverhampton Wanderers "A"	36	7	11	18	35	68	25
Darlaston	36	6	11	19	34	68	23
Halesowen Town	36	3	12	21	41	77	18
Hinckley Athletic	36	4	8	24	26	83	16

West Midlands (Regional) League 1972-1974

Atherstone Town, Bedworth United, Bromsgrove Rovers, Kidderminster Harriers, Redditch United and Tamworth all moved to the Southern League. Hednesford moved to the Midland League, swapping places with Heanor Town who moved in the opposite direction. Hereford United Reserves also joined the league.
Lower Gornal Athletic changed their name to Gornal Athletic.

The Division was reduced to 16 clubs.

1972-73

Premier Division

Warley County Borough	28	17	7	4	82	28	41
Brereton Social	28	15	9	4	44	25	39
Worcester City Reserves	28	15	7	6	40	24	37
Racing F.C. (Warwick)	28	15	6	7	49	20	36
Armitage	28	12	11	5	53	34	35
Tividale	28	14	6	8	63	27	34
Bilston Reserves	28	11	9	8	42	36	31
Baddesley Colliery	28	10	7	11	31	34	27
Oxley	28	11	4	13	52	53	26
Coventry Amateurs	28	7	12	9	23	28	26
Springvale	28	8	6	14	41	51	22
Rowley United	28	9	3	16	40	56	21
Tipton Town	28	6	6	16	23	47	18
Halesowen Town Reserves	28	5	6	17	30	87	16
Burton Albion Reserves	28	4	3	21	23	86	11

Solihull Amateurs were expelled from the league in March 1972 for breaches of rules and their record was deleted.
Baddesley Colliery disbanded, Racing F.C. (Warwick) moved to the Midland Combination and Burton Albion Reserves also left the league. West Shirley Athletic joined from the Midland Combination having changed their name from Westphalians. Chasetown joined from the Staffordshire County League (South), Langley Celtic joined from the West Midlands Metropolitan League while G.K.N. Sankey Reserves and Telford United Reserves also joined.

The Division was reduced to 15 clubs.

Premier Division

Bilston	30	21	7	2	71	25	49
Heanor Town	30	16	8	6	53	35	40
Brereton Social	30	15	9	6	49	23	39
Darlaston	30	12	11	7	58	34	35
Brierley Hill Alliance	30	15	5	10	49	46	35
Wolverhampton Wanderers "A"	30	14	6	10	54	44	34
Eastwood (Hanley)	30	14	5	11	57	54	33
Hereford United Reserves	30	13	5	12	40	39	31
Lye Town	30	13	4	13	54	46	30
Warley County Borough	30	9	11	10	38	44	29
Warley	*30*	*6*	*12*	*12*	*46*	*49*	*24*
G.K.N. Sankey	30	8	8	14	29	43	24
Gornal Athletic	30	8	7	15	25	53	23
Halesowen Town	30	7	5	18	38	69	19
Dudley Town	30	6	6	18	32	56	18
Hinckley Athletic	30	5	7	18	31	64	17

Wolverhampton Wanderers "A" moved to the Midland Combination, swapping leagues with Alvechurch who moved in the opposite direction.
The Division was increased to 17 clubs.

Division One

Tividale	28	22	3	3	90	24	47
Coventry Amateurs	28	17	5	6	58	26	39
Chasetown	28	15	3	10	52	38	33
Armitage	28	13	7	8	41	31	33
Oxley	28	14	4	10	50	46	32
Rowley United	28	13	5	10	42	38	31
Langley Celtic	28	14	3	11	53	48	31
Telford United Reserves	28	11	7	10	35	39	29
Worcester City Reserves	28	9	6	13	50	59	24
Tipton Town	28	8	8	12	37	49	24
G.K.N. Sankey Reserves	28	10	4	14	35	47	24
West Shirley Athletic	28	9	5	14	28	44	23
Springvale	28	7	4	17	34	52	18
Bilston Reserves	28	6	4	18	49	71	16
Halesowen Town Reserves	28	5	6	17	38	80	16

Staffordshire and Stoke Police joined from the Staffordshire County League (South). Bromsgrove Rovers Reserves, Nuneaton Borough Reserves, Stourbridge Reserves and Tamworth Reserves all also joined.
Langley Celtic changed their name to Langley.
The Division was increased to 19 clubs.

1973-74

Premier Division

Alvechurch	32	23	5	4	89	24	51
Bilston	32	25	1	6	75	28	51
Brierley Hill Alliance	32	22	5	5	65	31	49
Brereton Social	32	16	10	6	49	23	42
Lye Town	32	17	8	7	57	31	42
Hereford United Reserves	32	17	5	10	62	43	39
Darlaston	32	13	12	7	40	31	38
Dudley Town	32	16	4	12	49	42	36
Warley County Borough	32	11	9	12	55	50	31
Coventry Amateurs	32	10	10	12	39	41	30
Halesowen Town	32	11	5	16	54	78	27
Tividale	32	7	10	15	39	57	24
Heanor Town	32	11	2	19	34	54	24
Eastwood (Hanley)	32	8	6	18	32	70	22
Hinckley Athletic	32	5	8	19	27	65	18
G.K.N. Sankey	32	2	10	20	9	41	14
Gornal Athletic	32	0	6	26	18	84	6

Coventry Amateurs changed their name to Coventry Sporting.
G.K.N. Sankey moved to the Shropshire County League and Hereford United Reserves also left the league. Heanor Town moved to the Midland League, swapping leagues with Hednesford Town who moved in the opposite direction.
The Division was reduced to 16 clubs.

Division One

Armitage	36	22	9	5	84	39	53
Chasetown	36	21	8	7	88	47	50
Staffordshire and Stoke Police	36	18	13	5	70	39	49
Langley	36	18	11	7	52	33	47
Worcester City Reserves	36	19	7	10	68	43	45
Telford United Reserves	36	16	11	9	57	33	43
Nuneaton Borough Reserves	36	15	12	9	58	38	42
Tamworth Reserves	36	18	5	13	67	62	41
Stourbridge Reserves	36	16	6	14	52	46	38
Bilston Reserves	36	16	4	16	44	54	36
West Shirley Athletic	36	13	9	14	50	41	35
Tipton Town	36	11	12	13	58	59	34
Bromsgrove Rovers Reserves	36	11	11	14	60	66	33
Springvale	36	11	10	15	44	59	32
Rowley United	36	12	5	19	54	67	29
Oxley	36	10	6	20	70	95	26
Halesowen Town Reserves	36	7	6	23	41	83	20
Warley	36	7	3	26	37	86	17
G.K.N. Sankey Reserves	36	4	6	26	31	95	14

Staffordshire and Stoke police changed their name to Staffordshire Police and West Shirley Athletic changed their name to Shirley Town.
G.K.N. Sankey Reserves left the league. Ledbury Town joined from the Herefordshire League while both Hednesford Town Reserves and Stafford Rangers Reserves also joined.

The Division was increased to 20 clubs.

1974-75

Premier Division

Alvechurch	30	20	8	2	74	30	48
Brierley Hill Alliance	30	16	9	5	56	31	41
Lye Town	30	18	5	7	53	35	41
Brereton Social	30	14	9	7	40	30	37
Bilston	30	11	12	7	53	42	34
Dudley Town	30	12	10	8	47	38	34
Coventry Sporting	30	11	10	9	40	32	32
Darlaston	30	12	8	10	41	37	32
Hednesford Town	30	12	7	11	44	41	31
Eastwood (Hanley)	30	13	4	13	49	53	30
Armitage	30	10	7	13	45	50	27
Tividale	30	9	7	14	40	52	25
Warley County Borough	30	6	7	17	29	52	19
Gornal Athletic	30	6	6	18	26	59	18
Hinckley Athletic	30	5	7	18	29	47	17
Halesowen Town	30	3	8	19	30	67	14

Gresley Rovers joined from the East Midlands Regional League and V.S. Rugby joined from the United Counties League.

The Division was increased to 19 clubs.

Division One

Staffordshire Police	38	24	10	4	76	33	58
Chasetown	38	23	7	8	67	41	53
Stafford Rangers Reserves	38	21	9	8	82	36	51
Bilston Reserves	38	15	14	9	66	49	44
Worcester City Reserves	38	21	2	15	64	49	44
Rowley United	38	19	5	14	91	60	43
Langley	38	16	10	12	66	63	42
Nuneaton Borough Reserves	38	12	17	9	56	51	41
Bromsgrove Rovers Reserves	38	15	11	12	65	62	41
Shirley Town	38	15	8	15	56	56	38
Hednesford Town Reserves	38	10	17	11	48	55	37
Stourbridge Reserves	38	13	9	16	51	53	35
Tipton Town	38	14	7	17	78	82	35
Warley	38	14	7	17	51	63	35
Telford United Reserves	38	13	6	19	61	67	32
Springvale	38	10	11	17	44	66	31
Tamworth Reserves	38	12	6	20	59	88	30
Ledbury Town	38	8	8	22	57	100	24
Oxley	38	9	5	24	65	99	23
Halesowen Town Reserves	38	7	9	22	43	73	23

Stafford Rangers Reserves, Stourbridge Reserves and Tamworth Reserves all left the league. Oldswinford joined from the Redditch & South Warwickshire Sunday League. The club were champions of the Staffordshire County League (South) in 1973-74 but their ground did not meet newly set standards and so they had to play in Sunday football on a parks ground for a year until they were able to find a suitable ground. Willenhall Town joined from the Staffordshire County League (South) while Cheltenham Town Reserves, V.S. Rugby Reserves and Kidderminster Harriers Reserves also all joined.

The Division was increased to 21 clubs.

1975-76

Premier Division

Alvechurch	36	29	3	4	74	20	61
Bilston	36	24	6	6	74	25	54
Dudley Town	36	19	11	6	61	34	49
Tividale	36	21	7	8	75	46	49
Lye Town	36	16	13	7	60	36	45
Darlaston	36	18	9	9	59	42	45
Brereton Social	36	16	7	13	42	34	39
Armitage	36	15	9	12	64	52	39
Hednesford Town	36	12	13	11	61	52	37
Coventry Sporting	36	13	9	14	41	42	35
Eastwood (Hanley)	36	12	10	14	46	45	34
Brierley Hill Alliance	36	14	6	16	53	63	34
Halesowen Town	36	10	9	17	46	59	29
Gresley Rovers	36	8	11	17	51	65	27
V.S. Rugby	36	9	7	20	26	57	25
Gornal Athletic	36	10	5	21	32	71	25
Hinckley Athletic	36	6	9	21	21	69	21
Staffordshire Police	36	7	5	24	39	79	19
Warley County Borough	36	5	7	24	30	64	17

Walsall Reserves joined the league.

The Division was increased to 21 clubs.

Division One

Willenhall Town	40	32	4	4	115	26	68
Chasetown	40	28	8	4	94	30	64
Oldswinford	40	22	10	8	70	51	54
Warley	40	22	9	9	71	38	53
Bilston Reserves	40	20	12	8	81	40	52
Cheltenham Town Reserves	40	22	7	11	75	50	51
Shirley Town	40	20	8	12	74	49	48
Tipton Town	40	18	7	15	77	65	43
Telford United Reserves	40	17	9	14	61	55	43
Kidderminster Harriers Reserves	40	11	14	15	54	57	36
Nuneaton Borough Reserves	40	12	12	16	51	64	36
Worcester City Reserves	40	12	11	17	55	69	35
V.S. Rugby Reserves	40	13	9	18	42	59	35
Bromsgrove Rovers Reserves	40	12	10	18	52	69	34
Hednesford Town Reserves	40	13	7	20	56	63	33
Ledbury Town	40	10	12	18	63	79	32
Springvale	40	13	5	22	42	61	31
Langley	40	11	9	20	58	94	31
Halesowen Town Reserves	40	10	9	21	45	69	29
Rowley United	40	5	7	28	32	102	17
Oxley	40	4	7	29	30	108	15

Warley disbanded. Oxley merged with Whitmore Old Boys from the Midland Combination and continued playing in the WMRL as Wolverhampton United. Donnington Wood, G.K.N. Sankey and Shifnal Town all joined from the Shropshire County League, Lichfield and Burntwood Institute both joined from the Staffordshire County League (South), Wednesfield Social joined from the Wolverhampton & District Amateur League, Causeway Green joined from the West Midland Metropolitan League while Coventry Sporting Reserves, Atherstone Town Reserves and Redditch United Reserves also joined.

The Division was increased to 29 clubs that were split into two sections – A and B.

West Midlands (Regional) League 1976-1978

1976-77

Premier Division

Alvechurch	40	29	6	5	74	20	64
Lye Town	40	26	5	9	76	35	57
Hednesford Town	40	22	13	5	59	31	57
Brereton Social	40	20	11	9	69	46	51
Dudley Town	40	18	11	11	65	41	47
V.S. Rugby	40	17	12	11	48	41	46
Tividale	40	15	14	11	47	37	44
Coventry Sporting	40	14	16	10	46	40	44
Armitage	40	15	13	12	67	57	43
Hinckley Athletic	40	14	15	11	59	54	43
Bilston	40	15	11	14	47	48	41
Darlaston	40	16	8	16	49	55	40
Warley County Borough	40	10	18	12	40	48	38
Walsall Reserves	40	11	14	15	49	58	36
Eastwood (Hanley)	40	14	4	22	60	75	32
Willenhall Town	40	11	10	19	52	57	32
Gresley Rovers	40	8	13	19	54	66	29
Brierley Hill Alliance	40	7	15	18	46	78	29
Staffordshire Police	40	7	11	22	37	78	25
Gornal Athletic	40	5	13	22	37	76	23
Halesowen Town	40	5	9	26	46	86	19

Warley County Borough disbanded and Walsall Reserves also left.
The Division was reduced to 19 clubs.

Division One – Section A

Wednesfield Social	26	19	3	4	56	20	41
Tipton Town	26	16	7	3	64	25	39
Rowley United	26	17	2	7	55	45	36
Ledbury Town	26	14	4	8	56	32	32
Cheltenham Town Reserves	26	13	5	8	53	38	31
Oldswinford	26	11	7	8	57	42	29
Shirley Town	26	10	6	10	36	45	26
Causeway Green	26	11	3	12	38	42	25
V.S. Rugby Reserves	26	9	6	11	41	46	24
Langley	26	10	4	12	39	45	24
Worcester City Reserves	26	5	7	14	29	52	17
Coventry Sporting Reserves	26	5	4	17	31	57	14
Halesowen Town Reserves	26	4	5	17	38	65	13
Redditch United Reserves	26	4	5	17	30	69	13

Division One – Section B

Wolverhampton United	28	18	7	3	52	24	43
Donnington Wood	28	16	10	2	46	19	42
Telford United Reserves	28	19	4	5	52	25	42
Chasetown	28	14	6	8	43	26	34
G.K.N. Sankey	28	14	6	8	44	31	34
Burntwood Institute	28	11	5	12	40	44	27
Shifnal Town	28	8	10	10	50	48	26
Kidderminster Harriers Reserves	28	11	4	13	46	55	26
Bilston Reserves	28	9	7	12	37	36	25
Lichfield	28	8	9	11	32	35	25
Springvale	28	9	5	14	22	40	23
Nuneaton Borough Reserves	28	9	3	16	33	56	21
Hednesford Town Reserves	28	7	6	15	31	43	20
Atherstone Town Reserves	28	4	8	16	22	42	16
Bromsgrove Rovers Reserves	28	5	6	17	24	50	16

The two sections were split into Divisions One and Two. The 16 clubs in bold type above went into Division One, the remainder went into Division Two with the exception of Bilston Reserves and V.S. Rugby Reserves who both left the league. Three new clubs joined Division Two taking membership up to 14. These clubs were Brereton Town and Albrighton United (from the Shropshire County League) and Stafford South End from the Staffordshire County League (South).
Burntwood Institute changed their name to Burntwood.

Goal difference instead of goal average was used to decide positions when clubs have the same number of points from the next season.

1977-78

Premier Division

Hednesford Town	36	20	11	5	82	28	51
Alvechurch	36	20	10	6	71	33	50
Bilston	36	19	10	7	68	37	48
Lye Town	36	20	8	8	64	46	48
Willenhall Town	36	20	7	9	76	37	47
Eastwood (Hanley)	36	17	10	9	75	51	44
Tividale	36	16	11	9	46	35	43
Hinckley Athletic	36	16	10	10	54	43	42
Halesowen Town	36	17	7	12	55	40	41
Dudley Town	36	14	13	9	53	42	41
Brereton Social	36	18	5	13	58	50	41
Armitage	36	13	12	11	63	53	38
V.S. Rugby	36	12	9	15	56	49	33
Brierley Hill Alliance	36	11	7	18	40	60	29
Gresley Rovers	36	9	7	20	44	66	25
Coventry Sporting	36	7	10	19	24	67	24
Darlaston	36	7	9	20	35	66	23
Gornal Athletic	36	2	5	29	26	116	9
Staffordshire Police	**36**	**1**	**5**	**30**	**22**	**93**	**7**

Alvechurch moved to the Southern League and Eastwood (Hanley) moved to the Cheshire League.
The Division was reduced to 18 clubs.

Division One

Chasetown	30	20	7	3	49	20	47
Wednesfield Social	**30**	**19**	**5**	**6**	**60**	**27**	**43**
Causeway Green	30	11	11	8	38	30	33
Oldswinford	30	12	9	9	46	38	33
Ledbury Town	**30**	**10**	**12**	**8**	**45**	**36**	**32**
Lichfield	30	13	6	11	48	45	32
Shifnal Town	30	14	4	12	39	39	32
Telford United Reserves	30	12	6	12	52	46	30
Wolverhampton United	30	11	7	12	45	47	29
G.K.N. Sankey	30	8	13	9	33	35	29
Cheltenham Town Reserves	30	13	3	14	53	59	29
Donnington Wood	30	9	8	13	39	46	26
Tipton Town	30	8	10	12	36	44	26
Rowley United	30	8	7	15	39	55	23
Burntwood	30	7	8	15	28	56	22
Shirley Town	30	4	6	20	40	67	14

Rowley United disbanded. Rushall Olympic joined from the Staffordshire County League (South).
The Division was increased to 18 clubs.

Division Two

Worcester City Reserves	26	16	5	5	61	30	37
Atherstone Town Reserves	26	15	7	4	43	25	37
Nuneaton Borough Reserves	26	15	5	6	51	27	35
Stafford South End	26	14	5	7	48	27	33
Hednesford Town Reserves	26	14	5	7	53	41	33
Brereton Town	26	14	5	7	46	38	33
Albrighton United	26	10	5	11	35	44	25
Springvale	26	9	5	12	30	34	23
Halesowen Town Reserves	26	8	7	11	33	38	23
Langley	26	9	4	13	45	56	22
Coventry Sporting Reserves	26	9	3	14	28	51	21
Kidderminster Harriers Reserves	26	7	4	15	46	52	18
Bromsgrove Rovers Reserves	26	6	6	14	42	50	18
Redditch United Reserves	26	2	2	22	21	69	6

Redditch United Reserves left the league. Westfields joined from the Worcester & District League, Brewood joined from the Wolverhampton Amateur League, Ludlow Town joined from the Kidderminster League while Bridgnorth Sports and Alvechurch Reserves, Dudley Town Reserves, Tividale Reserves and Willenhall Town Reserves also joined.
The Division was increased to 18 clubs.

West Midlands (Regional) League 1978-1980

1978-79

Premier Division

Team	P	W	D	L	F	A	Pts
Willenhall Town	34	23	7	4	82	32	53
Lye Town	34	21	11	2	62	33	53
Dudley Town	34	21	8	5	53	23	50
Hednesford Town	34	19	10	5	59	26	48
Tividale	34	19	6	9	63	40	44
Bilston	34	15	10	9	50	34	40
Brierley Hill Alliance	34	17	5	12	67	47	39
Brereton Social	34	17	5	12	48	40	39
Darlaston	34	15	5	14	52	51	35
Coventry Sporting	34	12	6	16	39	48	30
Hinckley Athletic	34	12	5	17	42	52	29
Ledbury Town	34	10	7	17	57	63	27
V.S. Rugby	34	9	9	16	29	41	27
Wednesfield Social	34	7	12	15	27	45	26
Halesowen Town	34	8	8	18	35	55	24
Armitage	34	7	6	21	44	69	20
Gresley Rovers	34	4	7	23	27	67	15
Gornal Athletic	34	4	5	25	21	91	13

Blakenall, Malvern Town and Sutton Coldfield Town all joined from the Midland Combination.
The Division was increased to 22 clubs.

Division One

Team	P	W	D	L	F	A	Pts
Shifnal Town	34	20	11	3	83	38	51
Causeway Green	34	18	13	3	58	24	49
Cheltenham Town Reserves	34	18	13	3	47	26	49
Rushall Olympic	34	21	6	7	70	32	48
Donnington Wood	34	17	10	7	60	37	44
G.K.N. Sankey	34	14	10	10	56	40	38
Wolverhampton United	34	15	7	12	45	32	37
Oldswinford	34	14	8	12	45	44	36
Lichfield	34	10	13	11	33	37	33
Nuneaton Borough Reserves	34	10	12	12	43	51	32
Chasetown	34	7	16	11	34	43	30
Atherstone Town Reserves	34	11	7	16	45	58	29
Telford United Reserves	34	11	7	16	52	67	29
Staffordshire Police	34	11	6	17	49	65	28
Worcester City Reserves	34	7	11	16	42	56	25
Tipton Town	34	8	7	19	38	53	23
Shirley Town	34	6	6	22	26	69	18
Burntwood	34	3	7	24	26	80	13

Cheltenham Town Reserves left the league. Atherstone Town of the Southern League disbanded but a new club called Atherstone United was formed that took the place of Atherstone Town Reserves.
The Division was increased to 19 clubs.

Division Two

Team	P	W	D	L	F	A	Pts
Ludlow Town	34	19	8	7	54	39	46
Willenhall Town Reserves	34	17	9	8	68	41	43
Alvechurch Reserves	34	18	6	10	62	41	42
Kidderminster Harriers Reserves	34	18	5	11	70	41	41
Bridgnorth Sports	34	18	5	11	67	44	41
Brereton Town	34	17	7	10	60	50	41
Brewood	34	15	10	9	52	40	40
Stafford South End	34	14	10	10	61	48	38
Halesowen Reserves	34	14	8	12	61	64	36
Hednesford Town Reserves	34	11	10	13	45	51	32
Albrighton United	34	12	8	14	51	61	32
Dudley Town Reserves	34	13	5	16	47	50	31
Coventry Sporting Reserves	34	12	6	16	52	65	30
Bromsgrove Rovers Reserves	34	9	10	15	53	67	28
Tividale Reserves	34	11	4	19	44	64	26
Westfields	34	7	10	17	59	76	24
Langley	34	8	7	19	38	63	23
Springvale	34	5	8	21	23	62	18

Langley disbanded. Stourport Swifts joined from the Worcester & District League while five reserve sides joined: Ledbury Town, Lye Town, Malvern Town, Oswestry Town and Stourbridge.
The Division was increased to 20 clubs.

1979-80

Premier Division

Team	P	W	D	L	F	A	Pts
Sutton Coldfield Town	42	28	11	3	96	39	67
Lye Town	42	30	7	5	73	29	67
Willenhall Town	42	23	11	8	95	45	57
Hednesford Town	42	19	16	7	72	41	54
Brereton Social	42	20	11	11	86	45	51
Brierley Hill Alliance	42	20	11	11	62	49	51
Shifnal Town	42	19	10	13	72	53	48
Dudley Town	42	20	6	16	61	52	46
Coventry Sporting	42	16	10	16	64	67	42
Ledbury Town	42	13	15	14	62	71	41
Malvern Town	42	13	11	18	56	71	37
Halesowen Town	42	13	11	18	52	69	37
Hinckley Athletic	42	12	12	18	40	59	36
Tividale	42	13	9	20	70	75	35
Gresley Rovers	42	10	14	18	49	69	34
Armitage	42	12	9	21	39	55	33
V.S. Rugby	42	11	11	20	43	60	33
Blakenall	42	11	11	20	45	76	33
Wednesfield Social	42	10	12	20	44	66	32
Darlaston	42	9	13	20	42	86	31
Gornal Athletic	**42**	**7**	**16**	**19**	**52**	**69**	**30**
Bilston	42	8	13	21	50	79	29

Division One

Team	P	W	D	L	F	A	Pts
Rushall Olympic	**36**	**28**	**5**	**3**	**79**	**17**	**61**
Telford United Reserves	36	18	9	9	70	40	45
Oldswinford	36	17	9	10	52	35	43
Chasetown	36	17	8	11	57	43	42
Atherstone United	36	16	10	10	47	39	42
Burntwood	36	15	8	13	54	51	38
Willenhall Town Reserves	36	13	11	12	49	50	37
Causeway Green	36	15	7	14	43	54	37
Tipton Town	36	11	14	11	37	37	36
Donnington Wood	36	13	9	14	46	43	35
Staffordshire Police	36	11	12	13	55	53	34
Wolverhampton United	36	10	13	13	48	57	33
Lichfield	36	9	14	13	36	38	32
Nuneaton Borough Reserves	36	11	10	15	45	61	32
Worcester City Reserves	36	8	14	14	38	54	30
Ludlow Town	36	11	6	19	43	48	28
Shirley Town	36	8	11	17	26	51	27
Alvechurch Reserves	36	6	15	15	42	79	27
G.K.N. Sankey	36	9	7	20	41	58	25

The Division was increased to 22 clubs.

Division Two

Team	P	W	D	L	F	A	Pts
Brewood	**38**	**24**	**8**	**6**	**89**	**37**	**56**
Stafford South End	**38**	**20**	**8**	**10**	**82**	**58**	**48**
Hednesford Town Reserves	**38**	**21**	**6**	**11**	**65**	**51**	**48**
Brereton Town	38	20	7	11	72	51	47
Kidderminster Harriers Reserves	38	17	12	9	82	45	46
Oswestry Town Reserves	38	18	10	10	72	51	46
Coventry Sporting Reserves	38	17	11	10	84	60	45
Springvale	38	19	7	12	58	50	45
Westfields	38	18	8	12	58	41	44
Dudley Town Reserves	38	15	11	12	72	65	41
Lye Town Reserves	38	12	15	11	48	53	39
Bromsgrove Rovers Reserves	38	13	12	13	60	64	38
Stourport Swifts	38	13	12	13	59	64	38
Albrighton United	38	14	9	15	66	72	37
Stourbridge Reserves	38	13	10	15	67	53	36
Halesowen Town Reserves	38	7	11	20	47	75	25
Bridgnorth Sports	38	9	7	22	54	89	25
Ledbury Town Reserves	38	8	7	23	62	109	23
Malvern Town Reserves	38	5	9	24	38	91	19
Tividale Reserves	38	2	10	26	40	96	14

Dales United joined from the Herefordshire League, Tamworth Reserves joined from the Midland Combination, Great Wyrley joined from the Staffordshire County League (South) and Cheltenham Town Reserves also joined. nThe Division was increased to 21 clubs.

West Midlands (Regional) League 1980-1982

1980-81

Premier Division

Shifnal Town	42	31	7	4	89	33	69
Lye Town	42	27	9	6	80	36	63
Willenhall Town	42	25	11	6	93	41	61
Brereton Social	42	22	8	12	74	51	52
Hednesford Town	42	20	11	11	73	48	51
Coventry Sporting	42	19	12	11	75	54	50
Ledbury Town	42	19	10	13	74	52	48
Dudley Town	42	19	10	13	55	44	48
Sutton Coldfield Town	42	18	10	14	71	56	46
Bilston	42	18	10	14	78	65	46
Armitage	42	20	5	17	58	59	45
Rushall Olympic	42	15	13	14	50	52	43
Blakenall	42	14	15	13	55	58	43
Darlaston	42	17	5	20	68	95	39
Gresley Rovers	42	13	10	19	46	62	36
Halesowen Town	42	10	15	17	53	67	35
Wednesfield Social	42	11	11	20	52	67	33
V.S. Rugby	42	9	10	23	50	80	28
Tividale	42	5	17	20	35	64	27
Malvern Town	42	9	7	26	56	93	25
Brierley Hill Alliance	42	6	8	28	33	85	20
Hinckley Athletic	42	3	10	29	43	99	16

Brierley Hill Alliance disbanded.

Division One

Oldswinford	**42**	**32**	**5**	**5**	**95**	**33**	**69**
Chasetown	42	26	11	5	81	25	63
Atherstone United	42	23	13	6	80	33	59
Wolverhampton United	42	26	7	9	80	38	59
Worcester City Reserves	42	24	9	9	83	48	57
Donnington Wood	42	24	6	12	87	68	54
Willenhall Town Reserves	42	21	10	11	64	36	52
Brewood	42	18	10	14	58	58	46
Gornal Athletic	42	16	12	14	59	54	44
Tipton Town	42	19	4	19	73	82	42
Telford United Reserves	42	17	6	19	67	83	40
Causeway Green	42	15	9	18	50	47	39
Ludlow Town	42	15	8	19	71	73	38
Lichfield	42	14	9	19	57	73	37
Staffordshire Police	42	12	12	18	69	86	36
Hednesford Town Reserves	42	11	8	23	58	82	30
Nuneaton Borough Reserves	42	10	9	23	53	74	29
Alvechurch Reserves	42	9	11	22	58	92	29
Shirley Town	42	7	13	22	42	70	27
Stafford South End	42	10	7	25	59	101	27
Burntwood	42	8	9	25	39	82	25
G.K.N. Sankey	**42**	**7**	**8**	**27**	**42**	**87**	**22**

Alvechurch Reserves moved to the Midland Combination.

The Division was reduced to 20 clubs.

Division Two

Bromsgrove Rovers Reserves	**40**	**26**	**8**	**6**	**115**	**49**	**60**
Stourbridge Reserves	40	24	8	8	91	52	56
Westfields	40	24	8	8	89	60	56
Springvale	40	21	10	9	97	60	52
Brereton Town	40	20	9	11	87	65	49
Halesowen Town Reserves	40	20	8	12	91	74	48
Stourport Swifts	40	15	12	13	56	56	42
Albrighton United	40	16	10	14	67	84	42
Malvern Town Reserves	40	16	8	16	67	70	40
Kidderminster Harriers Reserves	40	15	9	16	83	68	39
Great Wyrley	40	16	7	17	72	67	39
Oswestry Town Reserves	40	14	8	18	68	84	36
Bridgnorth Sports	40	14	8	18	43	60	36
Lye Town Reserves	40	13	9	18	67	74	35
Ledbury Town Reserves	40	15	4	21	71	74	34
Cheltenham Town Reserves	40	14	6	20	72	98	34
Tividale Reserves	40	11	11	18	61	76	33
Coventry Sporting Reserves	40	11	11	18	60	80	33
Dales United	40	12	7	21	57	95	31
Dudley Town Reserves	40	10	8	22	39	56	28
Tamworth Reserves	40	5	7	28	40	91	17

Brereton Town, Kidderminster Harriers Reserves, Oswestry Town Reserves, Stourbridge Reserves and Tividale Reserves all left the league. Northpark United joined from the Staffordshire County League (South) and Bilston United, Dowty Ashchurch and Stafford Rangers Reserves also joined.

The Division was reduced to 20 clubs.

1981-82

Premier Division

Shifnal Town	42	26	11	5	82	36	63
Sutton Coldfield Town	42	26	9	7	80	43	61
Halesowen Town	42	24	8	10	84	45	56
Bilston	42	23	8	11	70	49	54
Ledbury Town	42	19	14	9	83	58	52
Rushall Olympic	42	16	18	8	72	54	50
Willenhall Town	42	18	11	13	64	46	47
V.S. Rugby	42	20	7	15	67	51	47
Blakenall	42	20	7	15	59	53	47
Dudley Town	42	17	12	13	61	52	46
Wednesfield Social	42	15	13	14	43	42	43
Lye Town	42	15	12	15	59	49	42
Hednesford Town	42	17	8	17	61	57	42
Coventry Sporting	42	13	11	18	43	54	37
Gresley Rovers	42	13	9	20	50	59	35
Hinckley Athletic	42	12	10	20	43	66	34
Tividale	42	13	6	23	56	82	32
Malvern Town	42	11	10	21	49	78	32
Armitage	42	10	11	21	43	69	31
Oldswinford	42	9	11	22	48	74	29
Brereton Social	42	7	10	25	47	100	24
Darlaston	**42**	**6**	**8**	**28**	**37**	**84**	**20**

Dudley Town, Sutton Coldfield Town and Willenhall Town all moved to the Southern League.

The Division was reduced to 20 clubs.

West Midlands (Regional) League 1982-1983

1982-83

Division One

Team	P	W	D	L	F	A	Pts
Atherstone United	38	23	11	4	79	30	57
Wolverhampton United	38	24	8	6	64	25	56
Chasetown	38	21	13	4	64	29	55
Tipton Town	38	22	8	8	67	31	52
Nuneaton Borough Reserves	38	22	7	9	71	35	51
Brewood	38	18	10	10	55	38	46
Donnington Wood	38	15	14	9	64	45	44
Causeway Green	38	17	7	14	55	49	41
Worcester City Reserves	38	13	10	15	56	59	36
Burntwood	38	12	11	15	51	54	35
Willenhall Town Reserves	38	14	7	17	52	58	35
Bromsgrove Rovers Reserves	38	12	10	16	43	55	34
Stafford South End	38	12	9	17	46	60	33
Ludlow Town	38	13	5	20	38	62	31
Staffordshire Police	38	13	4	21	47	86	30
Gornal Athletic	38	10	9	19	44	72	29
Lichfield	38	9	9	20	53	66	27
Telford United Reserves	38	7	10	21	43	63	24
Shirley Town	38	8	7	23	40	74	23
Hednesford Town Reserves	38	5	11	22	30	71	21

Staffordshire Police moved to the Staffordshire County League (North) while Burntwood, Telford United Reserves, Bromsgrove Rovers Reserves, Causeway Green and Worcester City Reserves also left the league.

The Division was reduced to 17 clubs.

Division Two

Team	P	W	D	L	F	A	Pts
G.K.N. Sankey	36	23	6	7	85	38	52
Northpark United	36	20	10	6	74	40	50
Bilston United	36	19	10	7	73	47	48
Lye Town Reserves	36	19	8	9	69	47	46
Cheltenham Town Reserves	36	16	10	10	63	41	42
Stourport Swifts	36	16	10	10	50	38	42
Springfield	36	18	5	13	63	54	41
Westfields	36	17	6	13	78	54	40
Dudley Town Reserves	36	16	7	13	47	38	39
Coventry Sporting Reserves	36	16	7	13	58	57	39
Stafford Rangers Reserves	36	15	6	15	64	58	36
Malvern Town Reserves	36	15	6	15	68	65	36
Ledbury Town Reserves	36	16	4	16	70	88	36
Albrighton United	36	11	7	18	51	62	29
Halesowen Town Reserves	36	10	8	18	49	70	28
Great Wyrley	36	11	4	21	52	79	26
Dales United	36	9	5	22	55	92	23
Dowty Ashchurch	36	8	6	22	41	76	22
Tamworth Reserves	36	2	5	29	27	93	9

Bridgnorth Sports resigned during the season and their record was expunged. Ledbury Town Reserves, Lye Town Reserves and Tamworth Reserves all left the league. Pelsall Villa, Harrisons and Oldswinford Reserves all joined from the Staffordshire County League (South) while Wolverhampton Casuals and Newport Town also joined.

The Division was reduced to 17 clubs.

1982-83

Premier Division

Team	P	W	D	L	F	A	Pts
Halesowen Town	38	28	6	4	124	37	62
Hinckley Athletic	38	24	7	7	59	32	55
Hednesford Town	38	22	4	12	64	53	48
Shifnal Town	38	19	9	10	78	48	47
Atherstone United	38	21	5	12	73	46	47
Bilston	38	19	7	12	82	50	45
V.S. Rugby	38	17	10	11	69	36	44
Armitage	38	18	8	12	61	51	44
Gresley Rovers	38	15	11	12	69	52	41
Tividale	38	18	5	15	52	48	41
Wednesfield Social	38	17	7	14	47	47	41
Wolverhampton United	38	14	12	12	50	47	40
Lye Town	38	13	10	15	50	49	36
Rushall Olympic	38	12	8	18	59	66	32
Blakenall	38	8	13	17	45	61	29
Coventry Sporting	38	7	14	17	40	64	28
Oldswinford	38	6	11	21	46	78	23
Brereton Social	38	8	6	24	43	89	22
Ledbury Town	38	6	7	25	45	117	19
Malvern Town	38	6	4	28	40	125	16

Bilston changed their name to Bilston Town. Coventry Sporting and V.S. Rugby were promoted to the Southern League and Ledbury Town also left the league. Cradley Town joined from the Midland Combination.

Division One

Team	P	W	D	L	F	A	Pts
Brewood	32	18	8	6	55	34	44
Chasetown	32	19	6	7	56	36	44
Tipton Town	32	19	5	8	65	39	43
Cheltenham Town Reserves	32	17	5	10	60	39	39
G.K.N. Sankey	32	15	6	11	47	38	36
Willenhall Town Reserves	32	13	10	9	51	46	36
Gornal Athletic	32	9	13	10	41	36	31
Donnington Wood	32	11	9	12	62	59	31
Nuneaton Borough Reserves	32	10	11	11	45	43	31
Northpark United	32	11	9	12	47	52	31
Ludlow Town	32	11	6	15	52	58	28
Shirley Town	32	12	3	17	42	56	27
Bilston United	32	10	6	16	47	67	26
Hednesford Town Reserves	32	8	9	15	39	53	25
Lichfield	32	9	7	16	44	65	25
Stafford South End	32	9	6	17	46	59	24
Darlaston	32	7	9	16	38	57	23

Stafford South End left the league. The Division was reduced to 16 clubs.

Division Two

Team	P	W	D	L	F	A	Pts
Great Wyrley	32	20	7	5	67	30	47
Harrisons	32	19	8	5	53	27	46
Stafford Rangers Reserves	32	18	9	5	75	32	45
Wolverhampton Casuals	32	20	5	7	55	30	45
Dudley Town Reserves	32	19	6	7	70	36	44
Dales United	32	17	5	10	60	48	39
Albrighton United	32	14	9	9	61	48	37
Stourport Swifts	32	16	4	12	57	44	36
Newport Town	32	10	12	10	39	39	32
Halesowen Town Reserves	32	10	10	12	46	52	30
Springvale	32	12	5	15	54	48	29
Westfields	32	10	7	15	55	59	27
Pelsall Villa	32	8	5	19	42	76	21
Oldswinford Reserves	32	6	6	20	38	60	18
Dowty Ashchurch	32	8	2	22	44	70	18
Coventry Sporting Reserves	32	5	7	20	27	83	17
Malvern Town Reserves	32	5	3	24	34	95	13

Albrighton United disbanded. Coventry Sporting Reserves and Stafford Rangers Reserves also left the league. Aero Lucas and Atherstone United Reserves joined the league.

The Division was reduced to 14 clubs.

West Midlands (Regional) League 1983-1985

1983-84

Premier Division

Halesowen Town	38	32	3	3	112	36	67
Hednesford Town	38	23	10	5	70	34	56
Atherstone United	38	17	11	10	63	44	45
Gresley Rovers	38	17	9	12	68	61	43
Lye Town	38	15	12	11	55	45	42
Wolverhampton United	38	17	7	14	53	55	41
Oldswinford	38	15	11	12	61	64	41
Armitage	38	17	5	16	67	61	39
Shifnal Town	38	13	12	13	59	56	38
Wednesfield Social	38	15	8	15	52	58	38
Tividale	38	12	12	14	53	48	36
Malvern Town	38	14	7	17	64	61	35
Rushall Olympic	38	11	11	16	55	59	33
Hinckley Athletic	38	12	9	17	51	61	33
G.K.N. Sankey	38	13	7	18	54	74	33
Brereton Social	38	10	12	16	46	62	32
Bilston Town	38	10	11	17	44	58	31
Blakenall	38	11	7	20	39	59	29
Chasetown	38	9	8	21	39	81	26
Cradley Town	***38***	***9***	***4***	***25***	***44***	***72***	***22***

Hednesford Town were promoted to the Southern League, swapping places with Tamworth who were relegated.

Division One

Tipton Town	30	18	11	1	65	28	47
Gornal Athletic	30	18	8	4	60	29	44
Northpark United	30	19	5	6	73	23	43
Harrisons	30	19	5	6	60	29	43
Cheltenham Town Reserves	30	13	10	7	51	37	36
Brewood	30	14	7	9	49	36	35
Great Wyrley	30	13	6	11	52	44	32
Darlaston	30	14	3	13	49	40	31
Dudley Town Reserves	30	9	9	12	31	43	27
Lichfield	30	10	6	14	34	44	26
Willenhall Town Reserves	30	6	10	14	33	58	22
Nuneaton Borough Reserves	30	8	6	16	31	60	22
Ludlow Town	30	8	4	18	38	64	20
Hednesford Town Reserves	30	5	9	16	36	58	19
Shirley Town	30	3	11	16	27	63	17
Bilston United	30	3	10	17	26	59	16

Cheltenham Town Reserves moved to the Midland Combination while both Hednesford Town Reserves and Willenhall Town Reserves also left. The Division was increased to 18 clubs.

Division Two

Halesowen Town Reserves	26	16	8	2	54	21	40
Westfields	26	17	5	4	50	21	39
Newport Town	26	17	2	7	54	24	36
Pelsall Villa	26	14	6	6	47	32	34
Donnington Wood	26	13	6	7	52	35	32
Wolverhampton Casuals	26	13	5	8	42	23	31
Springvale	26	14	2	10	43	37	30
Stourport Swifts	26	13	3	10	47	28	29
Dales United	26	11	5	10	44	40	27
Atherstone United Reserves	26	11	3	12	26	29	25
Aero Lucas	26	5	6	15	29	53	16
Oldswinford Reserves	26	2	8	16	28	70	12
Dowty Ashchurch	26	2	3	21	16	71	7
Malvern Town Reserves	26	1	4	21	20	68	6

Springvale changed their name to Springvale-Tranco. Halesowen Harriers joined from Sunday football (Birmingham Festival League), Ettingshall Holy Trinity and Bloxwich Town both joined from the Staffordshire County League (South) while Broseley Athletic, Harrisons Reserves, Jamaica City, Minworth and Stuarts Athletic also joined. The Division was increased to 17 clubs.

1984-85

Premier Division

Halesowen Town	38	28	6	4	96	36	62
Bilston Town	38	24	5	9	84	49	53
Atherstone United	38	20	8	10	64	40	48
Wednesfield Social	38	20	8	10	52	34	48
Tipton Town	38	19	10	9	67	52	48
Tividale	38	19	9	10	53	39	47
Tamworth	38	16	14	8	66	38	46
Gresley Rovers	38	16	8	14	62	56	40
Hinckley Athletic	38	14	10	14	63	59	38
Oldswinford	38	14	7	17	61	61	35
G.K.N. Sankey	38	11	13	14	47	50	35
Lye Town	38	11	12	15	47	47	34
Rushall Olympic	38	12	10	16	57	58	34
Brereton Social	38	12	10	16	58	83	34
Wolverhampton United	38	10	11	17	39	49	31
Chasetown	38	10	11	17	45	65	31
Malvern Town	38	9	12	17	49	57	30
Blakenall	38	7	10	21	40	69	24
Armitage	38	8	7	23	45	95	23
Shifnal Town	38	5	9	24	30	88	19

Bilston Town were promoted to the Southern League.

Division One

Harrisons	34	26	4	4	77	25	56
Wolverhampton Casuals	34	24	5	5	89	37	53
Westfields	34	21	9	4	74	39	51
Brewood	34	21	3	10	60	42	45
Darlaston	34	17	7	10	65	41	41
Newport Town	34	15	7	12	54	43	37
Dudley Town Reserves	34	15	4	15	57	45	34
Halesowen Town Reserves	34	13	8	13	57	52	34
Pelsall Villa	34	11	11	12	46	45	33
Gornal Athletic	34	10	11	13	45	53	31
Northpark United	34	11	8	15	56	58	30
Great Wyrley	34	11	8	15	49	55	30
Nuneaton Borough Reserves	34	11	6	17	34	62	28
Lichfield	34	10	6	18	42	51	26
Cradley Town	34	7	10	17	46	72	24
Ludlow Town	34	8	8	18	54	92	24
Shirley Town	34	9	5	20	39	71	23
Bilston United	34	4	4	26	32	93	12

Dudley Town disbanded their reserve side.

Division Two

Halesowen Harriers	32	28	1	3	108	21	57
Ettingshall Holy Trinity	32	22	6	4	70	25	50
Springvale-Tranco	32	21	3	8	84	41	45
Broseley Athletic	32	16	11	5	64	36	43
Bloxwich Town	32	16	7	9	57	39	39
Donnington Wood	32	16	6	10	72	51	38
Jamaica City	32	14	8	10	57	44	36
Stourport Swifts	32	14	6	12	68	42	34
Harrisons Reserves	32	12	7	13	54	70	31
Atherstone United Reserves	32	10	10	12	59	61	30
Aero Lucas	32	10	5	17	46	66	25
Dowty Ashchurch	32	9	6	17	33	53	24
Stuarts Athletic	32	6	10	16	42	66	22
Minworth	32	5	11	16	47	81	21
Dales United	32	5	8	19	36	74	18
Malvern Town Reserves	32	6	6	20	36	95	18
Oldswinford Reserves	32	5	3	24	35	103	13

Dales United, Malvern Town Reserves and Minworth left the league. Albright & Wilson, Chasetown Reserves, Clancey Halesowen, Metal Box Sports, Millfields and Wednesbury Town all joined. The Division was increased to 18 clubs.

1985-86
Premier Division

	P	W	D	L	F	A	Pts
Halesowen Town	38	31	4	3	108	28	66
Gresley Rovers	38	25	9	4	91	29	59
Atherstone United	38	26	7	5	90	48	59
Harrisons	38	22	9	7	82	40	53
Wednesfield Social	38	21	7	10	88	48	49
Lye Town	38	18	11	9	54	39	47
G.K.N. Sankey	38	15	12	11	59	64	42
Hinckley Athletic	38	15	11	12	60	50	41
Tamworth	38	15	8	15	68	52	38
Brereton Social	38	13	11	14	58	54	37
Rushall Olympic	38	14	9	15	63	65	37
Malvern Town	38	13	10	15	51	61	36
Shifnal Town	38	9	10	19	38	76	28
Oldswinford	38	9	9	20	46	68	27
Blakenall	38	9	8	21	38	61	26
Tividale	38	8	10	20	51	83	26
Chasetown	38	7	10	21	40	74	24
Wolverhampton United	38	8	8	22	31	66	24
Tipton Town	38	8	8	22	43	79	24
Armitage	38	7	3	28	44	118	17

Halesowen Town were promoted to the Southern League swapping places with Oldbury United who were relegated. Shifnal Town moved to the Shropshire County League.

Division One

	P	W	D	L	F	A	Pts
Halesowen Harriers	34	24	7	3	108	26	55
Wolverhampton Casuals	34	21	5	8	62	33	47
Westfields	34	19	7	8	67	32	45
Ettingshall Holy Trinity	34	17	9	8	69	39	43
Newport Town	34	16	9	9	68	46	41
Halesowen Town Reserves	34	14	9	11	50	43	37
Pelsall Villa	34	15	7	12	43	42	37
Great Wyrley	34	13	10	11	61	52	36
Nuneaton Borough Reserves	34	13	8	13	46	56	34
Cradley Town	34	12	9	13	48	62	33
Brewood	34	13	6	15	60	65	32
Darlaston	34	11	9	14	51	58	31
Bilston United	34	10	10	14	52	61	30
Gornal Athletic	34	9	8	17	43	53	26
Ludlow Town	34	8	9	17	51	64	25
Northpark United	34	9	6	19	43	84	24
Lichfield	**34**	**9**	**2**	**23**	**34**	**81**	**20**
Shirley Town	34	4	8	22	35	94	16

Shirley Town moved to the Midland Combination.
The Division was increased to 20 clubs.

Division Two

	P	W	D	L	F	A	Pts
Springvale-Tranco	**34**	**25**	**5**	**4**	**80**	**27**	**55**
Metal Box Sports	**34**	**23**	**6**	**5**	**66**	**32**	**52**
Broseley Athletic	**34**	**20**	**8**	**6**	**72**	**32**	**48**
Stourport Swifts	**34**	**16**	**12**	**6**	**60**	**36**	**44**
Aero Lucas	**34**	**18**	**6**	**10**	**66**	**45**	**42**
Millfields	34	15	7	12	48	41	37
Atherstone United Reserves	34	15	6	13	80	63	36
Donnington Wood	34	14	8	12	62	59	36
Bloxwich Town	34	12	10	12	49	54	34
Jamaica City	34	13	7	14	64	55	33
Chasetown Reserves	34	12	9	13	58	55	33
Harrisons Reserves	34	12	6	16	61	67	30
Albright & Wilson	34	11	5	18	58	63	27
Wednesbury Town	34	8	8	18	52	73	24
Dowty Ashchurch	34	10	4	20	29	63	24
Oldswinford Reserves	34	7	8	19	32	76	22
Clancey Halesowen	34	8	4	22	40	92	20
Stuarts Athletic	34	3	9	22	46	90	15

Hednesford Progressive joined from the Staffordshire Senior League while Hinton, Brewood Reserves, Gresley Rovers Reserves, Tamworth Reserves and Wolverhampton Casuals Reserves also joined.
The Division was increased to 20 clubs.

1986-87
Premier Division

	P	W	D	L	F	A	Pts
Atherstone United	38	29	4	5	115	30	62
Oldbury United	38	28	5	5	89	28	61
Wednesfield Social	38	26	5	7	80	32	57
Gresley Rovers	38	23	11	4	73	39	57
Tamworth	38	21	4	13	103	47	46
Malvern Town	38	20	6	12	74	51	46
Halesowen Harriers	38	19	6	13	75	51	44
Hinckley Athletic	38	18	6	14	70	67	42
Chasetown	38	12	15	11	64	63	39
Harrisons	38	15	8	15	60	56	38
G.K.N. Sankey	38	13	12	13	73	69	38
Rushall Olympic	38	13	8	17	60	63	34
Lye Town	38	12	9	17	41	56	33
Brereton Social	38	14	5	19	61	80	33
Tividale	38	12	8	18	54	71	32
Wolverhampton United	38	11	8	19	44	63	30
Oldswinford	38	7	8	23	49	93	22
Tipton Town	38	5	8	25	37	109	18
Armitage	38	5	5	28	37	113	15
Blakenall	38	4	5	29	38	116	13

Atherstone United were promoted to the Southern League and Armitage disbanded just before the start of the 1987-88 season.
The Division was reduced to 19 clubs.

Division One

	P	W	D	L	F	A	Pts
Westfields	**38**	**30**	**1**	**7**	**111**	**46**	**61**
Wolverhampton Casuals	38	26	5	7	92	58	57
Broseley Athletic	**38**	**23**	**6**	**9**	**88**	**47**	**52**
Metal Box Sports	38	21	9	8	81	43	51
Springvale-Tranco	38	21	7	10	86	47	49
Newport Town	38	21	5	12	95	64	47
Ettingshall Holy Trinity	38	18	11	9	59	36	47
Great Wyrley	38	18	10	10	75	58	46
Darlaston	38	15	10	13	73	64	40
Pelsall Villa	38	15	8	15	66	83	38
Brewood	38	14	8	16	83	74	36
Ludlow Town	38	14	5	19	64	81	33
Aero Lucas	38	11	9	18	43	65	31
Gornal Athletic	38	11	8	19	61	75	30
Nuneaton Borough Reserves	38	12	6	20	51	69	30
Cradley Town	38	9	10	19	54	74	28
Halesowen Town Reserves	38	9	6	23	44	91	24
Northpark United	**38**	**9**	**5**	**24**	**57**	**98**	**23**
Stourport Swifts	38	8	5	25	41	88	21
Bilston United	38	5	6	27	38	101	16

Halesowen Town Reserves and Metal Box Sports both left the league. Northpark United were relegated and changed their name to Claregate United. Rocester joined from the Staffordshire Senior League. Hednesford Progressive changed their name to Cannock Chase after promotion from Division Two. The Division was reduced to 19 clubs.

Division Two

	P	W	D	L	F	A	Pts
Donnington Wood	36	25	3	8	105	54	53
Millfields	**36**	**22**	**7**	**7**	**77**	**34**	**51**
Hinton	36	23	5	8	87	55	51
Hednesford Progressive	**36**	**18**	**11**	**7**	**70**	**50**	**47**
Atherstone United Reserves	36	20	6	10	86	40	46
Albright & Wilson	36	20	5	11	79	53	45
Wolverhampton Casuals Reserves	36	17	11	8	71	46	45
Jamaica City	36	17	4	15	73	65	38
Bloxwich Town	36	17	4	15	60	58	38
Gresley Rovers Reserves	36	15	7	14	69	54	37
Stuarts Athletic	36	15	3	18	68	72	33
Tamworth Reserves	36	13	6	17	61	88	32
Chasetown Reserves	36	12	7	17	67	70	31
Brewood Reserves	36	13	3	20	55	87	29
Lichfield	36	9	6	21	48	76	24
Oldswinford Reserves	36	6	11	19	46	91	23
Clancey Halesowen	36	7	9	20	38	86	23
Dowty Ashchurch	36	7	6	23	41	87	20
Harrisons Reserves	36	6	6	24	50	103	18

West Midlands (Regional) League 1987-1989

Wednesbury Town were expelled during the season and their record was deleted.
Atherstone United Reserves moved to the Midland Combination Reserve Division and Bloxwich Town, Dowty Ashchurch, Jamaica City, Oldswinford Reserves and Stuarts Athletic also left. Lye Town Reserves joined from the Kidderminster League, Mitchells & Butlers joined from the Birmingham Works League and Malvern Town Reserves, Springvale-Tranco Reserves, Moxley Rangers and Gornal Sports also joined.

The Division was reduced to 18 clubs.

1987-88

Premier Division

Tamworth	34	27	3	4	98	31	57
Oldbury United	34	25	6	3	91	39	56
Lye Town	34	22	8	4	65	27	52
Gresley Rovers	34	20	10	4	74	36	50
Chasetown	34	22	4	8	74	40	48
Halesowen Harriers	34	18	6	10	66	40	42
Malvern Town	34	15	6	13	59	47	36
Wednesfield Social	34	14	7	13	43	43	35
Rushall Olympic	34	13	7	14	43	44	33
Hinckley Athletic	34	11	9	14	58	58	31
Harrisons	34	13	5	16	54	61	31
Blakenall	34	11	7	16	42	49	29
Tividale	34	11	5	18	40	68	27
Westfields	34	10	6	18	60	64	26
Tipton Town	34	7	9	18	38	56	23
G.K.N. Sankey	34	7	7	20	46	73	21
Wolverhampton United	**34**	**4**	**4**	**26**	**25**	**88**	**12**
Oldswinford	34	1	1	32	16	128	3

Brereton Social resigned during the season and their record was deleted. They later replaced their reserves in the Staffordshire County League (South). Tamworth were promoted to the Southern League, swapping places with Paget Rangers who were relegated. Hinckley Town joined from the Central Midlands League. G.K.N. Sankey disbanded.

The Division was increased to 21 clubs.

Division One

Rocester	**36**	**28**	**6**	**2**	**91**	**27**	**62**
Stourport Swifts	**36**	**22**	**7**	**7**	**79**	**40**	**51**
Millfields	**36**	**20**	**11**	**5**	**60**	**38**	**51**
Wolverhampton Casuals	**36**	**20**	**8**	**8**	**74**	**48**	**48**
Great Wyrley	36	19	8	9	76	48	46
Ettingshall Holy Trinity	36	17	12	7	58	43	46
Newport Town	36	15	11	10	68	46	41
Donnington Wood	36	16	7	13	62	60	39
Nuneaton Borough Reserves	36	13	11	12	53	46	37
Aero Lucas	36	14	5	17	51	62	33
Springvale-Tranco	36	12	7	17	54	53	31
Cradley Town	36	12	7	17	45	62	31
Pelsall Villa	36	12	6	18	61	70	30
Ludlow Town	36	12	6	18	39	57	30
Brewood	36	8	13	15	44	51	29
Bilston United	36	7	10	19	49	79	24
Cannock Chase	36	8	8	20	51	92	24
Gornal Athletic	36	5	8	23	35	83	18
Darlaston	36	4	5	27	43	88	13

The Division was reduced to 18 clubs.

Division Two

Hinton	34	20	10	4	70	24	50
Chasetown Reserves	**34**	**19**	**9**	**6**	**77**	**37**	**47**
Moxley Rangers	34	18	11	5	54	28	47
Broseley Athletic	34	20	6	8	73	36	46
Malvern Town Reserves	34	18	9	7	64	35	45
Gresley Rovers Reserves	34	16	9	9	56	33	41
Lichfield	34	16	9	9	72	59	41
Tamworth Reserves	34	17	5	12	67	53	39
Gornal Sports	34	16	5	13	77	63	37
Wolverhampton Casuals Reserves	34	15	3	16	53	55	33
Albright & Wilson	34	13	6	15	60	45	32
Mitchells & Butlers	34	12	7	15	65	52	31
Clancey Halesowen	34	12	6	16	58	70	30
Lye Town Reserves	34	11	4	19	46	66	26
Harrisons Reserves	34	7	6	21	39	85	20
Brewood Reserves	34	7	3	24	42	87	17
Claregate United	34	5	6	23	34	101	16
Springvale-Tranco Reserves	34	5	4	25	34	112	14

Brewood Reserves, Claregate United and Springvale-Tranco Reserves left the league. Hill Top Rangers joined from the Mercian F.A., G.E.C. Blackheath joined from the Birmingham Works League and Hinckley Town Reserves and Rocester Reserves also joined.

The Division was reduced to 17 clubs.

Three points were awarded for a win from the next season.

1988-89   Premier Division

Blakenall	40	25	11	4	81	31	86
Gresley Rovers	40	24	13	3	100	30	85
Halesowen Harriers	40	23	9	8	74	43	78
Paget Rangers	40	23	8	9	91	41	77
Rushall Olympic	40	22	11	7	73	39	77
Oldbury United	40	22	10	8	89	49	76
Hinckley Town	40	23	6	11	96	38	75
Lye Town	40	20	7	13	61	42	67
Chasetown	40	19	9	12	54	48	66
Malvern Town	40	17	12	11	81	47	63
Rocester	40	14	15	11	67	49	57
Harrisons	40	12	10	18	50	71	46
Tividale	40	10	9	21	65	84	39
Hinckley Athletic	40	9	12	19	50	76	39
Wolverhampton Casuals	40	8	13	19	49	86	37
Wednesfield Social	40	9	8	23	33	82	35
Westfields	40	8	9	23	43	97	33
Millfields	40	9	5	26	42	85	32
Oldswinford	40	8	8	24	42	98	32
Tipton Town	40	8	6	26	30	86	30
Stourport Swifts	40	6	11	23	45	94	29

Wednesfield Social changed their name to Wednesfield.

Division One

Newport Town	34	24	6	4	71	27	78
Donnington Wood	34	22	6	6	79	43	72
Ettingshall Holy Trinity	34	21	6	7	71	44	69
Darlaston	34	20	8	6	83	42	68
Pelsall Villa	34	19	9	6	64	41	66
Chasetown Reserves	34	16	7	11	68	62	55
Ludlow Town	34	16	6	12	79	50	54
Springvale-Tranco	34	14	5	15	49	49	47
Aero Lucas	34	12	10	12	55	59	46
Hinton	34	13	7	14	56	65	46
Brewood	34	10	11	13	51	60	41
Cradley Town	34	10	8	16	43	61	38
Nuneaton Borough Reserves	34	9	9	16	50	56	36
Cannock Chase	34	10	6	18	52	72	36
Great Wyrley	34	9	4	21	62	76	31
Gornal Athletic	34	8	7	19	51	78	31
Wolverhampton United	34	6	6	22	42	76	24
Bilston United	34	4	5	25	25	90	17

Bilston United disbanded just before the start of the 1989-90 season and Aero Lucas also left the league.   The Division was reduced to 16 clubs.

West Midlands (Regional) League 1989-1991

Division Two

Broseley Athletic	32	20	5	7	73	44	65
Lichfield	32	19	6	7	72	40	63
Gresley Rovers Reserves	32	18	8	6	80	40	62
Gornal Sports	32	16	9	7	72	45	57
Mitchells & Butlers	32	17	6	9	70	56	57
Lye Town Reserves	32	14	8	10	55	51	50
G.E.C. Blackheath	32	12	10	10	51	64	46
Hill Top Rangers	32	14	4	14	73	69	46
Moxley Rangers	32	13	6	13	46	49	45
Albright & Wilson	32	13	5	14	55	62	44
Clancey Halesowen	32	11	10	11	65	58	43
Hinckley Town Reserves	32	12	6	14	63	67	42
Harrisons Reserves	32	11	6	15	48	59	39
Tamworth Reserves	32	8	5	19	41	63	29
Malvern Town Reserves	32	6	10	16	42	63	28
Rocester Reserves	32	5	6	21	46	80	21
Wolverhampton Casuals Reserves	32	4	8	20	34	76	20

Tamworth Reserves left the league. Wem Town joined from the Shropshire County League. Clancey Halesowen changed their name to Clancey Dudley.

1989-90
Premier Division

Hinckley Town	40	24	10	6	87	30	82
Rocester	40	25	7	8	85	44	82
Gresley Rovers	40	24	8	8	89	42	80
Blakenall	40	24	5	11	78	52	77
Lye Town	40	22	10	8	68	35	76
Hinckley Athletic	40	18	10	12	58	47	64
Wednesfield	40	16	14	10	60	44	62
Oldbury United	40	18	8	14	62	60	62
Halesowen Harriers	40	17	10	13	79	55	61
Chasetown	40	16	12	12	57	36	60
Paget Rangers	40	18	6	16	74	63	60
Harrisons	40	15	11	14	55	54	56
Malvern Town	40	15	10	15	62	62	55
Rushall Olympic	40	15	5	20	65	56	50
Stourport Swifts	40	12	10	18	40	59	46
Wolverhampton Casuals	40	10	9	21	41	80	39
Westfields	40	10	7	23	44	84	37
Oldswinford	40	10	5	25	39	82	35
Tividale	40	8	8	24	42	80	32
Millfields	40	6	9	25	39	90	27
Tipton Town	40	4	12	24	30	99	24

Millfields changed their name to West Bromwich Town. Hinckley Town were promoted to the Southern League and Harrisons disbanded. Ilkeston Town joined from the Central Midlands League. The Division was increased to 22 clubs.

Division One

Darlaston	30	23	4	3	81	35	73
Springvale-Tranco	30	19	6	5	82	41	63
Pelsall Villa	30	20	3	7	73	34	63
Newport Town	30	19	3	8	73	46	60
Ludlow Town	30	14	7	9	80	47	49
Donnington Wood	30	13	8	9	57	56	47
Ettingshall Holy Trinity	30	13	6	11	55	47	45
Gornal Athletic	30	12	6	12	60	51	42
Brewood	30	11	8	11	31	38	41
Cannock Chase	30	9	7	14	52	64	34
Great Wyrley	30	9	6	15	52	64	33
Nuneaton Borough Reserves	30	7	8	15	41	69	29
Wolverhampton United	30	7	7	16	37	71	28
Chasetown Reserves	30	7	6	17	43	60	27
Hinton	30	6	8	16	37	59	26
Cradley Town	30	2	5	23	21	93	11

Brewood moved to the Staffordshire County League and Springvale-Tranco disbanded.

Division Two

Hill Top Rangers	32	25	3	4	82	38	78
Broseley Athletic	32	19	7	6	76	39	64
Lichfield	32	19	6	7	84	44	63
Moxley Rangers	32	18	8	6	55	33	62
Wem Town	32	15	10	7	58	34	55
Clancey Dudley	32	16	5	11	69	43	53
Hinckley Town Reserves	32	15	5	12	48	41	50
Gresley Rovers Reserves	32	15	4	13	63	62	49
Gornal Sports	32	14	3	15	61	47	45
Mitchells & Butlers	32	12	8	12	55	51	44
Lye Town Reserves	32	11	8	13	53	56	41
Albright & Wilson	32	10	4	18	47	60	34
Malvern Town Reserves	32	9	4	19	35	70	31
Harrisons Reserves	32	9	4	19	39	77	31
Rocester Reserves	32	9	3	20	47	84	30
G.E.C. Blackheath	32	6	9	17	30	59	27
Wolverhampton Casuals Reserves	32	3	3	26	24	88	12

Harrisons Reserves disbanded. G.E.C. Blackheath changed their name to Blackheath Electromotors. Cheslyn Hay joined from the Staffordshire County League (South), Bloxwich Strollers joined from the Midland Combination while Oldbury United Reserves, Paget Rangers Reserves and Rushall Olympic Reserves also joined.

1990-91
Premier Division

Gresley Rovers	42	32	5	5	104	36	101
Chasetown	42	24	13	5	79	32	85
Oldbury United	42	23	14	5	75	37	83
Darlaston	42	20	11	11	89	67	71
Hinckley Athletic	42	20	10	12	76	51	70
Wednesfield	42	21	7	14	76	59	70
Ilkeston Town	42	19	12	11	75	49	69
West Bromwich Town	42	19	11	12	76	51	68
Lye Town	42	19	10	13	53	41	67
Halesowen Harriers	42	19	9	14	84	54	66
Rocester	42	18	12	12	72	44	66
Rushall Olympic	42	17	12	13	67	51	63
Stourport Swifts	42	15	13	14	74	56	58
Blakenall	42	14	16	12	56	59	58
Pelsall Villa	42	10	14	18	49	64	44
Wolverhampton Casuals	42	11	10	21	50	98	43
Paget Rangers	42	10	8	24	50	94	38
Oldswinford	42	9	10	23	60	89	37
Tividale	42	9	5	28	45	100	32
Westfields	42	9	11	22	49	87	32
Malvern Town	42	6	7	29	36	106	25
Tipton Town	42	4	8	30	27	97	20

Westfields had 6 points deducted.
Willenhall Town joined following relegation from the Southern League. The Division was reduced to 19 clubs.

Division One

Cradley Town	28	20	6	2	75	27	66
Ludlow Town	28	17	6	5	53	20	57
Cannock Chase	28	16	4	8	62	47	52
Moxley Rangers	28	15	5	8	37	31	50
Great Wyrley	28	13	5	10	45	38	44
Wolverhampton United	28	12	4	12	38	36	40
Donnington Wood	28	11	7	10	41	39	40
Ettingshall Holy Trinity	28	12	4	12	42	57	40
Newport Town	28	10	6	12	41	40	36
Broseley Athletic	28	9	7	12	34	39	34
Lichfield	28	11	1	16	37	47	34
Wem Town	28	9	5	14	38	46	32
Gornal Athletic	28	7	7	14	30	49	28
Hill Top Rangers	28	7	5	16	45	65	26
Chasetown Reserves	28	3	4	21	25	62	13

Hinton resigned from the league during the season and their record was deleted when it stood as follows: 9 2 1 6 10 27 7
They later joined the Herefordshire County League.

West Midlands (Regional) League 1991-1993

Newport Town moved to the Shropshire County League.
Knypersley Victoria joined from the Staffordshire Senior League.

The Division was increased to 20 clubs.

Division Two

Clancey Dudley	32	21	5	6	76	45	68
Oldbury United Reserves	32	20	6	6	57	26	66
Hinckley Town Reserves	32	20	4	8	87	32	64
Mitchells & Butlers	32	19	6	7	57	36	63
Gresley Rovers Reserves	32	18	7	7	78	39	61
Gornal Sports	32	18	6	8	67	33	60
Lye Town Reserves	32	15	9	8	63	43	54
Bloxwich Strollers	32	14	9	9	65	48	51
Rushall Olympic Reserves	32	14	5	13	62	51	47
Cheslyn Hay	32	11	6	15	57	72	39
Rocester Reserves	32	11	5	16	49	88	38
Albright & Wilson	32	9	9	14	60	56	36
Blackheath Electromotors	32	9	9	14	38	49	36
Paget Rangers Reserves	32	7	6	19	56	85	27
Wolverhampton Casuals Reserves	32	5	7	20	36	88	22
Malvern Town Reserves	32	2	11	19	36	77	17
Nuneaton Borough Reserves	32	1	6	25	22	98	9

Hinckley Town Reserves moved to the Midland Combination Reserve Division while Gresley Rovers Reserves and Paget Rangers Reserves also left the league. K Chell joined as a newly formed club, Manders joined (probably from the Wolverhampton Works League), Alvechurch Reserves joined from the Midland Combination Reserve Division, Park Rangers joined from the Staffordshire County League (South) while Cradley Town Reserves, Halesowen Harriers Reserves and Oldswinford Reserves also joined.

The Division was increased to 20 clubs.

1991-92

Premier Division

Gresley Rovers	36	24	7	5	83	37	79
Paget Rangers	36	20	5	11	81	44	65
Stourport Swifts	36	18	10	8	62	45	64
Blakenall	36	17	10	9	67	49	61
Chasetown	36	17	10	9	47	31	61
Rocester	36	17	8	11	64	52	59
Oldbury United	36	17	7	12	61	47	58
Rushall Olympic	36	16	9	11	61	38	57
Lye Town	36	14	11	11	51	34	53
Halesowen Harriers	36	13	11	12	63	52	50
Willenhall Town	36	14	6	16	56	63	48
Pelsall Villa	36	12	11	13	52	58	47
West Bromwich Town	36	11	11	14	41	60	44
Cradley Town	36	12	7	17	39	56	43
Hinckley Athletic	36	9	7	20	36	56	34
Malvern Town	**36**	**8**	**9**	**19**	**39**	**79**	**33**
Wednesfield	36	8	8	20	43	69	32
Westfields	36	6	12	18	48	74	30
Oldswinford	36	7	5	24	34	84	26

Gresley Rovers were promoted to the Southern League.
Alvechurch joined from the Southern League.

Division One

Ilkeston Town	38	31	6	1	121	30	99
Darlaston	38	22	11	5	83	34	77
Donnington Wood	38	21	12	5	77	43	75
Gornal Athletic	38	21	8	9	73	41	71
Knypersley Victoria	38	19	9	10	84	54	66
Ettingshall Holy Trinity	38	15	15	8	60	47	60
Hill Top Rangers	38	17	5	16	75	76	56
Cannock Chase	38	16	7	15	68	71	55
Ludlow Town	38	16	5	17	72	71	53
Moxley Rangers	38	14	9	15	32	42	51
Wolverhampton Casuals	38	13	11	14	51	59	50
Lichfield	38	14	5	19	57	50	47
Tipton Town	38	11	12	15	51	62	45
Wem Town	38	10	10	18	63	73	40
Wolverhampton United	38	8	14	16	63	80	38
Tividale	38	10	6	22	46	72	36
Oldbury United Reserves	38	8	11	19	34	68	35
Great Wyrley	38	9	6	23	45	86	33
Clancey Dudley	38	8	8	22	49	90	32
Broseley Athletic	38	8	8	22	38	93	32

Broseley Athletic and Clancey Dudley left the league.
The Division was reduced to 19 clubs.

Division Two

K Chell	38	28	4	6	128	39	88
Gornal Sports	**38**	**26**	**8**	**4**	**86**	**32**	**86**
Rushall Olympic Reserves	38	21	8	9	91	54	71
Park Rangers	38	22	5	11	91	68	71
Mitchells & Butlers	38	21	7	10	96	48	70
Manders	38	20	9	9	70	40	69
Lye Town Reserves	38	19	7	12	75	51	64
Albright & Wilson	38	18	6	14	74	56	60
Bloxwich Strollers	38	14	10	14	81	71	52
Oldswinford Reserves	38	16	4	18	79	85	52
Halesowen Harriers Reserves	38	14	6	18	63	65	48
Alvechurch Reserves	38	13	9	16	62	84	48
Chasetown Reserves	38	13	7	18	63	86	46
Cradley Town Reserves	38	12	9	17	74	102	45
Blackheath Electromotors	38	12	6	20	65	93	42
Malvern Town Reserves	38	10	9	19	63	68	39
Rocester Reserves	38	11	5	22	53	119	38
Wolverhampton Casuals Reserves	38	9	5	24	58	116	32
Cheslyn Hay	38	7	9	22	62	93	30
Nuneaton Borough Reserves	38	4	7	27	50	114	19

K Chell moved to the North West Counties League while Alvechurch Reserves, Malvern Town Reserves and Nuneaton Borough Reserves also left the league. Hinckley Athletic Reserves and Tividale Reserves both joined. Blackheath Electromotors changed their name to Blackheath Electrodrives.
The Division was reduced to 17 clubs.

1992-93

Premier Division

Oldbury United	36	24	8	4	80	39	80
Chasetown	36	23	11	2	66	28	80
Paget Rangers	36	21	7	8	84	54	70
Rocester	36	20	9	7	71	41	69
Stourport Swifts	36	19	9	8	69	38	66
Ilkeston Town	36	19	8	9	73	38	65
Rushall Olympic	36	17	7	12	61	53	58
Wednesfield	36	14	10	12	58	47	52
Alvechurch	36	14	5	17	58	65	47
West Bromwich Town	36	13	6	17	55	86	45
Pelsall Villa	36	10	12	14	60	54	42
Blakenall	36	9	13	14	57	75	40
Willenhall Town	36	12	4	20	49	69	40
Hinckley Athletic	36	11	6	19	56	68	39
Halesowen Harriers	36	8	9	19	44	62	33
Cradley Town	36	9	6	21	42	71	33
Oldswinford	36	9	6	21	39	80	33
Westfields	36	8	6	22	56	85	30
Lye Town	36	7	8	21	47	72	29

Oldswinford changed their name to Brierley Hill Town.
Alvechurch disbanded but a new club called Alvechurch Sports was formed and took their place in the Premier Division.

The Division was increased to 21 clubs.

Division One

Knypersley Victoria	36	26	3	7	105	34	81
Darlaston	36	25	6	5	69	27	81
Lichfield	36	23	6	7	75	42	75
Ettingshall Holy Trinity	36	20	11	5	69	34	71
Gornal Athletic	36	17	8	11	75	52	59
Cannock Chase	36	16	4	16	50	59	52
Wolverhampton United	36	14	7	15	60	69	49
Great Wyrley	36	12	12	12	44	53	48
Tividale	36	14	5	17	76	67	47
Hill Top Rangers	36	13	8	15	58	62	47
Donnington Wood	36	12	11	13	67	77	47
Malvern Town	36	12	10	14	56	71	46
Oldbury United Reserves	***36***	***10***	***13***	***13***	***52***	***67***	***43***
Moxley Rangers	36	11	11	14	48	53	41
Ludlow Town	36	10	9	17	55	78	39
Wolverhampton Casuals	36	11	5	20	57	72	38
Tipton Town	36	9	11	16	42	63	38
Gornal Sports	36	7	6	23	42	75	27
Wem Town	36	4	6	26	39	84	18

Moxley Rangers had 3 points deducted.
Gornal Sports changed their name to Bilston United.

Divisions One and Two were restructured. Division One was to be for first teams only while Division Two was replaced by a new Reserve Division. Stafford Town and Walsall Wood joined Division One from the Staffordshire Senior League while Bloxwich Strollers, Manders and Cheslyn Hay were promoted from Division Two and Oldbury United Reserves moved to the new 13-club Reserve Division. Division One was increased to 21 clubs.

Division Two

Rushall Olympic Reserves	32	23	4	5	87	42	73
Bloxwich Strollers	**32**	**23**	**2**	**7**	**99**	**39**	**71**
Chasetown Reserves	32	21	5	6	81	28	68
Rocester Reserves	32	20	6	6	104	49	66
Manders	**32**	**20**	**5**	**7**	**83**	**40**	**65**
Blackheath Electrodrives	32	17	5	10	69	56	56
Mitchells & Butlers	32	14	9	9	70	53	51
Hinckley Athletic Reserves	32	14	9	9	57	48	51
Lye Town Reserves	32	14	5	13	61	71	47
Albright & Wilson	32	13	5	14	53	62	44
Oldswinford Reserves	32	10	4	18	40	67	34
Halesowen Harriers Reserves	32	9	6	17	49	86	32
Cradley Town Reserves	32	8	4	20	38	68	28
Wolverhampton Casuals Reserves	32	7	5	20	44	87	26
Park Rangers	32	6	5	21	34	80	23
Cheslyn Hay	**32**	**4**	**6**	**22**	**44**	**87**	**18**
Tividale Reserves	32	5	3	24	38	88	18

Halesowen Harriers Reserves had 1 point deducted.
Albright & Wilson, Blackheath Electrodrives, Mitchells & Butlers and Park Rangers all moved to the Midland Combination. Oldswinford (renamed Brierley Hill Town) withdrew their reserves. Moxley Rangers Reserves and Walsall Wood Reserves both joined from the Staffordshire County League (South) and Pelsall Villa Reserves also joined to form the new reserve division of 13 members.

1993-94

Premier Division

Ilkeston Town	38	25	6	7	102	43	81
Stourport Swifts	38	24	7	7	83	37	79
Oldbury United	38	23	9	6	85	42	78
Blakenall	38	23	8	7	78	45	77
Paget Rangers	38	21	5	12	79	43	68
Knypersley Victoria	38	19	8	11	75	60	65
Rocester	38	20	4	14	83	63	64
Hinckley Athletic	38	18	7	13	77	58	61
Chasetown	38	18	6	14	51	57	60
Pelsall Villa	38	16	8	14	70	78	56
Willenhall Town	38	15	8	15	73	60	53
Wednesfield	38	13	11	14	65	63	50
Halesowen Harriers	38	15	5	18	63	66	50
Darlaston	38	12	12	14	61	74	48
Lye Town	38	10	10	18	43	67	40
Brierley Hill Town	38	11	5	22	56	83	38
Rushall Olympic	38	10	7	21	53	76	34
Westfields	38	7	7	24	58	92	28
Cradley Town	38	4	10	24	42	104	22
West Bromwich Town	38	3	3	32	37	123	12

Rushall Olympic had 3 points deducted.
Alvechurch Sports disbanded in mid-season and their record was deleted when it stood as follows: 13 7 2 4 23 14 23
Ilkeston Town were promoted to the Southern League and West Bromwich Town disbanded.

A new competition was formed called the Midland Football Alliance and Brierley Hill Town, Chasetown, Halesowen Harriers, Hinckley Athletic, Knypersley Victoria, Oldbury United, Paget Rangers, Rocester, Rushall Olympic and Willenhall Town all left to become founder members.

The division became all floodlit but was reduced to 19 clubs.

Division One

Stafford Town	**40**	**32**	**2**	**6**	**109**	**52**	**98**
Gornal Athletic	**40**	**30**	**4**	**6**	**92**	**35**	**94**
Tividale	**40**	**26**	**5**	**9**	**96**	**48**	**83**
Ludlow Town	**40**	**21**	**7**	**12**	**70**	**39**	**70**
Walsall Wood	**40**	**19**	**10**	**11**	**71**	**40**	**67**
Bloxwich Strollers	**40**	**20**	**3**	**17**	**101**	**68**	**63**
Wolverhampton United	40	18	8	14	89	70	62
Tipton Town	40	19	5	16	68	67	62
Malvern Town	**40**	**18**	**8**	**14**	**73**	**74**	**62**
Ettingshall Holy Trinity	**40**	**16**	**10**	**14**	**70**	**71**	**58**
Wolverhampton Casuals	40	17	5	18	73	63	56
Hill Top Rangers	**40**	**14**	**11**	**15**	**66**	**72**	**53**
Lichfield	40	14	12	14	66	60	50
Great Wyrley	40	13	9	18	63	85	48
Cannock Chase	40	12	11	17	60	84	47
Donnington Wood	40	11	10	19	50	54	43
Manders	**40**	**11**	**10**	**19**	**54**	**70**	**43**
Bilston United	**40**	**11**	**10**	**19**	**54**	**91**	**43**
Moxley Rangers	40	8	5	27	47	81	29
Wem Town	40	8	5	27	46	116	29
Cheslyn Hay	40	5	4	31	32	110	19

Lichfield had 4 points deducted.
Lichfield changed their name to Lichfield City. Cheslyn Hay moved to the Midland Combination and Donnington Wood disbanded. Goodyear joined from the Wolverhampton Works League, Morda United joined from the Mid-Wales League while Darlaston Reserves and Gornal Athletic Reserves also joined.

The Division was reduced to 20 clubs.

West Midlands (Regional) League 1994-1996

Reserve Division

Rushall Olympic Reserves	24	22	1	1	75	20	67
Rocester Reserves	24	16	5	3	73	31	53
Lye Town Reserves	24	13	3	8	59	44	42
Hinckley Athletic Reserves	24	10	7	7	50	33	37
Pelsall Villa Reserves	24	9	6	9	50	47	33
Wolverhampton Casuals Reserves	24	9	6	9	41	47	33
Oldbury United Reserves	24	10	3	11	42	49	33
Chasetown Reserves	24	10	3	11	47	41	30
Halesowen Harriers Reserves	24	7	8	9	43	53	29
Walsall Wood Reserves	24	8	1	15	33	52	25
Tividale Reserves	24	6	5	13	33	47	23
Cradley Town Reserves	24	4	8	12	28	47	20
Moxley Rangers Reserves	24	2	4	18	15	78	10

Chasetown Reserves had 3 points deducted.
Wolverhampton Casuals Reserves moved to the Midland Combination while Halesowen Harriers Reserves, Lye Town Reserves, Moxley Rangers Reserves and Walsall Wood Reserves also left. The remaining clubs were all promoted to Division One and the Reserve Division closed down.

1994-95
Premier Division

Pelsall Villa	36	28	3	5	83	31	87
Blakenall	36	27	4	5	101	22	85
Stourport Swifts	36	25	7	4	91	29	82
Stafford Town	36	21	5	10	85	53	67
Westfields	36	19	6	11	76	53	63
Walsall Wood	36	18	8	10	84	57	62
Darlaston	36	17	5	14	71	60	56
Bloxwich Strollers	36	15	5	16	50	60	50
Lye Town	36	15	4	17	67	59	49
Wednesfield	36	15	4	17	63	72	49
Gornal Athletic	36	12	10	14	53	54	46
Manders	36	13	6	17	58	83	45
Ludlow Town	36	10	14	12	43	52	44
Tividale	36	13	3	20	49	69	42
Cradley Town	36	11	7	18	46	71	37
Ettingshall Holy Trinity	36	9	6	21	63	78	33
Hill Top Rangers	36	8	4	24	46	98	28
Bilston United	*36*	*6*	*5*	*25*	*39*	*106*	*23*
Malvern Town	36	5	4	27	31	89	19

Stafford Town had 1 point deducted.
Cradley Town had 3 points deducted.
Blakenall were promoted to the Midland Football Alliance swapping places with Brierley Hill Town who were relegated. Manders disbanded.

Division One

Wolverhampton Casuals	38	29	2	7	126	53	89
Lichfield City	38	25	6	7	107	37	81
Morda United	38	24	4	10	92	45	76
Wem Town	38	20	5	13	69	60	65
Moxley Rangers	38	20	4	14	85	73	64
Rocester Reserves	38	18	10	10	91	66	61
Rushall Olympic Reserves	38	18	6	14	65	65	60
Tipton Town	38	18	5	15	80	52	59
Goodyear	38	17	8	13	81	68	59
Great Wyrley	38	15	11	12	85	56	56
Chasetown Reserves	38	15	11	12	73	59	56
Pelsall Villa Reserves	38	13	11	14	74	80	50
Hinckley Athletic Reserves	38	14	6	18	97	99	48
Oldbury United Reserves	38	14	7	17	77	71	46
Wolverhampton United	38	12	9	17	71	95	45
Tividale Reserves	38	10	10	18	45	67	39
Cannock Chase	38	10	7	21	57	98	37
Gornal Athletic Reserves	38	7	10	21	49	91	31
Cradley Town Reserves	38	8	5	25	57	93	29
Darlaston Reserves	38	3	3	32	31	184	12

Oldbury United Reserves and Rocester Reserves each had 3 points deducted.

Tividale Reserves had 1 point deducted.
Wem Town, Cradley Town Reserves, Darlaston Reserves and Pelsall Villa Reserves all left the league. Bandon joined from the Kidderminster League and Bromyard Town joined from the Herefordshire League. Brereton Social joined as a newly re-formed club, having disbanded in 1994 with financial problems after finishing bottom of the Midland League. Lichfield City had been playing on Breretons ground in 1994-95. Mahal and Sikh Hunters joined from the Staffordshire County League (South) and Pershore Town Reserves also joined.
The Division was increased to 21 clubs.

1995-96
Premier Division

Wednesfield	36	28	6	2	95	30	90
Pelsall Villa	36	27	5	4	97	30	86
Lye Town	36	20	11	5	80	34	71
Stafford Town	36	19	10	7	79	35	67
Stourport Swifts	36	19	10	7	74	50	67
Bloxwich Strollers	36	17	9	10	67	50	60
Walsall Wood	36	16	8	12	61	42	56
Gornal Athletic	36	16	7	13	55	42	55
Westfields	36	16	6	14	86	73	54
Ludlow Town	36	14	9	13	68	71	51
Ettingshall Holy Trinity	36	11	9	16	62	80	42
Tividale	36	10	9	17	65	80	39
Lichfield City	36	9	10	17	43	65	37
Malvern Town	36	9	9	18	34	67	36
Brierley Hill Town	36	10	4	22	49	73	34
Cradley Town	36	8	7	21	55	82	31
Wolverhampton Casuals	36	9	4	23	53	108	31
Darlaston	36	5	11	20	40	86	26
Hill Top Rangers	36	4	6	26	34	99	18

Pelsall Villa were promoted to the Midland Football Alliance.
Lichfield City moved to Sunday football.
Darlaston changed their name to Darlaston Town.
The Division was reduced to 18 clubs.

Division One

Goodyear	40	27	6	7	110	45	87
Wolverhampton United	**40**	**27**	**3**	**10**	**85**	**50**	**84**
Rocester Reserves	40	24	10	6	109	46	82
Morda United	40	26	4	10	87	54	82
Chasetown Reserves	40	23	6	11	92	69	75
Bandon	40	22	7	11	94	57	73
Tipton Town	40	21	10	9	78	41	73
Rushall Olympic Reserves	40	21	4	15	98	70	64
Bilston United	40	17	10	13	92	84	61
Brereton Social	40	14	12	14	65	62	54
Moxley Rangers	40	16	8	16	70	64	53
Bromyard Town	40	16	5	19	70	67	53
Hinckley Athletic Reserves	40	15	4	21	71	84	49
Gornal Athletic Reserves	40	13	5	22	42	91	44
Great Wyrley	40	13	4	23	55	103	43
Mahal	40	12	6	22	61	89	42
Oldbury United Reserves	40	11	7	22	68	87	40
Pershore Town Reserves	40	10	7	23	47	92	37
Tividale Reserves	40	10	6	24	51	92	36
Cannock Chase	40	7	9	24	54	97	30
Sikh Hunters	40	6	5	29	50	115	23

Rushall Olympic Reserves and Moxley Rangers each had 3 points deducted.
Moxley Rangers and Goodyear both disbanded and Hinckley Athletic Reserves and Rocester Reserves both left the league.

Division One was split into two sections, North and South.
The North Section was formed of 13 clubs: Brereton Social, Cannock Chase, Chasetown Reserves, Great Wyrley, Morda United, Rushall Olympic Reserves and Sikh Hunters, plus 6 new members – Blakenall Reserves, Brereton Town, Corestone Services, Heath Hayes, Sporting Khalsa and Wolverhampton Casuals Reserves.

The South Section was formed of 14 clubs: Bandon, Bilston United, Bromyard Town, Gornal Athletic Reserves, Mahal, Oldbury United Reserves, Pershore Town Reserves, Tipton Town and Tividale Reserves, plus 5 new members – Bustleholme, Cradley Town Reserves, Kington Town, Leominster Town and Smethwick Rangers.

1996-97
Premier Division

Wednesfield	34	26	5	3	103	25	83
Stourport Swifts	34	24	5	5	103	34	77
Bloxwich Strollers	34	23	7	4	84	29	76
Lye Town	34	20	6	8	82	40	66
Brierley Hill Town	34	20	5	9	83	44	65
Stafford Town	34	17	9	8	57	40	60
Wolverhampton Casuals	34	17	7	10	72	69	58
Gornal Athletic	34	15	8	11	55	48	53
Ludlow Town	34	15	7	12	63	57	52
Westfields	34	13	8	13	50	53	47
Tividale	34	12	8	14	53	78	44
Darlaston Town	34	10	9	15	49	60	39
Ettingshall Holy Trinity	34	8	7	19	42	81	31
Cradley Town	34	7	6	21	51	83	27
Malvern Town	34	6	8	20	47	70	26
Walsall Wood	34	6	6	22	35	72	24
Wolverhampton United	34	5	7	22	34	102	22
Hill Top Rangers	34	2	2	30	27	105	8

Wednesfield were promoted to the Midland Football Alliance and Hill Top Rangers reverted to junior football.
Clubs in italics were transferred from one regional section to the other.

Division One (North)

Great Wyrley	24	20	1	3	66	20	61
Blakenall Reserves	24	17	3	4	71	19	54
Brereton Town	24	15	5	4	61	31	50
Brereton Social	24	11	5	8	65	47	38
Morda United	24	11	4	9	50	45	37
Cannock Chase	24	11	3	10	56	57	36
Heath Hayes	24	9	5	10	38	49	32
Sikh Hunters	24	8	4	12	62	72	28
Corestone Services	24	7	7	10	36	59	28
Wolverhampton Casuals Reserves	24	8	3	13	45	75	27
Rushall Olympic Reserves	24	7	2	15	32	55	23
Chasetown Reserves	24	6	2	16	43	54	20
Sporting Khalsa	24	2	4	18	24	66	10

Sporting Khalsa moved back to Sunday football while Chasetown Reserves and Rushall Olympic Reserves also left. Lawson Mardon Star (formerly Star Aluminium), Lucas Flight Controls, Newport Town and Walsall Wood Reserves joined. Section increased to 15 clubs.

Division One (South)

Kington Town	26	22	2	2	91	35	68
Bustleholme	26	16	4	6	62	32	52
Bandon	26	15	3	8	70	31	48
Smethwick Rangers	26	14	5	7	50	35	47
Bromyard Town	26	14	2	10	63	43	44
Leominster Town	26	12	4	10	70	58	40
Tipton Town	26	12	4	10	58	55	40
Bilston United	26	11	4	11	57	52	37
Oldbury United Reserves	26	10	7	9	44	42	37
Mahal	26	10	6	10	51	44	36
Cradley Town Reserves	26	6	4	16	43	73	22
Tividale Reserves	26	5	4	17	31	81	19
Pershore Town Reserves	26	3	6	17	28	78	15
Gornal Athletic Reserves	26	1	7	18	27	86	10

Bilston United moved to the Wolverhampton League and Oldbury United Reserves also left the league.
Birmingham College of Food, Hinton, Wellington, Halesowen Harriers Reserves and Malvern Town Reserves all joined.

1997-98
Premier Division

Lye Town	34	26	6	2	91	35	84
Stourport Swifts	34	23	6	5	101	34	75
Brierley Hill Town	34	21	5	8	64	34	68
Kington Town	34	21	3	10	97	67	66
Bloxwich Strollers	34	18	4	12	81	49	58
Malvern Town	34	17	4	13	73	59	55
Wolverhampton Casuals	34	15	6	13	64	52	51
Gornal Athletic	34	15	5	14	56	50	50
Darlaston Town	34	15	3	16	78	70	48
Tividale	34	15	6	13	64	57	48
Ludlow Town	34	14	3	17	58	71	45
Stafford Town	34	12	7	15	49	57	43
Walsall Wood	34	11	7	16	49	64	40
Westfields	34	11	5	18	57	69	38
Bustleholme	34	11	3	20	48	76	36
Cradley Town	34	9	5	20	54	80	32
Ettingshall Holy Trinity	34	5	7	22	37	100	22
Wolverhampton United	34	2	5	27	19	116	11

Tividale had 3 points deducted.
Stourport Swifts were promoted to the Midland Football Alliance and Bloxwich Strollers disbanded. Dudley Town joined after re-forming.
The Division was increased to 21 clubs.

Division One (North)

Bandon	28	20	6	2	86	31	66
Lawson Mardon Star	28	19	3	6	100	48	60
Blakenall Reserves	28	17	4	7	78	33	55
Brereton Social	28	14	7	7	60	43	49
Heath Hayes	28	15	2	11	62	55	47
Great Wyrley	28	14	5	9	55	37	44
Morda United	28	13	5	10	47	47	44
Brereton Town	28	13	4	11	63	61	42
Newport Town	28	11	8	9	64	45	41
Sikh Hunters	28	10	4	14	46	53	34
Lucas Flight Controls	28	8	7	13	60	72	31
Wolverhampton Casuals Reserves	28	9	4	15	51	79	31
Corestone Services	28	6	2	20	37	78	20
Cannock Chase	28	6	2	20	40	102	20
Walsall Wood Reserves	28	3	1	24	33	98	10

Great Wyrley had 3 points deducted.
Brereton Town had 1 point deducted.
Lawson Mardon Star changed their name to Star following their promotion.
Blakenall Reserves and Brereton Town left the league.
Little Drayton Rangers, Sedgley White Lions, Shifnal Town Reserves, Wolverhampton Town and Wyrley Rangers joined.

Division One (South)

Smethwick Rangers	26	18	5	3	75	32	59
Tipton Town	26	18	4	4	71	26	58
Leominster Town	26	15	4	7	68	44	49
Halesowen Harriers Reserves	26	12	7	7	54	35	43
Bromyard Town	26	11	6	9	62	47	39
Tividale Reserves	26	11	7	8	38	36	37
Wellington	26	11	4	11	45	53	37
Cradley Town Reserves	26	10	6	10	52	40	36
Birmingham College of Food	26	11	3	12	55	48	36
Malvern Town Reserves	26	9	8	9	38	52	35
Mahal	26	10	2	14	54	62	32
Pershore Town Reserves	26	3	7	16	28	94	16
Hinton	26	4	3	19	33	67	15
Gornal Athletic Reserves	26	2	8	16	18	55	14

Tividale Reserves had 3 points deducted.
Birmingham College of Food and Gornal Athletic Reserves both left the league. Causeway United joined from the Birmingham A.F.A., Borgfield Celtic joined as a newly formed club and Lye Town Reserves also joined.

1998-99

Premier Division

Kington Town	40	32	3	5	120	39	99
Cradley Town	40	28	3	9	98	40	87
Stafford Town	40	27	5	8	89	38	86
Wolverhampton Casuals	40	24	5	11	99	72	77
Smethwick Rangers	40	21	8	11	88	52	71
Darlaston Town	40	21	7	12	81	63	70
Bandon	40	19	7	14	72	53	64
Malvern Town	40	16	12	12	76	62	60
Tipton Town	40	17	6	17	62	75	57
Bustleholme	40	16	7	17	63	71	55
Gornal Athletic	40	14	11	15	68	65	53
Lye Town	40	12	15	13	56	54	51
Star	40	14	8	18	55	63	50
Dudley Town	40	11	13	16	52	67	46
Tividale	40	12	9	19	55	69	45
Brierley Hill Town	40	11	12	17	57	74	45
Westfields	40	9	15	16	57	69	42
Ludlow Town	40	12	5	23	46	82	41
Ettingshall Holy Trinity	40	10	9	21	62	87	39
Walsall Wood	40	5	7	28	43	99	22
Wolverhampton United	**40**	**1**	**9**	**30**	**33**	**138**	**12**

Cradley Town promoted to the Midland Football Alliance.
The Division was increased to 22 clubs.

Division One (North)

Heath Hayes	**28**	**19**	**5**	**4**	**75**	**28**	**62**
Little Drayton Rangers	**28**	**19**	**6**	**3**	**74**	**24**	**60**
Lucas Flight Controls	28	18	4	6	91	37	58
Brereton Social	28	16	8	4	83	48	56
Newport Town	28	17	5	6	62	40	56
Great Wyrley	28	17	5	6	75	35	53
Cannock Chase	28	14	7	7	63	43	49
Sedgley White Lions	28	11	7	10	44	38	40
Morda United	28	9	3	16	55	72	30
Shifnal Town Reserves	28	9	2	17	42	66	29
Wolverhampton Casuals Reserves	28	8	4	16	53	79	28
Wyrley Rangers	28	6	5	17	39	92	23
Wolverhampton Town	28	3	7	18	35	71	16
Corestone Services	28	2	8	18	37	105	14
Walsall Wood Reserves	28	4	22	25	75	9	

Little Drayton Rangers and Great Wyrley each had 3 points deducted. Walsall Wood Reserves had 1 point deducted.
Brereton Social disbanded their Saturday side as they were unable to find a manager to run it. Wolverhampton Casuals Reserves, Wolverhampton Town and Wyrley Rangers also left the league. Shawbury United joined from the Shropshire County League and Heath Hayes Reserves also joined. The Division was reduced to 13 clubs.

Division One (South)

Wellington	26	22	1	3	115	17	67
Causeway United	**26**	**21**	**1**	**4**	**75**	**24**	**64**
Leominster Town	26	13	5	8	57	48	44
Bromyard Town	26	13	3	10	43	34	42
Tividale Reserves	26	12	4	10	48	49	40
Sikh Hunters	26	12	3	11	68	70	39
Halesowen Harriers Reserves	26	11	4	11	59	51	37
Malvern Town Reserves	26	9	7	10	45	54	34
Cradley Town Reserves	26	10	2	14	43	50	32
Hinton	26	10	2	14	53	68	32
Pershore Town Reserves	26	9	4	13	28	50	31
Mahal	26	7	5	14	42	67	26
Lye Town Reserves	26	8	1	17	44	91	25
Borgfield Celtic	26	3	2	21	36	83	11

Halesowen Harriers Reserves, Lye Town Reserves and Tividale Reserves all left the league. Bewdley Town joined from the Kidderminster League, Ledbury Town joined from the Midland Combination and Chaddesley Corbett also joined.
The Division was reduced to 12 clubs.

1999-2000

Premier Division

Stafford Town	42	35	4	3	113	31	109
Causeway United	42	34	2	6	88	35	104
Darlaston Town	42	30	5	7	115	64	95
Bandon	42	26	7	9	83	46	85
Wolverhampton Casuals	42	25	6	11	99	54	81
Kington Town	42	25	3	14	88	68	72
Tividale	42	19	9	14	66	58	66
Heath Hayes	42	19	4	19	64	66	61
Malvern Town	42	17	7	18	73	56	58
Little Drayton Rangers	42	16	10	16	64	66	58
Lye Town	42	15	9	18	65	66	54
Dudley Town	42	13	13	16	53	59	52
Gornal Athletic	42	14	4	24	58	75	46
Tipton Town	42	12	9	21	61	87	45
Smethwick Rangers	42	12	8	22	67	95	44
Ettingshall Holy Trinity	42	11	10	21	53	91	43
Ludlow Town	42	10	11	21	52	75	41
Brierley Hill Town	42	11	8	23	50	73	41
Bustleholme	42	10	9	23	69	95	39
Westfields	42	9	9	24	56	89	36
Walsall Wood	42	8	10	24	55	99	34
Star	42	8	9	25	37	81	33

Kington Town had 6 points deducted.
Stafford Town were promoted to the Midland Football Alliance and Bandon disbanded. Smethwick Rangers changed their name to Warley Rangers. The Division was increased to 23 clubs.

Division One (North)

Shawbury United	**24**	**18**	**3**	**3**	**75**	**19**	**57**
Wolverhampton United	24	16	2	6	55	23	50
Great Wyrley	24	16	2	6	57	31	50
Sedgley White Lions	24	13	8	3	48	18	47
Cannock Chase	24	15	2	7	67	46	47
Newport Town	24	13	4	7	44	28	43
Lucas Flight Controls	24	8	5	11	58	50	29
Shifnal Town Reserves	24	8	5	11	45	55	29
Morda United	24	8	1	15	40	61	25
Walsall Wood Reserves	24	6	5	13	35	59	23
Borgfield Celtic	24	4	5	15	38	75	17
Heath Hayes Reserves	24	3	5	16	28	71	14
Corestone Services	24	1	7	16	28	82	9

Corestone Services had 1 point deducted.
Borgfield Celtic and Cannock Chase both disbanded. Ounsdale joined from the Kidderminster League, Ecceshall Reserves joined from the Staffordshire County League (North), Brereton Social joined as a newly re-formed club after a seasons inactivity and Chasetown Reserves also joined as a newly re-formed side. Corestone Services changed their name to Wolverhampton Sports G.N.S.T. and Lucas Flight Controls changed their name to Lucas Sports. The Division was increased to 14 clubs.

Division One (South)

Bromyard Town	**22**	**17**	**2**	**3**	**75**	**27**	**53**
Wellington	**22**	**16**	**4**	**2**	**65**	**21**	**52**
Ledbury Town	22	14	2	6	65	35	44
Sikh Hunters	22	9	4	9	58	51	31
Hinton	22	10	1	11	40	52	31
Malvern Town Reserves	22	8	6	8	37	38	30
Leominster Town	22	8	3	11	41	53	27
Chaddesley Corbett	22	8	2	12	47	53	26
Bewdley Town	22	7	5	10	42	48	26
Pershore Town Reserves	22	7	3	12	47	66	24
Cradley Town Reserves	22	7	3	12	40	63	21
Mahal	22	3	1	18	26	76	10

Cradley Town Reserves had 3 points deducted.
Cradley Town Reserves left the league. Brintons Athletic joined from the Kidderminster League having changed their name from Brintons Chainwire and Bustleholme Reserves joined from the Midland Combination. Lye Town Reserves and Gornal Athletic Reserves both joined as newly formed sides.

2000-01
Premier Division

Team	P	W	D	L	F	A	Pts
Ludlow Town	44	34	9	1	100	35	111
Warley Rangers	44	29	7	8	129	54	94
Little Drayton Rangers	44	27	7	10	91	53	88
Darlaston Town	44	24	7	13	111	76	79
Causeway United	44	22	11	11	78	47	77
Shawbury United	44	22	6	16	77	59	72
Malvern Town	44	19	16	9	83	67	72
Kington Town	44	19	9	16	92	78	66
Lye Town	44	18	12	14	68	63	66
Wolverhampton Casuals	44	17	12	15	82	67	63
Wellington	44	19	6	19	69	75	63
Tividale	44	16	11	17	72	74	59
Star	44	15	12	17	77	69	57
Westfields	44	14	14	16	60	63	56
Heath Hayes	44	15	8	21	63	74	53
Bustleholme	44	15	6	23	79	91	51
Ettingshall Holy Trinity	44	14	9	21	58	80	51
Dudley Town	44	13	8	23	48	72	47
Bromyard Town	44	10	10	24	51	97	40
Walsall Wood	44	9	10	25	54	78	37
Gornal Athletic	44	10	7	27	59	105	37
Brierley Hill Town	44	10	7	27	48	125	37
Tipton Town	44	10	6	28	61	108	36

Malvern Town had 1 point deducted.
Ludlow Town were promoted to the Midland Football Alliance. Warley Rangers changed their name back to Smethwick Rangers. Brierley Hill Town merged with West Hagley and continued as Brierley & Hagley Alliance.
The Division was increased to 24 clubs.

Division One (North)

Team	P	W	D	L	F	A	Pts
Wolverhampton United	26	23	0	3	101	27	69
Ounsdale	26	22	1	3	85	21	67
Brereton Social	26	18	1	7	63	29	55
Newport Town	26	14	4	8	60	47	46
Lucas Sports	26	13	6	7	80	46	45
Great Wyrley	26	14	2	10	65	50	38
Eccleshall Reserves	26	10	5	11	37	37	35
Morda United	26	10	2	14	29	62	32
Walsall Wood Reserves	26	8	5	13	41	64	25
Sikh Hunters	26	8	1	17	45	71	25
Shifnal Town Reserves	26	7	3	16	39	67	23
Heath Hayes Reserves	26	5	5	16	34	72	20
Wolverhampton Sports G.N.S.T.	26	5	4	17	30	74	19
Chasetown Reserves	26	2	7	17	31	73	13

Great Wyrley had 6 points deducted.
Walsall Wood Reserves had 4 points deducted.
Shifnal Town Reserves had 1 point deducted.
Chasetown Reserves and Shifnal Town Reserves both left the league.
Wrockwardine Wood joined from the Bridgnorth League, Shenstone Pathfinder joined from the Birmingham A.F.A. and Marston Wolves joined from the Wolverhampton Combination. Darlaston Town Reserves and Wyrley Rangers also joined.
The Division was increased to 16 clubs.

Division One (South)

Team	P	W	D	L	F	A	Pts
Ledbury Town	22	16	2	4	99	37	49
Brintons Athletic	22	14	4	4	66	40	46
Sedgley White Lions	22	13	2	7	61	29	41
Chaddesley Corbett	22	11	6	5	55	39	39
Bewdley Town	22	12	2	8	58	37	38
Mahal	22	11	0	11	50	57	33
Hinton	22	8	6	8	36	47	30
Bustleholme Reserves	22	7	4	11	41	44	25
Malvern Town Reserves	22	9	1	12	37	55	25
Leominster Town	22	5	4	13	39	66	19
Lye Town Reserves	22	5	1	16	29	74	16
Pershore Town Reserves	22	4	2	16	19	65	14

Malvern Town Reserves had 3 points deducted.
Ledbury Town had 1 point deducted.
Gornal Athletic Reserves resigned during the season and their record at the time was deleted: 2 0 0 2 0 11 0
Pershore Town Reserves left the league. Malvern Rangers joined from the Worcester & District League, Ludlow Town Reserves joined from the Kidderminster League, Wyre Forest joined as a newly re-formed club having resigned from the Midland Combination during the 2000-01 season and Bridgnorth Town Reserves also joined.
The Division was increased to 14 clubs.

2001-02
Premier Division

Team	P	W	D	L	F	A	Pts
Causeway United	46	29	12	5	107	55	99
Tividale	46	27	10	9	94	57	88
Wolverhampton Casuals	46	26	8	12	89	69	86
Little Drayton Rangers	46	24	13	9	98	54	85
Westfields	46	24	9	13	89	53	81
Ledbury Town	46	26	3	17	103	85	81
Star	46	24	8	14	91	65	80
Kington Town	46	20	14	12	76	42	74
Malvern Town	46	20	11	15	87	57	71
Heath Hayes	46	19	13	14	60	54	70
Tipton Town	46	19	12	15	76	50	69
Brierley & Hagley Alliance	46	18	15	13	74	60	69
Wellington	46	18	11	17	63	69	65
Lye Town	46	16	15	15	59	47	63
Ettingshall Holy Trinity	46	16	13	17	66	73	61
Bustleholme	46	16	10	20	80	92	58
Wolverhampton United	46	15	11	20	79	81	56
Shawbury United	46	13	14	19	69	83	53
Darlaston Town	46	13	12	21	69	99	51
Bromyard Town	46	11	10	25	73	97	43
Gornal Athletic	46	7	15	24	54	113	36
Smethwick Rangers	46	11	3	32	70	147	36
Walsall Wood	46	7	12	27	52	96	33
Dudley Town	46	3	6	37	42	122	15

Tividale had 3 points deducted.
Causeway United were promoted to the Midland Football Alliance and Star moved to the Shropshire County League. Smethwick Rangers changed their name to Smethwick Sikh Temple.
The Division was reduced to 22 clubs.

Division One (North)

Team	P	W	D	L	F	A	Pts
Ounsdale	30	24	5	1	101	15	77
Great Wyrley	30	24	4	2	127	33	73
Brereton Social	30	22	5	3	83	31	71
Newport Town	30	16	5	9	69	48	53
Sikh Hunters	30	15	5	10	79	63	50
Morda United	30	13	9	8	43	36	48
Marston Wolves	30	13	8	9	58	45	47
Wrockwardine Wood	30	13	6	11	80	49	45
Shenstone Pathfinder	30	11	8	11	54	60	41
Lucas Sports	30	10	8	12	58	63	38
Wyrley Rangers	30	9	6	15	56	70	33
Eccleshall Reserves	30	9	5	16	41	60	32
Heath Hayes Reserves	30	7	8	15	50	70	29
Darlaston Town Reserves	30	4	4	22	35	88	16
Wolverhampton Sports G.N.S.T.	30	3	4	23	24	106	13
Walsall Wood Reserves	30	1	2	27	20	143	5

Great Wyrley had 3 points deducted.
Eccleshall Reserves moved to the Staffordshire County League, Darlaston Town Reserves were replaced by their demoted first team and Ounsdale disbanded. Bilston Town joined as a newly formed club after their Southern League predecessors of the same name had disbanded at the end of the season. Riverway joined from the Wolverhampton Combination, Ashbourne United joined from the Midland Regional Alliance and Shelfield Sports and Wednesbury Town also joined.
The Division was increased to 19 clubs.

West Midlands (Regional) League 2002-2004

Division One (South)

Sedgley White Lions	26	22	3	1	77	18	69
Bewdley Town	26	15	3	8	56	31	48
Hinton	26	13	7	6	54	44	46
Leominster Town	26	13	4	9	49	38	43
Wyre Forest	26	10	10	6	44	34	40
Brintons Athletic	26	12	3	11	41	47	39
Bridgnorth Town Reserves	26	11	5	10	50	45	38
Ludlow Town Reserves	26	11	4	11	62	50	37
Chaddesley Corbett	26	10	1	15	56	61	31
Mahal	26	8	4	14	37	50	28
Malvern Town Reserves	26	8	4	14	38	54	28
Lye Town Reserves	26	6	8	12	35	54	26
Malvern Rangers	26	7	4	15	47	63	25
Bustleholme Reserves	26	5	2	19	32	89	17

Brintons Athletic and Wyre Forest merged to form Wyre Forest Brintons. Blackheath Town joined as a newly formed club and Ledbury Town Reserves also joined.

2002-03
Premier Division

Westfields	42	32	6	4	119	30	102
Kington Town	42	31	6	5	121	51	99
Tipton Town	42	27	8	7	95	40	89
Little Drayton Rangers	42	26	5	11	113	66	83
Tividale	42	22	10	10	104	53	76
Malvern Town	42	22	9	11	96	49	75
Shawbury United	42	21	9	12	86	68	72
Lye Town	42	19	7	16	69	64	64
Ledbury Town	42	18	9	15	90	75	63
Brierley & Hagley Alliance	42	17	11	14	74	73	62
Wellington	42	16	10	16	59	69	58
Heath Hayes	42	15	12	15	72	75	57
Wolverhampton Casuals	42	17	5	20	71	91	56
Wolverhampton United	42	15	8	19	66	73	53
Smethwick Sikh Temple	42	11	11	20	58	83	44
Sedgley White Lions	42	11	9	22	48	74	42
Ettingshall Holy Trinity	42	12	5	25	65	92	41
Bustleholme	42	11	7	24	69	93	40
Bromyard Town	42	11	2	29	61	125	35
Dudley Town	42	7	9	26	46	112	30
Walsall Wood	**42**	**6**	**11**	**25**	**48**	**109**	**29**
Gornal Athletic	**42**	**7**	**7**	**28**	**41**	**106**	**28**

Westfields were promoted to the Midland Football Alliance, swapping places with Wednesfield who were relegated. Sedgley White Lions changed their name to Coseley Town. Little Drayton Rangers changed their name to Market Drayton Town.
The Division was reduced to 21 clubs.

Division One (North)

Newport Town	**34**	**29**	**3**	**2**	**105**	**28**	**90**
Bilston Town	34	28	4	2	125	29	88
Lucas Sports	34	25	3	6	124	51	78
Brereton Social	34	18	7	9	87	58	61
Ashbourne United	34	18	5	11	106	69	59
Morda United	34	16	5	13	65	57	53
Darlaston Town	34	14	8	12	76	75	50
Marston Wolves	34	14	6	14	65	58	48
Great Wyrley	34	13	7	14	84	69	46
Sikh Hunters	34	12	9	13	81	73	45
Heath Hayes Reserves	34	12	6	16	55	72	42
Wrockwardine Wood	34	10	7	17	45	77	37
Wednesbury Town	34	10	5	19	68	85	35
Shenstone Pathfinder	34	9	8	17	50	81	35
Riverway	34	9	7	18	52	91	34
Wyrley Rangers	34	10	3	21	42	82	33
Wolverhampton Sports G.N.S.T.	34	9	4	21	51	101	31
Walsall Wood Reserves	34	0	3	31	23	148	3

Shelfield Sports withdrew during the season and their record was deleted when it stood as follows: 16 5 1 10 40 41 16

Marston Wolves and Walsall Wood Reserves both left the league. Wrockwardine Wood disbanded just before the start of the 2003-04 season. Bilbrook joined from youth football and Eccleshall A.F.C. also joined. Lucas Sports changed their name to Goodrich.

The Division was reduced to 17 clubs.

Division One (South)

Bewdley Town	26	19	5	2	83	31	62
Hinton	26	17	1	8	74	42	52
Blackheath Town	26	14	8	4	65	36	50
Bridgnorth Town Reserves	26	14	6	6	58	34	48
Mahal	*26*	*13*	*5*	*8*	*55*	*46*	*44*
Chaddesley Corbett	26	12	6	8	50	37	42
Ludlow Town Reserves	26	10	8	8	61	51	38
Wyre Forest Brintons	26	11	3	12	58	60	36
Lye Town Reserves	26	10	5	11	36	38	35
Malvern Town Reserves	26	8	6	12	52	62	30
Bustleholme Reserves	26	5	5	16	38	70	20
Ledbury Town Reserves	26	5	4	17	38	76	19
Leominster Town	26	4	5	17	36	74	17
Malvern Rangers	26	4	5	17	33	80	17

Lye Town Reserves left the league. Tenbury United joined from the Kidderminster League, Reality Sports joined from Sunday football and Cradley Town Reserves also joined.

The Division was increased to 16 clubs.

2003-04
Premier Division

Malvern Town	38	29	3	6	138	38	90
Tipton Town	38	26	8	4	105	36	86
Kington Town	38	26	2	10	100	62	80
Shawbury United	38	21	10	7	73	56	73
Ledbury Town	38	22	6	10	96	60	72
Heath Hayes	38	20	6	12	81	48	66
Market Drayton Town	38	19	8	11	69	54	65
Tividale	38	18	8	12	81	55	62
Wellington	38	18	8	12	74	54	62
Lye Town	38	19	5	14	62	52	62
Bromyard Town	38	17	4	17	78	66	55
Brierley & Hagley Alliance	38	14	7	17	59	68	49
Bustleholme	38	13	3	22	76	85	42
Dudley Town	38	11	9	18	65	81	42
Ettingshall Holy Trinity	38	12	4	22	58	94	40
Wolverhampton United	**38**	**12**	**3**	**23**	**63**	**116**	**39**
Smethwick Sikh Temple	38	11	5	22	65	93	38
Wednesfield	38	11	4	23	49	125	37
Wolverhampton Casuals	38	7	2	29	51	106	23
Coseley Town	38	0	3	35	23	117	3

Newport Town resigned during the season and their record was deleted when it stood as follows: 25 10 7 8 45 44 37
Malvern Town were promoted to the Midland Football Alliance, swapping places with Pelsall Villa who were relegated.
Brierley & Hagley Alliance changed their name to Brierley & Hagley

West Midlands (Regional) League 2004-2005

Division One (North)

Team	P	W	D	L	F	A	Pts
Goodrich	30	24	0	6	73	39	72
Darlaston Town	30	23	2	5	101	42	71
Riverway	30	21	4	5	101	44	67
Great Wyrley	30	19	7	4	89	26	64
Wyrley Rangers	30	20	4	6	69	40	64
Eccleshall A.F.C.	30	17	4	9	58	32	55
Walsall Wood	30	14	5	11	59	53	47
Brereton Social	30	10	7	13	54	56	37
Wednesbury Town	30	11	3	16	51	73	36
Ashbourne United	30	9	4	17	47	62	31
Morda United	30	8	6	16	55	78	30
Sikh Hunters	30	8	5	17	38	65	29
Heath Hayes Reserves	30	8	4	18	40	74	28
Shenstone Pathfinder	*30*	*5*	*4*	*21*	*32*	*83*	*19*
Mahal	*30*	*4*	*6*	*20*	*47*	*93*	*18*
Bilbrook	*30*	*4*	*5*	*21*	*30*	*84*	*17*

Wolverhampton Sports G.N.S.T. resigned during the season and their record at the time was deleted: 15 2 1 12 16 54 7

Division One (South)

Team	P	W	D	L	F	A	Pts
Gornal Athletic	30	24	2	4	72	12	74
Bridgnorth Town Reserves	30	20	6	4	79	32	66
Bilston Town	30	21	4	5	88	35	64
Bewdley Town	30	17	4	9	67	40	55
Blackheath Town	30	15	4	11	53	42	49
Tenbury United	30	15	3	12	57	62	48
Malvern Town Reserves	30	12	6	12	48	44	42
Hinton	30	12	3	15	60	55	39
Ludlow Town Reserves	30	9	7	14	38	50	34
Leominster Town	30	10	3	17	48	76	33
Wyre Forest Brintons	30	9	6	15	40	68	33
Bustleholme Reserves	*30*	*8*	*8*	*14*	*51*	*52*	*32*
Cradley Town Reserves	*30*	*9*	*5*	*16*	*52*	*68*	*32*
Malvern Rangers	*30*	*8*	*7*	*15*	*36*	*65*	*31*
Chaddesley Corbett	*30*	*6*	*8*	*16*	*38*	*58*	*26*
Ledbury Town Reserves	30	4	6	20	20	88	18

Bilston Town had 3 points deducted.
Reality Sports resigned during the season and their record was deleted when it stood as follows: 27 2 2 23 21 97 8

The two regional sections of Division One were re-organised into Divisions One and Two. The clubs in the two regional sections printed in italics above were placed in Division Two. All of the remaining clubs were placed in Division One with the exception of Leominster Town and Ledbury Town Reserves (who both moved to the Herefordshire League), Morda United (who moved to the Shropshire County League), Wyre Forest Brintons (who demerged and joined the Kidderminster League as two separate clubs, Wyre Forest and Brintons), Sikh Hunters and Heath Hayes Reserves (who also both left the league) plus Goodrich and Gornal Athletic (who were both promoted to the Premier Division).

Division One was increased to 19 clubs by the addition of Stafford Town who joined from the Midland Football Alliance and Wolverhampton United who were demoted from the Premier Division.

Division Two was increased to 17 clubs by the addition of 10 new clubs: Bromyard Town Reserves from the Herefordshire League, Brereton Town, Cresswell Wanderers from youth football, Darlaston Town Reserves, Dudley United (who were a newly formed club), Ellesmere Rangers from the Shropshire County League, Kington Town Reserves, Parkfield Leisure and Sporting Khalsa (both from Sunday football) and Wednesfield Reserves.

2004-05

Premier Division

Team	P	W	D	L	F	A	Pts
Tipton Town	38	31	3	4	111	19	96
Market Drayton Town	38	23	6	9	76	47	75
Shawbury United	38	20	7	11	59	45	67
Ledbury Town	38	18	7	13	81	60	61
Wellington	38	18	6	14	84	65	60
Heath Hayes	38	18	6	14	67	54	60
Bromyard Town	38	16	8	14	67	62	56
Lye Town	38	16	8	14	63	59	56
Bustleholme	38	15	10	13	90	67	55
Gornal Athletic	38	15	9	14	55	47	54
Wolverhampton Casuals	38	15	9	14	67	73	54
Dudley Town	38	14	11	13	64	63	53
Kington Town	38	13	11	14	72	90	50
Smethwick Sikh Temple	38	15	4	19	60	71	49
Pelsall Villa	38	13	8	17	73	86	47
Tividale	38	12	10	16	56	69	46
Goodrich	38	11	11	16	40	60	44
Brierley & Hagley	38	7	9	22	46	86	30
Coseley Town	38	6	10	22	48	96	28
Wednesfield	38	4	7	27	49	109	19

Ettingshall Holy Trinity resigned during the season and their record was deleted when it stood as follows: 35 6 5 24 35 88 23
Tipton Town were promoted to the Midland Football Alliance, swapping places with Ludlow Town who were relegated. Coseley Town disbanded. Smethwick Sikh Temple changed their name to Smethwick Rangers.

Division One

Team	P	W	D	L	F	A	Pts
Great Wyrley	36	29	6	1	131	31	93
Bewdley Town	36	27	5	4	107	36	86
Wyrley Rangers	36	22	4	10	80	52	70
Riverway	36	20	5	11	93	64	65
Hinton	36	17	9	10	82	66	60
Walsall Wood	36	19	2	15	81	55	59
Stafford Town	36	16	8	12	71	59	56
Blackheath Town	36	16	8	12	58	49	56
Ashbourne United	36	17	6	13	57	49	56
Malvern Town Reserves	36	14	8	14	66	56	50
Darlaston Town	36	15	5	16	64	77	50
Brereton Social	36	13	9	14	75	65	48
Eccleshall A.F.C.	36	13	7	16	62	78	46
Tenbury United	36	11	12	13	58	59	45
Bridgnorth Town Reserves	36	7	13	16	47	75	34
Wednesbury Town	**36**	**8**	**6**	**22**	**55**	**97**	**30**
Bilston Town	36	8	5	23	62	95	29
Ludlow Town Reserves	36	5	6	25	31	98	21
Wolverhampton United	36	2	2	32	41	160	8

Ashbourne United had 1 point deducted.
Eccleshall A.F.C. moved to the Staffordshire County Senior League.

Division Two

Team	P	W	D	L	F	A	Pts
Parkfield Leisure	32	28	4	0	116	19	88
Cresswell Wanderers	32	25	2	5	91	34	77
Malvern Rangers	32	23	2	7	99	55	71
Ellesmere Rangers	32	21	5	6	108	38	68
Sporting Khalsa	32	18	5	9	85	50	59
Mahal	32	17	2	13	58	57	53
Shenstone Pathfinder	32	15	5	12	79	54	50
Bilbrook	32	14	1	17	63	64	43
Cradley Town Reserves	32	10	7	15	60	72	37
Bustleholme Reserves	32	10	5	17	53	62	35
Brereton Town	31	11	2	18	55	76	32
Kington Town Reserves	32	9	5	18	53	82	31
Darlaston Town Reserves	32	8	5	19	65	112	29
Wednesfield Reserves	31	9	2	20	61	120	29
Chaddesley Corbett	32	8	4	20	40	83	28
Dudley United	32	6	6	20	38	94	24
Bromyard Town Reserves	32	7	2	23	44	96	23

Brereton Town had 3 points deducted.
Kington Town Reserves had 1 point deducted.

West Midlands (Regional) League 2005-2007

Brereton Town vs Wednesfield Reserves was not played.
Penkridge Town joined from the Staffordshire County League while AFC Wulfrunians, Sedgley Town, Wolverhampton Development and Wyrley all joined as newly formed clubs and Bewdley Town Reserves joined as a newly formed side. Cradley Town Reserves, Kington Town Reserves and Wednesfield Reserves all left the league.

2005-06

Premier Division

Market Drayton Town	42	32	8	2	102	33	104
Gornal Athletic	42	25	11	6	74	32	86
Great Wyrley	42	24	14	4	94	36	85
Bewdley Town	42	23	8	11	100	52	77
Wyrley Rangers	42	22	10	10	81	40	76
Lye Town	42	20	11	11	64	44	71
Goodrich	42	18	16	8	86	66	70
Tividale	42	20	8	14	73	50	68
Wellington	42	19	8	15	64	62	65
Dudley Town	42	18	8	16	74	71	62
Wednesfield	42	18	5	19	56	66	59
Bustleholme	42	15	9	18	66	73	54
Heath Hayes	42	14	12	16	53	64	54
Pelsall Villa	42	16	5	21	61	69	53
Shawbury United	42	15	6	21	74	87	51
Ludlow Town	42	12	11	19	62	90	45
Brierley & Hagley	42	11	6	25	50	83	39
Bromyard Town	42	10	8	24	53	79	38
Wolverhampton Casuals	42	11	5	26	60	99	38
Smethwick Rangers	42	11	3	28	57	98	35
Kington Town	42	8	7	27	41	102	31
Ledbury Town	42	7	7	28	52	101	28

Great Wyrley and Smethwick Rangers each had 1 point deducted.
Ludlow Town had 2 points deducted.
Market Drayton Town were promoted to the Midland Football Alliance. Bridgnorth Town, Dudley Sports and Shifnal Town all joined from the Midland Combination. Heath Hayes moved to the Midland Combination, Kington Town moved to the Herefordshire League and Smethwick Rangers also left the league.

Division One

Ellesmere Rangers	36	26	6	4	78	25	84
Brereton Social	36	27	2	7	112	40	83
Parkfield Leisure	36	26	3	7	102	45	81
Walsall Wood	36	24	5	7	92	40	77
Blackheath Town	36	23	4	9	75	44	73
Bilston Town	36	23	1	12	103	63	70
Bridgnorth Town Reserves	36	16	4	16	71	69	52
Riverway	36	14	6	16	71	68	48
Stafford Town	36	14	6	16	78	80	48
Hinton	36	14	6	16	76	88	48
Malvern Town Reserves	36	14	3	19	71	77	45
Wolverhampton United	36	12	9	15	52	65	45
Cresswell Wanderers	36	13	5	18	64	81	44
Ludlow Town Reserves	36	9	10	17	60	89	37
Ashbourne United	36	10	6	20	43	70	36
Sporting Khalsa	36	11	3	22	64	98	33
Tenbury United	36	9	5	22	51	87	32
Malvern Rangers	36	8	2	26	51	99	26
Darlaston Town	36	5	2	29	41	127	17

Sporting Khalsa had 3 points deducted.
Ashbourne United moved to the Staffordshire County Senior League, Brereton Social and Walsall Wood both moved to the Midland Combination and Malvern Rangers also left the league.

Division Two

AFC Wulfrunians	26	22	4	0	83	7	70
Bilbrook	26	16	2	8	75	44	50
Shenstone Pathfinder	26	15	5	6	60	37	50
Penkridge Town	26	14	3	9	43	39	45
Wednesbury Town	26	11	9	6	75	46	42
Bustleholme Reserves	26	11	7	8	53	44	40
Chaddesley Corbett	26	11	5	10	52	43	38
Bewdley Town Reserves	26	11	5	10	44	54	38
Wyrley	26	9	4	13	41	53	31
Brereton Town	26	7	6	13	46	60	27
Wolverhampton Development	26	6	8	12	34	43	26
Dudley United	26	8	1	17	43	53	25
Mahal	26	3	9	14	36	68	18
Bromyard Town Reserves	26	3	2	21	23	117	11

Darlaston Town Reserves resigned during the season and their record was deleted when it stood as follows: 3 1 0 2 3 15 3
Sedgley Town resigned during the season and their record was deleted when it stood as follows: 16 2 1 13 21 51 7
Bromyard Town Reserves moved to the Herefordshire League. Heath Town Rangers, Penn Colts and Warstone Wanderers all joined as newly formed clubs and Gornal Athletic Reserves joined as a newly formed side.

2006-07

Premier Division

Shifnal Town	40	27	7	6	100	27	88
Tividale	40	22	12	6	84	49	78
Bewdley Town	40	20	15	5	92	55	75
Gornal Athletic	40	20	10	10	61	47	70
Dudley Town	40	20	7	13	67	46	67
Goodrich	40	21	4	15	83	69	67
Bridgnorth Town	40	20	9	11	83	49	66
Lye Town	40	19	9	12	83	57	66
Pelsall Villa	40	15	12	13	70	69	57
Wellington	40	15	10	15	66	73	55
Dudley Sports	40	14	9	17	56	58	51
Ellesmere Rangers	40	15	5	20	57	68	50
Wednesfield	40	13	9	18	46	76	48
Wyrley Rangers	40	12	10	18	50	68	45
Brierley & Hagley	40	12	7	21	55	80	43
Ledbury Town	40	12	5	23	51	97	41
Wolverhampton Casuals	40	9	13	18	53	72	40
Bromyard Town	40	11	7	22	56	83	40
Ludlow Town	40	11	7	22	49	78	40
Bustleholme	40	10	9	21	55	69	39
Shawbury United	40	10	8	22	55	82	38

Bridgnorth Town had 3 points deducted.
Wyrley Rangers had 1 point deducted.
Great Wyrley resigned during the season and their record was deleted when it stood as follows: 4 0 0 4 3 18 0
Shifnal Town were promoted to the Midland Football Alliance. Brierley & Hagley merged with Withymoor Colts to form Brierley & Withymoor. Wyrley Rangers disbanded.

2007-08

Premier Division

Bridgnorth Town	40	31	4	5	97	33	97
Bewdley Town	40	23	6	11	83	57	75
Shawbury United	40	21	9	10	86	59	72
Wednesfield	40	20	9	11	68	51	69
Dudley Town	40	20	9	11	56	48	69
AFC Wulfrunians	40	19	10	11	83	43	67
Ellesmere Rangers	40	20	7	13	71	52	67
Dudley Sports	40	19	12	9	64	46	66
Darlaston Town	40	17	12	11	71	57	63
Lye Town	40	18	8	14	80	58	62
Tividale	40	13	12	15	72	65	51
Pelsall Villa	40	14	9	17	67	71	51
Wellington	40	13	11	16	63	79	50
Ludlow Town	40	13	11	16	50	73	50
Goodrich	40	13	6	21	72	83	45
Gornal Athletic	40	10	12	18	46	63	42
Brierley & Withymoor	40	12	5	23	62	89	41
Wolverhampton Casuals	40	8	15	17	58	80	38
Ledbury Town	40	10	3	27	56	100	33
Bromyard Town	40	8	7	25	46	87	31
Bustleholme	40	7	5	28	55	112	26

Dudley Sports had 3 points deducted.
Wolverhampton Casuals had 1 point deducted.
Bridgnorth Town were promoted to the Midland Football Alliance and Brierley & Withymoor disbanded.

Division One

Birchills United	36	29	2	5	112	35	89
Bridgnorth Town Reserves	36	26	7	3	76	25	85
Heath Town Rangers	36	23	9	4	93	41	78
Stafford Town	36	22	5	9	106	53	71
Wolverhampton Development	36	19	7	10	78	58	64
AFC Wombourne United	36	18	7	11	61	55	61
Warstone Wanderers	36	18	7	11	77	59	58
Penn Croft	36	17	6	13	77	63	57
Malvern Town Reserves	36	13	8	15	58	63	47
Riverway	36	13	7	16	59	59	46
Blackheath Town	36	9	13	14	62	60	40
Wolverhampton United	36	10	9	17	45	68	39
Bilbrook	36	9	10	17	57	76	37
Cresswell Wanderers	36	11	4	21	50	81	37
Sporting Khalsa	36	9	9	18	54	84	36
Wednesbury Town	36	7	13	16	57	75	34
Shenstone Pathfinder	36	7	10	19	50	98	31
Gornal Athletic Reserves	36	6	4	26	37	104	22
Dudley United	36	5	5	26	38	90	20

Warstone Wanderers had 3 points deducted.
Hinton resigned during the season and their record was deleted when it stood as follows: 4 0 0 4 2 18 0
Cresswell Wanderers and Gornal Athletic Reserves both left the league.
Following their promotion, Birchills United changed their name to Bloxwich United while Wolverhampton Development changed their name to Warley Development.

Division Two

Wellington Amateurs	26	18	5	3	78	23	59
Bilston Town (2007)	26	17	6	3	78	37	57
Penkridge Town	26	14	5	7	61	33	47
Wyrley	26	14	4	8	53	39	46
Bustleholme Reserves	26	15	0	11	66	48	45
Stone Old Alleynians	26	12	9	5	48	30	45
Bentley Youth	26	10	6	10	56	54	36
Heath Town Rangers Reserves	26	11	3	12	48	55	36
Tenbury United	26	10	3	13	57	61	33
Powick	26	8	6	12	43	52	30
Black Country Rangers	26	8	4	14	44	56	28
Punjab United Sports	26	7	4	15	51	79	25
Mahal	26	5	4	17	38	65	19
Brereton Town	26	2	3	21	29	118	9

Division One

Darlaston Town	30	24	4	2	82	14	76
AFC Wulfrunians	30	22	2	6	81	23	68
Cresswell Wanderers	30	18	4	8	52	38	58
Stafford Town	30	16	8	6	74	47	56
Riverway	30	15	8	7	75	42	53
Blackheath Town	30	17	2	11	69	48	53
Bilston Town	30	15	7	8	63	44	52
Bridgnorth Town Reserves	30	12	5	13	41	37	41
Malvern Town Reserves	30	11	5	14	50	50	38
Hinton	30	11	2	17	55	72	35
Bilbrook	30	10	3	17	51	75	33
Tenbury United	30	10	3	17	49	75	33
Ludlow Town Reserves	30	10	3	17	40	69	33
Wolverhampton United	30	8	4	18	44	63	28
Sporting Khalsa	30	6	4	20	37	80	22
Parkfield Leisure	30	1	4	25	17	103	7

Ludlow Town Reserves moved to the Shropshire County League. Parkfield Leisure changed their name to Parkfield United. Penn Croft joined from the Birmingham A.F.A., Birchills United joined from the Wolverhampton Combination and AFC Wombourne United also joined from the Wolverhampton Combination having changed their name to Orton Vale. Bilston Town resigned but were re-formed as Bilston Town (2007) and joined Division Two of the WMRL.

Division Two

Heath Town Rangers	28	19	5	4	65	30	62
Shenstone Pathfinder	28	18	5	5	69	45	59
Gornal Athletic Reserves	28	13	9	6	59	43	48
Wolverhampton Development	28	13	8	7	57	36	47
Penn Colts	28	14	5	9	73	54	47
Wednesbury Town	28	12	6	10	63	49	42
Warstone Wanderers	28	10	7	11	60	58	37
Dudley United	28	10	7	11	51	54	36
Mahal	28	9	9	10	47	53	36
Chaddesley Corbett	28	9	6	13	52	61	33
Wyrley	28	9	6	13	57	70	33
Bustleholme Reserves	28	9	4	15	61	77	31
Penkridge Town	28	7	9	12	41	52	30
Bewdley Town Reserves	28	6	6	16	43	71	24
Brereton Town	28	2	8	18	44	89	14

Dudley United had 1 point deducted.
Chaddesley Corbett moved to the Kidderminster League and Bewdley Town Reserves also left. Wellington Amateurs joined from the Shropshire County League, Punjab United Sports joined from the Wolverhampton Combination, Powick joined from the Worcester & District League, Stone Old Alleynians joined from the Staffordshire County Senior League, Bentley Youth and Black Country Rangers both joined from youth football and Heath Town Rangers Reserves joined as a newly formed side.

West Midlands (Regional) League 2008-2010

Parkfield United resigned during the season and their record was deleted when it stood as follows: 22 2 1 19 19 86 7
Penn Colts resigned during the season and their record was deleted when it stood as follows: 20 5 1 14 39 58 16
Brereton Town moved to the Staffordshire County Senior League and Powick moved to the Worcester & District League while Bustleholme Reserves and Punjab United Sports also left the league. Hanwood United joined from the Shropshire County League, Lye Town Reserves joined from the Kidderminster League and Wrens Nest joined from the Dudley & Cradley Heath League. Ettingshall Park Farm joined from Sunday football and Trysull also joined from Sunday football having changed their name from AFC Codsall. Warstone Wanderers Reserves and Darlaston Town Reserves joined as newly formed sides.
Bentley Youth changed their name to Bentley.

2008-09

Premier Division

AFC Wulfrunians	40	28	3	9	89	47	87
Bloxwich United	40	27	4	9	123	50	85
Bewdley Town	40	26	7	7	107	52	85
Ellesmere Rangers	40	25	7	8	105	45	82
Dudley Town	40	24	7	9	91	55	79
Wellington	40	21	6	13	76	62	69
Darlaston Town	40	20	6	14	67	58	66
Heath Town Rangers	40	19	4	17	68	68	60
Wednesfield	40	16	11	13	68	59	59
Shawbury United	40	16	9	15	59	66	57
Lye Town	40	16	7	17	69	62	55
Dudley Sports	40	15	10	15	53	55	55
Tividale	40	15	8	17	63	64	53
Bromyard Town	40	14	8	18	61	67	50
Gornal Athletic	40	13	10	17	56	60	49
Goodrich	40	10	11	19	58	88	41
Ludlow Town	40	12	5	23	66	99	41
Pelsall Villa	40	7	13	20	53	72	34
Wolverhampton Casuals	40	10	2	28	60	113	32
Ledbury Town	40	8	7	25	68	128	31
Bustleholme	40	4	3	33	39	129	12

Heath Town Rangers had 1 point deducted.
Bustleholme had 3 points deducted.
Pelsall Villa moved to the Midland Combination, swapping places with Oldbury Athletic who joined from the same league.

Division One

Wellington Amateurs	32	24	3	5	86	20	75
Bilbrook	32	22	4	6	83	34	70
Bridgnorth Town Reserves	32	19	8	5	73	37	65
Stafford Town	32	17	4	11	95	62	55
Bilston Town (2007)	32	15	8	9	55	52	53
AFC Wombourne United	32	16	4	12	65	49	52
Penn Croft	32	15	2	15	63	58	47
Dudley United	32	13	5	14	50	50	44
Warstone Wanderers	32	12	7	13	58	64	43
Warley Development	32	13	3	16	71	66	42
Blackheath Town	32	10	12	10	47	45	42
Riverway	32	12	6	14	56	67	42
Malvern Town Reserves	32	10	8	14	58	76	38
Wolverhampton United	32	8	4	20	43	75	28
Shenstone Pathfinder	32	8	4	20	51	92	28
Wednesbury Town	32	8	3	21	43	93	27
Sporting Khalsa	32	6	3	23	39	96	21

Wednesbury Town left the league.

Division Two

Hanwood United	26	21	4	1	70	23	67
Trysull	26	17	3	6	63	23	54
Stone Old Alleynians	26	16	5	5	56	29	50
Wrens Nest	26	14	5	7	57	35	47
Black Country Rangers	26	12	8	6	55	42	44
Bentley	26	12	5	9	61	52	41
Darlaston Town Reserves	26	11	6	9	44	42	39
Penkridge Town	26	9	8	9	42	37	35
Wyrley	26	9	6	11	45	42	33
Heath Town Rangers Reserves	26	10	2	14	40	51	32
Mahal	26	6	4	16	51	65	22
Lye Town Reserves	26	6	1	19	33	70	19
Tenbury United	26	2	7	17	42	75	13
Ettingshall Park Farm	26	3	4	19	24	97	13

Stone Old Alleynians had 3 points deducted.
Warstone Wanderers Reserves resigned during the season and their record at the time was deleted: 18 6 0 12 31 54 18
Wem Town joined from the Shropshire County League, Pensnett Panthers joined from Sunday football and Malvern Rangers joined as a newly formed club. Lye Town Reserves left the league.

2009-10

Premier Division

Ellesmere Rangers	40	30	5	5	98	29	95
Bloxwich United	40	30	4	6	128	46	94
AFC Wulfrunians	40	28	4	8	83	31	88
Bustleholme	40	26	7	7	93	42	85
Dudley Town	40	24	6	10	86	52	78
Wellington	40	21	8	11	104	73	71
Tividale	40	22	5	13	76	61	71
Oldbury Athletic	40	23	1	16	89	67	70
Ledbury Town	40	18	8	14	78	77	62
Ludlow Town	40	19	4	17	92	74	61
Wednesfield	40	16	7	17	85	77	55
Bewdley Town	40	16	5	19	78	82	53
Darlaston Town	40	13	3	24	57	82	42
Bromyard Town	40	11	5	24	54	108	38
Dudley Sports	40	10	7	23	38	87	37
Wolverhampton Casuals	40	9	10	21	66	98	36
Gornal Athletic	40	9	8	23	47	81	35
Goodrich	40	9	8	23	50	89	35
Lye Town	40	9	5	26	49	106	32
Heath Town Rangers	40	10	4	26	53	98	31
Shawbury United	40	8	4	28	47	91	28

Wolverhampton Casuals had 1 point deducted.
Heath Town Rangers had 3 points deducted.
Ellesmere Rangers were promoted to the Midland Football Alliance, Ledbury Town moved to the Herefordshire League, Ludlow Town moved to the Shropshire County League and Oldbury Athletic disbanded.
Cradley Town and Shifnal Town both joined after relegation from the Midland Football Alliance.

Division One

Wellington Amateurs	32	25	4	3	110	22	79
Stafford Town	32	25	4	3	121	43	79
Hanwood United	32	19	6	7	85	46	63
Bilbrook	32	19	4	9	70	47	61
Warley Development	32	17	3	12	62	52	54
Blackheath Town	32	15	6	11	75	60	51
Warstone Wanderers	32	15	3	14	70	79	48
Trysull	32	12	6	14	59	60	42
AFC Wombourne United	32	12	6	14	53	55	42
Bridgnorth Town Reserves	32	13	3	16	64	76	42
Wolverhampton United	32	13	3	16	58	79	42
Bilston Town (2007)	32	10	8	14	55	65	38
Penn Croft	32	10	6	16	71	83	36
Shenstone Pathfinder	32	11	3	18	44	80	36
Riverway	*32*	*7*	*3*	*22*	*53*	*93*	*24*
Dudley United	32	7	3	22	41	94	24
Sporting Khalsa	32	4	5	23	43	100	17

Malvern Town Reserves resigned during the season and their record was deleted when it stood as follows: 10 0 1 9 10 37 1
They joined the Worcester & District League for the 2010-11 season.
Bilbrook, Dudley United and Warley Development all left the league.

Division Two

Black Country Rangers	22	18	2	2	89	28	56
Wem Town	22	17	1	4	95	27	52
Wyrley	22	15	3	4	58	35	48
Stone Old Alleynians	22	11	5	6	57	38	38
Penkridge Town	22	10	4	8	48	34	34
Malvern Rangers	22	10	2	10	55	47	32
Tenbury United	22	10	1	11	44	72	31
Bentley	22	7	2	13	53	70	23
Heath Town Rangers Reserves	22	7	1	14	43	83	22
Wrens Nest	22	6	1	15	38	76	19
Mahal	22	4	4	14	34	68	16
Ettingshall Park Farm	22	3	2	17	25	61	11

Darlaston Town Reserves resigned during the season and their record at the time was deleted: 18 2 0 16 30 87 6
Pennsett Panthers resigned during the season and their record at the time was deleted: 17 9 2 6 43 38 29
Bentley left the league. AFC Smethwick joined from the Midland Combination, Leominster Town joined from the Herefordshire League, St. Martins joined from the Shropshire County League and Penn Colts joined from youth football while Team Dudley joined as a newly formed club and Bilston Town (2007) Reserves and Warstones Wanderers Reserves both joined as newly formed sides.

2010-11

Premier Division

Tividale	38	31	4	3	123	33	97
Gornal Athletic	38	27	5	6	106	43	86
AFC Wulfrunians	38	27	2	9	117	41	83
Wednesfield	38	24	8	6	87	38	80
Bustleholme	38	21	11	6	81	59	74
Bewdley Town	38	22	7	9	98	55	73
Bloxwich United	38	20	8	10	89	72	68
Cradley Town	38	17	7	14	90	71	58
Shifnal Town	38	16	6	16	79	67	54
Wellington	38	15	5	18	76	67	50
Lye Town	38	14	6	18	69	72	48
Wolverhampton Casuals	38	14	3	21	58	71	42
Dudley Town	38	12	5	21	53	106	41
Dudley Sports	38	13	0	25	47	88	39
Stafford Town	38	11	5	22	69	105	38
Darlaston Town	38	11	3	24	51	98	36
Shawbury United	38	10	5	23	48	96	35
† Wolverhampton Sporting Comm.	38	9	3	26	55	88	30
Goodrich	38	9	2	27	53	116	29
Bromyard Town	38	8	3	27	48	111	27

Wolverhampton Casuals had 3 points deducted.

† Heath Town Rangers changed their name to Wolverhampton Sporting Community during the season.
Tividale were promoted to the Midland Football Alliance, swapping places with Malvern Town who were relegated from the same league.
Bloxwich United moved to the Midland Combination.
Pegasus Juniors joined from the Hellenic League.

Division One

Black Country Rangers	30	25	2	3	110	31	77
Wellington Amateurs	30	22	2	6	74	38	68
Sporting Khalsa	30	17	5	8	58	32	56
Wem Town	30	16	4	10	80	61	49
Hanwood United	30	14	6	10	52	45	48
Stone Old Alleynians	30	13	8	9	61	52	47
Warstone Wanderers	30	14	2	14	49	44	44
Blackheath Town	30	11	10	9	52	53	43
Bilston Town (2007)	30	10	12	8	68	59	42
Trysull	30	12	5	13	46	44	41
Penn Croft	30	11	6	13	57	85	39
Wyrley	30	9	8	13	42	59	35
Shenstone Pathfinder	30	7	4	19	53	77	25
Bridgnorth Town Reserves	30	6	3	21	43	81	21
AFC Wombourne United	30	4	8	18	41	75	20
Wolverhampton United	30	4	5	21	42	92	17

Wem Town had 3 points deducted.

Division Two

Malvern Rangers	24	18	3	3	89	33	57
St. Martins	24	17	2	5	66	32	53
Leominster Town	24	15	4	5	72	33	49
AFC Smethwick	24	13	8	3	62	28	47
Penkridge Town	24	14	2	8	78	48	44
Wrens Nest	24	12	5	7	53	49	41
Tenbury United	24	12	3	9	53	46	39
Mahal	24	10	5	9	51	58	35
Team Dudley	24	10	1	13	37	47	31
Riverway	24	5	3	16	38	75	18
Bilston Town (2007) Reserves	24	5	1	18	29	65	16
Ettingshall Park Farm	24	4	1	19	37	60	13
† Wolv. Sporting Community Res.	24	2	0	22	18	109	6

† Heath Town Rangers Reserves changed their name to Wolverhampton Sporting Community Reserves during the season.
Penn Colts and Warstones Wanderers Reserves both resigned during the season and their records were deleted.
Malvern Rangers and Bilston Town (2007) Reserves both left the league.
Red Star Alma and Sikh Hunters both joined from the Wolverhampton Combination, Malvern Town Reserves joined from the Worcester & District League, Haughmond joined from the Shropshire County League and Hereford Lads Club joined from the Herefordshire League.

West Midlands (Regional) League 2011-2013

2011-12

Premier Division

Team	P	W	D	L	F	A	Pts
Gornal Athletic	42	33	6	3	149	47	105
Black Country Rangers	42	32	6	4	158	62	102
Wolverhampton Casuals	42	25	10	7	100	47	85
Bewdley Town	42	26	6	10	88	53	84
AFC Wulfrunians	42	24	7	11	95	66	79
Wednesfield	42	23	8	11	91	64	77
Dudley Town	42	20	9	13	93	71	69
Cradley Town	42	19	8	15	98	74	65
Goodrich	42	17	11	14	73	68	62
Shawbury United	42	17	7	18	66	69	58
Wellington	42	17	7	18	79	83	58
Dudley Sports	42	17	7	18	60	82	58
Malvern Town	42	15	10	17	75	81	55
Sporting Khalsa	42	16	3	23	69	106	51
Lye Town	42	13	11	18	60	80	50
Shifnal Town	42	13	9	20	82	88	48
Pegasus Juniors	42	14	6	22	50	68	48
Stafford Town	42	12	10	20	80	101	46
Wolverhampton Sporting Comm.	42	10	12	20	43	63	42
Bustleholme	42	6	5	31	49	102	23
Bromyard Town	42	5	8	29	35	111	23
Darlaston Town	42	4	2	36	41	148	14

Gornal Athletic were promoted to the Midland Football Alliance, swapping places with Willenhall Town who were relegated from the same league. Stafford Town moved to the Midland Combination, swapping places with Bartley Green who joined from the same league. Goodrich disbanded.

Division One

Team	P	W	D	L	F	A	Pts
Wellington Amateurs	30	20	5	5	96	42	65
Hanwood United	30	18	8	4	72	35	62
AFC Wombourne United	30	18	7	5	74	40	61
AFC Smethwick	30	18	6	6	73	47	60
Stone Old Alleynians	30	16	9	5	72	36	57
Wyrley	30	14	4	12	48	54	46
Bridgnorth Town Reserves	30	12	6	12	57	55	42
Warstone Wanderers	30	12	4	14	60	59	40
Bilston Town (2007)	30	12	4	14	58	58	40
Trysull	30	11	5	14	50	51	38
Leominster Town	30	11	5	14	68	88	38
Wem Town	30	10	7	13	68	74	37
Shenstone Pathfinder	30	10	4	16	39	59	34
Penn Croft	30	8	7	15	49	59	31
Blackheath Town	30	5	4	21	41	82	19
Wolverhampton United	30	2	1	27	33	119	7

Division Two

Team	P	W	D	L	F	A	Pts
Haughmond	26	22	4	0	103	27	70
Hereford Lads Club	26	16	5	5	64	29	53
Mahal	26	14	6	6	63	40	48
Penkridge Town	26	14	5	7	70	54	47
St. Martins	26	13	5	8	75	53	44
Sikh Hunters	26	11	5	10	55	49	38
Team Dudley	26	11	3	12	55	58	36
Wrens Nest	26	11	1	14	54	55	34
Ettingshall Park Farm	26	10	4	12	45	50	34
Riverway	26	9	5	12	65	71	32
Tenbury United	26	9	4	13	57	69	31
Red Star Alma	26	6	2	18	29	62	20
Malvern Town Reserves	26	5	1	20	33	91	16
Wolv. Sporting Community Res.	26	4	4	18	28	88	16

Bartestree and Ledbury Town both joined from the Herefordshire League, Newport Town joined from the Shropshire County League, while Malvern Rangers, Gornal Athletic Reserves and Mahal Reserves also joined.

2012-13

Premier Division

Team	P	W	D	L	F	A	Pts
AFC Wulfrunians	42	35	1	6	140	42	106
Lye Town	42	33	6	3	124	43	105
Wolverhampton Casuals	42	30	7	5	113	48	97
Shawbury United	42	29	6	7	146	59	93
Black Country Rangers	40	29	1	10	144	61	88
Dudley Town	42	24	7	11	93	58	79
Pegasus Juniors	41	21	8	12	93	65	71
Bewdley Town	42	22	5	15	80	80	71
Cradley Town	42	18	6	18	82	77	60
Wolverhampton Sporting Comm.	42	18	6	18	75	74	60
Sporting Khalsa	42	17	6	19	85	89	57
Wellington Amateurs	42	16	8	18	79	86	56
Malvern Town	42	14	8	20	67	92	50
Bromyard Town	42	15	3	24	76	121	48
Wellington	41	14	5	22	64	93	47
Bartley Green	42	14	5	23	69	107	47
Dudley Sports	41	12	9	20	70	84	45
Wednesfield	41	12	5	24	58	75	41
Shifnal Town	42	11	5	26	66	107	38
Willenhall Town	42	8	6	28	62	118	30
Darlaston Town	40	6	1	33	42	134	19
Bustleholme	42	2	2	38	37	152	8

4 games were not played. AFC Wulfrunians were promoted to the Midland Football Alliance, swapping places with Ellesmere Rangers who were relegated from the same league. Darlaston Town disbanded.

Division One

Team	P	W	D	L	F	A	Pts
AFC Smethwick	32	24	2	6	101	39	74
Bilston Town (2007)	32	23	4	5	97	45	73
Wem Town	32	23	2	7	105	54	71
Haughmond	32	20	4	8	116	54	64
Hanwood United	32	18	4	10	67	54	58
AFC Wombourne United	32	17	3	12	78	65	54
Trysull	32	15	7	10	71	52	52
Wyrley	32	16	3	13	79	71	51
Mahal	32	15	5	12	85	71	50
Stone Old Alleynians	32	13	7	12	66	62	46
Shenstone Pathfinder	32	10	5	17	65	88	35
Penn Croft	32	8	5	19	71	126	29
Bridgnorth Town Reserves	32	7	4	21	54	88	25
Leominster Town	32	6	7	19	72	114	25
Wolverhampton United	32	6	6	20	52	100	24
St. Martins	32	6	6	20	62	113	24
Blackheath Town	32	5	6	21	44	89	21

Warstone Wanderers resigned during the season and their record was deleted. Bridgnorth Town of the Midland Football Alliance disbanded and their reserves place in the WMRL – Division One was taken by a newly formed replacement club called AFC Bridgnorth. Blackheath Town moved to the Birmingham A.F.A., Leominster Town moved to the Herefordshire League and AFC Wombourne United disbanded. AFC Smethwick changed their name to Smethwick Rangers following their promotion to the Premier Division.

Division Two

Team	P	W	D	L	F	A	Pts
Gornal Athletic Reserves	28	21	4	3	78	26	67
Ledbury Town	28	18	5	5	109	48	59
Hereford Lads Club	27	16	7	4	65	37	55
Bartestree	28	17	4	7	70	50	55
Penkridge Town	28	14	7	7	69	40	49
Malvern Rangers	28	12	8	8	59	49	44
Newport Town	27	12	7	8	68	49	43
Team Dudley	28	13	3	12	63	51	42
Sikh Hunters	27	10	5	12	51	54	32
Wrens Nest	28	10	2	16	64	70	32
Riverway	28	7	10	11	49	57	31
Wolv. Sporting Community Res.	28	8	2	18	57	96	26
Red Star Alma	28	7	4	17	41	69	25
Tenbury United	27	4	3	20	33	101	15
Malvern Town Reserves	28	3	1	24	35	114	10

2 games were not played.

Sikh Hunters and Tenbury United each had 3 points deducted.
Riverway had 1 point deducted.
Ettingshall Park Farm and Mahal Reserves both resigned during the season and their records were deleted.
Tenbury United moved to the Herefordshire League and Malvern Town Reserves moved to the Worcester & District League. Riverway changed their name to F.C. Stafford. AFC Ludlow joined from the Mercian Regional League while Bilbrook, Warstone Wanderers and Worcester Raiders joined as newly formed clubs and Wyrley Reserves joined as a newly formed side.

2013-14

Premier Division

Lye Town	42	31	8	3	141	39	101
Pegasus Juniors	42	32	4	6	127	44	100
Wolverhampton Casuals	42	31	5	6	128	68	98
Shawbury United	42	30	7	5	139	50	97
Black Country Rangers	42	29	2	11	120	58	86
Sporting Khalsa	42	26	4	12	130	63	82
Bewdley Town	42	20	5	17	94	75	65
Wellington	42	19	8	15	86	87	65
Dudley Town	42	19	6	17	101	87	63
Cradley Town	42	19	5	18	89	87	62
Ellesmere Rangers	42	18	7	17	91	87	61
Smethwick Rangers	42	16	5	21	87	100	53
Wellington Amateurs	42	15	6	21	78	88	51
Malvern Town	42	16	3	23	74	95	51
Wednesfield	42	14	8	20	72	79	50
Bilston Town (2007)	42	13	4	25	77	107	43
Dudley Sports	42	11	10	21	64	107	43
Wolverhampton Sporting Comm.	42	10	7	25	54	97	37
Shifnal Town	42	9	6	27	49	104	32
Willenhall Town	42	7	7	28	50	133	28
Bustleholme	*42*	*6*	*8*	*28*	*57*	*152*	*26*
Bromyard Town	*42*	*7*	*3*	*32*	*40*	*141*	*24*

Black Country Rangers had 3 points deducted.
Shifnal Town had 1 point deducted.
Bartley Green resigned and disbanded during the season and their record was deleted.
Lye Town were promoted to the Midland League and Gornal Athletic joined after relegation from the Midland Alliance.
Bilston Town (2007) changed their name to Bilston Town Community.

Division One

AFC Bridgnorth	**30**	**26**	**3**	**1**	**117**	**18**	**81**
Haughmond	**30**	**22**	**4**	**4**	**89**	**33**	**70**
Bartestree	30	18	7	5	80	36	61
Wem Town	30	17	3	10	91	59	54
Penn Croft	30	12	9	9	78	73	45
Hanwood United	30	15	1	14	68	64	43
Wyrley Juniors	30	13	4	13	70	69	43
Stone Old Alleynians	30	10	8	12	54	50	38
Gornal Athletic Reserves	30	10	8	12	62	71	38
Hereford Lads Club	30	12	2	16	58	68	38
Trysull	30	9	8	13	63	68	35
Shenstone Pathfinder	30	9	6	15	47	68	33
Ledbury Town	30	9	4	17	60	89	31
St. Martins	30	8	4	18	48	96	28
Mahal	30	7	3	20	47	93	24
Wolverhampton United	*30*	*5*	*2*	*23*	*29*	*106*	*17*

Hanwood United had 3 points deducted.
Gornal Athletic Reserves and Mahal both left the league.

Division Two

AFC Ludlow	**26**	**17**	**3**	**6**	**91**	**28**	**54**
Team Dudley	**26**	**17**	**3**	**6**	**83**	**39**	**54**
Worcester Raiders	**26**	**16**	**2**	**8**	**107**	**77**	**50**
Wrens Nest	**26**	**15**	**5**	**6**	**65**	**40**	**50**
Penkridge Town	26	15	5	6	75	56	50
Newport Town	26	11	7	8	80	57	40
Wolv. Sporting Comm. Reserves	26	13	4	9	53	73	40
Malvern Rangers	26	13	3	10	85	66	38
Warstone Wanderers	26	11	4	11	65	59	37
FC Stafford	26	11	3	12	77	53	36
Sikh Hunters	26	9	2	15	55	85	26
Red Star Alma	26	4	4	18	31	94	16
Wyrley Reserves	26	2	5	19	29	83	11
Bilboron	26	2	2	22	32	118	8

Wolverhampton Sporting Community Reserves and Sikh Hunters each had 3 points deducted.
Malvern Rangers had 4 points deducted.
Wolverhampton Sporting Community withdrew their reserve side and entered an Under-21 side into the Staffordshire County Senior League instead while Malvern Rangers merged with Powick of the Worcester & District League to form Powick Rangers who replaced Malvern Rangers in the WMRL – Division Two. Penkridge Town disbanded but a new club named Penkridge was formed as a replacement in 2015 and joined the Staffordshire County Senior League. Kington Town joined from the Herefordshire League, Oakengates Athletic joined from the Mercian Regional League while Bartley Green Illey and Darlaston Town (1874) joined as a newly formed replacement clubs. Malvern Town entered their newly formed Under-21 side having withdrawn their reserve side from the Worcester & District League while AFC Worcester Olympic, Gornal Colts and Tipton Youth all joined from junior football.

2014-15

Premier Division

Sporting Khalsa	42	38	3	1	143	25	117
AFC Bridgnorth	42	28	6	8	108	45	90
Gornal Athletic	42	28	6	8	102	45	90
Ellesmere Rangers	42	24	9	9	100	52	81
Malvern Town	42	23	9	10	110	59	78
Wolverhampton Casuals	42	22	7	13	94	81	73
Shawbury United	42	22	6	14	129	84	72
Haughmond	42	20	10	12	86	63	70
Pegasus Juniors	42	20	5	17	80	56	65
Black Country Rangers	42	17	9	16	98	93	60
Wellington	42	16	11	15	83	71	59
Dudley Sports	42	17	6	19	71	80	57
Bilston Town Community	42	16	5	21	67	93	53
Dudley Town	42	14	8	20	85	93	50
Cradley Town	42	13	5	24	83	124	44
Wolverhampton Sporting Comm.	42	12	6	24	70	99	42
Bewdley Town	42	11	7	24	72	95	40
Willenhall Town	42	9	12	21	68	104	39
Smethwick Rangers	42	11	6	25	76	116	39
Wellington Amateurs	42	10	5	27	50	122	35
Shifnal Town	*42*	*8*	*8*	*26*	*48*	*106*	*32*
Wednesfield	*42*	*5*	*7*	*30*	*53*	*170*	*22*

Sporting Khalsa were promoted to the Midland League, swapping places with Tipton Town who were relegated from the same league.
Bilston Town Community became known as Bilston Town.

West Midlands (Regional) League 2015-2017

Division One

Bromyard Town	28	20	4	4	92	34	64
Stone Old Alleynians	28	18	3	7	55	37	57
St. Martins	28	17	2	9	82	55	53
Wrens Nest	28	16	2	10	61	48	50
Hereford Lads Club	28	15	2	11	46	48	47
AFC Ludlow	28	12	8	8	65	39	44
Wem Town	28	12	4	12	71	59	40
Trysull	28	11	7	10	45	33	40
Shenstone Pathfinder	28	10	5	13	35	43	35
Bustleholme	28	10	3	15	45	79	33
Team Dudley	28	9	4	15	55	73	31
Penn Croft	28	8	5	15	60	82	29
Bartestree	28	6	9	13	58	72	27
Worcester Raiders	28	8	3	17	72	107	27
Wyrley	28	5	5	18	46	79	20

Ledbury Town resigned in early October 2014 and their record (Played 7, Lost 7) was deleted. They joined the Herefordshire League in 2015-16. Hanwood United resigned in early November 2014 and their record was deleted.

Division Two

Kington Town	30	21	5	4	78	29	68
FC Stafford	30	20	4	6	80	34	64
Darlaston Town (1874)	30	21	1	8	84	44	64
Warstone Wanderers	30	19	2	9	94	60	59
Powick Rangers	30	17	6	7	81	45	57
Sikh Hunters	30	14	9	7	55	41	51
Newport Town	30	14	6	10	76	48	48
Oakengates Athletic	30	14	4	12	60	49	46
Tipton Youth	30	14	2	14	61	60	44
Malvern Town U21	30	12	6	12	51	52	42
Wolverhampton United	30	11	6	13	55	55	39
Bartley Green Illey	30	9	4	17	44	51	31
Wyrley Reserves	30	6	5	19	33	72	23
Gornal Colts	30	6	3	21	40	114	21
Red Star Alma	30	5	5	20	37	80	20
AFC Worcester Olympic	30	1	4	25	31	126	7

Bilbrook resigned during the season and their record was deleted but they rejoined the league for the 2015-16 season.
AFC Worcester Olympic moved to the Cheltenham League, Oakengates Athletic moved to the Mercian Regional League and Bartley Green Illey disbanded. Wyrley Reserves also left the league. Old Wulfrunians and Wonder Vaults both joined from the Birmingham A.F.A. and Telford Juniors joined from the Mercian Regional League. Tividale Reserves and Wrens Nest Reserves also joined.

2015-16 Premier Division

Shawbury United	42	29	7	6	140	46	94
AFC Bridgnorth	42	29	6	7	123	43	93
Malvern Town	42	25	3	14	114	72	78
Wolverhampton Sporting Comm.	42	23	8	11	130	69	77
Haughmond	42	22	10	10	111	69	76
Wolverhampton Casuals	42	22	8	12	111	81	74
Dudley Sports	42	21	11	10	82	63	74
Cradley Town	42	20	10	12	89	63	70
Pegasus Juniors	42	21	3	18	87	77	66
Ellesmere Rangers	42	19	8	15	92	72	65
Wellington	42	16	13	13	86	67	61
Smethwick Rangers	42	18	7	17	89	99	61
Dudley Town	42	17	10	15	66	82	61
Stone Old Alleynians	42	18	4	20	74	85	58
Black Country Rangers	42	15	11	16	73	65	56
Bewdley Town	42	16	8	18	72	78	56
Gornal Athletic	42	12	5	25	67	94	41
Willenhall Town	42	10	7	25	63	110	37
Wellington Amateurs	42	9	7	26	46	115	34
Bilston Town	42	8	9	25	50	105	33
Bromyard Town	**42**	**9**	**5**	**28**	**66**	**134**	**32**
Tipton Town	**42**	**0**	**6**	**36**	**26**	**168**	**6**

Shawbury United were promoted to the Midland League.

Division One

Shifnal Town	32	25	3	4	81	34	78
Hereford Lads Club	32	21	4	7	77	37	67
AFC Ludlow	32	20	4	8	87	44	64
Wednesfield	32	18	8	6	70	37	62
Darlaston Town (1874)	32	15	9	8	84	52	54
St. Martins	32	17	2	13	82	69	53
Kington Town	32	15	5	12	72	64	50
Trysull	32	15	3	14	58	49	48
Wem Town	32	14	4	14	74	71	46
Wrens Nest	32	11	6	15	54	83	39
FC Stafford	32	9	8	15	50	69	35
Worcester Raiders	32	9	6	17	71	86	33
Shenstone Pathfinder	32	10	2	20	45	75	32
Team Dudley	32	8	6	18	56	78	30
Penn Croft	32	7	9	16	49	76	30
Bustleholme	32	8	5	19	50	90	29
Wyrley	32	5	6	21	44	90	21

Bartestree resigned during the season and their record was deleted. They subsequently joined the Herefordshire League in 2016-17. AFC Ludlow disbanded and Trysull also left the league.

Division Two

Newport Town	28	24	2	2	113	40	74
Old Wulfrunians	27	17	3	7	69	30	54
Warstone Wanderers	28	14	6	8	89	69	48
Wolverhampton United	28	14	5	9	60	63	47
Red Star Alma	28	12	8	8	69	56	44
Telford Juniors	28	10	10	8	60	45	40
Bilbrook	27	12	4	11	56	62	40
Powick Rangers	26	10	8	8	53	40	38
Gornal Colts	28	9	5	14	69	86	32
Malvern Town U21	27	8	7	12	53	60	31
Wonder Vaults	28	9	4	15	56	68	31
Tipton Youth	27	8	3	16	68	79	27
Sikh Hunters	27	7	5	15	52	101	23
Tividale Reserves	21	5	4	12	43	60	19
Wrens Nest Reserves	28	4	6	18	37	88	18

Sikh Hunters had 3 points deducted.
Tividale Reserves resigned with 7 games still to play but their record was allowed to stand.
Red Star Alma moved to the Staffordshire County Senior League and Bilbrook, Powick Rangers, Tividale Reserves and Wrens Nest Reserves also left the league. AFC Broseley and Allscott both joined from the Mercian Regional League, Azaad Sports and Emerald Athletic both joined from the Wolverhampton Combination while Bewdley Town Reserves and West Bromwich United both also joined. Malvern Town U21 were replaced by Malvern Town Reserves.

2016-17 Premier Division

Haughmond	38	32	3	3	135	42	99
Wolverhampton Casuals	38	27	3	8	122	70	84
Wolverhampton Sporting Comm.	38	24	10	4	122	43	81
Malvern Town	38	25	4	9	120	56	79
Wellington	38	20	8	10	95	65	68
Bewdley Town	38	20	6	12	118	82	66
Ellesmere Rangers	38	20	5	13	97	77	65
AFC Bridgnorth	38	17	4	17	67	76	55
Pegasus Juniors	38	17	3	18	85	74	54
Cradley Town	38	16	5	17	76	70	53
Shifnal Town	38	15	8	15	76	76	53
Stone Old Alleynians	38	12	13	13	70	64	49
Black Country Rangers	38	13	10	15	73	72	49
Willenhall Town	**38**	**15**	**3**	**20**	**74**	**99**	**48**
Bilston Town	38	12	7	19	73	90	43
Smethwick Rangers	38	12	4	22	53	91	40
Dudley Sports	38	9	7	22	49	92	34
Dudley Town	38	9	4	25	52	114	31
Wellington Amateurs	38	7	2	29	45	147	23
Gornal Athletic	**38**	**2**	**3**	**33**	**28**	**130**	**9**

Wolverhampton Sporting Community had 1 point deducted.

Haughmond were promoted to the Midland League, swapping places with Tividale who were relegated from the same league.

Division One

Hereford Lads Club	30	26	2	2	121	32	80
Wednesfield	30	22	3	5	114	45	69
Worcester Raiders	30	18	5	7	83	61	59
Newport Town	30	18	4	8	89	54	58
Old Wulfrunians	30	17	5	8	78	52	56
Tipton Town	30	17	4	9	61	52	55
Darlaston Town (1874)	30	13	5	12	53	50	44
St. Martins	30	11	2	17	65	94	35
Wem Town	30	9	6	15	59	78	33
Bustleholme	30	9	4	17	58	77	31
Wrens Nest	30	8	6	16	55	82	30
Bromyard Town	30	8	4	18	48	79	28
Wyrley	30	7	6	17	38	87	27
FC Stafford	30	8	5	17	67	98	26
Kington Town	30	7	4	19	53	80	25
Team Dudley	30	7	5	18	53	74	26

FC Stafford had 3 points deducted.
Shenstone Pathfinder and Penn Croft both resigned during the season and their records were deleted. Shenstone Pathfinder joined the Staffordshire County Senior League for the 2017-18 season. F.C. Stafford left the league.

Division Two

Telford Juniors	26	18	3	5	100	40	57
West Bromwich United	26	18	3	5	79	29	57
Allscott	26	16	7	3	79	36	52
AFC Broseley	26	14	2	10	53	51	44
Gornal Colts	26	12	3	11	60	51	39
Warstone Wanderers	26	12	3	11	66	63	39
Sikh Hunters	26	10	4	12	60	77	34
Wolverhampton United	26	11	1	14	60	89	31
Wonder Vaults	26	10	3	13	57	66	30
Tipton Youth	26	8	6	12	52	65	30
Malvern Town Reserves	26	8	5	13	53	64	29
Bewdley Town Reserves	26	8	3	15	58	69	27
Emerald Athletic	26	7	6	13	44	83	27
Azaad Sports	26	4	3	19	40	78	12

Allscott, Azaad Sports, Wolverhampton United and Wonder Vaults all had 3 points deducted.
Azaad Sports and Emerald Athletic both moved to the Wolverhampton & District Sunday League while Malvern Town Reserves and West Bromwich United also both left the league. Tipton Youth merged with Bilbrook Juniors to form AFC Bilbrook who replaced Tipton Youth in the WMRL – Division Two. Church Stretton and Rock Rovers both joined from the Mercian Regional League and Ludlow joined as a newly re-formed club. AFC Bridgnorth withdrew their reserve side from the Mercian Regional League and entered their Development side in the WMRL – Division Two while FC Darlaston, Market Drayton Town Reserves and Oldbury United also joined.

2017-18

Premier Division

Wolverhampton Sporting Comm.	38	34	2	2	148	29	104
Tividale	38	28	5	5	121	49	89
Malvern Town	38	26	5	7	113	65	83
Black Country Rangers	38	23	8	7	111	56	77
Wednesfield	38	23	5	10	101	63	74
Ellesmere Rangers	38	22	5	11	106	68	71
Bewdley Town	38	19	6	13	91	70	63
Cradley Town	38	19	5	14	85	63	62
Wolverhampton Casuals	38	18	3	17	121	95	57
Wellington	38	17	5	16	82	75	56
Bilston Town	38	16	5	17	80	85	53
Hereford Lads Club	38	16	3	19	73	90	51
Stone Old Alleynians	38	14	3	21	76	92	45
Smethwick Rangers	38	9	6	23	49	85	33
Shifnal Town	38	10	3	25	58	111	33
Dudley Sports	38	9	5	24	61	110	32
Dudley Town	38	8	7	23	44	100	31
AFC Bridgnorth	38	8	6	24	50	91	30
Pegasus Juniors	38	7	7	24	37	109	28
Wellington Amateurs	**38**	**3**	**8**	**27**	**38**	**139**	**17**

Wolverhampton Sporting Community were promoted to the Midland League from where Haughmond and Shawbury United were relegated. Ellesmere Rangers and Stone Old Alleynians both moved to the North-West Counties League and Pershore Town joined from the Midland League.

Division One

Wem Town	32	23	4	5	95	34	73
Newport Town	32	21	6	5	106	39	69
Old Wulfrunians	32	20	8	4	58	27	68
St. Martins	32	20	0	12	87	46	60
Gornal Athletic	32	18	5	9	71	47	59
Darlaston Town (1874)	32	17	7	8	79	63	58
Worcester Raiders	32	17	7	8	72	59	58
Team Dudley	32	15	7	10	90	68	52
Allscott	32	13	3	16	55	65	42
Tipton Town	32	12	4	16	60	71	40
Bustleholme	32	12	3	17	68	85	39
Wrens Nest	32	11	2	19	56	79	35
Bromyard Town	32	10	3	19	60	87	33
Kington Town	32	8	3	21	51	81	27
Telford Juniors	32	7	3	22	48	87	24
Wyrley	32	6	5	21	39	86	23
Willenhall Town	32	3	8	21	34	105	17

Kington Town moved to the Herefordshire League and St. Martins moved to the North-West Counties League. Droitwich Spa joined from the Midland League.

Division Two

Sikh Hunters	28	23	4	1	105	25	73
Wolverhampton United	28	20	4	4	85	26	64
Gornal Colts	28	19	5	4	92	57	62
Bewdley Town Reserves	28	15	7	6	93	48	52
Warstone Wanderers	28	17	1	10	114	71	52
Rock Rovers	28	14	4	10	75	71	46
Church Stretton	28	13	5	10	68	49	44
Oldbury United	28	10	5	13	56	61	35
AFC Bilbrook	28	9	6	13	51	74	33
Ludlow	28	8	5	15	58	79	29
FC Darlaston	28	8	5	15	51	76	29
Wonder Vaults	28	8	3	17	56	83	27
AFC Broseley	28	7	6	15	43	92	27
Market Drayton Town Reserves	28	4	6	18	45	93	18
AFC Bridgnorth Development	28	1	2	25	29	116	5

AFC Bilbrook, AFC Broseley, Bewdley Town Reserves, Market Drayton Town Reserves and Oldbury United all left the league. Hawkins Sports joined, having resigned from the Staffordshire County Senior League during the 2016-17 season and Tipton Town Reserves also joined.
Wonder Vaults changed their name to AFC Bentley.

West Midlands (Regional) League 2018-2019

2018-19

Premier Division

Tividale	38	29	4	5	133	32	91
Haughmond	38	28	3	7	118	38	87
Wolverhampton Casuals	38	25	7	6	111	44	82
Malvern Town	38	26	4	8	103	36	82
Wednesfield	38	24	6	8	86	54	78
Bewdley Town	38	21	7	10	82	53	70
Hereford Lads Club	38	19	6	13	80	52	63
Black Country Rangers	38	18	6	14	88	79	60
Wellington	38	17	6	15	80	72	57
Dudley Town	38	15	9	14	72	70	54
Cradley Town	38	15	5	18	67	79	50
AFC Bridgnorth	38	13	9	16	64	75	48
Bilston Town	38	12	6	20	59	91	42
Pershore Town	38	11	6	21	66	100	39
Dudley Sports	38	9	10	19	50	91	37
Shawbury United	38	10	6	22	63	111	36
Smethwick Rangers	38	10	5	23	33	103	35
Wem Town	38	9	2	27	38	101	29
Shifnal Town	38	8	4	26	62	91	28
Pegasus Juniors	38	4	3	31	26	109	15

Tividale and Haughmond were both promoted to the Midland League from where Wolverhampton Sporting Community were relegated. Littleton also joined from the Midland League. Hereford Lads Club, Malvern Town and Wellington moved to the Hellenic League and Pegasus Juniors also moved to the Hellenic League, having changed their name to Hereford Pegasus.

Division One

Worcester Raiders	**32**	**24**	**7**	**1**	**98**	**37**	**79**
Darlaston Town (1874)	**32**	**25**	**3**	**4**	**100**	**34**	**78**
Droitwich Spa	32	22	3	7	107	31	69
Sikh Hunters	32	20	4	8	99	46	64
Team Dudley	32	18	5	9	82	55	59
Wrens Nest	32	16	6	10	67	64	54
Wellington Amateurs	32	14	4	14	68	67	46
Old Wulfrunians	32	14	4	14	48	51	46
Allscott	32	13	3	16	56	64	42
Wyrley	32	12	4	16	41	57	40
Bromyard Town	32	11	6	15	62	78	39
Newport Town	**32**	**11**	**4**	**17**	**62**	**68**	**37**
Gornal Athletic	32	11	3	18	53	79	36
Tipton Town	32	7	9	16	55	66	30
Bustleholme	32	8	2	22	51	107	26
Willenhall Town	32	5	5	22	37	89	20
Telford Juniors	**32**	**3**	**4**	**25**	**35**	**128**	**13**

Division Two

Gornal Colts	**20**	**14**	**3**	**3**	**55**	**28**	**45**
Church Stretton	19	12	3	4	62	26	42
FC Darlaston	**19**	**11**	**5**	**3**	**56**	**29**	**41**
AFC Bentley	20	10	3	7	48	55	33
Hawkins Sports	20	9	4	7	66	43	31
Ludlow	20	9	3	8	57	42	30
AFC Bridgnorth Development	20	9	2	9	42	48	29
Warstone Wanderers	20	7	4	9	41	51	25
Rock Rovers	19	6	1	12	43	56	19
Wolverhampton United	19	4	5	10	41	72	17
Tipton Town Reserves	20	0	1	19	24	85	1

Church Stretton and FC Darlaston each had 3 points added. Hawkins Sports moved to the Staffordshire County Senior League and Rock Rovers disbanded. Tipton Town Reserves and Wolverhampton United also left the league. Coven Athletic joined from the Staffordshire County Senior League, Walsall Town Swifts joined as a newly formed club and Worcester Raiders Reserves also joined.

SHROPSHIRE & DISTRICT LEAGUE 1890-1900

Shrewsbury School has a tradition of playing football (or dowling as it was known there) that goes back for centuries and it was largely because of this tradition that the game became popular in Shropshire much earlier than in virtually every other area of the country. There were already several clubs playing in Shrewsbury in the late 1860s and with the game having spread further into the county, the Shropshire F.A. was founded in 1877. The Shropshire Senior Cup was first played for in the 1877-78 season and the only older football competitions anywhere in the world are the Birmingham Senior Cup, the Sheffield & Hallamshire Cup and the oldest of all, the F.A. Cup itself.

When the growing industrial cities of the North and the Midlands began to take up the game, the earliest clubs often found it difficult to get fixtures against enough local teams of sufficient strength and so had to travel further afield to find worthwhile opponents. Thus it was that the established teams in the small market towns of Shropshire once played host to some of the Premier League club of today.

Wolverhampton Wanderers started life as St. Lukes and it was under that title that they twice visited Shifnal in the 1879-80 season, and were beaten, both by Shifnal Mechanics in November and by Shifnal Wanderers in January. Notice that Wolves were not of sufficient status to play Shifnal's top club, Shifnal Town who did however have annual home fixtures with Aston Villa. In the same era, Oswestry often beat Everton in their annual home and away fixtures, while the Toffees also came to grief on Boxing Day 1881 when their first XI were thrashed 5-1 by one of Shropshires lesser sides, Ellesmere.

Once professionalism was legalised in 1885 though, the best players from rural areas soon gravitated to the large cities where the gate receipts meant that they could pay the best wages (or expenses as they were usually described!). Even so, Shropshire still had enough strong teams left to form one of the earliest leagues and only two years after the Football League was formed in 1888, the Shropshire & District League came into being "to help to improve the standard of football in the county".

The intended 8 founder members were Ironbridge, Ludlow, Newport, Oswestry, Shifnal Town, Shrewsbury Town, St. Georges and Wellington Town. Shifnal, though, were having financial difficulties and withdrew because of a lack of signed-up players just a few days before the start of the season. Whitchurch quickly accepted an invitation to replace them.

Of those founder members, Ironbridge and St. Georges had already played one season of league football, having been founder members of the Birmingham & District League a year earlier, but it was not long before the best of the Shropshire Leagues clubs began to move in the opposite direction and the League closed down in 1900, its strength having already being significantly diluted.

There were a number of attempts to replace the league but it was not until the Shropshire County League was formed in 1950 that any of these was successful. This, after a number of transformations, has now become the Shropshire Premier League but neither in its current form nor in any of its previous incarnations has it been as strong a competition as the original Shropshire & District League.

Shropshire & District League 1890-1898

1890-91

Ironbridge	14	11	0	3	40	12	22
Shrewsbury Town	14	9	1	4	42	21	19
Newport	14	8	0	6	21	27	16
Wellington Town	14	6	2	6	26	25	14
St. Georges	14	6	1	7	35	24	13
Ludlow	14	4	2	8	18	26	10
Whitchurch	14	5	0	9	25	44	10
Oswestry	14	4	0	10	14	42	8

Ironbridge vs Oswestry and Newport vs Oswestry were not played.
Ironbridge and Newport were each awarded a win.
Ludlow resigned and disbanded but a replacement club was quickly formed and played friendlies in the 1891-92 season. Oswestry also left the league. Nantwich, Stafford Rangers and Wolverhampton Wanderers Reserves all joined.
The League was increased to 9 clubs.

1891-92

Wolverhampton Wanderers Res.	16	15	1	0	89	10	31
Nantwich	16	8	2	6	44	36	18
Stafford Rangers	16	8	2	6	35	31	18
St. Georges	16	7	3	6	44	41	17
Ironbridge	16	6	4	6	61	53	16
Shrewsbury Town	16	6	4	6	48	48	16
Newport	16	4	4	8	35	64	12
Wellington Town	16	2	4	10	20	44	8
Whitchurch	16	3	2	11	23	72	8

Wolverhampton Wanderers Reserves moved to the Birmingham & District League and Nantwich moved to The Combination.
Hereford Town and Newtown both joined.

1892-93

Newtown	16	8	6	2	72	24	22
Ironbridge	16	9	3	4	41	34	21
St. Georges	16	8	4	4	47	38	20
Shrewsbury Town	16	7	6	3	45	37	20
Wellington Town	16	5	7	4	48	35	17
Stafford Rangers	16	7	3	6	31	34	17
Hereford Town	16	5	4	7	20	35	14
Newport	16	4	3	9	30	43	11
Whitchurch	16	0	2	14	23	77	2

Stafford Rangers moved to the Birmingham & District League.
Market Drayton and Oswestry United both joined.
The League was increased to 10 clubs.

1893-94

St. Georges	18	12	2	4	48	23	26
Newtown	18	12	1	5	68	28	25
Shrewsbury Town	17	11	2	4	60	37	24
Wellington Town	18	6	5	7	40	45	17
Market Drayton	18	7	2	9	34	50	16
Hereford Town	17	7	1	9	55	44	15
Ironbridge	18	6	3	9	36	51	15
Whitchurch	18	6	3	9	47	65	15
Newport	18	5	3	10	34	51	13
Oswestry United	18	4	4	10	35	63	12

Hereford Town vs Shrewsbury Town was not played.
Market Drayton moved to the North Staffordshire & District League.
Wrockwardine Wood joined the league.

1894-95

St. Georges	17	12	4	1	44	18	28
Oswestry United	18	10	5	3	53	25	25
Shrewsbury Town	17	8	4	5	42	28	20
Hereford Town	18	5	8	5	34	25	18
Newtown	17	8	2	7	42	35	18
Wrockwardine Wood	17	6	4	7	30	34	16
Ironbridge	18	6	3	9	38	47	15
Wellington Town	18	4	5	9	45	63	13
Whitchurch	18	4	4	10	30	54	12
Newport	18	4	3	11	21	50	11

Wrockwardine Wood vs Newtown and St. Georges vs Shrewsbury Town were not played.
Shrewsbury Town moved to the Birmingham & District League.
Market Drayton joined from the North Staffordshire & District League.

1895-96

Hereford Town	18	14	1	3	69	22	29
Wrockwardine Wood	18	11	4	3	46	21	26
Wellington Town	18	9	5	4	54	37	23
Newtown	18	10	2	6	48	29	22
St. Georges	18	9	3	6	53	28	21
Ironbridge	18	8	4	6	49	43	20
Market Drayton	18	6	2	10	31	41	14
Newport	18	5	1	12	29	58	11
Whitchurch	18	3	2	13	19	78	8
Oswestry United	18	3	0	15	30	71	6

Newtown and Oswestry United both moved to the Welsh League and Hereford Town moved to the Birmingham & District League. Leominster and Wem joined, both having previously just played friendlies and cup ties.
The League was reduced to 9 clubs.

1896-97

Wellington Town	16	12	4	0	55	18	28
Wrockwardine Wood	14	8	3	3	46	15	19
St. Georges	14	7	4	3	30	20	18
Newport	16	7	4	5	33	31	18
Ironbridge	16	7	2	7	44	31	16
Market Drayton	14	5	2	7	35	36	12
Whitchurch	14	4	1	9	19	71	9
Wem	16	3	3	10	27	53	9
Leominster	16	3	1	12	32	46	7

Four games were not played.
Leominster reverted to playing just friendlies and cup ties and Whitchurch disbanded. Newtown and Oswestry United both joined from the Welsh League and Shrewsbury Town Reserves also joined.
The League was increased to 10 clubs.

1897-98

Wellington Town	18	15	1	2	64	18	31
Newtown	18	13	1	4	64	21	27
Ironbridge	18	10	4	4	48	26	24
St. Georges	18	10	2	6	44	32	22
Newport	18	8	5	5	36	35	21
Oswestry United	18	8	1	9	36	40	17
Market Drayton	18	7	2	9	32	45	16
Wrockwardine Wood	18	6	1	11	35	44	13
Shrewsbury Town Reserves	18	2	1	15	19	69	5
Wem	18	1	2	15	19	67	4

Market Drayton moved to the North Staffordshire & District League, Oswestry United moved to The Combination and Wellington Town moved to the Birmingham & District League. Singleton & Coles continued playing in the Wellington & District League under that title but became Shrewsbury Towns reserve side. Walsall Reserves and Welshpool United joined, both having played just cup-ties and friendlies in 1897-98.
The League was reduced to 8 clubs.

1898-99

Ironbridge	11	7	3	1	32	7	17
Walsall Reserves	12	8	1	3	30	10	17
St. Georges	12	8	1	3	30	17	17
Newtown	11	5	2	4	26	15	12
Wem	12	4	2	6	10	21	10
Welshpool United	12	3	1	8	19	47	7
Newport	12	0	2	10	3	33	2

Wrockwardine Wood failed to fulfil any fixtures after 27th December 1898 and it was eventually decided that their record should be deleted at the league's meeting in April 1899: *9 2 1 6 15 36 5*
Ironbridge vs Newtown was not played.
St. Georges and Walsall Reserves both moved to the Birmingham & District League and Newtown moved to The Combination.
Bridgnorth, Singleton & Coles and St. Georges United all joined from the Wellington & District League and Stafford Christ Church joined from the Cannock & District League.

1899-1900

Ironbridge	14	12	1	1	56	12	25
Singleton & Coles	13	8	2	3	46	27	18
St. Georges United	13	6	3	4	36	29	15
Bridgnorth	14	5	3	6	37	35	13
Newport	14	4	3	7	22	32	11
Stafford Christ Church	13	5	0	8	34	32	10
Wem	14	3	3	8	14	46	9
Welshpool United	13	3	1	9	13	45	7

St. Georges United vs Welshpool United was not played. Stafford Christ Church vs Singleton & Coles was played but the result has not been found.
Ironbridge moved to the Birmingham & District League, Newport decided to suspend all activity for a year, Wem decided to play only cup ties and friendlies and St. Georges United and Stafford Christ Church both disbanded. With only Bridgnorth, Singleton & Coles and Welshpool United wishing to continue in the league, it had to close down. Bridgnorth and Singleton & Coles both joined the Wellington & District League in 1899-1900, while Welshpool United played just cup ties and friendlies.

BIRMINGHAM COMBINATION 1892-1954

(Formerly the Birmingham & District Junior League)

Even after the formation of the Birmingham League in 1889, there were still a large number of established clubs in the Birmingham area who were not attached to any league. The Birmingham F.A. already had two cup competitions – the Senior Cup and the Junior Cup – and so it was logical to have a league for both classes of clubs as well.

Thus, in 1892, the Birmingham & District Junior League was formed with 8 of the area's leading junior clubs – Aston St. James, Bournbrook, Bournville, Ellen Street Victoria, Hamstead, Kings Heath Albion, Park Mills and Soho Villa. These 8 were all from the city of Birmingham itself but the league soon expanded its area of coverage and by 1908, its status had grown to the extent that it changed its name to the Birmingham Combination.

For many years, the Combination acted as an unofficial second division to the Birmingham League and many of the area's leading clubs played in the Birmingham Combination, including future Football League clubs Hereford United and Cheltenham Town. In the 1930s, the strength of the Combination had increased to the level where it equalled that of the Birmingham League and when that league suffered a crisis, the Combination briefly became the stronger of the two.

The Birmingham League recovered after the war and during the 1952-53 season it suggested a merger between the two but the Combination refused. Six of the Combination's best clubs then moved across to the League and it was the Combination's turn to suggest a merger but with six new members, there was now no advantage in that for the League. A year later all but one of the remaining Combination clubs also resigned to join the League leaving the Combination with no alternative but to close down.

Note: Particularly in the early years of the league, very few tables were published and many of those published contained errors. Additional research has succeeded in correcting many of those errors by summing up results. Tables that still contain errors have the unbalanced totals in italics below the relevant columns.

BIRMINGHAM & DISTRICT JUNIOR LEAGUE

1892-93

	P	W	D	L	F	A	Pts
Soho Villa	13	10	1	2	47	19	21
Bournville	14	8	3	3	29	20	19
Park Mills	13	7	2	4	48	20	16
Hamstead	11	7	0	4	41	25	14
Bournbrook	14	5	0	9	31	58	10
Aston St. James	11	4	1	6	18	30	9
Kings Heath Albion	12	2	1	9	12	29	5
Ellen Street Victoria	10	2	0	8	12	37	4

Note: No published tables have been found at any point during this season and so the table given above has been compiled using all results found. The 7 missing games may not have been played as they would not have affected the destiny of the championship.
Aston St. James, Bournbrook, Ellen Street Victoria, Hamstead and Kings Heath Albion all left the league. Calthorpe Rovers, Causeway Green Villa, Coles Farm Unity, Coombs Wood, Lozells, Oldbury Town and Redditch Excelsior all joined.

The League was increased to 10 clubs.

1893-94

	P	W	D	L	F	A	Pts
Coombs Wood	18	12	4	2	50	21	28
Oldbury Town	18	11	3	4	45	30	25
Lozells	18	9	3	6	48	40	21
Coles Farm Unity	17	8	3	6	42	35	19
Bournville	16	7	4	5	40	30	18
Redditch Excelsior	18	7	3	8	48	50	17
Causeway Green Villa	18	7	2	9	36	45	16
Park Mills	16	7	0	9	33	37	14
Soho Villa	18	3	4	11	33	44	10
Calthorpe Rovers	17	2	2	13	25	68	6

Note: Several tables were published during the season but often contained obvious errors and no end of season table has been found. The table above has been compiled after correcting errors and adding in missing and late season results as found. The 3 missing games were probably not played.
Oldbury Town moved to the Birmingham League and Bournville, Calthorpe Rovers and Coles Farm Unity also left the league. Bournbrook, Ellen Street Victoria, Kings Heath Albion, Smethwick Wesleyan Rovers and Windsor Street Gas all joined.

The League was increased to 11 clubs.

1894-95

	P	W	D	L	F	A	Pts
Lozells	20	17	1	2	63	28	35
Coombs Wood	20	15	3	2	83	25	31
Smethwick Wesleyan Rovers	20	10	3	7	47	38	23
Soho Villa	20	10	3	7	47	57	23
Bournbrook	20	11	0	9	61	49	20
Windsor Street Gas	20	7	5	8	31	41	19
Park Mills	20	8	1	11	51	52	17
Redditch Excelsior	20	7	1	12	40	46	15
Causeway Green Villa	20	6	2	12	46	60	14
Kings Heath Albion	20	7	0	13	39	53	14
Ellen Street Victoria	20	2	1	17	24	83	5

Bournbrook and Coombs Wood each had 2 points deducted.
Coombs Wood and Ellen Street Victoria left the league.
Bournville, Calthorpe Rovers and Harborne joined.

The League was increased to 12 clubs.

1895-96

	P	W	D	L	F	A	Pts
Bournbrook	22	15	4	3	69	24	34
Smethwick Wesleyan Rovers	22	16	2	4	63	34	34
Windsor Street Gas	22	13	3	6	48	41	29
Redditch Excelsior	22	9	5	8	46	39	23
Soho Villa	21	11	1	9	58	47	23
Causeway Green Villa	22	9	4	9	56	40	22
Lozells	21	10	2	9	47	45	22
Park Mills	19	8	4	7	42	41	20
Bournville	21	7	2	12	43	63	16
Calthorpe Rovers	22	6	2	14	51	61	14
Kings Heath Albion	21	5	2	14	27	69	12
Harborne	19	1	3	15	20	66	5

Note: No end of season table has been found and tables published during the season often contained errors and so the table above has been compiled from results found. The Lozells vs Bournbrook result was not found but, as Bournbrook were declared champions, they must have won that game. The missing game has therefore been included in the table as a win for Bournbrook and a defeat for Lozells but without any additions to the clubs Goals For or Goals Against records. The 5 missing games are believed to have been played but the results have not been found.

1896-97

	P	W	D	L	F	A	Pts
Bournbrook	20	14	3	3	54	22	31
Soho Villa	20	14	2	4	59	27	30
Bournville	20	11	5	4	63	30	27
Smethwick Wesleyan Rovers	20	10	7	3	51	27	27
Lozells	20	12	3	5	48	34	27
Calthorpe Rovers	20	8	2	10	41	65	18
Windsor Street Gas	20	7	3	10	25	41	17
Redditch Excelsior	20	7	2	11	40	44	16
Harborne	20	4	7	9	33	42	15
Causeway Green Villa	20	4	2	14	25	55	10
Park Mills	20	0	2	18	21	73	2

Kings Heath Albion resigned during the season and their record was deleted.
Causeway Green Villa moved to the West Midland League and Windsor Street Gas also left the league. Bromsgrove Rovers and Evesham Wanderers joined from the Studley & District League and Kings Norton Metal Works joined from the Redditch Junior League.
Bournville changed their name to Bournville Athletic.

1897-98

	P	W	D	L	F	A	Pts
Bournville Athletic	22	20	1	1	93	23	41
Bournbrook	22	15	2	5	52	23	32
Redditch Excelsior	22	13	3	6	52	33	29
Soho Villa	22	12	3	7	46	37	27
Evesham Wanderers	22	11	2	9	61	49	24
Kings Norton Metal Works	22	11	0	11	36	45	22
Harborne	22	8	5	9	46	45	21
Smethwick Wesleyan Rovers	22	6	5	11	35	42	17
Park Mills	22	7	3	12	51	62	17
Bromsgrove Rovers	22	7	3	12	27	43	17
Calthorpe Rovers	22	4	2	16	32	80	10
Lozells	22	2	3	17	24	73	7

Evesham Wanderers merged with Evesham Old Boys at the end of the season but resigned and disbanded shortly afterwards. Lozells also left the league and are thought to have disbanded. Coombs Wood joined from the West Midland League and Redditch Town joined from the Studley & District League. Leamington Town and Warwick United also joined, having played only friendlies and cup ties in 1897-98.

The League was increased to 14 clubs.

Birmingham Combination 1898-1904

1898-99

Bournville Athletic	26	24	1	1	115	26	49
Coombs Wood	26	16	2	8	53	33	34
Warwick United	26	14	4	8	58	41	32
Park Mills	26	13	3	10	76	60	29
Kings Norton Metal Works	26	11	7	8	51	42	29
Soho Villa	26	14	1	11	52	49	29
Bournbrook	26	13	1	12	60	52	27
Bromsgrove Rovers	26	11	4	11	34	44	26
Redditch Excelsior	26	10	4	12	51	70	24
Leamington Town	26	8	6	12	60	64	22
Harborne	26	7	6	13	43	55	20
Calthorpe Rovers	26	8	2	16	35	60	18
Redditch Town	26	4	6	16	45	73	14
Smethwick Wesleyan Rovers	26	4	3	19	37	101	11

Redditch Town disbanded and Calthorpe Rovers and Park Mills also left.
Eadies (Redditch) joined from the Redditch League, Oldbury Town joined from the Walsall & District League and Windsor Street Gas also joined.

1899-1900

Bournville Athletic	24	16	4	4	103	38	36
Leamington Town	24	17	2	5	71	35	36
Oldbury Town	24	15	2	7	79	37	32
Warwick United	24	14	3	7	68	39	31
Bromsgrove Rovers	24	12	4	8	48	43	28
Redditch Excelsior	24	11	4	9	66	53	26
Soho Villa	24	11	2	11	56	63	24
Smethwick Wesleyan Rovers	24	10	2	12	50	63	22
Kings Norton Metal Works	24	10	1	13	57	64	21
Windsor Street Gas	24	7	3	14	47	64	17
Bournbrook	24	6	4	14	50	74	16
Eadies (Redditch)	24	5	2	17	39	99	12
Harborne	24	4	3	17	26	88	11

Coombs Wood withdrew at the end of January 1900 with financial problems. Their record was deleted: 15 5 2 8 20 33 12
A replacement club called Coombs Wood Tube Works was formed and played cup-ties and friendlies in 1900-01.
Eadies (Redditch) withdrew just before the start of the 1900-01 season and instead joined the Redditch, Studley & District League (a merger of the Redditch and Studley leagues) and Warwick United disbanded. Smethwick Wesleyan Rovers changed their name to Smethwick Town. Foleshill Great Heath joined from the Coventry & North Warwickshire League.

The League was reduced to 12 clubs.

1900-01

Bournville Athletic	18	14	1	3	71	20	29
Oldbury Town	18	11	3	4	57	32	25
Leamington Town	18	8	5	5	27	23	21
Redditch Excelsior	18	9	2	7	40	42	20
Foleshill Great Heath	18	8	3	7	36	30	19
Bournbrook	18	7	2	9	31	41	16
Kings Norton Metal Works	17	3	7	7	32	31	13
Soho Villa	17	6	1	10	34	52	13
Bromsgrove Rovers	18	5	3	10	24	54	13
Smethwick Town	18	3	3	12	17	44	9

Soho Villa failed to send a team to Kings Norton on 30th April leaving one game unplayed. Windsor Street Gas resigned and disbanded before playing any games. Harborne withdrew in March 1901 and their record at the time was deleted: 13 0 2 11 13 59 2
They also later disbanded.
Langley St. Michaels joined from the Handsworth & District League and Selly Oak St. Marys joined from the Aston & District League. Witton Shell Department also joined, having been playing in both the Handsworth League and the Aston League. Smethwick Town left and are thought to have disbanded.

1901-02

Bournville Athletic	22	15	3	4	63	43	33
Langley St. Michaels	22	13	4	5	55	33	30
Soho Villa	22	14	2	6	65	41	30
Foleshill Great Heath	22	13	2	7	57	35	28
Kings Norton Metal Works	22	11	5	6	46	34	27
Bournbrook	22	6	6	10	45	42	18
Leamington Town	22	7	4	11	43	47	18
Oldbury Town	22	6	6	10	39	45	18
Witton Shell Department	22	7	4	11	25	35	18
Bromsgrove Rovers	22	7	3	12	29	56	17
Redditch Excelsior	22	7	2	13	40	60	16
Selly Oak St. Marys	22	3	5	14	31	67	11

Coombs Wood Tube Works joined from the Handsworth & District League.

The league was increased to 13 clubs.

1902-03

Bournville Athletic	22	16	3	3	64	25	35
Soho Villa	22	12	4	6	72	31	28
Langley St. Michaels	22	11	4	7	39	28	26
Leamington Town	22	11	4	7	45	36	26
Coombs Wood Tube Works	22	8	9	5	33	28	25
Foleshill Great Heath	22	8	7	7	45	41	23
Redditch Excelsior	22	8	5	9	45	43	21
Selly Oak St. Marys	22	7	6	9	53	73	20
Oldbury Town	22	6	7	9	28	36	19
Bromsgrove Rovers	22	8	2	12	44	48	18
Bournbrook	22	7	2	13	27	49	16
Kings Norton Metal Works	22	2	3	17	26	77	7
					521	515	

Witton Shell Department resigned on 17th January and their record at the time was deleted: 9 1 0 8 12 44 2
They disbanded shortly afterwards.
Brades Park and Saltley Gas both joined the league. Saltley Gas are thought to have been a newly formed club while Brades Park played in the Birmingham Junior Cup in 1902-03 but are thought not to have played in any league. They are thought to have been formed in 1902.

The League was increased to 14 clubs.

1903-04

Foleshill Great Heath	26	17	4	5	76	47	38
Soho Villa	26	16	5	5	60	42	37
Bournville Athletic	26	16	3	7	68	33	35
Langley St. Michaels	26	13	6	7	34	34	32
Coombs Wood Tube Works	26	14	4	8	67	54	32
Leamington Town	26	12	7	7	52	46	31
Brades Park	26	14	2	10	68	49	30
Saltley Gas	26	11	5	10	61	52	27
Bournbrook	26	10	4	12	52	51	24
Oldbury Town	26	9	5	12	42	51	23
Redditch Excelsior	26	10	2	14	50	64	22
Bromsgrove Rovers	26	4	6	16	34	58	14
Selly Oak St. Marys	26	2	6	18	31	98	10
Kings Norton Metal Works	26	3	3	20	33	76	9

Erdington joined from the Central Birmingham League while Selly Oak St. Marys disbanded. Saltley Gas changed their name to Birmingham Gas.

Birmingham Combination 1904-1909

1904-05

Coombs Wood Tube Works	26	18	3	5	69	36	39
Bromsgrove Rovers	26	15	3	8	62	42	33
Oldbury Town	26	14	5	7	53	45	33
Soho Villa	26	13	4	9	54	43	30
Foleshill Great Heath	26	12	6	8	56	45	30
Langley St. Michaels	26	11	5	10	67	56	27
Erdington	26	12	2	12	62	56	26
Kings Norton Metal Works	26	9	7	10	42	47	25
Bournbrook	26	9	7	10	51	60	25
Bournville Athletic	26	9	6	11	54	61	24
Birmingham Gas	26	7	9	10	35	43	23
Leamington Town	26	8	6	12	34	45	22
Brades Park	26	8	5	13	49	59	21
Redditch Excelsior	26	1	4	21	36	86	6

Redditch Excelsior disbanded but were replaced by a newly formed club simply called Redditch. Oldbury Town moved to the Walsall & District League, Leamington Town moved to the Coventry & North Warwickshire League and Brades Park disbanded. Cradley Heath St. Lukes and Rowley United both joined from the West Midland League and Churchfield also joined, having previously played just cup-ties and friendlies.

1905-06

Coombs Wood Tube Works	26	16	4	6	73	33	36
Bournbrook	26	15	6	5	63	42	36
Cradley Heath St. Lukes	26	16	4	6	76	53	36
Erdington	26	16	2	8	79	58	34
Redditch	26	15	3	8	86	58	33
Rowley United	26	12	6	8	77	61	30
Bournville Athletic	26	10	6	10	59	72	26
Kings Norton Metal Works	26	10	4	12	61	57	24
Langley St. Michaels	26	7	10	9	62	65	24
Bromsgrove Rovers	26	9	4	13	75	83	22
Soho Villa	26	7	5	14	35	62	19
Churchfield	26	5	8	13	39	65	18
Foleshill Great Heath	26	5	3	18	42	64	13
Birmingham Gas	26	4	5	17	41	81	13
					868	854	

Birmingham Gas left the league and are thought to have joined the newly formed Birmingham Works F.A. as City Gas (a separate Works F.A. club called Nechells Gas changed their name to Birmingham Gas in January 1907). Foleshill Great Heath moved to the Coventry & North Warwickshire League while Churchfield are thought to have disbanded. Nuneaton Town joined from the Coventry & North Warwickshire League, Oldbury Town joined from the Walsall & District League and Brades Park also joined, having re-formed after a season of inactivity.

1906-07

Nuneaton Town	24	17	4	3	86	39	38
Redditch	24	17	1	6	76	37	35
Cradley Heath St. Lukes	24	13	6	5	67	32	32
Kings Norton Metal Works	24	13	5	6	62	46	31
Coombs Wood Tube Works	24	10	8	6	50	42	28
Bromsgrove Rovers	24	12	2	10	68	60	26
Rowley United	24	9	4	11	56	70	22
Erdington	24	8	4	12	70	70	20
Langley St. Michaels	24	8	4	12	57	64	20
Brades Park	24	7	5	12	45	89	19
Bournbrook	24	6	5	13	53	61	17
Bournville Athletic	24	7	3	14	45	67	17
Oldbury Town	24	1	5	18	29	87	7

Soho Villa resigned at the start of February and their record was deleted when it stood as follows: 15 2 2 11 22 60 6
They continued to play cup-ties and friendlies in 1906-07 but moved into youth football in the 1907-08 season.
Kings Norton Metal Works changed their name to Stirchley United and Oldbury Town disbanded. Bilston United, Darlaston, Wednesbury Old Athletic and Willenhall Pickwick all joined from the Walsall & District League.
The League was increased to 16 clubs.

1907-08

Darlaston	30	21	6	3	83	32	48
Bilston United	30	22	3	5	89	35	47
Cradley Heath St. Lukes	30	19	5	6	102	47	43
Nuneaton Town	30	16	4	10	93	65	36
Willenhall Pickwick	30	16	3	11	71	51	35
Wednesbury Old Athletic	30	15	4	11	67	60	34
Coombs Wood Tube Works	30	12	5	13	70	64	29
Stirchley United	30	12	4	14	62	70	28
Redditch	30	11	6	13	63	73	28
Bournbrook	30	8	10	12	61	84	26
Langley St. Michaels	30	9	6	15	54	76	24
Bromsgrove Rovers	30	10	4	16	46	71	24
Erdington	30	8	6	16	58	77	22
Rowley United	30	7	7	16	69	89	21
Brades Park	30	6	8	16	45	84	20
Bournville Athletic	30	4	7	19	44	99	15

Brades Park and Erdington both disbanded while Hednesford Town and Willenhall Swifts both joined from the Walsall & District League.

The league changed its name to the Birmingham Combination.

BIRMINGHAM COMBINATION

1908-09

Willenhall Pickwick	30	20	6	4	129	54	46
Cradley Heath St. Lukes	30	20	3	7	91	52	43
Darlaston	30	20	1	9	102	46	41
Wednesbury Old Athletic	30	16	6	8	82	54	38
Bilston United	30	15	6	9	78	62	36
Redditch	30	15	5	10	67	52	35
Bournbrook	30	14	3	13	59	83	31
Willenhall Swifts	30	13	4	13	56	48	30
Hednesford Town	30	14	1	15	64	72	29
Nuneaton Town	30	12	3	15	81	62	27
Stirchley United	30	12	3	15	75	95	27
Bromsgrove Rovers	30	11	2	17	50	94	24
Coombs Wood Tube Works	30	9	4	17	87	99	22
Rowley United	30	8	4	18	53	87	20
Langley St. Michaels	30	5	6	19	32	94	16
Bournville Athletic	30	6	3	21	52	104	15

Rowley United disbanded and St. Georges Victoria joined from the Walsall & District League. Langley St. Michaels did not apply for re-election by the required date and so Cannock Town from the Walsall & District League were elected in their place. Langley St. Michaels appealed against their exclusion and their appeal was upheld, so both they and Cannock Town were given places in the league which was extended to 17 clubs.

Note: Newly elected St. Georges Victoria were often referred to in the press as Wellington St. Georges, presumably to avoid confusion with other clubs that also had "St. Georges" as part of their name. However Wellington St. Georges was never the clubs official name. nor was there any direct connection with an earlier club that disbanded in February 1900 whilst members of the Birmingham League. That earlier club was simply called St. Georges but was also often referred to as Wellington St. Georges. St. Georges Victoria had previously been known as Trench Victoria but changed their name in 1902 when they moved from Trench to St. Georges and took over the ground used by the earlier club. Trench and St. Georges are both villages a short distance east of Wellington, Shropshire.

Birmingham Combination 1909-1915

1909-10

Hednesford Town	30	24	3	3	93	39	51
Cradley Heath St. Lukes	30	21	6	3	80	41	48
Wednesbury Old Athletic	30	18	4	8	76	44	40
Darlaston	30	16	7	7	78	60	39
Coombs Wood Tube Works	30	16	6	8	86	49	38
Willenhall Pickwick	30	15	5	10	82	51	35
Nuneaton Town	30	14	7	9	79	53	35
Bilston United	30	11	8	11	66	62	30
Cannock Town	30	12	4	14	68	69	28
Willenhall Swifts	30	12	2	16	71	69	26
Bromsgrove Rovers	30	9	5	16	65	70	23
St. Georges Victoria	30	8	7	15	62	80	23
Redditch	30	9	4	17	62	71	22
Bournbrook	30	7	3	20	64	127	17
Stirchley United	30	5	3	22	51	129	13
Bournville Athletic	30	4	4	22	43	112	12
Langley St. Michaels	15	0	1	14	14	90	1

Langley St. Michaels resigned and disbanded on 13th January 1910 and their record was deleted.
Wednesbury Old Athletic moved to the Birmingham League and Birmingham Trams joined from the Birmingham Wednesday League.

1910-11

Darlaston	30	25	0	5	115	52	50
Nuneaton Town	30	22	0	8	93	44	44
Willenhall Swifts	30	19	4	7	86	42	42
Hednesford Town	30	16	6	8	85	42	38
Willenhall Pickwick	30	18	2	10	85	49	38
Redditch	30	16	4	10	95	64	36
Birmingham Trams	30	16	4	10	71	50	36
Cannock Town	30	16	3	11	61	54	35
Cradley Heath St. Lukes	29	13	2	14	74	72	28
Coombs Wood Tube Works	30	13	2	15	62	81	28
Stirchley United	29	9	7	13	58	85	25
Bilston United	30	8	7	15	70	77	23
Bromsgrove Rovers	30	7	4	19	59	96	18
St. Georges Victoria	30	7	4	19	52	90	18
Bournbrook	30	6	1	23	41	116	13
Bournville Athletic	30	1	4	25	30	123	6

Stirchley United failed to appear at Cradley Heath on 29th April and the outstanding game was never played.
Darlaston and Willenhall Swifts both moved to the Birmingham League and Stirchley United disbanded. The club was in financial difficulties and after being evicted from their ground for non-payment of rent at the end of March, had to complete their home games at a different ground.
Halesowen joined from the Birmingham League, Atherstone Town joined from the Coventry & North Warwickshire League and Dudley Phoenix joined as a newly formed club.

1911-12

Cradley Heath St. Lukes	30	21	2	7	99	50	44
Atherstone Town	30	16	8	6	72	41	40
Birmingham Trams	30	18	4	8	58	37	40
Willenhall Pickwick	30	18	3	9	66	43	39
Bournbrook	30	19	0	11	85	60	38
Hednesford Town	30	14	7	9	74	42	35
Nuneaton Town	30	15	5	10	77	58	35
Bilston United	30	15	3	12	64	55	33
Redditch	30	14	3	13	63	56	31
Bromsgrove Rovers	30	11	5	14	51	54	27
Coombs Wood Tube Works	30	11	4	15	48	52	26
Bournville Athletic	30	10	4	16	40	62	24
Cannock Town	30	9	5	16	51	81	23
St. Georges Victoria	30	9	1	20	56	105	19
Dudley Phoenix	30	7	4	19	42	89	18
Halesowen	30	2	4	24	38	99	8

St. Georges Victoria left the league and played just cup-ties and friendlies during 1912-13. Stafford Rangers joined from the Birmingham League.

1912-13

Stafford Rangers	30	23	4	3	91	27	50
Hednesford Town	30	23	2	5	81	28	48
Nuneaton Town	30	16	6	8	71	44	38
Redditch	30	15	5	10	77	59	35
Bilston United	30	14	6	10	62	58	34
Cradley Heath St. Lukes	30	13	5	12	64	57	31
Atherstone Town	30	13	5	12	73	69	31
Cannock Town	30	13	5	12	62	70	31
Willenhall Pickwick	30	9	11	10	71	60	29
Bournville Athletic	30	11	4	15	52	65	26
Birmingham Trams	30	10	5	15	58	63	25
Dudley Phoenix	30	9	6	15	66	75	24
Bournbrook	30	10	4	16	53	76	24
Coombs Wood Tube Works	30	8	5	17	41	73	21
Bromsgrove Rovers	30	7	6	17	41	66	20
Halesowen	30	6	1	23	32	105	13

Dudley Phoenix disbanded while Coombs Wood Tube Works resigned following a major industrial dispute at the works. They joined the Birmingham Suburban League in 1913-14. Bloxwich Strollers joined from the Walsall & District League and Tamworth Castle who had been playing just cup-ties and friendlies in 1912-13, also joined.

1913-14

Redditch	30	22	2	6	105	46	46
Stafford Rangers	30	19	6	5	85	48	44
Hednesford Town	30	17	8	5	64	30	42
Bournbrook	30	15	6	9	57	39	36
Nuneaton Town	30	15	6	9	61	43	36
Willenhall Pickwick	30	15	6	9	61	52	36
Bilston United	30	15	5	10	63	42	35
Bloxwich Strollers	30	15	1	14	65	73	31
Tamworth Castle	30	11	8	11	60	61	30
Birmingham Trams	30	10	7	13	51	49	27
Cradley Heath St. Lukes	30	12	3	15	62	65	27
Bournville Athletic	30	9	8	13	46	56	26
Atherstone Town	30	11	4	15	56	70	26
Bromsgrove Rovers	30	11	3	16	43	61	25
Halesowen	30	2	4	24	29	107	8
Cannock Town	30	1	3	26	44	110	5

Hinckley United from the Leicestershire Senior League were elected in place of Halesowen who joined the Birmingham Suburban League.

1914-15

Nuneaton Town	30	20	5	5	79	41	45
Redditch	30	18	6	6	80	39	42
Cradley Heath St. Lukes	30	16	5	9	73	45	37
Hinckley United	30	14	8	8	74	57	36
Stafford Rangers	30	14	7	9	75	53	35
Bloxwich Strollers	30	14	7	9	69	49	35
Hednesford Town	30	14	6	10	65	42	34
Birmingham Trams	30	13	8	9	63	44	34
Willenhall Pickwick	30	13	5	12	57	55	31
Bilston United	30	14	2	14	55	51	30
Atherstone Town	30	11	5	14	51	69	27
Bournville Athletic	30	8	9	13	57	69	25
Tamworth Castle	30	9	3	18	50	81	21
Cannock Town	30	10	1	19	34	80	21
Bournbrook	30	7	5	18	36	72	19
Bromsgrove Rovers	30	3	2	25	45	116	8

Birmingham Combination 1915-1923

1915-19

War was declared in August 1914 and by July 1915, 60% of players who were registered with the league had volunteered to join the armed forces. It was therefore decided to suspend the competition until it was possible to resume.

Nuneaton Town were elected to the Birmingham League in 1915 but because of the war, were unable to play in it until 1919 when Hednesford Town also moved to it. Bournbrook moved to the Birmingham Suburban League in 1915 but ceased activity at the end of the 1915-16 season and did not re-form after the war. Willenhall Pickwick merged with Willenhall Swifts of the Birmingham League in 1919 and the merged club continued in that competition in 1919-20 as Willenhall. Also in 1919, Redditch changed their name to Redditch Town and four new clubs joined the league:

Halesowen, who had played in the Birmingham Suburban League in 1914-15 after leaving the Birmingham Combination in 1914.
Rugby Town, who had joined the Northamptonshire League in 1914-15 but had to resign in October 1914 because of the war. They had played in the Coventry & North Warwickshire League in 1913-14.
Burton All Saints, who were playing in the Trent Valley League in 1913-14 but that league closed down shortly after the outbreak of war.
Talbot Stead, who had been formed in 1913 and after playing just friendlies in 1913-14, joined the Walsall Junior League in 1914-15.

Dudley Bean Athletic disbanded while Bilston United, Burton All Saints, Cannock Town, Redditch Town, Stafford Rangers and Tamworth Castle all moved to the Birmingham League. Leamington Town joined from the Coventry & North Warwickshire League, Newhall Swifts joined from the Burton & District League, Wolseley Athletic joined from the Birmingham Works F.A. and West Birmingham joined from the Birmingham Suburban League. Round Oak also joined, having been playing cup-ties and friendlies.

The League was reduced to 16 clubs.

1919-20

Cradley Heath St. Lukes	30	21	5	4	105	34	47
Stafford Rangers	30	18	4	8	72	44	40
Tamworth Castle	30	16	5	9	60	44	37
Rugby Town	30	14	8	8	73	45	36
Redditch Town	30	16	4	10	65	57	36
Burton All Saints	30	15	4	11	77	66	34
Bloxwich Strollers	30	13	7	10	63	52	33
Halesowen	30	11	7	12	60	51	29
Bilston United	30	12	4	14	55	60	28
Cannock Town	30	12	4	14	54	61	28
Hinckley United	30	11	5	14	67	84	27
Talbot Stead	30	10	7	13	57	74	27
Bournville Athletic	30	7	9	14	53	67	23
Atherstone Town	30	9	1	20	54	87	19
Birmingham Trams	30	5	8	17	37	79	18
Bromsgrove Rovers	30	6	6	18	36	83	18

Oakengates Town joined as a newly formed club and Harper, Sons & Bean joined from the Birmingham Works F.A., changing their name to Dudley Bean Athletic.

The League was increased to 18 clubs.

1920-21

Cannock Town	34	21	4	9	72	48	46
Talbot Stead	34	21	3	10	65	46	45
Rugby Town	34	18	7	9	77	41	43
Bilston United	34	19	5	10	87	55	43
Redditch Town	34	18	6	10	75	44	42
Cradley Heath St. Lukes	34	16	7	11	85	44	39
Oakengates Town	34	15	8	11	76	74	38
Burton All Saints	34	14	10	10	62	62	38
Atherstone Town	34	16	5	13	70	58	37
Stafford Rangers	34	13	10	11	69	56	36
Bloxwich Strollers	34	11	11	12	56	63	33
Tamworth Castle	34	10	12	12	56	70	32
Bromsgrove Rovers	34	12	7	15	63	84	31
Halesowen	34	12	5	17	71	76	29
Hinckley United	34	10	5	19	67	86	25
Dudley Bean Athletic	34	9	5	20	64	99	23
Birmingham Trams	34	7	7	20	53	82	21
Bournville Athletic	34	4	3	27	31	111	11

1921-22

Cradley Heath St. Lukes	30	20	7	3	90	36	47
Rugby Town	30	18	7	5	76	36	43
Oakengates Town	30	16	4	10	69	49	36
Leamington Town	30	14	8	8	58	42	36
Hinckley United	30	15	6	9	83	63	36
Bromsgrove Rovers	30	13	8	9	56	36	34
Halesowen	30	15	4	11	82	59	34
Newhall Swifts	30	15	4	11	76	61	34
Birmingham Trams	30	12	3	15	67	71	27
West Birmingham	30	9	6	15	59	74	24
Atherstone Town	30	8	8	14	50	77	24
Bournville Athletic	30	7	9	14	49	68	23
Bloxwich Strollers	30	8	6	16	42	67	22
Talbot Stead	30	9	4	17	40	89	22
Wolseley Athletic	30	7	5	18	53	90	19
Round Oak	30	7	5	18	42	74	19

Cradley Heath St. Lukes moved to the Birmingham League and Talbot Stead moved to the Walsall Senior League. Foleshill Great Heath joined as a newly re-formed club and Wellington St. Georges joined from the Walsall Senior League. This Wellington St. Georges were the third club from the Shropshire village of St. Georges to play in Birmingham-based leagues and had been formed after the end of the Great War. As with the earlier two St. Georges clubs, the "Wellington" prefix was only ever used outside the locality.

1922-23

Oakengates Town	28	15	7	6	85	42	37
Bloxwich Strollers	28	16	5	7	61	48	37
Hinckley United	28	16	4	8	76	56	36
Halesowen	28	15	6	7	73	54	36
Birmingham Trams	28	15	4	9	66	55	34
Wellington St. Georges	28	14	3	11	66	45	31
Bromsgrove Rovers	28	11	7	10	55	52	29
Round Oak	28	10	8	10	63	58	28
Foleshill Great Heath	28	11	5	12	55	49	27
Rugby Town	28	11	5	12	56	53	27
Wolseley Athletic	28	10	4	14	35	68	24
Leamington Town	28	7	7	14	52	67	21
Bournville Athletic	28	5	10	13	41	68	20
Atherstone Town	28	6	5	17	55	68	17
Newhall Swifts	28	7	2	19	34	90	16

West Birmingham resigned at the end of December, 1922 and their record at the time was deleted: 16, 2, 3, 11, 25, 47, 7
They moved immediately to the Birmingham Alliance where they took over the fixtures of Nechells, who had resigned from the Alliance.
Oakengates Town moved to the Birmingham League while Newhall Swifts also resigned and it is believed that they returned to the Burton & District League. Lichfield City United, Sunbeam Motors, Walsall Reserves and Walsall Wood all joined from the Walsall Senior League while Tamworth Castle joined from the Birmingham League.

The League was increased to 18 clubs.

1923-24

Hinckley United	34	27	1	6	130	62	55
Walsall Reserves	34	21	8	5	94	32	50
Wellington St. Georges	34	19	5	10	91	44	43
Sunbeam Motors	34	17	7	10	82	61	41
Halesowen	34	16	7	11	75	49	39
Wolseley Athletic	34	14	11	9	78	64	39
Bloxwich Strollers	34	17	2	15	74	65	36
Foleshill Great Heath	34	14	7	13	68	72	35
Round Oak	34	15	4	15	66	66	34
Bromsgrove Rovers	34	13	7	14	60	62	33
Birmingham Trams	34	14	5	15	66	79	33
Walsall Wood	34	15	2	17	69	74	32
Lichfield City United	34	13	5	16	41	58	31
Rugby Town	34	11	6	17	54	73	28
Tamworth Castle	34	10	8	16	62	91	28
Leamington Town	34	10	3	21	51	95	23
Bournville Athletic	34	9	2	23	47	91	20
Atherstone Town	34	4	4	26	48	118	12

Wellington St. Georges moved to the Birmingham League and Round Oak moved to the Cradley Heath League. Wednesbury Old Athletic joined from the Birmingham League and Hereford United joined as a newly formed club.

1924-25

Bloxwich Strollers	34	26	4	4	96	40	56
Walsall Reserves	34	20	8	6	93	27	48
Hinckley United	34	21	4	9	101	56	46
Halesowen	34	20	4	10	86	53	44
Leamington Town	34	17	10	7	71	44	44
Sunbeam Motors	34	16	8	10	83	68	40
Bromsgrove Rovers	34	17	5	12	74	58	39
Birmingham Trams	34	14	8	12	61	51	36
Rugby Town	34	16	3	15	88	73	35
Bournville Athletic	34	13	7	14	74	75	33
Hereford United	34	12	8	14	71	70	32
Walsall Wood	34	13	6	15	64	74	32
Atherstone Town	34	11	7	16	68	90	29
Lichfield City United	34	13	1	20	45	86	27
Tamworth Castle	34	5	12	17	56	95	22
Foleshill Great Heath	34	7	6	21	53	95	20
Wolseley Athletic	34	7	1	26	50	105	15
† Nuneaton Town Reserves	34	4	6	24	40	114	14

† Wednesbury Old Athletic resigned and disbanded in mid-December 1924 but Nuneaton Town Reserves (of the Northamptonshire League) took over Wednesbury's record and completed their fixtures. At the time of resignation, this record was: 12 0 1 11 9 44 1
Nuneaton Town Reserves also completed their own fixtures in the Northamptonshire League before resigning from the competition at the end of the season.
Wolseley Athletic moved to the Midland Amateur League and also joined the Birmingham Works F.A.. Lichfield City United disbanded. Gresley Rovers joined from the Central Alliance and Dudley Bean joined from the Stafford & District League.

1925-26

Leamington Town	34	24	4	6	114	48	52
Rugby Town	34	23	4	7	97	47	50
Hinckley United	34	22	6	6	122	62	50
Hereford United	34	20	4	10	96	65	44
Dudley Bean	34	17	8	9	87	61	42
Halesowen	34	18	4	12	82	70	40
Gresley Rovers	34	17	3	14	79	76	37
Bournville Athletic	34	16	4	14	91	82	36
Walsall Reserves	34	13	8	13	71	63	34
Tamworth Castle	34	12	9	13	85	102	33
Nuneaton Town Reserves	34	14	4	16	80	81	32
Bloxwich Strollers	34	13	4	17	83	106	30
Birmingham Trams	34	11	7	16	85	94	29
Atherstone Town	34	11	4	19	70	82	26
Walsall Wood	34	11	1	22	52	102	23
Bromsgrove Rovers	34	9	4	21	60	77	22
Sunbeam Motors	34	6	5	23	59	125	17
Foleshill Great Heath	34	3	9	22	66	136	15

Nuneaton Town joined from the Southern League, replacing their reserves who moved to the Nuneaton Combination. Walsall Wood resigned with financial difficulties but decided to suspend activity rather than disband. Evesham Town joined from the Midland Amateur League.

1926-27

Hinckley United	34	25	3	6	136	49	53
Walsall Reserves	34	25	2	7	100	48	52
Leamington Town	34	22	4	8	99	53	48
Tamworth Castle	34	20	5	9	84	78	45
Bloxwich Strollers	34	21	2	11	108	77	44
Hereford United	34	20	2	12	113	64	42
Nuneaton Town	34	19	2	13	93	69	40
Sunbeam Motors	34	15	2	17	85	101	32
Evesham Town	34	13	4	17	84	89	30
Bournville Athletic	34	12	5	17	85	91	29
Rugby Town	34	12	5	17	70	86	29
Gresley Rovers	34	14	0	20	93	118	28
Atherstone Town	34	12	3	19	72	84	27
Bromsgrove Rovers	34	10	6	18	57	91	26
Birmingham Trams	34	8	7	19	71	104	23
Foleshill Great Heath	34	9	4	21	53	118	22
Dudley Bean	34	7	7	20	55	85	21
Halesowen	34	9	3	22	56	109	21

Foleshill Great Heath and Dudley Bean both disbanded.
Market Harborough Town joined from the Northamptonshire League and Walsall LMS joined from the Midland Amateur League.

1927-28

Walsall Reserves	34	22	3	9	97	63	47
Bloxwich Strollers	34	20	3	11	81	64	43
Hereford United	34	19	4	11	104	62	42
Halesowen	34	20	2	12	89	76	42
Market Harborough Town	34	18	5	11	93	67	41
Leamington Town	34	19	3	12	83	69	41
Evesham Town	34	16	8	10	66	55	40
Gresley Rovers	34	16	4	14	79	71	36
Hinckley United	34	15	5	14	84	75	35
Sunbeam Motors	34	16	1	17	106	99	33
Birmingham Trams	34	14	5	15	79	81	33
Bromsgrove Rovers	34	13	6	15	83	80	32
Atherstone Town	34	13	4	17	72	76	30
Walsall LMS	34	13	4	17	80	94	30
Nuneaton Town	34	11	4	19	75	90	26
Rugby Town	34	11	0	23	73	131	22
Bournville Athletic	34	6	8	20	69	106	20
Tamworth Castle	34	6	7	21	81	135	19

Birmingham Combination 1928-1933

Hereford United and Walsall Reserves both moved to the Birmingham League and Tamworth Castle disbanded. Cannock Town and Darlaston joined both from the Birmingham League and Birmingham "A" also joined. Birmingham "A" were the 3rd team of Birmingham F.C. (now Birmingham City) who, as Birmingham Colts, had played occasional friendlies and cup-ties in 1927-28.

1928-29

Nuneaton Town	34	24	4	6	100	46	52
Leamington Town	34	23	4	7	111	54	50
Market Harborough Town	34	20	3	11	97	66	43
Evesham Town	34	17	7	10	79	53	41
Darlaston	34	17	7	10	107	77	41
Gresley Rovers	34	16	8	10	81	60	40
Birmingham "A"	34	14	9	11	93	76	37
Rugby Town	34	15	7	12	78	72	37
Hinckley United	34	17	3	14	96	91	37
Bromsgrove Rovers	34	16	4	14	96	91	36
Bloxwich Strollers	34	14	6	14	82	75	34
Bournville Athletic	34	13	4	17	63	84	30
Halesowen	34	11	5	18	69	102	27
Birmingham Trams	34	7	11	16	64	88	25
Sunbeam Motors	34	9	6	19	60	97	24
Cannock Town	34	8	6	20	57	97	22
Walsall LMS	34	8	5	21	43	89	21
Atherstone Town	34	6	3	25	64	122	15

Sunbeam Motors resigned when the parent company insisted that in future, only company employees could play for the club.
Redditch Town joined from the Birmingham League.

1929-30

Market Harborough Town	34	24	6	4	128	53	54
Birmingham "A"	34	24	5	5	112	45	53
Evesham Town	34	21	3	10	101	61	45
Darlaston	34	19	6	9	93	66	44
Redditch Town	34	18	7	9	99	69	43
Nuneaton Town	34	17	7	10	103	61	41
Rugby Town	34	17	4	13	92	82	38
Bloxwich Strollers	34	15	6	13	78	76	36
Leamington Town	34	15	5	14	83	69	35
Gresley Rovers	34	13	5	16	62	66	31
Atherstone Town	34	11	5	18	64	94	27
Walsall LMS	34	9	7	18	60	90	25
Bromsgrove Rovers	34	11	3	20	60	93	25
Hinckley United	34	11	3	20	78	128	25
Bournville Athletic	34	9	7	18	59	101	25
Birmingham Trams	34	9	6	19	62	87	24
Halesowen	34	10	4	20	67	95	24
Cannock Town	34	6	5	23	54	119	17

There were no changes to the leagues membership.

1930-31

Nuneaton Town	34	24	4	6	126	61	52
Evesham Town	34	22	5	7	101	60	49
Hinckley United	34	20	5	9	124	68	45
Market Harborough Town	34	18	6	10	108	66	42
Redditch Town	34	18	5	11	100	58	41
Birmingham "A"	34	16	8	10	95	66	40
Darlaston	34	15	9	10	112	70	39
Gresley Rovers	34	17	4	13	86	81	38
Walsall LMS	34	15	8	11	89	86	38
Atherstone Town	34	16	4	14	127	105	36
Cannock Town	34	15	6	13	92	80	36
Leamington Town	34	14	5	15	90	97	33
Birmingham Trams	34	10	7	17	73	96	27
Bromsgrove Rovers	34	12	3	19	73	104	27
Bournville Athletic	34	10	5	19	71	109	25
Halesowen	34	10	5	19	80	134	25
Rugby Town	34	5	1	28	64	169	11
Bloxwich Strollers	34	2	4	28	59	160	8

There were no changes to the membership of the league.

1931-32

Birmingham "A"	34	27	3	4	120	41	57
Nuneaton Town	34	26	3	5	137	56	55
Redditch Town	34	23	2	9	147	65	48
Darlaston	34	19	3	12	105	74	41
Market Harborough Town	34	18	2	14	96	90	38
Atherstone Town	34	15	6	13	120	79	36
Birmingham Trams	34	17	2	15	73	105	36
Hinckley United	34	15	3	16	81	82	33
Halesowen Town	34	14	5	15	79	102	33
Bromsgrove Rovers	34	14	2	18	87	106	30
Bloxwich Strollers	34	14	2	18	78	114	30
Cannock Town	34	11	6	17	80	94	28
Walsall LMS	34	13	2	19	71	92	28
Evesham Town	34	10	6	18	73	90	26
Leamington Town	34	10	4	20	81	112	24
Gresley Rovers	34	8	8	18	69	101	24
Bournville Athletic	34	9	5	20	59	101	23
Rugby Town	34	8	6	20	51	103	22

It was decided to increase membership to 20 clubs. Walsall LMS moved to the Walsall & District League while Wolverhampton Wanderers "A" joined from the Staffordshire County League, Cheltenham Town joined from the Gloucestershire Northern Senior League and Dudley Town joined from the Worcestershire Combination. Bloxwich Strollers resigned and disbanded on 5th August and so the league operated with 19 clubs. Bloxwich quickly re-formed as an amateur club and joined the Walsall & District League.

1932-33

Redditch Town	36	28	1	7	124	61	57
Birmingham "A"	36	26	4	6	132	46	56
Cheltenham Town	36	20	7	9	93	61	47
Nuneaton Town	36	18	9	9	107	68	45
Wolverhampton Wanderers "A"	36	17	9	10	103	53	43
Atherstone Town	36	18	7	11	106	74	43
Cannock Town	36	19	4	13	99	79	42
Market Harborough Town	36	16	3	17	95	87	35
Dudley Town	36	16	3	17	86	91	35
Halesowen Town	36	15	5	16	96	103	35
Rugby Town	36	14	6	16	64	89	34
Evesham Town	36	16	1	19	76	92	33
Hinckley United	36	14	3	19	98	110	31
Gresley Rovers	36	13	3	20	71	91	29
Bournville Athletic	36	12	5	19	72	115	29
Leamington Town	36	12	3	21	72	122	27
Darlaston	36	6	11	19	80	122	23
Birmingham Trams	36	9	3	24	64	115	21
Bromsgrove Rovers	36	7	5	24	74	133	19

Cannock Town and Nuneaton Town both moved to the Birmingham League, Gresley Rovers moved to the Central Combination and Market Harborough Town moved to the United Counties League. Walsall Reserves joined from the Birmingham League, Tamworth joined as a newly formed club and West Bromwich Albion "A" joined from the Midland Midweek League.

The League was reduced to 18 clubs.

1933-34

Dudley Town	34	23	6	5	93	35	52
Hinckley United	34	23	2	9	102	61	48
Wolverhampton Wanderers "A"	34	22	3	9	131	54	47
Bromsgrove Rovers	34	20	3	11	93	72	43
Cheltenham Town	34	17	8	9	81	53	42
Walsall Reserves	34	18	5	11	84	56	41
West Bromwich Albion "A"	34	19	2	13	109	73	40
Birmingham "A"	34	18	3	13	111	95	39
Darlaston	34	15	6	13	96	84	36
Redditch Town	34	15	4	15	82	91	34
Atherstone Town	34	15	4	15	73	87	34
Leamington Town	34	14	4	16	87	84	32
Bournville Athletic	34	10	5	19	74	113	25
Rugby Town	34	9	5	20	52	95	23
Halesowen Town	34	9	4	21	73	136	22
Tamworth	34	8	4	22	77	112	20
Birmingham Trams	34	8	2	24	72	130	18
Evesham Town	34	6	4	24	66	125	16

Birmingham "A" left the league but continued playing in the expanded Midland Midweek League and also played various friendlies.
Market Harborough Town joined from the Northamptonshire League.

1934-35

Wolverhampton Wanderers "A"	32	27	1	4	127	39	55
Dudley Town	32	20	4	8	69	41	44
West Bromwich Albion "A"	32	18	6	8	83	57	42
Walsall Reserves	32	17	5	10	94	58	39
Leamington Town	32	17	5	10	73	58	39
Tamworth	32	16	5	11	88	58	37
Bromsgrove Rovers	32	14	7	11	81	72	35
Birmingham Trams	32	13	8	11	57	49	34
Darlaston	32	13	6	13	78	67	32
Cheltenham Town	32	14	4	14	70	61	32
Atherstone Town	32	12	3	17	69	93	27
Hinckley United	32	10	4	18	66	83	24
Market Harborough Town	32	9	5	18	56	91	23
Bournville Athletic	32	8	6	18	58	95	22
Halesowen Town	32	9	2	21	53	98	20
Redditch Town	32	9	2	21	53	107	20
Evesham Town	32	8	3	21	58	106	19

Rugby Town resigned in mid-December and their record was deleted when it stood as follows: 12 0 2 10 13 56 2
The league accepted Banbury Spencers application to complete Rugby Town's fixtures but this was blocked by the Oxfordshire F.A. who insisted that their first team continued to play in the Oxfordshire Senior League rather than their reserves which is what Banbury had proposed.
Dudley Town moved to the Birmingham League and Cheltenham Town moved to the Southern League. Gloucester City and Cheltenham Town Reserves both joined from the Gloucestershire Northern Senior League, Banbury Spencer joined from the Oxfordshire Senior League, Shirley Town joined from the Birmingham Suburban League and Aston Villa "A" also joined. Aston Villa Colts had been playing in the Midland Midweek League, in which they continued, and also friendlies.

The League was increased to 20 clubs.

1935-36

Aston Villa "A"	36	25	3	8	126	54	53
West Bromwich Albion "A"	36	25	3	8	119	71	53
Wolverhampton Wanderers "A"	36	23	4	9	99	58	50
Gloucester City	36	21	6	9	99	62	48
Tamworth	36	22	2	12	118	65	46
Walsall Reserves	36	21	3	12	98	57	45
Cheltenham Town Reserves	36	19	6	11	79	61	44
Darlaston	36	16	8	12	86	70	40
Banbury Spencer	36	16	5	15	88	90	37
Birmingham Trams	36	13	9	14	66	64	35
Shirley Town	36	14	4	18	86	94	32
Halesowen Town	36	14	3	19	88	115	31
Evesham Town	36	13	5	18	73	107	31
Leamington Town	36	12	6	18	65	84	30
Atherstone Town	36	10	7	19	82	93	27
Bromsgrove Rovers	36	9	7	20	65	100	25
Redditch Town	36	8	8	20	66	108	24
Hinckley United	36	9	5	22	60	133	23
Bournville Athletic	36	2	6	28	50	127	10

Market Harborough Town resigned and disbanded on 9th December but the team still fulfilled their away fixture on 14th December after which their record was deleted: 11 0 1 10 10 47 1
Birmingham "A" rejoined after 2 years of friendlies and the Midland Midweek League.

1936-37

Walsall Reserves	38	29	2	7	144	50	60
West Bromwich Albion "A"	38	27	5	6	110	43	59
Banbury Spencer	38	22	5	11	96	88	49
Wolverhampton Wanderers "A"	38	20	7	11	105	58	47
Tamworth	38	21	5	12	124	85	47
Cheltenham Town Reserves	38	18	10	10	99	63	46
Aston Villa "A"	38	20	6	12	85	55	46
Birmingham Trams	38	19	6	13	100	83	44
Darlaston	38	19	5	14	102	59	43
Shirley Town	38	17	6	15	99	83	40
Redditch Town	38	15	6	17	87	96	36
Gloucester City	38	13	6	19	69	81	32
Halesowen Town	38	13	5	20	69	88	31
Evesham Town	38	12	7	19	76	113	31
Atherstone Town	38	12	5	21	85	127	29
Birmingham "A"	38	11	5	22	63	83	27
Bromsgrove Rovers	38	10	6	22	61	135	26
Hinckley United	38	10	4	24	73	146	24
Leamington Town	38	9	5	24	44	88	23
Bournville Athletic	38	8	4	26	63	130	20

Coventry City bought out Leamington Town who ceased to exist as a separate entity. Coventry took over Leamington's Windmill Ground and their "A" side played there, replacing Leamington in the Birmingham Combination. Leamington had been acting as a nursery club for Coventry since 1932.

Birmingham Combination 1937-1941

1937-38

Darlaston	38	31	2	5	135	34	64
Aston Villa "A"	38	29	3	6	145	47	61
West Bromwich Albion "A"	38	19	13	6	96	51	51
Tamworth	38	20	8	10	119	71	48
Birmingham "A"	38	21	5	12	86	68	47
Coventry City "A"	38	19	6	13	98	57	44
Banbury Spencer	38	19	6	13	105	68	44
Walsall Reserves	38	18	8	12	107	71	44
Evesham Town	38	18	5	15	75	89	41
Shirley Town	38	17	6	15	81	82	40
Birmingham Trams	38	17	6	15	63	79	40
Wolverhampton Wanderers "A"	38	16	7	15	101	66	39
Gloucester City	38	15	8	15	96	85	38
Atherstone Town	38	13	10	15	77	104	36
Cheltenham Town Reserves	38	11	11	16	67	97	33
Redditch Town	38	12	3	23	81	111	27
Halesowen Town	38	6	5	27	63	137	17
Bromsgrove Rovers	38	5	7	26	49	135	17
Hinckley United	38	6	3	29	49	144	15
Bournville Athletic	38	4	6	28	43	140	14

Birmingham Trams changed their name to Birmingham City Transport and Shirley Town changed their name to Solihull Town.

1938-39

Aston Villa "A"	38	26	8	4	130	38	60
Walsall Reserves	38	27	5	6	129	54	59
Birmingham "A"	38	24	4	10	124	48	52
Darlaston	38	26	0	12	120	52	52
Tamworth	38	22	7	9	112	64	51
West Bromwich Albion "A"	38	22	5	11	101	52	49
Wolverhampton Wanderers "A"	38	22	4	12	101	63	48
Gloucester City	38	16	12	10	73	61	44
Coventry City "A"	38	20	3	15	112	86	43
Birmingham City Transport	38	19	5	14	91	86	43
Redditch Town	38	14	9	15	74	74	37
Cheltenham Town Reserves	38	17	1	20	91	110	35
Solihull Town	38	14	4	20	68	83	32
Banbury Spencer	38	11	8	19	68	87	30
Hinckley United	38	9	10	19	77	116	28
Halesowen Town	38	8	7	23	77	137	23
† Nuneaton Borough	38	9	4	25	66	127	22
Atherstone Town	38	9	2	27	74	170	20
Bromsgrove Rovers	38	6	6	26	62	128	18
Bournville Athletic	38	4	6	28	51	165	14

† Evesham Town resigned on 25th October, 1938. Nuneaton Borough from the Central Amateur League took over their record and completed their fixtures. The record was as follows: 8 1 0 7 11 42 2
Evesham Town Reserves (funded by the supporters association) continued playing in the Redditch League until March when they, too, resigned and the club was disbanded. Nuneaton's record in the Central Amateur League was deleted.
Bournville Athletic moved to the Central Amateur League and Stourbridge joined from the Birmingham League.

1939-40

Stourbridge	3	3	0	0	10	2	6
Tamworth	2	2	0	0	4	2	4
West Bromwich Albion "A"	2	2	0	0	5	3	4
Bromsgrove Rovers	3	1	1	1	15	5	3
Nuneaton Borough	2	1	1	0	5	3	3
Cheltenham Town Reserves	1	1	0	0	3	0	2
Hinckley United	2	1	0	1	5	3	2
Wolverhampton Wanderers "A"	2	1	0	1	4	3	2
Solihull Town	2	1	0	1	4	4	2
Walsall Reserves	2	1	0	1	2	2	2
Aston Villa "A"	3	1	0	2	3	4	2
Banbury Spencer	2	1	0	1	3	4	2
Redditch Town	2	1	0	1	3	5	2
Birmingham City Transport	2	1	0	1	3	8	2
Coventry City "A"	2	0	1	1	5	6	1
Darlaston	2	0	1	1	3	4	1
Atherstone Town	1	0	0	1	2	3	0
Birmingham "A"	2	0	0	2	2	6	0
Gloucester City	2	0	0	2	1	4	0
Halesowen Town	1	0	0	1	0	11	0

The table shown above is as it was on 3rd September 1939 when war was declared and the competition was immediately abandoned.
Following a relaxation of government restrictions, it was decided to organise an emergency competition that consisted of 10 clubs who had indicated that they would be able to compete. This emergency competition commenced on 4th November and the 10 clubs who initially indicated that they would be able to take part were Birmingham City Transport, Bromsgrove Rovers, Coventry City "A", Darlaston, Nuneaton Borough, Redditch Town, Solihull Town, Stourbridge, Tamworth and Wolverhampton Wanderers "A". However, before the competition began, Coventry City "A" withdrew and were replaced by Sutton Town who had been playing in the Walsall Senior League before the war.

Emergency Competition 1939-40

Solihull Town "A"	16	13	2	1	89	28	28
Stourbridge	18	13	2	3	73	37	28
Darlaston	18	10	5	3	65	31	25
Bromsgrove Rovers	18	10	2	6	57	42	22
Nuneaton Borough	18	6	7	5	47	42	19
Tamworth	18	8	3	7	54	60	19
Sutton Town	18	5	2	11	26	55	12
Redditch Town	16	4	1	11	36	53	9
† Solihull Town "B"	16	4	1	11	34	56	9
Wolverhampton Wanderers "A"	16	0	1	15	19	96	1

The outstanding 4 games were not played.
† Birmingham City Transport found it impossible to continue and resigned on 7th December. Solihull Town were able to field two sides and so Solihull Town "B" took over City Transports record and completed their fixtures while the existing Solihull Town side became known as Solihull Town "A". BCT's record was as follows: 5 1 0 4 8 26 2

1940-41

Six clubs – Aston Villa, Birmingham, Darlaston, Nuneaton Borough, Solihull Town and West Bromwich Albion indicated that they would be able to field teams in the 1940-41 season but this was insufficient to form a league. Aston Villa, Birmingham and West Bromwich Albion therefore joined the emergency Birmingham League competition but the other 3 clubs found themselves unable to take part. The Birmingham Combination then closed down until the war ended in 1945.

1945

Re-forming the Birmingham Combination

Plans to revive the league began in the spring of 1945 and by the end of May, 18 clubs had signified their willingness to take part. Of these, 11 were amongst the 20 members of the league in the brief pre-war part of the 1939-40 season – Atherstone Town, Banbury Spencer, Birmingham City Transport, Bromsgrove Rovers, Darlaston, Hinckley United, Nuneaton Borough, Stourbridge, Tamworth, Walsall Reserves and Wolverhampton Wanderers "A". Of the other 9 pre-war members, Coventry City decided to replace their "A" team with their reserves as the London Combination, in which their reserves had been playing before the war, was not ready to resume operations while Birmingham (who changed their name to Birmingham City) also replaced their "A" team with their reserves as they had decided not to rejoin the Central League. Aston Villa and West Bromwich Albion did rejoin the Central League but were not ready to field 3 sides and so their "A" teams resigned from the Birmingham Combination.

There were 5 more pre-war members of the Combination who did not rejoin the league for the 1945-46 season: Halesowen, Redditch Town and Solihull Town had all disbanded during the war and had not yet been re-formed while Gloucester City were not yet ready to resume activity. Cheltenham Town were able to resume in the Southern League but were not yet ready to field a reserve side capable of competing in the Birmingham Combination. They did, however, enter a side to be made up of amateurs in the Cheltenham League.

As well as 13 pre-war members, there were 5 new members. Four of these – Dudley Town, Hednesford, Kidderminster Harriers and Stafford Rangers – had been playing in the Birmingham League in 1938-39. Dudley Town had disbanded during that season but had since re-formed. The fifth new member was Moor Green, who had been playing in the Central Amateur League before the war.

However, the constitution was not yet settled. Hinckley United withdrew not long before the start of the season as their ground was not yet ready for use and Worcester City Reserves, another pre-war member of the Birmingham League, replaced them. Finally in this transitional season in which so much rebuilding needed to be done, Stafford Rangers withdrew just a week before the start of the season as they were unable to raise a team but their withdrawal came so late that there was no time to find a replacement and so the league went ahead in 1945-46 with 17 clubs.

1945-46

Darlaston	32	22	4	6	117	62	48
Nuneaton Borough	32	19	4	9	113	58	42
Bromsgrove Rovers	32	19	4	9	103	91	42
Atherstone Town	32	18	4	10	91	64	40
Dudley Town	32	17	6	9	92	65	40
Kidderminster Harriers	32	15	6	11	75	57	36
Birmingham City Reserves	32	16	4	12	83	65	36
Stourbridge	32	17	2	13	90	78	36
Coventry City Reserves	32	12	5	15	73	80	29
Moor Green	32	13	3	16	85	94	29
Walsall Reserves	32	11	6	15	63	82	28
Wolverhampton Wanderers "A"	32	11	5	16	83	93	27
Banbury Spencer	32	10	7	15	56	79	27
Worcester City Reserves	32	12	1	19	76	102	25
Hednesford	32	9	6	17	65	89	24
Tamworth	32	9	5	18	76	108	23
Birmingham City Transport	32	4	4	24	43	117	12

Redditch Town and Stafford Rangers were both now able to resume activity and were elected back to the league. West Bromwich Albion were able to re-form their "A" side and they too were elected back to the league. The league would thus have been extended to 20 clubs but Birmingham City Reserves resigned just before the start of the new season, reducing it to 19. Birmingham had committed to playing in both the Football Combination and the Central League and would be unable to run a fourth side in the Combination.

1946-47

Bromsgrove Rovers	36	23	4	9	105	57	50
Walsall Reserves	36	22	3	11	95	71	47
Darlaston	36	21	3	12	116	70	45
Nuneaton Borough	36	19	4	13	84	64	42
Atherstone Town	36	18	6	12	85	73	42
Tamworth	36	18	5	13	88	68	41
Stafford Rangers	36	18	5	13	81	70	41
Dudley Town	36	18	5	13	76	71	41
Stourbridge	36	16	7	13	72	75	39
Banbury Spencer	36	15	6	15	86	65	36
Kidderminster Harriers	36	16	4	16	104	84	36
Wolverhampton Wanderers "A"	36	16	4	16	72	67	36
Redditch Town	36	17	2	17	83	96	36
West Bromwich Albion "A"	36	14	5	17	83	90	33
Moor Green	36	13	5	18	71	108	31
Hednesford	36	12	4	20	85	103	28
Worcester City Reserves	36	10	4	22	68	99	24
Birmingham City Transport	36	5	8	23	51	107	18
Coventry City "A"	36	6	6	24	56	123	18

Kidderminster Harriers and Worcester City Reserves both moved to the Birmingham League. Bedworth Town joined as a newly formed club and Hinckley United rejoined having re-formed as Hinckley Athletic. Birmingham City had resigned from the Central League and so re-entered their "A" team.

The League was increased to 20 clubs.

1947-48

Atherstone Town	38	30	1	7	108	41	61
Banbury Spencer	38	29	3	6	106	42	61
Bedworth Town	38	24	6	8	102	65	54
Tamworth	38	24	5	9	96	63	53
Bromsgrove Rovers	38	21	8	9	101	67	50
Nuneaton Borough	38	18	8	12	94	67	44
Darlaston	38	19	6	13	92	73	44
Dudley Town	38	17	8	13	69	56	42
West Bromwich Albion "A"	38	18	5	15	86	86	41
Stourbridge	38	16	8	14	85	65	40
Walsall Reserves	38	15	9	14	76	74	39
Wolverhampton Wanderers "A"	38	12	12	14	68	75	36
Stafford Rangers	38	14	6	18	69	88	34
Hednesford	38	14	4	20	86	98	32
Birmingham City "A"	38	8	11	19	57	79	27
Redditch Town	38	11	4	23	64	90	26
Birmingham City Transport	38	7	9	22	59	108	23
Moor Green	38	6	8	24	55	112	20
Hinckley Athletic	38	7	5	26	61	112	19
Coventry City "A"	38	3	8	27	50	123	14

Coventry City "A" moved to the Walsall Senior League, swapping places with Bilston who joined from that league.

Birmingham Combination 1948-1953

1948-49

Bedworth Town	38	30	5	3	129	38	65
Nuneaton Borough	38	23	9	6	93	45	55
Stourbridge	38	22	9	7	104	55	53
Bromsgrove Rovers	38	23	6	9	109	57	52
Hednesford	38	21	9	8	99	64	51
Tamworth	38	19	10	9	97	58	48
Walsall Reserves	38	20	7	11	87	65	47
Wolverhampton Wanderers "A"	38	15	11	12	73	71	41
Banbury Spencer	38	15	10	13	75	68	40
West Bromwich Albion "A"	38	15	9	14	97	87	39
Redditch Town	38	14	10	14	66	85	38
Stafford Rangers	38	14	7	17	66	74	35
Bilston	38	13	7	18	62	85	33
Darlaston	38	11	8	19	66	88	30
Dudley Town	38	9	11	18	54	75	29
Hinckley Athletic	38	10	9	19	62	97	29
Atherstone Town	38	10	7	21	82	96	27
Birmingham City "A"	38	7	7	24	56	86	21
Moor Green	38	7	7	24	58	111	21
Birmingham City Transport	38	1	4	33	40	170	6

Birmingham City disbanded its "A" team and Lockheed (Leamington) joined from the Central Amateur League.

1949-50

Bedworth Town	38	28	6	4	111	43	62
Bromsgrove Rovers	38	25	9	4	98	42	59
Nuneaton Borough	38	24	3	9	5	92	40	57
Atherstone Town	38	24	5	9	79	51	53
Walsall Reserves	38	20	5	13	88	60	45
Hinckley Athletic	38	19	7	12	71	49	45
Tamworth	38	16	12	10	80	61	44
Banbury Spencer	38	19	5	14	63	52	43
Stourbridge	38	18	3	17	81	75	39
Dudley Town	38	16	7	15	57	72	39
Moor Green	38	13	7	18	62	73	33
Bilston	38	14	3	21	63	73	31
Hednesford	38	12	7	19	65	84	31
Stafford Rangers	38	10	11	17	53	71	31
Wolverhampton Wanderers "A"	38	11	8	19	61	68	30
Darlaston	38	12	6	20	71	93	30
Redditch Town	38	13	3	22	63	69	29
West Bromwich Albion "A"	38	7	14	17	54	62	28
Lockheed (Leamington)	38	10	4	24	49	96	24
Birmingham City Transport	38	2	3	33	34	161	7

Birmingham City Transport moved to the Birmingham Works League and Wolverhampton Wanderers "A" resigned whilst maintaining their membership of the Birmingham League.
Rugby Town joined from the United Counties League and Sutton Town joined from the Walsall Senior League.

1950-51

Hednesford	38	24	8	6	112	53	56
Nuneaton Borough	38	26	3	9	112	65	55
Redditch Town	38	20	11	7	87	43	51
Stourbridge	38	23	5	10	82	55	51
Walsall Reserves	38	18	9	11	85	55	45
Stafford Rangers	38	21	3	14	82	56	45
Bromsgrove Rovers	38	16	9	13	76	66	41
Bedworth Town	38	18	4	16	59	77	40
Lockheed (Leamington)	38	17	2	19	65	67	36
Tamworth	38	16	3	19	92	98	35
Sutton Town	38	13	9	16	51	78	35
Banbury Spencer	38	13	8	17	64	75	34
Atherstone Town	38	12	9	17	83	81	33
Hinckley Athletic	38	14	5	19	64	74	33
Darlaston	38	14	5	19	67	80	33
Rugby Town	38	12	8	18	57	87	32
Dudley Town	38	11	7	20	59	68	29
Moor Green	38	9	11	18	61	92	29
Bilston	38	12	5	21	60	96	29
West Bromwich Albion "A"	38	6	6	26	39	91	18

There were no changes to the league's membership.

1951-52

Stourbridge	38	28	6	4	99	49	62
Redditch Town	38	24	8	6	112	58	56
Hednesford	38	23	5	10	92	48	51
Nuneaton Borough	38	22	7	9	109	75	51
Bromsgrove Rovers	38	19	4	15	73	62	42
Tamworth	38	18	6	14	92	91	42
Stafford Rangers	38	16	9	13	83	72	41
Walsall Reserves	38	18	4	16	100	89	40
Lockheed (Leamington)	38	16	7	15	80	71	39
Dudley Town	38	15	7	16	67	74	37
Moor Green	38	14	7	17	71	80	35
Hinckley Athletic	38	16	3	19	77	84	35
Darlaston	38	15	4	19	77	84	34
Rugby Town	38	13	7	18	69	73	33
Banbury Spencer	38	13	7	18	76	87	33
West Bromwich Albion "A"	38	12	7	19	64	74	31
Bilston	38	11	9	18	74	111	31
Bedworth Town	38	12	6	20	89	88	30
Atherstone Town	38	11	3	24	64	103	25
Sutton Town	38	4	4	30	40	118	12

Nuneaton Borough moved to the Birmingham League and Stafford Rangers moved to the Cheshire League.

1952-53

Redditch Town	34	21	7	6	84	60	49
Hednesford	34	20	6	8	81	46	46
Stourbridge	34	19	3	12	71	57	41
Rugby Town	34	16	8	10	64	38	40
Bilston	34	16	6	12	75	61	38
Atherstone Town	34	14	9	11	85	75	37
Dudley Town	34	17	2	15	67	71	36
Moor Green	34	16	4	14	64	70	36
Bromsgrove Rovers	34	12	11	11	65	79	35
Hinckley Athletic	34	14	6	14	67	69	34
Walsall Reserves	34	11	11	12	56	57	33
Darlaston	34	14	3	17	53	59	31
Banbury Spencer	34	12	6	16	73	65	30
Tamworth	34	11	8	15	55	64	30
Lockheed (Leamington)	34	10	6	18	56	68	26
Sutton Town	34	9	6	19	44	84	24
West Bromwich Albion "A"	34	10	3	21	54	73	23
Bedworth Town	34	9	5	20	49	67	23

In the published final tables for 1952-53, Bilston were shown with 36 points with exactly the same record (Won 16, Drawn 6, Lost 12). They finished their programme shortly before the end of the season and were then shown with 38 points but this was reduced to 36 in the final table. No reason has been found for such a note saying they had points deducted and so, in the table above, it has been assumed that the 36 was just a mistake and that Bilstons points total should be 38.

Bromsgrove Rovers, Dudley Town, Hednesford, Redditch, Stourbridge and Walsall Reserves all moved to the Birmingham League. Birch Coppice joined from the Tamworth & Trent Valley League and Gresley Rovers joined from the Central Alliance.

1953-54

Rugby Town	26	17	3	6	64	35	37
Bilston	26	14	6	6	67	37	34
Atherstone Town	26	13	7	6	60	42	33
Banbury Spencer	26	14	4	8	49	36	32
Lockheed (Leamington)	26	13	5	8	50	27	31
Hinckley Athletic	26	9	10	7	41	39	28
Tamworth	26	11	5	10	53	48	27
Bedworth Town	26	10	6	10	45	54	26
Gresley Rovers	26	10	4	12	65	58	24
West Bromwich Albion "A"	26	10	4	12	46	50	24
Darlaston	26	9	5	12	42	47	23
Birch Coppice	26	6	9	11	37	57	21
Moor Green	26	5	5	16	32	61	15
Sutton Town	26	3	3	20	32	92	9

All members of the Birmingham Combination moved to the Birmingham League with the exception of West Bromwich Albion "A" who moved to the Warwickshire Combination.

The Birmingham Combination then closed down.

STAFFORDSHIRE COUNTY LEAGUE (SOUTH) 1892-1996

(Also including the Walsall & District Junior League, the Walsall & District League and the Walsall Senior League)

Although its history was by no means continuous, the Staffordshire County League (South) could trace its origins back to 17th May 1892 when representatives of local clubs met at the Peoples Coffee House in Digbeth, Walsall and formed the Walsall & District Junior League.

The league began operations in September that year with 9 founder members – Bloxwich Strollers, Brownhills Albion, Cannock Town, Cotterills (Darlaston), Lichfield Leomansley, Tettenhall Wood, Walsall Rangers, Wolverhampton Presbyterians and Wolverhampton St. Chads.

Note: Most of the published tables were incomplete or contained errors. Additional research, which is ongoing, has enabled many to be corrected but where it has not yet been possible to correct the errors, totals are shown in italics below the relevant columns.

WALSALL & DISTRICT JUNIOR LEAGUE 1892-97

1892-93

Brownhills Albion	12	8	3	1	47	21	19
Bloxwich Strollers	12	8	1	3	35	31	17
Cannock Town	12	6	1	5	35	27	13
Tettenhall Wood	12	5	1	6	29	36	11
Wolverhampton Presbyterians	12	5	1	6	34	23	11
Wolverhampton St. Chads	12	3	1	8	27	44	7
Cotterills (Darlaston)	12	2	2	8	23	48	6

Walsall Rangers and Lichfield Leomansley both resigned during the season and their records were deleted.
Tettenhall Wood and Wolverhampton St Chads both left the league.
Hartshill Unity, Walsall Unity, Wednesbury Old Athletic, Willenhall Pickwick and Wordsley Olympic all joined.
The League was increased to 10 members.

1893-94

Willenhall Pickwick	16	11	1	4	46	25	23
Wolverhampton Presbyterians	16	10	1	5	39	28	21
Cotterills (Darlaston)	16	9	2	5	34	23	20
Bloxwich Strollers	16	6	3	7	33	24	15
Walsall Unity	16	6	3	7	37	34	15
Brownhills Albion	16	8	2	6	29	30	14
Cannock Town	16	5	4	7	32	39	14
Hartshill Unity	16	5	2	9	25	36	10
Wordsley Olympic	16	2	2	12	28	64	6

Hartshill Unity had 2 points deducted.
Brownhills Albion had 4 points deducted.
Wednesbury Old Athletic resigned during the season and their record was deleted.
Cotterills (Darlaston), Hartshill Unity and Wordsley Olympic all left the league. Bilston United, Coseley and Hednesford Town all joined.

Staffordshire County League (South) 1894-1900

1894-95

Willenhall Pickwick	15	10	3	2	55	30	23
Hednesford Town	16	10	2	4	47	33	22
Brownhills Albion	14	7	4	3	37	21	18
Bilston United	15	7	4	4	44	33	18
Walsall Unity	16	6	2	8	35	43	14
Wolverhampton Presbyterians	16	5	4	7	33	42	14
Cannock Town	16	4	3	9	40	48	11
Bloxwich Strollers	15	5	1	9	31	48	11
Coseley	15	2	3	10	26	49	7
					348	347	

The table above is the latest found, after games played on 15th April when there were 4 games still to play. The result of one of those games was found and is included above. The other 3 may not have been played.
Coseley left the league and Walsall Wood Athletic joined.

1895-96

Bilston United	14	11	0	3	44	16	22
Hednesford Town	14	10	2	2	35	16	22
Brownhills Albion	14	10	0	4	38	17	18
Willenhall Pickwick	14	7	2	5	25	22	16
Bloxwich Strollers	14	5	0	9	21	31	10
Walsall Unity	14	4	1	9	30	44	9
Walsall Wood Athletic	14	3	1	10	22	39	7
Cannock Town	14	3	0	11	23	53	6

Brownhills Albion had 2 points deducted.
Wolverhampton Presbyterians resigned during the season and their record was deleted.
Darlaston and Rushall Olympic both joined the league.

The league was increased to 10 clubs.

1896-97

Bloxwich Strollers	18	15	1	2	61	18	31
Darlaston	17	11	1	5	66	29	23
Willenhall Pickwick	17	9	4	4	38	32	22
Bilston United	18	10	1	7	41	20	21
Hednesford Town	17	7	4	6	29	36	18
Walsall Unity	18	5	3	10	38	46	13
Walsall Wood Athletic	18	4	5	9	30	52	13
Rushall Olympic	18	6	1	11	35	61	13
Cannock Town	17	6	0	11	28	45	12
Brownhills Albion	18	4	3	11	29	50	11
		77	23	76	395	389	177

Two games were not played.
Walsall Unity left the league. Oldbury Town joined from the Birmingham & District League and Wednesbury Old Athletic also joined.

1897

Many of the league's members were now of senior status and so the league changed its name to Walsall & District League.
In 1898, a new Walsall & District Junior League was formed to cater for the areas junior clubs. This league later changed its name to Walsall & District Minor League.

WALSALL & DISTRICT LEAGUE 1897-1910

1897-98

Brownhills Albion	20	13	4	3	63	25	30
Oldbury Town	20	12	4	4	46	40	28
Darlaston	20	11	5	4	61	28	27
Bilston United	20	10	4	6	68	23	24
Walsall Wood Athletic	20	10	4	6	39	43	22
Wednesbury Old Athletic	20	9	3	8	45	49	19
Cannock Town	20	7	5	8	38	47	19
Bloxwich Strollers	20	6	4	10	22	48	16
Hednesford Town	20	5	4	11	39	42	14
Willenhall Pickwick	20	4	2	14	33	59	10
Rushall Olympic	20	3	1	16	22	72	7

Walsall Wood Athletic and Wednesbury Old Athletic each had 2 points deducted.
Rushall Olympic left the league. Hednesford Swifts and Walsall Unity both joined.

The League was increased to 12 clubs.

1898-99

Willenhall Pickwick	22	18	1	3	92	30	37
Bilston United	22	16	1	5	76	32	33
Hednesford Town	22	15	3	4	55	28	33
Wednesbury Old Athletic	22	13	1	8	53	38	27
Hednesford Swifts	22	10	3	9	45	44	23
Darlaston	22	9	5	8	58	57	23
Brownhills Albion	22	10	3	9	46	52	21
Cannock Town	22	7	1	14	54	68	15
Walsall Unity	22	6	5	11	40	64	15
Bloxwich Strollers	22	5	3	14	29	52	13
Oldbury Town	22	4	3	15	38	60	11
Walsall Wood Athletic	22	3	3	16	22	83	9

Brownhills Albion and Walsall Unity each had 2 points deducted.
Oldbury Town moved to the Birmingham & District Junior League and Walsall Wood Athletic moved to the Walsall & District Junior League.
Cheslyn Hay Villa joined from the Cannock & District League and Tipton Victoria joined from the West Midland League.

1899-1900

Wednesbury Old Athletic	20	13	4	3	58	22	30
Hednesford Town	20	13	3	4	43	21	29
Bloxwich Strollers	20	10	6	4	47	30	26
Darlaston	20	11	1	8	40	35	23
Willenhall Pickwick	20	7	4	9	35	34	18
Bilston United	20	6	5	9	36	38	17
Cheslyn Hay Villa	20	7	2	11	38	50	16
Tipton Victoria	20	7	2	11	27	41	16
Brownhills Albion	20	6	4	10	33	51	16
Hednesford Swifts	20	6	3	11	27	47	15
Cannock Town	20	5	4	11	27	42	14

Walsall Unity resigned in January 1900 and their record was deleted.
Bridgtown Amateurs joined from the Walsall & District Junior League.

The League was increased to 12 clubs.

Staffordshire County League (South) 1900-1906

1900-01

Bilston United	22	16	4	2	56	22	36
Bloxwich Strollers	22	16	2	4	68	29	34
Wednesbury Old Athletic	22	11	5	6	49	28	27
Hednesford Town	19	9	6	4	51	20	24
Darlaston	19	10	3	6	36	34	23
Cheslyn Hay Villa	22	7	5	10	36	50	19
Willenhall Pickwick	21	8	2	11	43	48	18
Cannock Town	21	7	2	12	43	59	16
Brownhills Albion	22	7	2	13	33	69	16
Hednesford Swifts	22	6	4	12	36	46	14
Bridgtown Amateurs	22	4	5	13	26	52	13
Tipton Victoria	20	5	2	13	29	55	12
					506	512	

Hednesford Swifts had 2 points deducted.
Tipton Victoria resigned and disbanded shortly before the end of the season but their record was allowed to stand. The following 5 games were not played: Hednesford Town vs Tipton Victoria, Willenhall Pickwick vs Tipton Victoria, Hednesford Town vs Darlaston, Darlaston vs Hednesford Town and Cannock Town vs Darlaston.
Cheslyn Hay Villa moved to the Walsall & District Junior League.
The League was reduced to 10 clubs.

1901-02

Bilston United	18	11	3	4	44	24	25
Hednesford Town	18	11	2	5	46	18	24
Wednesbury Old Athletic	18	10	4	4	38	23	24
Cannock Town	18	6	6	6	32	34	18
Darlaston	18	7	3	8	36	43	17
Bridgtown Amateurs	18	7	2	9	30	29	16
Brownhills Albion	18	6	4	8	39	42	16
Bloxwich Strollers	18	6	4	8	23	25	16
Hednesford Swifts	18	5	4	9	27	32	14
Willenhall Pickwick	18	4	2	12	25	59	10
					340	329	

Stafford Rangers Reserves and Walsall Reserves both joined, neither having played in a league in 1901-02.
The League was increased to 12 clubs.

1902-03

Bloxwich Strollers	22	15	4	3	47	18	34
Bilston United	22	13	4	5	56	34	30
Hednesford Town	22	13	3	6	58	26	29
Wednesbury Old Athletic	22	11	5	6	51	36	27
Darlaston	22	10	6	6	47	39	26
Bridgtown Amateurs	22	9	7	6	38	35	25
Brownhills Albion	22	8	5	9	38	38	21
Cannock Town	22	9	2	11	41	44	20
Stafford Rangers Reserves	22	5	5	12	40	52	15
Willenhall Pickwick	22	6	3	13	32	59	15
Hednesford Swifts	22	5	4	13	30	58	14
Walsall Reserves	22	2	4	16	19	58	8

Hednesford Swifts disbanded.
Birchills Villa joined from the Walsall & District Junior League.

1903-04

Darlaston	22	17	3	2	85	16	37
Wednesbury Old Athletic	22	14	6	2	61	30	34
Cannock Town	22	9	6	7	30	27	24
Brownhills Albion	22	9	6	7	36	36	24
Willenhall Pickwick	22	9	5	8	45	37	23
Bloxwich Strollers	22	10	3	9	36	41	23
Bilston United	22	10	2	10	44	32	22
Hednesford Town	22	7	5	10	27	45	19
Bridgtown Amateurs	22	5	8	9	24	31	18
Stafford Rangers Reserves	22	5	6	11	45	57	16
Walsall Reserves	22	3	7	12	21	59	13
Birchills Villa	22	3	5	14	19	59	11
					473	470	

Walsall Reserves resigned from the league.

Rushall Olympic joined from the Walsall & District Junior League, St. Georges Victoria joined from the Wellington & District League and Willenhall Swifts joined from the Wolverhampton & District League.

The League was increased to 14 clubs.

1904-05

Wednesbury Old Athletic	26	18	3	5	84	35	39
Darlaston	26	15	7	4	62	31	37
Hednesford Town	26	15	5	6	72	42	35
Bilston United	26	14	7	5	62	31	35
Bloxwich Strollers	26	16	2	8	60	33	34
Bridgtown Amateurs	26	14	4	8	54	37	32
Willenhall Pickwick	26	12	3	11	47	45	27
St. Georges Victoria	26	10	5	11	45	35	25
Willenhall Swifts	26	7	8	11	44	50	22
Brownhills Albion	26	10	2	14	34	48	22
Cannock Town	26	9	3	14	37	63	21
Stafford Rangers Reserves	26	7	5	14	35	70	19
Birchills Villa	26	3	4	19	26	66	10
Rushall Olympic	26	2	2	22	17	93	6

Birchills Villa and Rushall Olympic both moved to the Walsall & District Junior League. Walsall Reserves were re-formed and re-joined the league, Halesowen joined from the Birmingham & District League and Oldbury Town joined from the Birmingham & District Junior League.
A newly re-formed club called Ironbridge were also elected at the A.G.M. but withdrew before the start of the season as they could not secure a ground. Ironbridge Swifts had been playing in the Wellington & District League in 1904-05 but resigned and disbanded during the season when they lost the use of their Hill Top ground at Madeley Wood.

The League was increased to 15 clubs.

1905-06

Darlaston	26	18	3	5	73	34	39
Halesowen	26	16	5	5	69	41	37
Wednesbury Old Athletic	26	16	4	6	82	53	36
Bilston United	26	14	5	7	65	36	33
Willenhall Pickwick	26	14	3	9	56	46	31
Bloxwich Strollers	26	13	5	8	58	51	31
St. Georges Victoria	26	14	2	10	68	49	30
Bridgtown Amateurs	26	10	3	13	52	54	23
Brownhills Albion	26	9	3	14	41	48	21
Cannock Town	26	7	5	14	42	54	19
Willenhall Swifts	26	6	7	13	44	61	19
Hednesford Town	26	7	4	15	36	65	18
Stafford Rangers Reserves	26	5	4	17	31	72	14
Oldbury Town	26	4	5	17	31	84	13

Walsall withdrew and disbanded their reserve side at the end of January and their record was deleted: 16 0 2 14 11 73 2
Halesowen moved to the Birmingham & District League, Oldbury Town moved to the Birmingham & District Junior League, Stafford Rangers Reserves moved to the Stone, Stafford & District League and Bridgtown Amateurs disbanded. Wellington Town joined from the Birmingham & District League and Short Heath United joined from the Wolverhampton & District League.

The league was reduced to 12 clubs.

Staffordshire County League (South) 1906-1910

1906-07

Willenhall Swifts	22	16	2	4	62	39	34
Darlaston	22	13	5	4	67	35	31
Bilston United	22	13	3	6	61	28	29
Hednesford Town	22	11	4	7	46	40	26
St. Georges Victoria	22	10	5	7	63	50	25
Willenhall Pickwick	22	9	4	9	54	51	22
Wednesbury Old Athletic	22	9	3	10	51	48	21
Bloxwich Strollers	22	8	4	10	36	41	20
Cannock Town	22	8	3	11	39	50	19
Wellington Town	22	6	2	14	40	63	14
Brownhills Albion	22	5	4	13	40	58	12
Short Heath United	22	4	1	17	26	78	9
					585	581	

Brownhills Albion had 2 points deducted for fielding an ineligible player.
Bilston United, Darlaston, Wednesbury Old Athletic and Willenhall Pickwick all moved to the Birmingham & District Junior League. Brownhills Albion also left the league. Cheslyn Hay United and West Cannock Colliery both joined from the Walsall & District Junior League, Walsall Reserves re-formed and re-joined and Rushall Red Cross joined as a newly formed club.

1907-08

St. Georges Victoria	20	14	4	2	75	22	32
Willenhall Swifts	20	15	2	3	60	25	32
Hednesford Town	20	14	1	5	74	33	29
Wellington Town	20	13	1	6	46	35	27
Cannock Town	20	11	3	6	66	38	25
Walsall Reserves	20	9	4	7	50	30	22
West Cannock Colliery	20	7	3	10	29	46	17
Rushall Red Cross	20	5	4	11	27	45	14
Bloxwich Strollers	20	6	0	14	35	60	12
Cheslyn Hay United	20	3	1	16	24	74	7
Short Heath United	20	1	1	18	23	98	3
					509	506	

Hednesford Town and Willenhall Swifts both moved to the Birmingham Combination and Wellington Town moved to the Birmingham & District League. Bloxwich Strollers disbanded. Aldridge Amateurs had resigned from the Walsall & District Junior League during the 1907-08 season but re-formed and joined the league as Aldridge. Brownhills Town joined from the Lichfield League and Rugeley joined as a newly formed club.
West Cannock Colliery changed their name to West Cannock Athletic.
A new second division was formed with 7 founder members – 3rd South Staffordshire Regiment (who were based in Lichfield), Cannock Central and Chadsmoor Athletic (both newly formed clubs), Chase Terrace Rangers and Chasetown Rovers (both from the Lichfield League), Pelsall Villa and Walsall Wood (both from the Walsall & District Junior League).

1908-09

Division One

St. Georges Victoria	14	10	0	4	52	29	20
West Cannock Athletic	14	10	0	4	40	30	20
Cannock Town	14	9	0	5	48	20	18
Cheslyn Hay United	14	9	0	5	50	32	18
Walsall Reserves	14	6	2	6	29	21	14
Brownhills Town	14	6	1	7	24	37	13
Rugeley	14	3	0	11	26	45	6
Rushall Red Cross	14	1	1	12	13	68	3

Short Heath United resigned and disbanded at the end of October 1908 and their record was deleted: 2 1 0 1 4 3 2
Aldridge were suspended sine die and their record was deleted when it stood as follows: 11 3 1 7 13 39 7
Cannock Town and St. Georges Victoria both moved to the Birmingham Combination, Rugeley moved to the Stafford & District League and Rushall Red Cross disbanded. Brownhills Town changed their name to Brownhills Albion.

Division Two

Pelsall Villa	10	7	1	2	32	9	15
Chasetown Rovers	10	6	2	2	26	9	14
Chadsmoor Athletic	10	5	3	2	23	20	11
Chase Terrace Rangers	10	3	3	4	23	16	9
Cannock Central	10	4	1	5	26	32	9
3rd South Staffordshire Regiment	10	0	0	10	5	49	0

Chadsmoor Athletic had 2 points deducted for fielding ineligible players.
Walsall Wood resigned in January 1909 and their record was deleted when it stood as follows: 2 1 0 1 5 6 2
Pelsall Villa moved to the Walsall Alliance and 3rd South Staffordshire Regiment left the league but were replaced by 2nd Royal Warwickshire Regiment. Chase Terrace Rangers disbanded. Darlaston's newly formed reserve side joined, Walsall Wood Ramblers and Bloxwich Strollers both joined as newly re-formed clubs.

Divisions One and Two merged to form a single division of 11 clubs.

1909-10

West Cannock Athletic	16	11	1	4	44	18	23
Brownhills Albion	16	9	2	5	41	23	20
Darlaston Reserves	16	8	3	5	39	28	19
2nd Royal Warwickshire Regiment	16	8	1	7	51	41	17
Walsall Reserves	16	7	3	6	32	28	17
Cannock Central	14	7	1	6	22	31	15
Bloxwich Strollers	16	7	0	9	33	58	14
Cheslyn Hay United	15	4	1	10	31	49	9
Chasetown Rovers	15	3	0	12	25	42	6

The results of the two outstanding games have not been found.
Walsall Wood Ramblers resigned from the league in January 1910 and their record was deleted: 3 2 0 1 5 6 4
Chadsmoor Athletic resigned from the league at the end of March 1910 and their record was deleted: 12 3 2 7 23 37 8
Walsall Reserves resigned as the club would now be playing in both the Southern League and the Birmingham League while Darlaston disbanded their reserve side and 2nd Royal Warwickshire Regiment also resigned. That left only 6 members of the league – Bloxwich Strollers, Brownhills Albion, Cannock Central, Chasetown Rovers, Cheslyn Hay United and West Cannock Athletic who all joined the Walsall Alliance, West Cannock Athletic changing their name to West Cannock Juniors.
Those 6 teams were joined by Boney Hay Albion, Bridgtown Amateurs, Burntwood Victoria, Little Bloxwich Wanderers, Newtown Swifts, Norton Primitives and Norton United all of whom were already members of the Walsall Alliance plus Brownhills Recreation who joined from the Walsall Church & Chapel League and 5th South Staffordshire Regiment, thus comprising a 15-club Walsall Alliance. However, the number of clubs increased to 16 when 2nd Royal Warwickshire Regiment were allowed to join the league at the start of October 1910.

The original Walsall & District League was then defunct but the Walsall Alliance changed its name to Walsall & District League.

WALSALL & DISTRICT LEAGUE
1910-20
(Previously the Walsall Alliance)

1910-11

2nd Royal Warwickshire Regiment	20	15	2	3	69 18	32
Bloxwich Strollers	20	13	2	5	33 24	28
Bridgtown Amateurs	19	10	3	6	38 38	23
Cheslyn Hay United	20	10	2	8	38 33	22
Cannock Central	20	9	2	9	37 44	20
Brownhills Albion	19	8	3	8	46 38	19
Chasetown Rovers	20	9	2	9	23 28	18
Brownhills Recreation	20	8	1	11	36 41	17
Norton Primitives	20	8	5	7	34 38	17
Burntwood Victoria	20	2	6	12	21 54	10
Newtown Swifts	20	1	4	15	24 43	6

Cannock Central and Chasetown Rovers each had 2 points deducted.
Norton Primitives had 4 points deducted.
Five clubs resigned during the season and their records were deleted:
West Cannock Juniors resigned in late October 1910 when their record stood as follows: 4 1 1 2 3 13 3
Little Bloxwich Wanderers resigned in early March 1911 when their record stood as follows: 12 3 0 9 17 38 6
Norton United resigned in late March 1911 at which point their record stood as follows: 17 1 2 14 15 75 4
5th South Staffordshire Regiment resigned in late March 1911 when their records stood as follows: 16 5 4 7 27 26 14
Boney Hay Albion resigned in late April 1911 at which point their record stood as follows: 19 4 6 9 22 32 14
2nd Royal Warwickshire Regiment left the league as they were leaving their Lichfield barracks. 5th South Staffordshire Regiment, Boney Hay Albion, Burntwood Victoria and Chasetown Rovers all moved to the Lichfield & District League and Cannock Central disbanded as they had lost their ground. Shelfield Villa joined from the Willenhall & District League and Hednesford United joined as a newly formed club.
Norton Primitives changed their name to Norton Athletic and Brownhills Recreation changed their name to Brownhills Town.

1911-12
The clubs played each other 4 times

Bloxwich Strollers	21	14	3	4	61 28	31
Brownhills Albion	17	10	4	3	43 22	24
Norton Athletic	24	10	4	10	46 46	24
Shelfield Villa	24	10	4	10	54 50	24
Bridgtown Amateurs	24	6	6	12	37 49	18
Cheslyn Hay United	21	10	3	8	25 25	17
Newtown Swifts	23	2	2	19	16 73	6
		62	26	64	282 293	144

Cheslyn Hay United had 6 points deducted.
Hednesford United were expelled on 15th April for failing to fulfil fixtures. They had already had 6 points deducted and their record at the time of expulsion was deleted: 10 6 2 2 21 13 8
They moved to the newly formed Cannock Chase League in 1912-13.
Brownhills Town were expelled in late March for failure to follow league orders. Their record was deleted: 12 2 3 7 15 32 7
The club later disbanded.
Bridgtown Amateurs and Cheslyn Hay United both moved to the Cannock Chase League while Brownhills Albion and Newtown Swifts disbanded. Pelsall Villa joined as a newly formed club while 2nd North Midland Royal Engineers, Walsall Wood Y.M.F. and Walsall Wood Colliery also joined.

1912-13

Shelfield Villa	10	7	1	2	37	15	15
Pelsall Villa	11	7	1	3	25	11	15
Walsall Wood Y.M.F.	10	5	2	3	23	20	12
Bloxwich Strollers	12	5	1	6	20	25	11
Norton Athletic	10	4	2	4	17	21	10
Walsall Wood Colliery	10	1	1	8	9	28	3
2nd North Midland Royal Eng.	7	2	0	5	4	20	2
					135	140	

2nd North Midland Royal Engineers had 2 points deducted. They resigned from the league in March 1913 but their record was allowed to stand.
At the end of the season, Bloxwich Strollers moved to the Birmingham Combination while Walsall Wood Colliery and 2nd North Midland Royal Engineers also left. Bloxwich Juniors and Sutton Town both joined.
Norton Athletic joined the Lichfield & District League before the start of the new season but had not resigned from the Walsall League and were ordered by the Walsall F.A. to play in both leagues.

Separately, a new league with two divisions was formed for clubs playing on parks pitches and called the Walsall & District Junior League.

1913-14
The clubs played each other home and away twice except Norton Athletic who were allowed to play every other club home and away just once.

Walsall Wood Y.M.F.	12	8	1	3	24	12	17
Shelfield Villa	12	7	3	2	31	18	17
Pelsall Villa	12	2	4	6	17	26	8
Sutton Town	12	1	4	7	17	32	6
					89	88	

Bloxwich Juniors resigned early in the season and their record was deleted. Norton Athletic also failed to complete their fixtures and their playing record was subsequently deleted: 3 1 1 1 7 16 3

1914-20
The league was planned to operate during the 1914-15 season with 7 clubs with Boldmere Rovers, Little Bloxwich Wanderers and Little Bloxwich Catholics joining the 4 clubs who completed the 1913-14 season. The league was still hoping for further clubs to join and Bridgtown Amateurs and Clayhanger Villa are thought to have joined, making a 9-club league. However no league tables have been found for the 1914-15 season and it is possible that, following the outbreak of war, the league had to be abandoned during the season. It did not operate between 1915 and 1919. The Walsall & District League appears to have been revived at some point during the 1919-20 season, but again, no league tables have been found.

Staffordshire County League (South) 1920-1931

WALSALL SENIOR LEAGUE 1920-23

In 1920, the Walsall Senior League was formed with 16 founder members (their 1919-20 league is shown in brackets where known). Chasetown Colliery, Lichfield City United, Rushall Olympic, Walsall Wood (all from the Lichfield & District League), Bloxwich Strollers Reserves, Brownhills Albion, Cannock Town Reserves, Dudley Bean Athletic Reserves, Hednesford Town Reserves, Rugeley (a newly formed club), Stafford Rangers Reserves, Sunbeam Motors, Walsall Reserves, Wellington St. Georges, Wellington Town Reserves and Willenhall Reserves.

1920-21

Sunbeam Motors	28	20	3	5	69	39	43
Wellington St. Georges	28	19	3	6	84	39	41
Chasetown Colliery	28	14	7	7	69	52	35
Willenhall Reserves	28	15	4	9	71	43	34
Walsall Wood	28	15	4	9	61	49	34
Wellington Town Reserves	28	15	3	10	91	58	33
Hednesford Town Reserves	28	16	1	11	66	46	33
Rugeley	28	11	5	12	55	70	27
Rushall Olympic	28	9	7	12	32	55	25
† Brownhills Town	28	9	5	14	45	79	23
Stafford Rangers Reserves	28	7	8	13	39	53	22
Cannock Town Reserves	28	7	7	14	46	67	21
Walsall Reserves	28	6	7	15	46	65	19
Bloxwich Strollers Reserves	28	6	4	18	38	78	16
Lichfield City United	28	6	4	18	40	87	16
	420	175		173	852	880	422

† Dudley Bean Athletic Reserves resigned from the league in November 1920 and their record and outstanding fixtures were taken over by Brownhills Town: 8 3 1 4 16 20 7
Brownhills Albion resigned from the league in December 1920 and their record was deleted: 9 0 0 9 6 63 0

Shrewsbury Town Reserves, Bilston United Reserves and Nuneaton Town Reserves all joined.

The league was increased to 18 clubs.

1921-22

Shrewsbury Town Reserves	34	23	5	6	100	44	51
Bilston United Reserves	34	23	5	6	80	43	51
Wellington St. Georges	34	21	4	9	114	43	46
Stafford Rangers Reserves	34	22	2	10	89	51	46
Walsall Reserves	34	20	5	9	88	59	45
Nuneaton Town Reserves	34	20	3	11	87	56	43
Walsall Wood	34	17	5	12	79	70	39
Rushall Olympic	34	17	4	13	54	59	38
Wellington Town Reserves	34	15	7	12	76	71	37
Sunbeam Motors	34	15	4	15	74	80	34
Willenhall Reserves	34	14	5	15	61	64	33
Hednesford Town Reserves	34	10	6	18	53	49	26
Lichfield City United	34	10	4	20	46	87	24
Cannock Town Reserves	34	9	4	21	50	70	22
Brownhills Town	34	6	8	20	49	82	20
Chasetown Colliery	34	9	2	23	54	93	20
Rugeley	34	6	7	21	44	90	19
Bloxwich Strollers Reserves	34	8	2	24	36	103	18
					1234	1214	

Chasetown Colliery and Rugeley both moved to the Lichfield & District League, Wellington St. Georges moved to the Birmingham Combination while Bloxwich Strollers Reserves and Nuneaton Town Reserves also both left the league. Talbot Stead joined from the Birmingham Combination and Tamworth Castle Reserves also joined.

1922-23

Sunbeam Motors	26	20	2	4	85	25	42
Lichfield City United	26	17	4	5	69	32	38
Walsall Reserves	26	15	6	5	72	26	36
Shrewsbury Town Reserves	26	14	5	7	62	31	33
Willenhall Reserves	26	12	5	9	49	44	29
Walsall Wood	26	13	2	11	57	42	28
Bilston United Reserves	26	12	3	11	42	55	27
Stafford Rangers Reserves	26	11	3	12	54	56	25
Wellington Town Reserves	26	11	3	12	49	71	25
Rushall Olympic	26	10	3	13	37	50	23
Hednesford Town Reserves	26	8	4	14	35	52	20
Talbot Stead	26	7	4	15	48	40	18
Brownhills Town	26	4	6	16	32	69	14
Tamworth Castle Reserves	26	2	2	22	35	117	6
					726	710	

Cannock Town Reserves fulfilled no fixtures after December 1922 and their record was deleted in April 1923: 10 0 1 9 11 33 1
Lichfield City United, Sunbeam Motors, Walsall Reserves and Walsall Wood all moved to the Birmingham Combination. Several other clubs also resigned leaving too few members to enable the league to continue and it closed down. Stafford Rangers Reserves and Wellington Town Reserves both joined the Stafford & District League, Rushall Olympic joined the Walsall Parks League, Brownhills Town joined the Lichfield & District League and Tamworth Castle Reserves joined the Trent Valley League.

WALSALL & DISTRICT LEAGUE 1924-1939

In 1924, it was decided to revive the Walsall & District League, at a lower level than the Walsall Senior League and with two divisions. No tables have been found for the period between 1924 and 1927 but members of Division One in 1924-25 included Blakenall, Bloxwich St. Peters, Bradley United, Brownhills Town, Burntwood Villa, Cannock Chase Colliery, Leamore Athletic, Leighs Wood Primitives, Little Bloxwich Wanderers, Pelsall, Short Heath United and Wednesbury Town.
In 1925-26, the league operated with a single division consisting of Aldridge St. Marys, Brownhills Town, Burntwood Villa, Cannock Chase Colliery, Chase Terrace Rangers, Chasetown, Hednesford Town Reserves, Leamore Athletic, Pelsall, Pelsall Villa, Rushall Olympic, Short Heath United, Talbot Stead, Walsall Wood Colliery, Wednesbury Town and West Cannock. There was again a single division in 1926-27 and amongst the members were Blakenall, Chase Terrace Rangers, Chasetown, Essington Villa, Hednesford Town Reserves, Leamore, Pelsall, Pelsall Villa, Short Heath United and Wednesbury Town.
No information has been found about the league between 1927 and 1930 and it may have again closed down until being revived in 1930 with 13 members: N1st South Staffordshire Regiment, Blakenall Villa, Brereton Social, Brownhills West Athletic, Cannock Chase Colliery, Darlaston Reserves, Leamore Social, Norton Athletic, Pelsall Villa, Shelfield Y.M.F., Short Heath United, Walsall Wood Primitives and Walsall Wood Y.M.F..

1930-31

Cannock Chase Colliery	19	17	2	0	78	29	36
Darlaston Reserves	19	11	5	3	68	36	27
Walsall Wood Primitives	19	12	2	5	51	39	26
Short Heath United	21	9	7	5	85	47	25
Pelsall Villa	19	11	2	6	72	45	24
Brereton Social	19	11	1	7	64	63	23
Blakenall Villa	22	9	2	11	38	60	20
1st South Staffordshire Regiment	16	8	1	7	56	45	17
Brownhills West Athletic	20	5	2	13	34	79	12
Shelfield Y.M.F.	16	3	1	12	29	50	7
Norton Athletic	16	2	2	12	32	73	6
† Burntwood Villa	19	1	0	18	23	100	2
	225	99	27	99	630	666	225

Table is latest found, before games played on 25th April. It is not known how many of the 20 outstanding fixtures were played.

Staffordshire County League (South) 1931-1936

Leamore Social resigned from the league early in the season and their record was deleted: 2 0 0 2 2 14 0
† Walsall Wood Y.M.F. resigned from the league during January 1931 and Burntwood Villa took over their record and completed their fixtures. Walsall Wood's record was: 9 0 0 9 6 57 0
Brownhills West Athletic and Burntwood Villa both moved to the Lichfield & District League, Short Heath United moved to the Wolverhampton Amateur League while Norton Athletic, Darlaston Reserves, 1st South Staffordshire Regiment and Shelfield Y.M.F. also left. Chase Terrace Victoria, Hazel Slade Rovers and Hednesford Town Reserves all joined from the Rugeley & District League, Rugeley Villa joined from the Stafford & District League while Cannock Town Reserves and Wednesbury Town also joined. Walsall Wood Primitives changed their name to Walsall Wood.

1931-32

Hazel Slade Rovers	20	15	1	4	59	28	31
Cannock Chase Colliery	20	13	3	4	72	37	29
Blakenall Villa	20	13	3	4	54	31	29
Walsall Wood	20	10	2	8	47	47	22
Brereton Social	20	8	3	9	63	58	19
Cannock Town Reserves	20	8	3	9	51	50	19
Chase Terrace Victoria	20	8	2	10	40	53	18
Pelsall Villa	20	7	3	10	39	43	17
Rugeley Villa	20	6	4	10	34	58	16
Wednesbury Town	20	3	4	13	43	74	10
Hednesford Town Reserves	20	3	4	13	37	65	10
					539	544	

Wednesbury Town left the league. Bilston Borough joined as a newly formed club after Bilston Town of the Birmingham & District League had disbanded and Bloxwich joined as a newly formed club after Bloxwich Strollers of the Birmingham Combination had disbanded. Walsall LMS joined from the Birmingham Combination, Stafford Rangers Reserves joined from the Staffordshire County League while Brownhills U.M. and Mid-Cannock Colliery also joined.

1932-33

Bilston Borough	22	15	5	2	74	19	35
Blakenall Villa	22	16	2	4	68	32	34
Walsall Wood	21	15	1	5	80	26	31
Brereton Social	21	12	4	5	65	32	28
Cannock Chase Colliery	22	12	2	8	86	41	26
Hazel Slade Rovers	22	12	2	8	59	52	26
Chase Terrace Victoria	22	11	2	9	55	57	24
Bloxwich	22	6	6	10	31	53	18
Pelsall Villa	22	5	3	14	44	64	13
Stafford Rangers Reserves	22	4	3	15	43	79	11
Rugeley Villa	22	4	3	15	38	83	11
Mid-Cannock Colliery	22	3	1	18	23	99	7
	115		113	666	637	264	

The latest table found was dated 6th May when 6 games were outstanding. The results of 5 of these were found and are included above but the 6th result has remained elusive.
Brownhills U.M., Cannock Town Reserves, Hednesford Town Reserves and Walsall LMS all left during the season and their records were deleted. Mid-Cannock Colliery and Pelsall Villa both left the league. Lichfield Amateurs, Kings Own Royal Regiment, Sherwood Foresters and Streetly Works all joined.

1933-34

Walsall Wood	26	19	4	3	76	34	42
Cannock Chase Colliery	26	18	4	4	108	41	40
Streetly Works	26	17	3	6	71	33	37
Sherwood Foresters	26	16	4	6	75	35	36
Bloxwich	26	16	2	8	71	54	34
Bilston Borough	26	15	2	9	78	43	32
Blakenall Villa	26	13	2	11	55	36	28
Kings Own Royal Regiment	26	9	5	12	57	68	23
Lichfield Amateurs	26	9	5	12	60	73	23
Chase Terrace Victoria	26	8	1	17	48	70	17
Brereton Social	26	7	2	17	37	79	16
Hazel Slade Rovers	26	6	3	17	50	87	15
Stafford Rangers Reserves	26	6	3	17	39	112	15
Rugeley Villa	26	3	2	21	35	104	8
	162		160	860	869	366	

Blakenall Villa, Kings Own Royal Regiment, Rugeley Villa and Stafford Rangers Reserves all left the league. Handford Greatrex, Kings Shropshire Light Infantry, Metro Shaft, Wellington St. Georges, Wellington Town Reserves and Wrockwardine Wood all joined.

1934-35

Cannock Chase Colliery	30	23	4	3	124	28	50
Streetly Works	29	21	2	6	98	48	44
Wrockwardine Wood	30	20	0	10	91	39	40
Metro Shaft	29	17	4	8	80	73	38
Hazel Slade Rovers	30	15	7	8	76	62	37
Bilston Borough	29	16	2	11	88	50	34
Wellington Town Reserves	29	14	4	11	84	79	32
Walsall Wood	30	12	6	12	79	57	30
Chase Terrace Victoria	25	9	7	9	46	93	23
Bloxwich	30	6	10	14	67	82	22
Sherwood Foresters	29	9	4	16	71	95	22
Kings Shropshire Light Infantry	30	9	3	18	66	107	21
Handford Greatrex	30	7	6	17	62	98	20
Wellington St. Georges	30	8	4	18	55	95	20
Lichfield Amateurs	28	7	4	17	48	78	18
Brereton Social	30	4	5	21	34	94	13
	197		199	1169	1178	464	

The table shown is the latest found, as at 24th May.
The 6 outstanding fixtures may not have been played.
Chase Terrace Victoria had 2 points deducted.
Brereton Social, Handford Greatrex, Kings Shropshire Light Infantry, Lichfield Amateurs and Sherwood Foresters all left the league. Donnington Wood and Stafford Rangers Reserves both joined.

1935-36

Bilston Borough	24	15	3	6	78	46	33
Wellington Town Reserves	21	12	3	6	61	39	27
Donnington Wood	21	12	2	7	63	38	26
Walsall Wood	19	11	3	5	59	29	25
Cannock Chase Colliery	18	12	1	5	53	33	25
Wrockwardine Wood	21	10	5	6	45	43	25
Metro Shaft	19	6	6	7	36	53	18
Streetly Works	18	7	2	9	45	42	16
Hazel Slade Rovers	19	4	5	10	23	40	13
Stafford Rangers Reserves	15	2	4	9	25	37	8
Wellington St. Georges	14	3	2	9	20	41	8
Bloxwich	17	3	2	12	22	62	8
Chase Terrace Victoria	12	2	3	7	20	51	7
	238	99	41	98	550	554	239

The table shown is the latest found, as at 2nd May when 37 fixtures were outstanding. Most of these were probably not played as several clubs were finding it difficult to continue because of the economic slump.
Bloxwich, Chase Terrace Victoria, Metro Shaft, Stafford Rangers Reserves, Streetly Works, Wellington St. Georges and Wellington Town Reserves all left the league. Shrewsbury Town Reserves and Walsall "A" both joined.

Staffordshire County League (South) 1936-1948

1936-37

Cannock Chase Colliery	14	10	1	3	44	17	21
Wrockwardine Wood	14	7	5	2	47	25	19
Bilston Borough	14	8	2	4	44	23	18
Walsall Wood	14	9	0	5	39	29	18
Shrewsbury Town Reserves	13	5	3	5	29	27	13
Donnington Wood	14	5	3	6	30	31	13
Walsall "A"	14	2	1	11	22	56	5
Hazel Slade Rovers	13	2	0	11	12	58	4
		48	15	47	267	266	111

The table shown is as at 1st May.
The outstanding fixture may not have been played.

Subsidiary Competition – Section 1

Cannock Chase Colliery	6	5	0	1	35	7	10
Walsall Wood	6	4	1	1	22	11	9
Walsall "A"	6	0	2	4	8	15	2
Hazel Slade Rovers	6	1	0	5	5	34	2
		10	3	11	70	67	23

Subsidiary Competition – Section 2

Bilston Borough	6	4	1	1	21	13	9
Wrockwardine Wood	6	2	2	2	15	14	6
Donnington Wood	6	2	1	3	7	12	5
Shrewsbury Town Reserves	6	2	0	4	12	15	4
					55	54	

Donnington Wood, Hazel Slade Rovers, Shrewsbury Town Reserves and Wrockwardine Wood all left the league. Brereton Social, Brownhills Albion, English Electric, Harrisons Colliery, Heath Hayes, Mid-Cannock Colliery, Pelsall and Sutton Town all joined.

1937-38

Cannock Chase Colliery	17	15	2	0	63	21	32
Bilston Borough	17	10	6	1	55	18	26
Walsall Wood	18	9	4	5	44	24	22
Brownhills Albion	17	9	2	6	43	30	20
English Electric	16	7	4	5	43	23	18
Sutton Town	17	6	1	10	29	47	13
Brereton Social	18	5	3	10	34	65	13
Pelsall	18	4	3	11	46	54	11
Walsall "A"	18	4	2	12	33	64	10
Harrisons Colliery	18	3	3	12	24	48	9
					414	394	

The table shown is as at 7th May.
Outstanding fixtures may not have been played.
Heath Hayes changed their name to Hednesford H&S just before the season started and acted as Hednesford Reserves. They resigned from the league at the beginning of March and their record was deleted when it stood as follows: 11   2   2   7   18   33   6
Mid-Cannock Colliery resigned at the end of April and their record (with 2 points deducted) was deleted: 9   1   1   7   7   41   1

1938-39

Cannock Chase Colliery	19	14	3	2	55	20	31
Walsall Wood	19	11	4	4	49	26	26
Wellington Town Reserves	20	10	5	5	39	38	25
English Electric	20	9	4	7	43	29	22
Bilston Borough	18	9	2	7	39	31	20
Sutton Town	19	6	6	7	37	42	18
Brownhills Albion	18	8	0	10	44	51	16
Brereton Social	18	7	1	10	47	54	15
Walsall "A"	20	4	5	11	34	61	13
Wolverhampton Wanderers "B"	19	4	4	11	30	43	12
Donnington Wood	18	3	4	11	26	48	10

The table shown is as at 6th May.
Outstanding fixtures may not have been played.
The league closed when war was declared. It was revived in 1945 as the Walsall Senior League with 11 founder members Brereton Social, Cannock Chase Colliery, English Electric, Hadley Castle Works, Hawkins United, Ogley Hay, R.A.F. Lichfield, R.A.F. Stafford, Rugeley W.M.C., Walsall Trinity and Walsall Wood.

WALSALL SENIOR LEAGUE 1945-50

1945-46

Walsall Wood	20	16	2	2	90	32	34
Ogley Hay	17	10	2	5	58	29	22
Cannock Chase Colliery	17	10	0	7	64	41	20
English Electric	17	9	1	7	52	29	19
Hadley Castle Works	15	8	2	5	47	47	18
Hawkins United	17	7	2	8	51	60	16
Brereton Social	20	8	0	12	56	81	16
Walsall Trinity	17	6	3	8	40	47	15
Rugeley W.M.C.	19	7	1	11	49	77	15
R.A.F. Stafford	11	4	3	4	31	28	11
R.A.F. Lichfield	18	0	2	16	28	88	2
					566	559	

The table shown is as at 30th March. Although more games were played, no record of the results has been found.   Hawkins United, R.A.F. Lichfield and R.A.F. Stafford all left the league. Bilston, Chase Terrace United, Hednesford Reserves, Rugeley Villa, Stafford Rangers Reserves, Stourbridge Reserves and Sutton Coldfield Athletic all joined.

1946-47

Walsall Wood	27	21	5	1	117	32	47
Walsall Trinity	27	19	3	5	118	54	41
Cannock Chase Colliery	26	17	4	5	116	50	38
Brereton Social	27	17	2	8	94	47	36
Bilston	23	14	2	7	77	44	30
Rugeley W.M.C.	26	14	2	10	94	77	30
Ogley Hay	24	12	4	8	68	58	28
Stafford Rangers Reserves	28	12	1	15	79	72	25
Rugeley Villa	25	9	6	10	66	58	24
Chase Terrace United	28	10	3	15	72	77	23
Stourbridge Reserves	28	8	5	15	71	78	21
Hednesford Reserves	26	8	3	15	67	107	19
English Electric	26	7	1	18	49	138	15
Hadley Castle Works	22	2	2	18	27	84	6
Sutton Coldfield Athletic	23	2	0	21	34	126	4
		172	43	171	1149	1102	387

A very severe winter left a huge backlog of fixtures and, despite the season being extended until 31st May, the remaining games were left unplayed. English Electric and Hadley Castle Works both left the league. Darlaston Reserves, Dudley Town Reserves, Halesowen Town Reserves, Lye Town Reserves and Sutton Town all joined.

1947-48

Bilston	34	24	4	6	98	36	52
Stafford Rangers Reserves	34	23	6	5	96	40	52
Walsall Trinity	34	20	5	9	115	60	45
Sutton Town	34	21	2	11	110	54	44
Walsall Wood	34	17	9	8	98	62	43
Cannock Chase Colliery	34	14	10	10	93	86	38
Brereton Social	34	18	1	15	86	85	37
Hednesford Reserves	34	14	8	12	82	65	36
Ogley Hay	34	16	4	14	58	71	36
Stourbridge Reserves	34	16	2	16	72	66	34
Halesowen Town Reserves	32	13	6	13	65	45	32
Lye Town Reserves	34	10	11	13	79	89	31
Dudley Town Reserves	33	13	4	16	72	67	30
Sutton Coldfield Athletic	34	14	1	19	79	124	29
Darlaston Reserves	34	12	2	20	60	84	26
Rugeley W.M.C.	33	9	4	20	69	117	22
Rugeley Villa	34	3	6	25	41	110	12
Chase Terrace United	34	3	5	26	43	113	11
		260			258 1418	1394	610

The two outstanding games were not played.
Bilston moved to the Birmingham Combination and were replaced by their reserves. Dudley Town Reserves, Halesowen Town Reserves, Lye Town Reserves, Rugeley Villa and Stourbridge Reserves all also left the league. Coventry City "A" joined from the Birmingham Combination, Brierley Hill Alliance Reserves joined as a newly formed club and English Electric also joined.

Staffordshire County League (South) 1948-1952

STAFFORDSHIRE COUNTY LEAGUE (SOUTH) 1950-1996

1948-49

Team	P	W	D	L	F	A	Pts
Sutton Town	30	24	4	2	73	32	52
Brereton Social	30	23	5	2	116	52	51
Walsall Trinity	30	19	7	4	83	36	45
Coventry City "A"	30	17	6	7	62	40	40
Stafford Rangers Reserves	30	17	3	10	85	57	37
Walsall Wood	30	16	5	9	78	56	37
Ogley Hay	30	13	7	10	69	62	33
Bilston Reserves	30	15	3	12	67	61	33
Hednesford Reserves	30	15	3	12	83	73	33
Rugeley W.M.C.	30	10	5	15	66	67	25
Cannock Chase Colliery	30	7	7	16	53	93	21
Brierley Hill Alliance Reserves	30	8	4	18	68	90	20
Darlaston Reserves	30	7	4	19	53	70	18
English Electric	30	6	6	18	49	92	18
Sutton Coldfield Athletic	30	8	0	22	78	110	16
Chase Terrace United	30	3	3	24	38	109	9
		208			200 1121 1100		488

Brierley Hill Alliance Reserves moved to the Worcestershire Combination while Coventry City "A" and Darlaston Reserves both also left. Newport Town, Tamworth Reserves and West Bromwich Albion "B" all joined.

1949-50

Team	P	W	D	L	F	A	Pts
Walsall Trinity	30	24	3	3	101	41	51
Walsall Wood	30	18	7	5	80	40	43
Ogley Hay	30	16	8	6	67	39	40
Newport Town	30	16	7	7	84	44	39
Brereton Social	30	15	7	8	78	56	37
Hednesford Reserves	30	14	7	9	73	62	35
Tamworth Reserves	30	14	6	10	83	70	34
Sutton Town	30	14	4	12	61	44	32
Sutton Coldfield Athletic	30	11	7	12	67	66	29
English Electric	30	11	4	15	71	65	26
West Bromwich Albion "B"	30	8	7	15	49	65	23
Bilston Reserves	30	8	6	16	57	71	22
Rugeley W.M.C.	30	9	4	17	45	89	22
Stafford Rangers Reserves	30	6	9	15	40	72	21
Cannock Chase Colliery	30	5	5	20	41	87	15
Chase Terrace United	30	4	2	24	33	109	10
		193			93 194 1030 1020		479

Sutton Town moved to the Birmingham Combination and were replaced by their reserves. English Electric and Stafford Rangers Reserves both left the league. Baddesley Liberals, Beaudesert Sports, Bloxwich Strollers and Shelfield Athletic all joined.

The name of the league was changed to Staffordshire County League.

The "(South)" was added later to distinguish it from the Staffordshire County League (North) which operated in the Stoke-on-Trent area.

1950-51

Team	P	W	D	L	F	A	Pts
Brereton Social	34	24	5	5	114	55	53
Walsall Trinity	34	24	2	8	114	47	50
Shelfield Athletic	34	23	3	8	95	40	49
Bloxwich Strollers	34	20	6	8	126	68	46
Walsall Wood	34	18	9	7	91	48	45
Hednesford Reserves	34	18	3	13	100	75	39
Newport Town	34	14	9	11	66	73	37
Tamworth Reserves	34	16	4	14	70	83	36
Sutton Town Reserves	34	14	4	16	65	61	32
Baddesley Liberals	34	13	5	16	86	91	31
West Bromwich Albion "B"	34	10	10	14	81	72	30
Bilston Reserves	34	12	6	16	58	80	30
Ogley Hay	34	13	3	18	62	85	29
Chase Terrace United	34	13	2	19	82	105	28
Sutton Coldfield Athletic	34	12	2	20	80	107	26
Rugeley W.M.C.	34	7	6	21	53	118	20
Cannock Chase Colliery	34	7	6	21	38	98	20
Beaudesert Sports	34	6	2	26	60	139	14
		264			87 261 1441 1445		615

Walsall Wood moved to the Worcestershire Combination and Bilston Reserves also left the league. Stafford Rangers Reserves joined.

1951-52

Team	P	W	D	L	F	A	Pts
Shelfield Athletic	32	23	6	3	89	30	52
Bloxwich Strollers	32	24	4	4	98	34	52
Walsall Trinity	32	20	7	5	115	51	47
Sutton Coldfield Athletic	32	16	8	8	84	58	40
Baddesley Liberals	32	15	7	10	99	74	37
Newport Town	32	15	6	11	85	69	36
West Bromwich Albion "B"	32	15	4	13	79	56	34
Ogley Hay	32	13	8	11	55	61	34
Hednesford Reserves	32	13	8	11	63	71	34
Brereton Social	32	12	5	15	57	72	29
Stafford Rangers Reserves	32	11	5	16	72	82	27
Cannock Chase Colliery	32	11	3	18	66	87	25
Rugeley W.M.C.	32	12	1	19	60	91	25
Sutton Town Reserves	32	10	5	17	60	99	25
Tamworth Reserves	32	6	10	16	64	92	22
Chase Terrace United	32	9	4	19	57	105	22
Beaudesert Sports	32	2	4	26	38	79	8
		227			95 222 1241 1211		549

Bloxwich Strollers moved to the Birmingham & District League and were replaced by their reserves. Newport Town and Sutton Town Reserves also both left the league. Armitage, Atherstone Town Reserves and Nuneaton Borough Reserves all joined.

Staffordshire County League (South) 1952-1957

1952-53

Shelfield Athletic	34	26	4	4	128	41	56
Stafford Rangers Reserves	34	24	5	5	101	59	53
Walsall Trinity	34	20	10	4	103	42	50
Baddesley Liberals	32	21	3	8	121	39	45
West Bromwich Albion "B"	34	19	7	8	90	47	45
Nuneaton Borough Reserves	34	19	3	12	76	53	41
Armitage	34	18	3	13	93	96	39
Brereton Social	34	16	6	12	73	67	38
Sutton Coldfield Athletic	34	17	0	17	88	107	34
Rugeley W.M.C.	34	14	2	18	80	106	30
Bloxwich Strollers Reserves	31	14	1	16	58	80	29
Beaudesert Sports	34	11	5	18	49	88	27
Tamworth Reserves	33	12	1	20	83	103	25
Chase Terrace United	34	11	2	21	75	87	24
Hednesford Reserves	34	10	4	20	68	93	24
Ogley Hay	34	9	3	22	59	124	21
Atherstone Town Reserves	34	9	3	22	56	123	21
Cannock Chase Colliery	33	3	3	27	31	117	9
	605	273	65	267	1432	1472	611

The outstanding games were not played.
Atherstone Town Reserves and Beaudesert Sports both left the league.
Walsall "A" joined from the Birmingham & District League while Burton Albion Reserves and Goodyears also joined.

1953-54

Shelfield Athletic	36	31	4	1	133	44	66
Baddesley Liberals	36	27	3	6	139	61	57
Goodyears	36	26	4	6	133	52	56
Walsall Trinity	36	23	5	8	121	71	51
Stafford Rangers Reserves	36	20	6	10	94	57	46
Armitage	36	18	4	14	91	78	40
Nuneaton Borough Reserves	36	17	5	14	80	60	39
Burton Albion Reserves	36	17	4	15	77	73	38
Rugeley W.M.C.	36	14	8	14	84	90	36
Brereton Social	36	15	3	18	85	80	33
Tamworth Reserves	36	14	5	17	88	95	33
Hednesford Reserves	35	12	4	19	95	107	28
West Bromwich Albion "B"	36	10	8	18	69	80	28
Cannock Chase Colliery	36	12	4	20	83	100	28
Ogley Hay	36	11	4	21	78	97	26
Walsall "A"	36	11	4	21	82	99	26
Sutton Coldfield Athletic	36	11	4	21	72	112	26
Bloxwich Strollers Reserves	36	6	5	25	59	145	17
Chase Terrace United	36	5	3	28	71	122	13
	683	300	87	296	1734	1623	687

Baddesley Liberals, Nuneaton Borough Reserves, Sutton Coldfield Athletic and Walsall "A" left the league. Rugeley W.M.C. also left and Rugeley Villa joined. Lichfield St. Chads also joined.

1954-55

Shelfield Athletic	30	28	2	0	131	27	58
Goodyears	30	17	6	7	79	50	40
Walsall Trinity	30	17	3	10	84	54	37
Armitage	30	17	3	10	79	67	37
Tamworth Reserves	30	15	5	10	77	54	35
West Bromwich Albion "B"	30	14	6	10	60	62	34
Stafford Rangers Reserves	30	15	2	13	65	63	32
Ogley Hay	30	12	4	14	70	72	28
Rugeley Villa	30	10	8	12	53	77	28
Burton Albion Reserves	30	12	2	16	68	68	26
Brereton Social	30	10	5	15	61	70	25
Chase Terrace United	30	10	5	15	56	96	25
Lichfield St. Chads	30	7	7	16	63	71	21
Hednesford Reserves	30	7	6	17	60	84	20
Cannock Chase Colliery	30	7	5	18	58	103	19
Bloxwich Strollers Reserves	30	8	0	22	38	88	16
	206	69	205	1102	1106	481	

Burton Albion Reserves, Hednesford Reserves and West Bromwich Albion "B" all left the league. Baddesley Colliery, Hadley Castle Works, Sutton Town Reserves, Walsall "A" and Wrockwardine Wood all joined.

1955-56

Shelfield Athletic	34	31	1	2	165	39	63
Walsall Trinity	34	28	3	3	134	55	59
Stafford Rangers Reserves	34	21	3	10	106	67	45
Hadley Castle Works	34	20	3	11	109	66	43
Armitage	34	19	2	13	93	80	40
Tamworth Reserves	34	17	5	12	89	81	39
Wrockwardine Wood	34	18	3	13	83	86	39
Brereton Social	34	14	7	13	94	93	35
Rugeley Villa	34	13	8	13	90	82	34
Ogley Hay	34	13	7	14	98	88	33
Lichfield St. Chads	34	15	3	16	109	110	33
Goodyears	34	13	6	15	75	89	32
Baddesley Colliery	34	12	4	18	91	111	28
Cannock Chase Colliery	34	11	5	18	67	81	27
Walsall "A"	34	9	4	21	56	92	22
Sutton Town Reserves	34	7	4	23	56	139	18
Bloxwich Strollers Reserves	34	7	3	24	45	115	17
Chase Terrace United	34	5	2	27	55	117	12
		273	73	266	1615	1591	619

Hadley Castle Works, Sutton Town Reserves and Wrockwardine Wood all left the league. Bloxwich Strollers Reserves also left but their first team had resigned from the Birmingham & District League during January 1956 and they joined the new Second Division of the Staffordshire County League (South), along with 7 other clubs – Blakenall, Brereton Colliery, Brookside Rangers, Pelsall Cricket & Sports, Penkridge Town, Rushall Olympic and Walsall Wood Reserves.

1956-57

Division One

Armitage	26	21	1	4	99	37	43
Shelfield Athletic	26	20	1	5	109	37	41
Baddesley Colliery	26	18	2	6	93	46	38
Stafford Rangers Reserves	26	16	3	7	78	45	35
Walsall Trinity	26	15	2	9	90	42	32
Rugeley Villa	26	12	5	9	75	65	29
Goodyears	26	12	5	9	88	71	29
Tamworth Reserves	26	12	3	11	74	78	27
Brereton Social	26	10	4	12	90	68	24
Walsall "A"	26	9	3	14	82	72	21
Ogley Hay	26	8	4	14	61	88	20
Lichfield St. Chads	26	4	3	19	48	103	11
Cannock Chase Colliery	26	4	1	21	35	131	9
Chase Terrace United	26	1	3	22	31	110	5
					1053	993	

Division Two

Rushall Olympic	14	13	0	1	66	21	26
Blakenall	14	9	0	5	60	33	18
Penkridge Town	14	9	0	5	64	42	18
Brookside Rangers	14	7	2	5	45	31	16
Pelsall Cricket & Sports	14	6	1	7	44	57	13
Brereton Colliery	14	4	2	8	28	64	10
Bloxwich Strollers	14	3	0	11	31	65	6
Walsall Wood Reserves	14	1	3	10	25	52	5
					363	365	

Bloxwich Strollers, Brereton Colliery, Brookside Rangers, Pelsall Cricket & Sports and Penkridge Town all left the league.

Darlaston Reserves joined and the two divisions merged so that the league reverted to a single division.

Staffordshire County League (South) 1957-1963

1957-58

Shelfield Athletic	34	30	3	1	159	39	63
Rushall Olympic	34	22	7	5	127	60	51
Walsall Trinity	34	22	5	7	113	57	49
Armitage	34	17	11	6	118	70	45
Stafford Rangers Reserves	34	19	6	9	104	63	44
Goodyears	34	17	8	9	120	70	42
Tamworth Reserves	34	17	5	12	94	64	39
Brereton Social	34	15	6	13	120	75	36
Rugeley Villa	34	15	6	13	109	76	36
Blakenall	34	16	3	15	98	89	35
Walsall Wood Reserves	34	14	6	14	73	84	34
Walsall "A"	34	12	4	18	77	104	28
Ogley Hay	34	7	10	17	73	95	24
Baddesley Colliery	34	10	2	22	79	121	22
Darlaston Reserves	34	8	4	22	68	140	20
Cannock Chase Colliery	34	5	5	24	46	140	15
Lichfield St. Chads	34	3	8	23	52	116	14
Chase Terrace United	34	5	2	27	45	163	12
		254	101	257	1675	1626	609

Shelfield Athletic moved to the Worcestershire Combination and were replaced by their reserves. Baddesley Colliery, Cannock Chase Colliery and Lichfield St. Chads left the league. English Electric and Old Woden joined.

1958-59

Stafford Rangers Reserves	32	24	4	4	107	48	52
Blakenall	32	21	9	2	132	55	51
Rushall Olympic	32	23	3	6	115	61	49
Armitage	31	22	4	5	132	68	48
Walsall "A"	32	21	5	6	85	47	47
Ogley Hay	32	17	5	10	107	78	39
Walsall Trinity	32	17	3	12	77	54	37
Tamworth Reserves	31	15	2	14	67	66	32
Brereton Social	32	14	2	16	78	83	30
English Electric	32	13	3	16	91	95	29
Goodyears	32	12	3	17	65	94	27
Walsall Wood Reserves	32	9	7	16	56	70	25
Old Woden	32	9	1	22	69	115	19
Rugeley Villa	32	7	2	23	66	120	16
Darlaston Reserves	32	5	4	23	46	106	14
Chase Terrace United	32	5	4	23	68	129	14
Shelfield Athletic Reserves	32	4	6	22	53	121	14
		238	67	237	1414	1410	543

One game was not played.
Darlaston Reserves, Shelfield Athletic Reserves and Stafford Rangers Reserves all left the league. Metro Old Park and Pelsall Sports both joined.

1959-60

Brereton Social	30	24	2	4	137	52	50
Rushall Olympic	30	22	4	4	91	49	48
Chase Terrace United	30	21	4	5	88	45	46
Blakenall	30	20	5	5	108	50	45
Armitage	30	17	4	9	113	57	38
Pelsall Sports	29	15	4	10	81	72	34
Ogley Hay	30	14	2	14	85	71	30
Walsall "A"	30	14	1	15	68	62	29
Metro Old Park	30	12	3	15	58	62	27
Rugeley Villa	30	10	5	15	46	65	25
Tamworth Reserves	30	10	3	17	84	77	23
English Electric	30	8	7	15	68	98	23
Walsall Trinity	30	8	3	19	55	78	19
Old Woden	30	6	4	20	50	105	16
Walsall Wood Reserves	30	6	1	23	53	123	13
Goodyears	29	5	2	22	41	88	12
					1226	1154	

One game was not played.
Blakenall moved to the Worcestershire Combination and were replaced by their reserves. Goodyears and Old Woden also both left the league. Stafford Rangers Reserves joined.

1960-61

Rushall Olympic	28	24	4	0	130	28	52
Brereton Social	28	16	6	6	104	50	38
Pelsall Sports	28	18	2	8	95	47	38
Stafford Rangers Reserves	28	14	7	7	72	54	35
Chase Terrace United	28	13	7	8	81	77	33
English Electric	28	14	4	10	84	65	32
Walsall "A"	28	13	6	9	83	72	32
Metro Old Park	28	12	7	9	61	72	31
Armitage	28	14	2	12	91	55	30
Blakenall Reserves	28	10	4	14	64	78	24
Walsall Trinity	28	9	5	14	64	91	23
Rugeley Villa	28	8	2	18	48	57	18
Tamworth Reserves	28	9	0	19	68	90	18
Walsall Wood Reserves	28	4	2	22	34	87	10
Ogley Hay	28	2	3	23	37	106	7
		180	61	179	1116	1029	421

Blakenall Reserves and Walsall Wood Reserves both moved to the Worcestershire Combination while Ogley Hay also left the league. Chase Terrace Old Scholars and Hednesford Reserves both joined. Pelsall Sports reformed as Pelsall Villa.

1961-62

Rushall Olympic	26	21	2	3	85	31	44
Brereton Social	26	19	5	2	106	47	43
Walsall "A"	26	18	1	7	73	35	37
Stafford Rangers Reserves	26	16	5	5	62	38	37
Armitage	26	16	3	7	82	54	35
Metro Old Park	26	12	3	11	61	55	27
English Electric	26	11	5	10	58	37	27
Chase Terrace Old Scholars	26	10	2	14	64	68	22
Pelsall Villa	26	8	5	13	53	58	21
Tamworth Reserves	26	7	4	15	53	77	18
Walsall Trinity	26	6	3	17	50	84	15
Chase Terrace United	26	5	3	18	49	85	13
Rugeley Villa	26	5	2	19	40	75	12
Hednesford Reserves	26	2	6	18	46	86	10
		156	49	159	882	830	361

Stafford Rangers Reserves left the league and Rickerscote joined.

1962-63

Rushall Olympic	26	20	5	1	96	34	45
Brereton Social	26	18	2	6	96	48	38
Metro Old Park	26	16	5	5	73	45	37
Armitage	26	14	4	8	67	48	32
Chase Terrace Old Scholars	26	13	5	8	77	56	31
Hednesford Reserves	26	10	7	9	76	54	27
Pelsall Villa	26	11	4	11	66	54	26
Walsall "A"	26	10	4	12	51	52	24
Walsall Trinity	26	8	6	12	62	75	22
Chase Terrace United	26	9	3	14	61	71	21
English Electric	26	8	4	14	49	61	20
Rickerscote	26	7	4	15	51	72	18
Tamworth Reserves	26	7	4	15	54	95	18
Rugeley Villa	26	1	3	22	43	136	5
					922	901	

Rickerscote and Rugeley Villa both left the league.
Bilston Reserves, Dudley Town Reserves, Etching Hill Athletic, North Warwick Colliery, Oxley and Stafford Town all joined.

Staffordshire County League (South) 1963-1968

1963-64

Hednesford Reserves	34	24	6	4	89	47	54
Metro Old Park	34	21	8	5	82	58	50
Rushall Olympic	34	23	3	8	116	43	49
Oxley	34	20	4	10	91	59	44
Chase Terrace Old Scholars	34	19	4	11	93	75	42
Pelsall Villa	34	16	8	10	93	60	40
Tamworth Reserves	34	13	9	12	59	61	35
Bilston Reserves	34	16	2	16	80	77	34
Walsall Trinity	34	14	3	17	76	76	31
Dudley Town Reserves	34	10	11	13	63	65	31
Brereton Social	34	13	5	16	87	94	31
Armitage	34	13	4	17	63	77	30
Chase Terrace United	34	11	4	19	75	93	26
English Electric	34	11	4	19	69	113	26
North Warwick Colliery	34	10	5	19	68	107	25
Etching Hill Athletic	34	9	5	20	49	88	23
Walsall "A"	34	8	6	20	49	83	22
Stafford Town	34	9	3	22	56	82	21
					260	258	614

Metro Old Park, North Warwick Colliery and Walsall "A" all left the league.
Beaudesert, Blackheath Town and Causeway Green Swifts all joined.
Second Division re-formed with 8 clubs, 6 of whom were the reserve sides of First Division clubs – Blackheath Town, Chase Terrace Old Scholars, English Electric, Etching Hill Athletic, Pelsall Villa and Stafford Town. The other 2 clubs were Bentley Estate and Trinity P.E..

1964-65

Division One

Rushall Olympic	34	26	4	4	95	34	56
Oxley	34	27	1	6	128	48	55
Hednesford Reserves	34	23	5	6	132	38	51
Chase Terrace Old Scholars	34	20	3	11	99	59	43
Brereton Social	34	17	7	10	96	75	41
Bilston Reserves	34	14	8	12	77	72	36
Pelsall Villa	34	16	2	16	63	88	34
Dudley Town Reserves	34	14	5	15	113	88	33
Tamworth Reserves	34	15	3	16	72	78	33
Walsall Trinity	34	11	10	13	71	71	32
Etching Hill Athletic	34	15	2	17	75	82	32
Blackheath Town	34	14	5	15	82	84	33
Armitage	34	13	4	17	86	89	30
Chase Terrace United	34	11	4	19	75	92	26
Stafford Town	34	7	9	18	75	109	23
English Electric	34	7	9	18	55	103	23
Beaudesert	34	8	5	21	72	139	21
Causeway Green Swifts	34	4	2	28	52	144	10
					1518	1493	

Bilston Reserves, Causeway Green Swifts, English Electric, Dudley Town Reserves and Hednesford Reserves all left the league. Kingston joined and Bentley Estate and Trinity P.E. were both promoted from Division Two after which Division Two closed down. Bentley Estate changed their name to Bentley.

Division Two

Bentley Estate	14	12	2	0	81	20	26
Trinity P.E.	14	7	4	3	53	29	18
Chase Terrace Old Scholars Reserves	14	8	2	4	51	31	18
English Electric Reserves	14	7	3	4	39	25	17
Pelsall Villa Reserves	14	5	3	6	37	39	13
Etching Hill Athletic Reserves	14	3	6	5	36	40	12
Blackheath Town Reserves	14	3	1	10	31	58	7
Stafford Town Reserves	14	2	0	12	15	98	4
					47	21	44	343	340	115

1965-66

Kingston	30	28	1	1	120	34	57
Rushall Olympic	30	22	3	5	110	42	47
Blackheath Town	30	19	4	7	79	43	42
Oxley	30	18	3	9	91	62	39
Walsall Trinity	30	17	5	8	66	53	39
Chase Terrace Old Scholars	30	12	9	9	64	55	33
Bentley	30	11	5	14	75	63	27
Stafford Town	30	11	5	14	59	78	27
Etching Hill Athletic	30	11	5	14	60	81	27
Brereton Social	30	12	2	16	73	66	26
Pelsall Villa	30	9	7	14	69	80	25
Armitage	30	8	7	15	57	91	23
Chase Terrace United	30	8	4	18	47	89	20
Tamworth Reserves	30	6	5	19	64	92	17
Trinity P.E.	30	7	3	20	52	112	17
Beaudesert	30	5	4	21	56	94	14
					1142	1135	

Bentley and Tamworth Reserves both left the league.
Darlaston Amateurs, Rising Brook and Tipton Sports all joined.

1966-67

Oxley	32	23	3	6	107	41	49
Rushall Olympic	32	22	2	8	88	41	46
Kingston	32	22	2	8	87	48	46
Chase Terrace Old Scholars	32	18	5	9	64	54	41
Walsall Trinity	32	18	4	10	84	58	40
Brereton Social	32	17	4	11	83	64	38
Darlaston Amateurs	32	15	8	9	83	67	38
Armitage	32	14	9	9	82	57	37
Tipton Sports	32	13	6	13	69	79	32
Pelsall Villa	32	12	4	16	59	64	28
Blackheath Town	32	13	3	16	73	78	29
Etching Hill Athletic	32	9	9	14	68	83	27
Stafford Town	32	10	4	18	52	82	24
Chase Terrace United	32	11	2	19	52	83	24
Trinity P.E.	32	6	5	21	40	96	17
Rising Brook	32	6	5	21	52	104	17
Beaudesert	32	5	1	26	40	92	11
					1183	1191	

Beaudesert, Stafford Town, Tipton Sports and Trinity P.E. all left the league.
Ashmore Park, Oldswinford and St. Georges all joined.

1967-68

Oxley	30	20	5	5	90	29	45
Rushall Olympic	30	21	2	7	87	44	44
Brereton Social	30	18	6	6	78	46	42
Walsall Trinity	30	19	2	9	81	38	40
Rising Brook	30	17	3	10	72	52	37
Kingston	30	14	7	9	67	45	35
Oldswinford	30	15	5	10	75	51	35
Chase Terrace Old Scholars	30	14	6	10	55	53	34
Pelsall Villa	30	13	5	12	69	65	31
Darlaston Amateurs	30	12	7	11	63	68	31
Armitage	30	11	6	13	61	57	28
Ashmore Park	30	10	5	15	56	60	25
Chase Terrace United	30	8	2	20	45	67	18
Blackheath Town	30	8	2	20	46	82	18
Etching Hill Athletic	30	4	3	23	42	123	11
St. Georges	30	2	2	26	38	123	6
					1033	1005	

Brereton Social and Oxley both moved to the West Midlands Regional League. Chase Terrace United, Etching Hill Athletic and St. Georges also left the league. Kingswinford United, Lichfield, Staffordshire Police, Trinity St. George and Willenhall Town all joined.

Staffordshire County League (South) 1968-1972

1968-69

Kingswinford United	30	21	5	4	72	30	47
Pelsall Villa	30	18	7	5	63	31	43
Blackheath Town	30	17	7	6	84	42	41
Staffordshire Police	30	16	5	9	52	30	37
Armitage	30	16	4	10	67	53	36
Rushall Olympic	30	16	1	13	70	54	33
Willenhall Town	30	14	5	11	52	49	33
Walsall Trinity	30	12	7	11	61	55	31
Chase Terrace Old Scholars	30	13	7	10	56	56	33
Oldswinford	30	12	6	12	59	47	30
Darlaston Amateurs	30	12	6	12	61	61	30
Ashmore Park	30	10	5	15	44	61	25
Lichfield	30	7	11	12	41	49	25
Rising Brook	30	8	5	17	45	76	21
Kingston	30	3	3	24	26	89	9
Trinity St. George	30	2	2	26	33	103	6

Ashmore Park, Kingston and Trinity St. George all left the league.
Great Wyrley Wednesday, Newport Athletic and West Midlands Constabulary all joined. Staffordshire Police changed their name to Staffordshire & Stoke Police.
The Second Division was re-formed with 14 founder members – Aldridge Athletic, B.R.D. Sports, Burntwood Institute, Kings Hill Crowns, Little Bloxwich, New Invention Sports, Norton Canes Old Boys, Orchard, Park Rangers, Rising Brook Reserves, Walsall Trinity Reserves, Walsall Wood Reserves, Whittington Villa and Willenhall Town Reserves.

1969-70

From 1970 onwards, coverage of the league became increasingly scarce. Its fixtures often continued for a week or more after most other leagues had finished and beyond the date when local papers were printing results. As a result, complete tables were often not found nor was it clear whether outstanding games were ever played. Where the tables below are incomplete, the latest found is given together with its publication date.

Promoted clubs are in bold type, relegated clubs are in bold italics.

Division One (15th May 1970)

Kingswinford United	30	22	3	5	91	35	47
Oldswinford	28	22	1	5	85	38	45
Staffordshire & Stoke Police	30	19	7	4	61	34	40
Armitage	30	19	5	6	74	37	43
Great Wyrley Wednesday	28	15	4	9	69	52	34
Chase Terrace Old Scholars	29	14	5	10	54	49	33
West Midlands Constabulary	30	13	2	15	56	51	28
Rising Brook	30	12	4	14	52	53	28
Lichfield	30	10	6	14	56	64	26
Rushall Olympic	30	9	8	13	52	63	26
Pelsall Villa	30	10	4	16	53	80	24
Darlaston Amateurs	30	8	7	15	47	72	23
Walsall Trinity	26	7	6	13	47	68	20
Willenhall Town	29	6	7	16	37	56	19
Newport Athletic	30	8	3	19	49	88	19
Blackheath Town	30	4	6	20	29	70	14
					198	194	474

Division Two (15th May 1970)

Burntwood Institute	26	19	7	0	105	21	45
Little Bloxwich	25	16	5	4	84	32	37
New Invention Sports	26	16	2	8	69	40	34
Aldridge Athletic	26	14	6	6	56	40	34
B.R.D. Sports	26	13	6	7	60	43	32
Park Rangers	23	13	5	5	52	29	31
Whittington Villa	26	14	3	9	55	52	31
Orchard	26	11	7	8	51	40	29
Norton Canes Old Boys	23	7	5	11	45	75	19
Walsall Wood Reserves	26	6	3	17	38	62	15
Walsall Trinity Reserves	24	4	6	14	37	78	14
Willenhall Town Reserves	26	5	3	18	25	71	13
Kings Hill Crowns	25	6	1	18	53	83	13
Rising Brook Reserves	26	3	1	22	26	90	7

B.R.D. Sports, Kings Hill Crowns, Norton Canes Old Boys, Orchard and Walsall Trinity Reserves all left the league.
Boney Hay Albion, Brownhills Institute, Darlaston Amateurs Reserves, Great Wyrley Wednesday Reserves, John Harper, Lichfield Reserves, R.A.F. Stafford, Walsall "A" and Wednesbury Town all joined.

1970-71

Division One (28th May 1971)

Kingswinford United	29	22	4	3	86	27	48
Great Wyrley Wednesday	30	21	4	5	85	42	46
Armitage	30	17	8	5	74	46	42
Staffordshire & Stoke Police	30	16	8	6	62	28	40
Rushall Olympic	30	16	4	10	60	47	36
Chase Terrace Old Scholars	29	12	10	7	59	35	34
Oldswinford	30	13	6	11	71	49	32
Rising Brook	30	13	6	11	62	53	32
Lichfield	30	12	6	12	61	55	30
Willenhall Town	30	10	8	12	41	45	28
Pelsall Villa	30	11	4	15	49	57	26
Newport Athletic	30	9	6	15	54	62	24
West Midlands Constabulary	30	8	5	17	56	85	21
Darlaston Amateurs	30	7	5	18	54	73	19
Blackheath Town	30	6	4	20	52	106	16
Walsall Trinity	**30**	**1**	**2**	**27**	**34**	**146**	**4**

Armitage moved to the West Midlands Regional League.
G.E.C. Witton joined.

Division Two (28th May 1971)

Little Bloxwich	32	27	3	2	113	21	57
Burntwood Institute	**33**	**24**	**5**	**4**	**119**	**40**	**53**
Park Rangers	33	22	6	5	99	40	50
Great Wyrley Wednesday Reserves	33	20	4	9	99	48	44
Brownhills Institute	34	16	9	9	84	51	41
Aldridge Athletic	34	16	7	11	76	64	39
Walsall "A"	34	15	5	14	73	65	35
Darlaston Amateurs Reserves	33	15	3	15	80	66	33
New Invention Sports	33	13	7	13	69	80	33
Boney Hay Albion	33	13	6	14	50	75	32
John Harper	34	14	3	17	73	65	31
Walsall Wood Reserves	34	12	6	16	64	92	30
Rising Brook Reserves	34	12	5	17	53	67	29
Whittington Villa	34	9	9	16	56	65	27
Willenhall Town Reserves	34	8	7	19	49	61	23
R.A.F. Stafford	33	9	3	21	61	87	21
Lichfield Reserves	31	7	6	18	55	80	20
Wednesbury Town	34	0	2	32	18	224	2

Darlaston Amateurs Reserves, John Harper, New Invention Sports, Park Rangers, R.A.F. Stafford and Wednesbury Town all left the league. Bolehall Swifts, Ogley Hay, Rowley Regis and Wednesfield Town all joined.

1971-72

Division One

Great Wyrley Wednesday	30	23	4	3	84	30	50
Rising Brook	30	19	6	5	74	42	44
Staffordshire & Stoke Police	30	18	6	6	77	37	42
Rushall Olympic	30	16	4	10	70	54	36
Kingswinford United	30	15	5	10	70	39	35
Chase Terrace Old Scholars	30	14	5	11	76	49	33
Newport Athletic	30	12	7	11	67	50	31
Oldswinford	30	13	5	12	64	65	31
Pelsall Villa	30	11	8	11	60	70	30
Willenhall Town	30	11	5	14	51	55	27
Darlaston Amateurs	30	8	9	13	51	71	25
Burntwood Institute	30	8	8	14	52	67	24
West Midlands Constabulary	30	9	5	16	51	83	23
Lichfield	30	9	4	17	50	66	22
G.E.C. Witton	30	2	10	18	35	85	14
Blackheath Town	30	5	3	22	25	94	13

Staffordshire County League (South) 1972-1974

Chase Terrace Old Scholars changed their name to Chasetown and moved to the West Midlands (Regional) League. Blackheath Town also left. Dudley St. James and Wrens Nest United both joined. Great Wyrley Wednesday changed their name to Great Wyrley and G.E.C. Witton changed their name to G.E.C. Social.

Division Two

Rowley Regis	30	22	5	3	73	23	49
Little Bloxwich	30	20	6	4	76	30	46
Ogley Hay	30	17	6	7	73	35	40
Wednesfield Town	30	17	6	7	84	42	40
Aldridge Athletic	30	17	4	9	77	47	38
Walsall Wood Reserves	30	16	3	11	51	36	35
Great Wyrley Wednesday Reserves	30	15	4	11	78	61	34
Walsall "A"	30	15	3	12	61	59	33
Rising Brook Reserves	30	9	7	14	47	48	25
Brownhills United	30	9	6	15	52	65	24
Boney Hay Albion	30	10	4	16	47	60	24
Willenhall Town Reserves	30	9	4	17	43	63	22
Bolehall Swifts	30	8	6	16	61	91	22
Whittington Villa	30	8	5	17	41	70	21
Walsall Trinity	30	7	3	20	50	116	17
Lichfield Reserves	30	3	4	23	31	99	10

Whittington Villa left the league.
G.E.C. Social Reserves, Joseph Lucas and Owenhills all joined.

1972-73

Division One

Staffordshire & Stoke Police	33	26	5	2	99	24	57
Oldswinford	34	24	3	7	94	36	51
Burntwood Institute	34	20	8	6	96	44	48
Kingswinford United	34	19	7	8	105	48	45
Little Bloxwich	34	17	11	6	76	39	45
Great Wyrley	34	15	9	10	81	60	39
Willenhall Town	34	16	6	12	66	54	38
Wrens Nest United	34	17	3	14	77	72	37
Rising Brook	34	14	8	12	97	48	36
Pelsall Villa	33	12	11	10	52	47	35
Rowley Regis	33	13	7	13	62	50	33
Dudley St. James	34	10	10	14	74	69	30
Lichfield	32	10	8	14	64	64	28
Darlaston Amateurs	33	9	9	15	71	68	27
Rushall Olympic	34	10	4	20	84	100	24
West Midlands Constabulary	34	7	4	23	59	111	18
G.E.C. Social	34	5	5	24	51	136	15
Newport Athletic	34	0	0	34	27	265	0

Three games were not played.
Staffordshire & Stoke Police moved to the West Midlands Regional League and Rowley Regis moved to the Midland Combination. G.E.C. Social, Little Bloxwich and Newport Athletic also left the league.
Fourways Rangers joined.

Division Two

Ogley Hay	30	25	3	2	99	31	53
Walsall Wood Reserves	30	18	8	4	65	35	44
Wednesfield Town	30	19	4	7	96	43	42
Owenhills	30	16	8	6	89	52	40
Bolehall Swifts	30	16	5	9	67	33	37
Willenhall Town Reserves	30	13	11	6	65	35	37
Aldridge Athletic	30	16	3	11	57	52	35
Rising Brook Reserves	30	13	7	10	57	36	33
Walsall "A"	30	11	5	14	72	63	27
Walsall Trinity	30	9	5	16	47	80	23
Boney Hay Albion	30	11	1	18	44	77	23
Brownhills United	30	8	5	17	48	66	21
Lichfield Reserves	30	8	5	17	48	78	21
Joseph Lucas	30	9	2	19	41	93	20
Great Wyrley Reserves	30	5	6	19	41	81	16
G.E.C. Social Reserves	30	2	4	24	32	113	8

G.E.C. Social Reserves left the league. Burntwood Swifts, Chasewood United, Fourways Rangers Reserves, Penkridge Town and Wednesfield Town Reserves joined.

1973-74

Division One

Oldswinford	34	26	6	2	90	35	58
Ogley Hay	34	22	8	4	80	31	52
Burntwood Institute	34	22	6	6	84	41	50
Rising Brook	34	20	4	10	76	48	44
Lichfield	34	18	7	9	52	39	43
Darlaston Amateurs	34	15	7	12	73	74	37
Willenhall Town	34	11	14	9	51	40	36
Great Wyrley	34	12	10	12	78	76	34
Bolehall Swifts	34	13	7	14	60	65	33
Rushall Olympic	34	14	4	16	77	69	32
Pelsall Villa	34	11	9	14	59	62	31
‡ **Owenhills**	**34**	**12**	**6**	**16**	**72**	**76**	**30**
Kingswinford United	34	9	7	18	44	58	25
Fourways Rangers	34	10	5	19	48	66	25
Dudley St. James	34	8	8	18	58	83	24
Wednesfield Town	34	9	5	20	52	77	23
West Midlands Constabulary	34	7	5	22	56	109	19
Wrens Nest United	34	5	6	23	48	109	16

‡ Owenhills were relegated as their ground did not meet new standards for top division clubs.
Dudley St. James and Ogley Hay both left the league while Oldswinford moved to the Redditch & South Warwickshire Sunday League as their ground did not meet new standards. After finding a new ground, Oldswinford moved to the West Midlands Regional League in 1975. West Midlands Constabulary merged with Birmingham City Police of the Midland Combination to form West Midlands Police. Their first team continued in the Midland Combination and their reserves replaced West Midlands Constabulary in the Staffordshire County League (South). West Midlands College and Gornal Athletic Reserves both joined.
Division One was renamed the Premier Division and Division Two was renamed Division One.

Division Two

Walsall "A"	30	25	4	1	103	25	54
Brownhills United	30	22	5	3	94	28	49
Aldridge Athletic	30	18	4	8	79	38	40
Rising Brook Reserves	30	16	6	8	70	46	38
Penkridge Town	30	16	4	10	66	41	36
Walsall Trinity	30	13	8	9	60	55	34
Willenhall Town Reserves	30	12	8	10	61	43	32
Great Wyrley Reserves	30	13	4	13	55	69	30
Boney Hay Albion	30	10	9	11	63	58	29
Burntwood Swifts	30	10	8	12	67	67	28
Wednesfield Town Reserves	30	10	4	16	46	62	24
Walsall Wood Reserves	30	8	6	16	46	83	22
Lichfield Reserves	30	9	3	18	45	64	21
Fourways Rangers Reserves	30	7	3	20	47	87	17
Chasewood United	30	6	4	20	40	79	13
Joseph Lucas	30	3	4	23	35	132	10

Chasewood United had 3 points deducted.
Chasewood United, Joseph Lucas and Walsall "A" all left the league.
Goscote, Lichfield Athletic, Walsall Amateurs and Walsall Pegasus all joined.

1974-75
Premier Division

Willenhall Town	30	23	5	2	94	20	51
Rising Brook	30	19	9	2	74	26	47
Pelsall Villa	30	20	6	4	66	29	46
Rushall Olympic	30	19	4	7	76	44	42
Burntwood Institute	30	17	3	10	73	37	37
Lichfield	30	11	11	8	60	39	33
West Midlands College	30	13	6	11	54	63	32
Great Wyrley	30	13	3	14	68	56	29
West Midlands Police Reserves	30	11	6	13	44	59	28
Kingswinford United	30	11	6	13	39	57	28
Darlaston Amateurs	30	6	9	15	46	65	21
Fourways Rangers	30	6	8	16	42	67	20
Wednesfield Town	30	6	7	17	45	77	19
Gornal Athletic Reserves	30	6	6	18	44	73	18
Bolehall Swifts	30	6	3	21	33	91	15
Wrens Nest United	30	5	4	21	42	97	14

Willenhall Town moved to the West Midlands Regional League and Gornal Athletic Reserves also left the league. Hall End Amateurs and Harrisons joined. Rising Brook changed their name to Stafford South End.

Division One (15th May 1975)

Walsall Amateurs	34	26	1	7	118	50	53
Aldridge Athletic	34	20	9	5	68	38	49
Brownhills United	29	19	5	5	89	26	43
Willenhall Town Reserves	31	20	3	8	81	38	43
Walsall Pegasus	34	18	6	10	90	64	42
Rising Brook Reserves	33	17	6	10	66	51	40
Penkridge Town	31	16	7	8	62	39	39
Burntwood Swifts	34	15	5	14	73	68	35
Lichfield Athletic	34	13	6	15	63	54	32
Boney Hay Albion	33	12	8	13	52	75	32
# Owenhills	28	12	7	9	60	49	31
Great Wyrley Reserves	34	12	6	16	62	75	30
Walsall Trinity	34	9	8	17	54	79	26
Fourways Rangers Reserves	34	9	7	18	44	89	25
Goscote	33	7	7	19	50	77	21
Wednesfield Town Reserves	34	8	4	22	51	123	20
Walsall Wood Reserves	33	6	7	20	42	74	19
Lichfield Reserves	33	4	5	24	42	93	13

Owenhills were omitted from the table published on 15th May. The previous table found was a month earlier, dated 17th April, and the record shown above is as it was on that date.

Walsall Trinity, Walsall Wood Reserves and Wednesfield Town Reserves all left the league. G.E.C. Measurements joined, Heath Hayes Cons. and Warley Reserves all joined.

1975-76
Premier Division (14th May 1976)

Lichfield	30	23	6	1	81	14	52
Burntwood Institute	32	22	5	5	97	33	49
Stafford South End	29	22	2	5	83	23	46
Harrisons	32	15	8	9	81	57	38
West Midlands Police Reserves	32	17	3	12	67	44	37
Fourways Rangers	29	15	6	8	58	52	36
Great Wyrley	27	16	3	8	65	37	35
Kingswinford United	31	12	7	12	62	61	31
Pelsall Villa	31	13	4	14	67	63	30
Hall End Amateurs	32	11	8	13	49	58	30
Rushall Olympic	32	9	8	15	48	68	26
Darlaston Amateurs	32	9	5	18	54	73	23
Lichfield Athletic	32	10	3	19	55	77	23
West Midlands College	30	7	8	15	55	85	22
Wednesfield Town	31	8	5	18	73	78	21
Bolehall Swifts	32	8	5	19	49	78	21
Wrens Nest United	30	1	4	27	25	168	6

Burntwood Institute and Lichfield both moved to the West Midlands Regional League, West Midlands Police Reserves moved to the Midland Combination and Wrens Nest United also left the league. Aston University and Rising Brook both joined.

Division One (14th May 1976)

Penkridge Town	32	24	5	3	96	36	53
Willenhall Town Reserves	31	19	5	7	68	35	43
Walsall Amateurs	30	20	2	8	89	45	42
Heath Hayes Cons.	32	17	7	8	66	41	41
G.E.C. Measurements	30	16	8	6	61	31	40
Stafford South End Reserves	31	18	4	9	72	47	40
Warley Reserves	31	15	4	12	47	41	34
Walsall Pegasus	27	15	3	9	89	42	33
Aldridge Athletic	32	13	7	12	54	51	33
Brownhills United	31	11	6	14	50	55	28
Burntwood Swifts	32	11	4	17	50	70	26
Great Wyrley Reserves	30	10	5	15	68	74	25
Owenhills	29	8	3	18	38	71	19
Goscote	30	8	3	19	35	70	19
Lichfield Reserves	32	7	5	20	43	95	19
Fourways Rangers Reserves	31	6	3	22	40	102	15
Boney Hay Albion	31	5	2	24	29	89	12

Boney Hay Albion and Owenhills both left the league and Warley Reserves disbanded. Wolverhampton United were formed by the merger of Oxley of the West Midlands Regional League and Whitmore Old Boys of the Midland Combination. Their reserves joined Division One of the Staffordshire County League (South).

1976-77
Premier Division (20th May 1977)

Great Wyrley	30	23	3	4	91	32	49
Willenhall Town Reserves	30	19	7	4	68	32	45
Wednesfield Town	28	18	2	8	87	40	38
Aston University	30	16	6	8	51	46	38
Rising Brook	29	15	4	10	79	60	34
Pelsall Villa	30	12	9	9	57	49	33
Fourways Rangers	30	13	6	11	45	40	32
Stafford South End	29	11	6	12	54	46	28
Rushall Olympic	30	11	6	13	62	62	28
Lichfield Athletic	30	10	8	12	43	53	28
Harrisons	30	7	9	14	55	85	23
Hall End Amateurs	30	8	6	16	32	62	22
Kingswinford United	30	7	6	17	47	69	20
Darlaston Amateurs	28	5	10	13	35	53	20
West Midlands College	30	6	8	16	47	84	20
Bolehall Swifts	28	6	2	20	36	76	14

Stafford South End moved to the Midland Combination while Lichfield Athletic and Rising Brook also left the league. Birmingham University, Dudley College, McKechnie Sports and Northicote all joined. Darlaston Amateurs left and Darlaston Reserves joined.

Division One (20th May 1977)

Heath Hayes Cons.	25	20	3	2	94	23	43
Penkridge Town	26	18	6	2	80	18	42
Walsall Amateurs	25	19	2	4	79	27	40
Goscote	26	15	6	5	66	34	36
Wolverhampton United Reserves	26	14	3	9	57	37	31
Walsall Pegasus	26	12	4	10	48	42	28
G.E.C. Measurements	26	12	1	13	37	65	25
Aldridge Athletic	26	9	5	12	41	49	23
Brownhills United	26	9	4	13	53	51	22
Lichfield Reserves	26	8	4	14	43	53	20
Great Wyrley Reserves	26	7	4	15	33	78	18
Burntwood Swifts	26	8	1	17	61	77	17
Fourways Rangers Reserves	26	4	1	21	27	89	9
Stafford South End Reserves	26	2	4	20	35	111	8

Burntwood Swifts left the league and Harrisons Reserves joined.

Staffordshire County League (South) 1977-1980

1977-78

Premier Division (20th May 1978)

Birmingham University	29	22	2	5	89	39	46
Northicote	29	18	6	5	64	34	42
Great Wyrley	30	16	9	5	87	44	41
Willenhall Town Reserves	25	18	4	3	71	17	40
McKechnie Sports	32	17	4	11	70	64	38
Rushall Olympic	31	15	8	8	67	64	38
Darlaston Reserves	30	16	4	10	50	38	36
Kingswinford United	30	16	4	10	63	54	36
Aston University	28	11	6	11	44	55	28
Hall End Amateurs	32	9	8	15	56	69	26
Harrisons	30	10	4	16	47	61	24
Bolehall Swifts	31	8	7	16	42	65	23
Wednesfield Town	28	8	5	15	55	67	21
Dudley College	27	7	6	14	39	59	20
Fourways Rangers	30	6	7	17	40	51	19
Pelsall Villa	32	5	7	20	44	73	17
West Midlands College	32	4	3	25	26	100	11

Rushall Olympic and Willenhall Town Reserves both moved to the West Midlands Regional League. Mile Oak Rovers Reserves and Wednesfield Social Reserves both joined.

Division One (20th May 1978)

Brownhills United	24	19	2	3	67	32	40
Wolverhampton United Reserves	23	17	2	4	76	24	36
Heath Hayes Cons.	24	14	6	4	66	42	34
Aldridge Athletic	24	11	7	6	53	35	29
Walsall Amateurs	23	14	2	7	58	36	30
Penkridge Town	24	11	3	10	59	38	25
G.E.C. Measurements	24	12	1	11	59	58	25
Goscote	24	10	3	11	53	51	23
Lichfield Reserves	24	7	3	14	46	69	17
Harrisons Reserves	24	6	4	14	33	56	16
Great Wyrley Reserves	24	5	5	14	37	63	15
Walsall Pegasus	24	4	4	16	49	75	12
Fourways Rangers Reserves	24	3	2	19	28	105	8

Fourways Rangers Reserves, Harrisons Reserves and Walsall Amateurs all left the league. Bilston United, Bloxwich 77, Etching Hill Athletic and Stafford South End Reserves all joined.

1978-79

Premier Division (11th May 1979)

Great Wyrley	21	19	1	1	77	12	39
Wednesfield Social Reserves	27	15	9	3	66	34	39
Wolverhampton United Reserves	27	15	6	6	57	31	36
Birmingham University	28	16	4	8	67	50	36
Northicote	25	17	1	7	72	28	35
Mile Oak Rovers Reserves	25	16	3	6	64	31	35
Aston University	27	11	9	7	61	51	31
Kingswinford United	22	12	5	5	58	35	29
Darlaston Reserves	31	8	8	15	50	57	24
Dudley College	23	10	2	11	39	37	22
Fourways Rangers	25	7	8	10	48	50	22
McKechnie Sports	25	8	5	12	38	45	21
Hall End Amateurs	28	9	3	16	55	81	21
Pelsall Villa	29	5	8	16	44	80	18
Bolehall Swifts	28	7	4	17	39	82	18
Harrisons	28	6	3	19	40	93	15
Wednesfield Town	26	5	4	17	33	74	14
West Midlands College	23	4	5	14	30	67	13

Mile Oak Rovers Reserves moved to the Midland Combination while Darlaston Reserves, Hall End Amateurs, McKechnie Sports, Northicote and Wednesfield Social Reserves also left the league. Northpark United joined.

Division One (11th May 1979)

Penkridge Town	20	16	2	2	63	18	34
Goscote	20	15	1	4	74	28	31
Stafford F.C. Reserves	23	13	2	8	50	35	28
Bloxwich 77	21	15	1	5	53	26	31
Etching Hill Athletic	18	11	2	5	55	18	24
Aldridge Athletic	21	8	4	9	45	38	20
Bilston United	24	9	4	11	53	61	22
Brownhills United	20	8	2	10	45	40	18
Heath Hayes Cons.	21	9	4	8	44	30	22
Great Wyrley Reserves	17	7	0	10	32	42	14
Lichfield Reserves	16	4	1	11	22	34	9
G.E.C. Measurements	20	1	3	16	20	69	5
Walsall Pegasus	21	1	2	18	24	141	4

Bilston United moved to the Midland Combination and were replaced by their reserves. Brownhills United and Goscote also left the league. Aldridge Athletic Reserves, Brocton, Chasetown Reserves, Chasewood United, Hednesford Progressive, Northpark United Reserves and Oldswinford Reserves all joined.
G.E.C. Measurements changed their name to G.E.C. St. Leonards.

1979-80

Premier Division (25th April 1980)

Great Wyrley	25	19	4	2	68	28	42
Aldridge Athletic	24	17	2	5	51	26	36
Northpark United	20	14	3	3	41	19	31
Wolverhampton United Reserves	25	14	3	8	58	32	31
Stafford South End Reserves	28	13	4	11	53	45	30
Pelsall Villa	28	12	6	10	51	45	30
Birmingham University	27	11	6	10	60	54	28
Harrisons	26	11	5	10	58	60	27
Penkridge Town	26	10	4	12	53	50	24
Dudley College	25	9	3	13	42	54	21
Fourways Rangers	26	8	3	15	44	60	19
Wednesfield Town	25	6	6	13	35	50	18
Aston University	25	5	7	13	42	57	17
Bolehall Swifts	27	7	3	17	49	62	17
Kingswinford United	16	7	2	7	26	28	16
West Midlands College	25	3	5	17	31	94	11
					762	764	

Great Wyrley moved to the West Midlands Regional League and Bolehall Swifts moved to the Midland Combination. Stafford South End Reserves and West Midlands College also left the league. Bilston Reserves, New World, Oldbury United Reserves and Wheaton Aston all joined.

Division One (25th April 1980)

Hednesford Progressive	24	20	1	3	76	20	41
Etching Hill Athletic	25	18	2	5	64	19	38
Oldswinford Reserves	21	16	1	4	61	24	33
Bloxwich 77	22	13	6	3	72	22	32
Chasewood United	25	14	4	7	70	38	32
Northpark United Reserves	24	12	6	6	65	46	30
Brocton	25	13	2	10	55	41	28
Chasetown Reserves	27	11	1	15	54	53	23
Heath Hayes Cons.	25	9	5	11	54	60	23
Great Wyrley Reserves	22	8	2	12	40	54	18
Aldridge Athletic Reserves	28	6	5	17	48	78	17
G.E.C. St. Leonards	25	7	3	15	38	67	17
Walsall Pegasus	27	7	2	18	46	88	16
Lichfield Reserves	23	6	3	14	40	69	15
Bilston United Reserves	27	3	1	23	18	132	7
					801	811	

Bilston United Reserves left the league. Ashley, Boney Hay Albion, Deeleys Rovers, Peelers and Pelsall Cricket & Sports all joined. Bloxwich 77 changed their name to Bloxwich.

Staffordshire County League (South) 1980-1983

1980-81

Premier Division (29th May 1981)

New World	32	23	6	3	95	28	52
Wolverhampton United Reserves	32	21	4	7	70	39	46
Pelsall Villa	32	17	8	7	54	35	42
Northpark United	32	14	12	6	64	37	40
Aldridge Athletic	32	14	8	10	61	39	36
Bilston Reserves	32	14	7	11	56	37	35
Oldbury United Reserves	32	10	14	8	47	45	34
Fourways Rangers	32	11	11	10	41	40	33
Dudley College	32	13	6	13	57	60	32
Harrisons	32	12	7	13	73	61	31
Penkridge Town	32	11	9	12	56	58	31
Birmingham University	32	11	8	13	53	52	30
Kingswinford United	32	12	6	14	55	57	30
Wednesfield Town	32	9	7	16	47	61	25
Great Wyrley Reserves	32	4	11	17	41	75	19
Wheaton Aston	31	5	4	22	39	122	14
Aston University	31	2	8	21	36	99	12

Northpark United moved to the West Midlands Regional League while Aldridge Athletic, Aston University, Birmingham University, Dudley College, Great Wyrley Reserves, and Wolverhampton United Reserves also left. Ettingshall Holy Trinity joined. Following their promotion from Division One, Bloxwich changed their name to Bloxwich Town.

Division One (29th May 1981)

Hednesford Progressive	31	21	9	1	79	31	51
Bloxwich	33	22	7	4	91	30	51
Deeleys Rovers	34	23	7	4	105	37	53
Pelsall Cricket & Sports	33	22	6	5	86	41	50
Boney Hay Albion	34	22	6	6	86	42	50
Chasetown Reserves	33	21	3	9	82	51	45
Oldswinford Reserves	33	18	5	10	93	51	41
Ashley	34	14	8	12	59	56	36
Lichfield Reserves	34	11	8	15	64	65	30
Brocton	34	13	4	17	61	66	30
Northpark United Reserves	32	11	7	14	53	58	29
Chasewood United	34	9	10	15	60	74	28
Etching Hill Athletic	34	10	4	20	65	84	24
G.E.C. St. Leonards	34	7	6	21	49	93	20
Peelers	34	6	8	20	42	95	20
Aldridge Athletic Reserves	34	4	11	19	35	91	19
Heath Hayes Cons.	34	8	2	24	57	118	18
Walsall Pegasus	33	1	5	27	37	121	7

Although a complete table has not been found, the final records of the top 4 clubs were as below:

Hednesford Progressive	34	23	9	2	88	39	55
Bloxwich	34	23	7	4	97	31	53
Deeleys Rovers	34	23	7	4	105	37	53
Pelsall Cricket & Sports	34	23	6	5	84	41	52

Aldridge Athletic Reserves, Etching Hill Athletic and Walsall Pegasus all left the league. Bloxwich A.F.C., Bradley Memorial, Pelsall Villa Reserves and Rugeley Athletic all joined.

1981-82

Premier Division (14th May 1982)

Bloxwich Town	26	22	3	1	70	18	47
New World	26	20	4	2	61	17	44
Pelsall Villa	26	13	7	6	46	36	33
Ettingshall Holy Trinity	24	14	4	6	45	26	32
Oldbury United Reserves	26	11	6	9	40	39	28
Hednesford Progressive	24	11	3	10	44	41	25
Northpark United Reserves	26	9	7	10	38	40	25
Harrisons	25	8	3	14	39	49	19
Bilston Reserves	26	7	5	14	39	49	19
Wheaton Aston	26	6	7	13	43	58	19
Penkridge Town	26	6	7	13	38	52	19
Wednesfield Town	26	5	9	12	23	40	19
Kingswinford United	25	5	5	15	21	51	15
Fourways Rangers	26	4	6	16	25	48	14
					572	564	

Pelsall Villa and Harrisons both moved to the West Midlands Regional League and Oldbury United Reserves moved to the Midland Combination. Wheaton Aston also left. Aldridge and Rushall Olympic Reserves both joined. Kingswinford United changed their name to Kingswinford Town.

Division One (14th May 1982)

Pelsall Cricket & Sports	30	20	3	7	72	33	43
Bloxwich A.F.C.	29	16	11	2	69	33	43
Boney Hay Albion	30	17	6	7	82	53	40
Oldswinford Reserves	29	17	5	7	75	33	39
Ashley	29	13	10	6	56	48	36
Bradley Memorial	30	14	5	11	69	54	33
Rugeley Athletic	28	13	6	9	44	42	32
Deeleys Rovers	30	14	3	13	56	48	31
Pelsall Villa Reserves	30	11	8	11	41	44	30
Brocton	30	11	7	12	45	53	29
Chasetown Reserves	29	9	10	10	39	43	28
Chasewood United	29	11	4	14	50	61	26
Lichfield Reserves	27	9	5	13	43	54	23
G.E.C. St. Leonards	30	7	1	22	29	73	15
Heath Hayes Cons.	30	5	4	21	52	80	14
Peelers	30	3	2	25	18	88	8

Oldswinford Reserves moved to the West Midlands Regional League and Boney Hay Albion also left the league. Aldridge Reserves, Bloxwich A.F.C. Reserves, Moxley Rangers and Wednesbury Town all joined.

1982-83

Premier Division (30th April 1983)

New World	28	21	3	4	74	23	45
Ettingshall Holy Trinity	26	19	3	4	63	15	41
Bloxwich Town	28	17	7	4	64	28	41
Bloxwich A.F.C.	28	11	9	8	57	53	31
Pelsall Cricket & Sports	27	11	8	8	46	31	30
Bilston Reserves	25	12	4	9	46	39	28
Aldridge	26	9	9	8	39	40	27
Fourways Rangers	23	10	4	9	46	47	24
Kingswinford Town	27	9	6	12	39	41	24
Wednesfield Town	26	9	5	12	40	49	23
Penkridge Town	24	6	7	11	25	42	19
Chasewood United	22	6	4	12	35	56	16
Rushall Olympic Reserves	27	6	3	18	36	69	15
Hednesford Progressive	25	5	4	16	43	73	14
Northpark United Reserves	28	4	4	20	28	75	12

Bloxwich A.F.C., Kingswinford Town and New World all moved to the Midland Combination. Bilston Reserves changed their name to Bilston Town Reserves.

Staffordshire County League (South) 1983-1988

Division One (30th April 1983)

Rugeley Athletic	25	17	4	4	62	21	38
Moxley Rangers	27	14	9	4	57	39	37
Bradley Memorial	27	16	3	8	68	39	35
Brocton	26	16	3	7	63	37	35
Wednesbury Town	28	14	6	8	72	50	34
Chasetown Reserves	26	16	1	9	54	32	33
Deeleys Rovers	28	13	6	9	51	45	32
Pelsall Villa Reserves	27	14	3	10	41	44	31
Ashley	26	11	6	9	39	31	28
Heath Hayes Cons.	24	10	2	12	55	55	22
Aldridge Reserves	24	8	4	12	35	42	20
Bloxwich A.F.C. Reserves	27	6	3	18	34	69	15
Peelers	26	6	3	17	28	57	15
Lichfield Reserves	27	3	5	19	39	81	11
G.E.C. St. Leonards	26	2	4	20	23	79	8

G.E.C. St. Leonards and Peelers both left the league. Bloxwich Strollers, Dudley, Handrahan Timbers, Pelsall Cricket & Sports Reserves, Rushall, Tranco and Wednesbury Town Reserves all joined.

1983-84

Premier Division

Hednesford Progressive	30	23	4	3	99	27	50
Ettingshall Holy Trinity	30	20	7	3	66	20	47
Pelsall Cricket & Sports	30	21	4	5	72	36	46
Bloxwich Town	30	14	9	7	53	37	37
Fourways Rangers	30	11	9	10	52	45	31
Wednesbury Town	30	13	5	12	58	55	31
Moxley Rangers	30	13	5	12	62	61	31
Chasewood United	30	11	7	12	56	53	29
Northpark United Reserves	30	10	7	13	52	62	27
Aldridge	30	9	8	13	45	59	26
Bilston Town Reserves	30	8	9	13	37	64	25
Penkridge Town	30	10	4	16	50	52	24
Rugeley Athletic	30	8	6	16	50	61	22
Rushall Olympic Reserves	30	8	6	16	40	71	22
Bradley Memorial	30	5	11	14	45	67	21
Wednesfield Town	30	3	5	22	34	101	11

Bloxwich Town and Ettingshall Holy Trinity both moved to the West Midlands Regional League and Hednesford Progressive moved to the Staffordshire Senior League. Aldridge, Bilston Town Reserves and Northpark United Reserves also left the league. Following their promotion from Division One, Tranco merged with Springvale of the West Midlands Regional League to form Springvale-Tranco whose reserves replaced Tranco in the Staffordshire County League.

Division One (12th May 1984)

Brocton	29	20	3	6	71	29	43
Pelsall Villa Reserves	27	20	2	5	75	31	42
Tranco	30	17	3	10	66	48	37
Bloxwich A.F.C. Reserves	28	16	4	8	52	35	36
Ashley	27	16	3	8	54	30	35
Chasetown Reserves	29	14	5	10	53	33	33
Rushall	28	14	5	9	52	34	33
Bloxwich Strollers	28	15	3	10	51	46	33
Deeleys Rovers	30	12	8	10	55	41	32
Heath Hayes Cons.	30	9	9	12	56	60	27
Pelsall Cricket & Sports Reserves	29	10	6	13	43	60	26
Handrahan Timbers	30	9	7	14	49	59	25
Dudley	30	10	3	17	46	65	23
Aldridge Reserves	28	6	1	21	26	72	13
Lichfield Reserves	29	5	2	22	25	81	12
Wednesbury Town Reserves	28	2	6	20	26	78	10
					800	802	

Aldridge Reserves, Dudley and Pelsall Cricket & Sports Reserves all left the league. Hawkins Sports, Moxley Rangers Reserves, Penkridge Town Reserves, Riley Sports and Yew Tree Estate all joined.

1984-85

Premier Division (9th May 1985)

The table of 9th May showed only the top 12 clubs.
* The records of the bottom 2 clubs are as printed on 2nd May.

Chasetown Reserves	25	20	2	3	55	18	42
Wednesbury Town	26	17	5	4	78	33	39
Deeleys Rovers	26	14	6	6	56	36	34
Penkridge Town	25	11	9	5	46	34	31
Moxley Rangers	24	10	9	5	46	30	29
Fourways Rangers	25	10	6	9	41	30	26
Wednesfield Town	26	10	4	12	44	63	24
Rushall Olympic Reserves	23	10	3	10	45	40	23
Pelsall Cricket & Sports	24	7	9	8	33	36	23
Bradley Memorial	23	9	5	9	35	40	23
Pelsall Villa Reserves	26	6	2	18	30	62	14
Rugeley Athletic	26	6	2	18	25	52	14
* Chasewood United	22	4	3	15	25	50	11
* Springvale-Tranco Reserves	21	3	4	14	24	58	10

Chasetown Reserves and Wednesbury Town both moved to the West Midlands Regional League. Other changes are not known.

Division One (9th May 1985)

The table of 9th May showed only the top 12 clubs.
* The records of the bottom 2 clubs are as printed on 2nd May.

Bloxwich Strollers	26	21	3	2	66	21	45
Riley Sports	25	14	7	4	65	29	35
Brocton	26	15	3	8	47	38	33
Yew Tree Estate	25	13	5	7	71	40	31
Handrahan Timbers	26	12	6	8	48	38	30
Ashley	25	12	3	10	45	32	27
Heath Hayes Cons.	25	11	4	10	59	53	26
Bloxwich A.F.C. Reserves	25	12	2	11	50	57	26
Lichfield Reserves	23	11	1	11	38	41	23
Hawkins Sports	26	8	7	11	41	49	23
Rushall	26	5	7	14	35	45	17
Wednesbury Town Reserves	24	7	3	14	39	74	17
* Penkridge Town Reserves	25	3	4	18	32	76	10
* Moxley Rangers Reserves	23	2	5	16	28	60	9

Changes to membership are not known.

1985-87

Although the league operated during these two seasons, no tables or results have been found in any of the local newspapers.
Handrahan Timbers joined the Midland Combination in 1986.
Moxley Rangers and Springvale-Tranco Reserves both joined the West Midlands Regional League in 1987.
Brereton Social resigned from the West Midlands Regional League during the 1987-88 season and replaced their reserves in the Staffordshire County League (South).

1987-88

Premier Division (9th April 1988)

18 later results have been added to the table below:

Brereton Social	24	17	4	3	71	44	38
Yew Tree Estate	20	12	5	3	55	25	29
Chasewood United	24	13	2	9	65	47	28
Armitage	22	11	4	7	48	32	26
Fourways Rangers	23	11	4	8	42	34	26
Heath Hayes Cons.	17	11	2	4	37	17	24
White Horse	20	8	7	5	44	29	23
Hawkins Sports	22	9	4	9	47	55	22
Punjab Rovers	22	9	4	9	34	49	22
Pelsall Villa Reserves	23	6	9	8	35	38	21
Wednesfield Town	20	5	5	10	28	43	15
Brocton	22	5	4	13	30	45	14
Penkridge Town	21	4	4	13	27	42	12
Rushall	22	0	2	20	22	76	2
					585	576	

Staffordshire County League (South) 1988-1991

Division One (26th March 1988)

21 later results have been added to the table below:

Chamberlin & Hill	22	18	1	3	94	28	37
Tipton Sports & Social	24	13	6	5	52	30	32
Sikh Hunters	20	14	2	4	58	29	30
Tipton Town Reserves	23	11	5	7	66	41	27
West Bromwich United	22	12	3	7	42	35	27
Toll End Wesley	17	10	5	2	46	19	25
Albright & Wilson	23	9	4	10	53	51	22
Moxley Rangers Reserves	22	9	3	10	51	36	21
Elmwood Dynamo	18	7	3	8	30	32	17
Park Rangers	22	5	4	13	29	52	14
Rugeley Athletic	21	4	3	14	38	64	11
Bell Rovers	22	5	1	16	27	77	11
Palfrey	20	1	0	19	14	105	2
					600	599	

Palfrey and Rugeley Athletic both left the league. Aldersley Rovers, Bilston Community College, Cheslyn Hay, Chubb Sports, G.E.C. Stafford, James Bridge and Mitchells & Butlers Reserves all joined

1988-89

Premier Division (15th April 1989)

27 later results have been added to the table below:

Heath Hayes Cons.	26	20	3	3	70	30	43
Brereton Social	29	20	3	6	88	50	43
Toll End Wesley	26	16	6	4	77	40	38
Chamberlin & Hill	26	17	4	5	66	43	38
Armitage	26	16	3	7	68	37	35
Penkridge Town	28	13	6	9	51	37	32
Chasewood United	28	12	6	10	64	58	30
Brocton	27	12	4	11	49	40	28
Fourways Rangers	27	12	3	12	47	49	27
Pelsall Villa Reserves	28	8	7	13	62	79	23
Tipton Town Reserves	26	7	8	11	44	47	22
Punjab Rovers	28	8	6	14	45	64	22
White Horse	28	7	6	15	41	53	20
Yew Tree Estate	28	7	4	17	53	100	18
Hawkins Sports	25	4	3	18	41	72	11
Wednesfield Town	30	1	4	25	42	120	6
					908	919	

Heath Hayes Cons. moved to the Staffordshire Senior League and Chasewood United also left the league.

Division One (15th April 1989)

16 later results have been added to the table below:

Tipton Sports & Social	27	24	1	2	93	26	49
Bilston Community College	28	19	7	2	110	31	45
G.E.C. Stafford	25	14	5	6	53	47	33
Sikh Hunters	22	14	4	4	62	35	32
Bell Rovers	25	12	4	9	62	43	28
West Bromwich United	27	10	5	12	59	54	25
Moxley Rangers Reserves	28	11	3	14	43	56	25
Chubb Sports	30	8	9	13	37	55	25
Albright & Wilson	28	10	4	14	49	61	24
Aldersley Rovers	22	11	2	9	38	52	24
Mitchells & Butlers Reserves	27	8	6	13	44	68	22
Rushall	22	9	4	10	38	50	21
James Bridge	25	7	4	14	34	43	18
Cheslyn Hay	26	6	2	18	41	71	14
Elmwood Dynamo	25	4	6	15	25	56	14
Park Rangers	25	4	5	16	27	62	13
					815	810	

Albright & Wilson, Chubb Sports, Elmwood Dynamo and Rushall all left the league. Cannock Chase Reserves, Chase Tyres, Lichfield Reserves, Toll End Wesley Reserves joined.

1989-90

Premier Division (12th May 1990)

Bilston Community College	27	22	4	1	120	24	48
Brocton	30	17	7	6	57	33	41
Penkridge Town	28	18	4	6	70	42	40
Toll End Wesley	28	14	8	6	70	48	36
Brereton Social	30	15	5	10	69	63	35
Tipton Sports & Social	28	14	3	11	49	38	31
Punjab Rovers	28	12	6	10	68	59	30
Chamberlin & Hill	25	13	3	9	54	45	29
Armitage 90	28	11	7	10	73	62	29
Pelsall Villa Reserves	26	11	6	9	55	48	28
White Horse	30	11	5	14	49	60	27
Wednesfield Town	29	9	6	14	54	79	24
Fourways Rangers	29	9	3	17	51	76	21
Tipton Town Reserves	29	4	5	20	30	83	13
Hawkins Sports	30	3	6	21	33	92	12
Yew Tree Estate	29	2	4	23	45	100	8
		185			187 947	952	452

Armitage 90 moved to the Staffordshire Senior League and Fourways Rangers, Punjab Rovers, White Horse and Yew Tree Estate also all left the league.

Division One (12th May 1990)

Sikh Hunters	22	16	4	2	70	29	36
Aldersley Rovers	25	17	2	6	63	24	36
G.E.C. Stafford	24	15	5	4	67	29	35
Lichfield Reserves	26	14	6	6	54	29	34
James Bridge	25	13	6	6	60	43	32
Cannock Chase Reserves	25	11	4	10	55	52	26
Chase Tyres	26	10	5	11	48	55	25
Cheslyn Hay	26	8	8	10	47	45	24
Moxley Rangers Reserves	26	8	7	11	35	44	23
Toll End Wesley Reserves	26	8	6	12	42	50	22
Mitchells & Butlers Reserves	25	8	2	15	34	52	18
West Bromwich United	26	5	6	15	35	65	16
Bell Rovers	25	6	3	16	46	66	15
Park Rangers	26	4	4	18	35	77	12
	353	143	68	142	691	660	354

Cheslyn Hay moved to the West Midlands Regional League and were replaced by their reserves. Aldersley Rovers, Bell Rovers, Cannock Chase Reserves and Chase Tyres all left the league.
A.F.C. Thatch, Brownhills Town and Walsall Martial Arts joined.

1990-91

Premier Division (18th May 1991)

Brereton Social	26	19	2	5	82	38	40
Brocton	25	17	4	4	72	36	38
Sikh Hunters	23	17	3	3	75	26	37
Bilston Community College	23	18	1	4	64	19	37
Toll End Wesley	26	13	3	10	52	33	29
G.E.C. Stafford	26	11	6	9	47	43	28
Chamberlin & Hill	25	10	6	9	41	74	26
Tipton Town Reserves	25	11	2	12	44	51	24
Pelsall Villa Reserves	25	9	3	13	37	47	21
Penkridge Town	26	7	6	13	38	53	20
Tipton Sports & Social	25	7	5	13	49	53	19
Lichfield Reserves	26	5	4	17	34	59	14
Hawkins Sports	26	5	4	17	45	82	14
Wednesfield Town	26	3	1	22	30	92	7
	353	152	50	151	710	706	354

Brocton, Chamberlin & Hill, Pelsall Villa Reserves and Wednesfield Town all left the league

Staffordshire County League (South) 1991-1995

Division One (18th May 1991)

A.F.C. Thatch	20	14	4	2	53	18	32
Walsall Martial Arts	19	13	3	3	51	29	29
James Bridge	20	8	8	4	35	26	24
Park Rangers	20	9	5	6	39	35	23
Moxley Rangers Reserves	20	6	7	7	22	24	19
Mitchells & Butlers Reserves	20	8	2	10	32	35	18
West Bromwich United	19	6	4	9	34	40	16
Cheslyn Hay Reserves	20	5	6	9	27	36	16
Brownhills Town	20	7	2	11	29	40	16
*** Missing club	–	–	–	–	–	–	–
Toll End Wesley Reserves	20	3	4	13	27	52	10
	198	79	45	74	349	335	203

*** The table dated 18th May was the only one found during the season. One club was omitted from this table and it has not been possible to identify it, although it has been possible to calculate that they finished in 10th place.

Park Rangers moved to the West Midlands Regional League while Cheslyn Hay Reserves, James Bridge, and West Bromwich United also all left. Cannock Town, Highfield Social, Mahal, Rugeley Athletic, Rugeley Moderation, Walsall Wood Reserves and West Bromwich B.H. all joined.

1991-92

Premier Division

Bilston Community College	22	16	5	1	85	22	37
Toll End Wesley	22	14	5	3	77	34	33
Sikh Hunters	22	14	4	4	73	38	32
Lichfield Reserves	22	12	4	6	41	36	28
Walsall Martial Arts	22	11	5	6	56	38	27
Hawkins Sports	22	9	6	7	39	41	24
Brereton Social	22	8	5	9	48	56	21
Tipton Sports & Social	22	5	5	12	36	53	15
A.F.C. Thatch	22	6	3	13	34	62	15
G.E.C. Stafford	22	4	5	13	28	52	13
Tipton Town Reserves	22	5	2	15	34	61	12
Penkridge Town	22	2	3	17	22	64	7
					573	557	

A.F.C. Thatch, Brereton Social, Penkridge Town and Walsall Martial Arts all left the league. Beechdale Social and Bloxwich Town Reserves both joined.

Division One

Cannock Town	18	12	3	3	54	22	27
Brownhills Town	18	12	2	4	37	16	26
Walsall Wood Reserves	18	12	0	6	43	24	24
Rugeley Athletic	18	7	6	5	28	20	20
Mahal	18	9	1	8	38	38	19
Moxley Rangers Reserves	18	7	3	8	29	22	17
Highfield Social	18	6	3	9	23	50	15
West Bromwich B.H.	18	6	1	11	23	41	13
Mitchells & Butlers Reserves	18	3	4	11	23	37	10
Toll End Wesley Reserves	18	3	3	12	19	47	9

Rugeley Moderation resigned and their record was deleted. Highfield Social left the league. Clancey Dudley joined from the West Midlands Regional League and Rocket Pool also joined.

1992-93

Premier Division

Bilston Community College	20	16	2	2	71	16	34
Cannock Town	20	14	3	3	63	34	31
Toll End Wesley	20	11	3	6	44	18	25
Brownhills Town	20	11	2	7	54	35	24
G.E.C. Stafford	20	11	1	8	57	35	23
Beechdale Social	20	10	3	7	44	37	23
Sikh Hunters	20	6	5	9	35	52	17
Lichfield Reserves	20	7	2	11	39	57	16
Tipton Sports & Social	20	5	3	12	28	47	13
Tipton Town Reserves	20	3	2	15	32	80	8
Bloxwich Town Reserves	20	1	4	15	14	70	6

Hawkins Sports resigned during the season and their record was deleted when it stood as follows: 8 2 0 6 18 38 4

Bilston Community College moved to the Midland Combination and Cannock Town moved to the Staffordshire Senior League. Bloxwich Town Reserves and Lichfield Reserves also left the league.

Division One

Mahal	16	11	1	4	53	22	23
West Bromwich B.H.	16	9	5	2	47	29	23
Moxley Rangers Reserves	16	7	3	6	27	18	17
Mitchells & Butlers Reserves	16	6	4	6	22	27	16
Walsall Wood Reserves	16	7	2	7	28	34	16
Rugeley Athletic	16	4	7	5	26	28	15
Toll End Wesley Reserves	16	4	5	7	33	44	13
Clancey Dudley	16	3	5	8	31	41	11
Rocket Pool	16	3	4	9	21	45	10

Moxley Rangers Reserves and Walsall Wood Reserves both moved to the West Midlands Regional League while Clancey Dudley, Mitchells & Butlers Reserves and Toll End Wesley Reserves also left the league. Tipton Rovers joined.

The two divisions merged into one for the 1993-94 season.

1993-94

Beechdale Social	22	14	5	3	59	37	33
Tipton Sports & Social	22	14	3	5	72	35	31
Brownhills Town	22	13	3	6	49	27	29
Mahal	22	11	6	5	57	40	28
Toll End Wesley	22	9	9	4	56	40	27
G.E.C. Stafford	22	7	10	5	40	39	24
Tipton Rovers	22	6	8	8	42	44	20
Sikh Hunters	22	7	4	11	57	55	18
West Bromwich B.H.	22	7	4	11	44	62	18
Rugeley Athletic	22	6	5	11	45	63	17
Tipton Town Reserves	22	5	4	13	26	44	14
Rocket Pool	22	1	3	18	32	93	5

Brownhills Town moved to the Midland Combination and Beechdale Social, G.E.C. Stafford, Rugeley Athletic, Toll End Wesley and West Bromwich B.H. also left the league. Brocton Reserves, Bustleholme, Chubb Sports, Union Locks, Willenhall Town Reserves and Yew Tree Albion all joined.

1994-95

Mahal	21	15	2	4	75	32	32
Willenhall Town Reserves	22	15	2	5	63	37	32
Tipton Sports & Social	21	15	1	5	60	26	31
Sikh Hunters	19	12	2	5	41	28	26
Yew Tree Albion	22	12	1	9	48	47	25
Chubb Sports	21	11	1	9	53	36	23
Tipton Town Reserves	21	8	4	9	49	45	20
Bustleholme	20	8	4	8	44	42	20
Tipton Rovers	21	8	2	11	54	52	18
Rocket Pool	21	6	1	14	33	64	13
Brocton Reserves	22	5	0	17	36	84	10
Union Locks	21	1	2	18	26	84	4
	252	116			114	582	577	254

Tipton Rovers and Tipton Sports & Social both moved to the Midland Combination while Mahal and Sikh Hunters both moved to the West Midlands Regional League. Rocket Pool, Willenhall Town Reserves and Yew Tree Albion also left the league. Corestone Services, Greets Green and Sporting Khalsa all joined. As only 8 clubs wished to play in the league, it was planned to close down in 1995 but by the time the decision was taken, it was too late for those 8 clubs to find another league for 1995-96 and so it was agreed to continue for one last season.

1995-96

Bustleholme	5	4	1	0	15	3	9
Sporting Khalsa	4	4	0	0	15	3	8
Greets Green	5	2	1	2	7	7	5
Brocton Reserves	5	2	1	2	3	6	5
Corestone Services	5	2	0	3	6	10	4
Union Locks	4	1	1	2	7	9	3
Tipton Town Reserves	4	1	0	3	3	8	2
Chubb Sports	4	0	0	4	1	11	0

The table shown is as at 7th October 1995. No further results or tables for the league were found after this date and the league closed down at the end of the season.

Bustleholme, Corestone Services and Sporting Khalsa all moved to the West Midlands Regional League and Tipton Town Reserves moved to the Midland Combination.

MIDLAND COMBINATION

Formation

The Midland Combination was formed as the Worcestershire Combination after a meeting held at the Seven Stars Hotel, Oldswinford near Stourbridge on 28th April 1927. This meeting was organised by Mr S. Bloye and Mr E.J. Rivers who worked at Stewarts & Lloyds' Coombs Wood works. They felt there was a need for a league for amateur clubs, particularly in the north of the county.

The 10 founder members were: Bewdley, Blackheath Town, Cookley St. Peters, Halesowen Labour, Highley Colliers, Kidderminster Harriers Reserves, Oldbury Town, Old Carolians, Stewarts & Lloyds and Stourbridge Reserves.

The Worcestershire Combination changed its name to the Midland Combination in 1968, a year after the neighbouring Warwickshire Combination closed down.

Some of the published tables contained errors. Additional research has found corrections for many of these, totals that still do not balance are shown below the relevant columns in italics.

Abbreviations used:

WMRL = West Midlands Regional League.

BYOB = Birmingham Youths & Old Boys F.A.

WWMA = Warwickshire & West Midland Alliance.

SCL(S) = Staffordshire County League (South)

& DL = & District League.

WORCESTERSHIRE COMBINATION

1927-28

Blackheath Town	18	12	2	4	74	29	26
Kidderminster Harriers Reserves	18	12	2	4	61	25	26
Stourbridge Reserves	18	12	2	4	88	42	26
Halesowen Labour	18	11	1	6	61	45	23
Oldbury Town	18	7	4	7	55	54	18
Stewart & Lloyds	18	7	2	9	65	58	16
Highley Colliers	18	6	1	11	50	64	13
Bewdley	18	6	0	12	41	80	12
Old Carolians	18	4	2	12	52	85	10
Cookley St. Peters	18	3	4	11	29	94	10

Highley Colliers left and were replaced by Halesowen St. John.

1928-29

Blackheath Town	16	12	2	2	66	32	26
Halesowen Labour	16	10	2	4	57	35	22
Stourbridge Reserves	16	9	3	4	62	43	21
Stewart & Lloyds	16	8	1	7	48	41	17
Oldbury Town	17	6	3	8	43	39	15
Bewdley	17	4	6	7	56	58	14
Cookley St. Peters	13	5	2	6	32	43	12
Halesowen St. John	18	5	2	11	48	76	12
Kidderminster Harriers Reserves	8	3	2	3	27	21	8
Old Carolians	17	3	1	13	44	104	7
					483	*492*	

Not all fixtures were completed.

Blackheath Town, Stourbridge Reserves, Oldbury Town, Cookley St. Peters, Halesowen St. John, Kidderminster Harriers Reserves and Old Carolians all left the league. Dudley Town and Netherton Liberals joined from the Cradley Heath & DL and Hanbury Conservatives also joined.

Midland Combination 1929-1935

1929-30

First Series

Halesowen Labour	10	7	1	2	48	23	15
Netherton Liberals	10	6	1	3	29	19	13
Bewdley	10	6	0	4	25	21	12
Dudley Town	10	3	1	6	28	35	7
Stewart & Lloyds	10	3	1	6	20	40	7
Hanbury Conservatives	10	2	2	6	22	34	6

Second Series

Dudley Town	10	8	1	1	27	7	17
Bewdley	10	6	0	4	38	26	12
Stewart & Lloyds	10	6	0	4	31	23	12
Halesowen Labour	10	5	0	5	27	32	10
Hanbury Conservatives	10	3	0	7	19	36	6
Netherton Liberals	10	1	1	8	10	28	3

Hanbury Conservatives left the league. Stourport Swifts joined from the Kidderminster League and Brintons, Bromley, Bromsgrove Rovers Reserves, Burton Delingpole, Lye & Wollescote, Round Oak, Stoke Works and Wordsley Olympic also joined.

1930-31

Halesowen Labour	25	19	2	4	135	51	40
Dudley Town	25	18	2	5	92	43	38
Lye & Wollescote	26	16	5	5	89	69	37
Burton Delingpole	25	17	2	6	104	53	36
Round Oak	24	11	4	9	71	44	26
Bromley	25	12	2	11	72	56	26
Wordsley Olympic	25	11	1	13	81	76	23
Bewdley	26	10	3	13	68	87	23
Stewart & Lloyds	25	9	3	13	64	86	21
Stoke Works	25	7	5	13	58	76	19
Brintons	26	8	3	15	60	97	19
Stourport Swifts	25	7	4	14	48	93	18
Netherton Liberals	26	5	2	19	32	90	12
Bromsgrove Rovers Reserves	16	3	0	13	23	76	6

Bromsgrove Rovers Reserves did not complete their fixtures and left at the end of the season.
Lye & Wollescote were reformed as Lye Town. Stewart & Lloyds left the league. Brierley Hill Alliance Reserves, Coombs Wood, B.T.H. and Stourbridge Reserves joined.

1931-32

Dudley Town	30	22	4	4	115	55	48
Brierley Hill Alliance Reserves	30	21	3	6	109	57	45
Brintons	30	22	2	6	104	54	46
Coombs Wood	30	16	6	8	108	65	38
Round Oak	30	17	3	10	98	83	37
Lye Town	30	14	8	8	100	64	36
Bromley	30	16	3	11	77	64	35
Burton Delingpole	30	15	2	13	104	96	32
Halesowen Labour	30	12	7	11	93	101	31
B.T.H.	30	14	2	14	73	88	30
Stourbridge Reserves	30	10	6	14	79	91	26
Wordsley Olympic	30	10	3	17	67	104	23
Stourport Swifts	30	9	4	17	80	93	22
Netherton Liberals	30	8	3	19	66	99	19
Stoke Works	30	4	1	25	62	120	9
Bewdley	30	1	1	28	36	137	3

Dudley Town moved to the Birmingham Combination and Stourport Swifts moved to the Kidderminster League.
Stoke Works, Halesowen Labour, Brintons and Burton Delingpole all left the league. Woodside Wanderers, Coombs Wood Works, Darby End Institute and Tarmac joined.

1932-33

Tarmac	26	19	2	5	100	31	40
Lye Town	26	19	1	6	125	58	39
Bromley	26	15	4	7	77	45	34
Woodside Wanderers	26	16	1	9	104	50	33
Brierley Hill Alliance Reserves	26	15	2	9	76	56	32
Round Oak	26	14	3	9	73	69	31
Stourbridge Reserves	26	14	2	10	69	62	30
Darby End Institute	26	12	4	10	73	77	28
Wordsley Olympic	26	10	1	15	69	88	21
Netherton Liberals	26	9	2	15	55	73	20
Coombs Wood Works	26	9	2	15	53	91	20
Bewdley	26	7	2	17	54	99	16
B.T.H.	26	6	2	18	48	98	14
Coombs Wood	26	3	0	23	29	108	6

Coombs Wood left the league.
Horseley Sports, Greets Green Wesley and Catshill Village joined.

1933-34

Woodside Wanderers	30	26	1	3	157	38	53
Tarmac	30	22	4	4	132	44	48
Brierley Hill Alliance Reserves	30	20	3	7	88	64	43
Lye Town	30	17	4	9	100	63	38
Horseley Sports	30	16	5	9	97	59	37
Darby End Institute	30	16	4	10	90	62	36
Coombs Wood Works	30	15	3	12	61	83	33
Greets Green Wesley	30	15	2	13	64	75	32
Netherton Liberals	30	11	7	12	64	67	29
Stourbridge Reserves	30	11	6	13	71	77	28
Catshill Village	30	10	3	17	68	94	23
Bromley	30	8	5	17	62	90	21
Wordsley Olympic	30	6	6	18	52	115	18
Bewdley	30	7	1	22	46	100	15
Round Oak	30	4	5	21	64	118	13
B.T.H.	30	4	5	21	44	111	13

Coombs Wood Works, Horseley Sports and Darby End Institute left the league. Dudley Town Reserves joined.

1934-35

Catshill Village	26	19	3	4	117	45	41
Lye Town	26	18	3	5	82	46	39
Dudley Town Reserves	26	16	3	7	81	41	35
Tarmac	26	16	3	7	70	40	35
Netherton Liberals	26	13	4	9	70	42	30
Greets Green Wesley	26	12	4	10	60	54	28
Woodside Wanderers	26	12	4	10	58	49	28
Stourbridge Reserves	26	11	4	11	61	78	26
Bromley	26	9	4	13	50	68	22
Bewdley	26	8	4	14	57	70	20
Wordsley Olympic	26	8	2	16	50	90	18
Brierley Hill Alliance Reserves	26	6	4	16	42	74	16
B.T.H.	26	6	4	16	57	98	16
Round Oak	26	3	4	19	51	111	10

Round Oak and Woodside Wanderers left the league. Whiteheath joined.

1935-36

Team	P	W	D	L	F	A	Pts
Lye Town	24	21	0	3	119	40	42
Catshill Village	24	18	4	2	90	33	40
Netherton Liberals	24	12	7	5	70	47	31
Tarmac	24	13	2	9	66	35	28
Greets Green Wesley	24	9	7	8	44	48	25
Brierley Hill Alliance Reserves	24	11	2	11	71	57	24
Bewdley	24	11	2	11	60	87	24
Whiteheath	24	9	3	12	57	77	21
Dudley Town Reserves	24	8	4	12	71	75	20
Stourbridge Reserves	24	5	5	14	50	79	15
Wordsley Olympic	24	5	5	14	49	86	15
Bromley	24	6	3	15	51	96	15
B.T.H.	24	5	2	17	46	84	12

Greets Green Wesley left the league.
Goodyears and Halesowen Town Reserves joined.

1936-37

Team	P	W	D	L	F	A	Pts
Catshill Village	26	23	2	1	110	25	48
Goodyears	25	17	4	4	72	32	38
Lye Town	26	18	2	6	97	46	38
Netherton Liberals	24	17	3	4	78	31	37
Tarmac	25	13	5	7	68	41	31
Dudley Town Reserves	26	11	5	10	46	50	27
Bewdley	25	10	2	13	50	64	22
Halesowen Town Reserves	26	9	4	13	54	71	22
Stourbridge Reserves	26	10	1	15	61	65	21
Wordsley Olympic	24	7	4	13	62	72	18
Whiteheath	25	6	3	16	45	72	15
Bromley	20	3	4	13	32	71	10
Brierley Hill Alliance Reserves	25	4	1	20	39	97	9
B.T.H.	21	3	2	16	20	97	8

Not all fixtures were completed.
Tarmac, Dudley Town Reserves, Halesowen Town Reserves, Wordsley Olympic, Whiteheath, Bromley and B.T.H. all left the league. Stourport Swifts joined from the Kidderminster League and Jack Moulds Athletic, Wrockwardine Wood and Worcester City Reserves also joined.

1937-38

Team	P	W	D	L	F	A	Pts
Catshill Village	20	16	1	3	70	32	33
Lye Town	20	14	2	4	76	31	30
Jack Moulds Athletic	20	9	7	4	38	29	25
Netherton Liberals	20	10	4	6	42	36	24
Goodyears	20	10	3	7	54	44	23
Wrockwardine Wood	20	9	4	7	50	38	22
Stourport Swifts	20	7	2	11	49	53	16
Stourbridge Reserves	20	6	3	11	38	50	15
Worcester City Reserves	20	5	4	11	47	69	14
Brierley Hill Alliance Reserves	20	4	5	11	40	66	13
Bewdley	20	2	1	17	26	82	5

Bewdley, Brierley Hill Alliance Reserves and Worcester City Reserves left Bridgnorth Town, Woodsetton, Weoley Castle and Stourbridge Glazed Brickworks joined.

1938-39

Team	P	W	D	L	F	A	Pts
Catshill Village	20	17	2	1	84	25	36
Wrockwardine Wood	21	15	2	4	62	33	32
Lye Town	21	14	3	4	75	42	31
Bridgnorth Town	22	11	1	10	60	57	23
Goodyears	21	8	4	9	51	61	20
Netherton Liberals	22	8	4	10	38	53	20
Woodsetton	21	8	3	10	51	38	19
Jack Moulds Athletic	16	7	2	7	31	30	16
Weoley Castle	22	7	2	13	40	61	16
Stourport Swifts	22	5	5	12	43	51	15
Stourbridge Glazed Brickworks	21	6	3	12	42	66	15
Stourbridge Reserves	21	3	1	17	24	84	7

Not all fixtures were completed.

1939-48

The Worcestershire Combination closed down upon the outbreak of war in 1939 and was not restarted until 1948. Of the pre-war members, only Jack Moulds Athletic, Stourport Swifts and Stourbridge Reserves rejoined. They were joined by 13 new members: Bournville Athletic, British Legion (Austin), Bromsgrove Rovers Reserves, Dudley Town Reserves, Halesowen Town Reserves, Handsworth Wood, High Duty Alloys, Kingswinford Wanderers, Lye Town Reserves, Moor Green Reserves, Round Oak, Smethwick Highfield and Wordsley.

1948-49

Team	P	W	D	L	F	A	Pts
Jack Moulds Athletic	30	23	5	2	106	35	51
Smethwick Highfield	30	19	4	7	91	56	42
Halesowen Town Reserves	30	18	3	9	99	55	39
Stourport Swifts	30	14	7	9	72	64	35
Lye Town Reserves	30	14	7	9	73	73	35
Moor Green Reserves	30	14	6	10	72	57	34
British Legion (Austin)	30	14	6	10	78	70	34
Stourbridge Reserves	30	13	5	12	87	67	31
Round Oak	30	12	5	13	74	74	29
Kingswinford Wanderers	30	12	5	13	70	85	29
Bromsgrove Rovers Reserves	30	13	2	15	73	61	28
Dudley Town Reserves	30	11	4	15	68	78	26
Bournville Athletic	30	10	6	14	59	76	26
Handsworth Wood	30	5	6	19	47	88	16
High Duty Alloys	30	4	5	21	57	94	13
Wordsley	30	4	4	22	39	132	12

High Duty Alloys moved to the Redditch & DL and Dudley Town Reserves also left. Brierley Hill Alliance Reserves joined from the Walsall Senior League, Boldmere St. Michaels Reserves joined from the BYOB and Herman Smith and Cradley Heath Reserves also joined.

1949-50

Team	P	W	D	L	F	A	Pts
Bournville Athletic	34	25	3	6	95	34	53
Jack Moulds Athletic	34	22	5	7	112	49	49
Smethwick Highfield	34	22	5	7	115	59	49
Bromsgrove Rovers Reserves	34	22	5	7	99	58	49
Brierley Hill Alliance Reserves	34	16	9	9	97	66	41
Stourport Swifts	34	17	7	10	74	60	41
Halesowen Town Reserves	34	14	6	14	74	72	34
Stourbridge Reserves	34	16	2	16	71	76	34
Herman Smith	34	11	8	15	57	85	30
Kingswinford Wanderers	34	12	5	17	71	83	29
Lye Town Reserves	34	12	5	17	68	85	29
Cradley Heath Reserves	34	12	5	17	56	72	29
Boldmere St. Michaels Reserves	34	11	6	17	63	60	28
Handsworth Wood	34	12	4	18	69	88	28
Moor Green Reserves	34	9	10	15	54	84	28
British Legion (Austin)	34	12	2	20	82	104	26
Round Oak	34	9	4	21	76	105	22
Wordsley	34	3	7	24	49	142	13

Stourport Swifts moved to the Kidderminster League and Round Oak, Wordsley and Cradley Heath Reserves also left. Paget Rangers joined from the Central Amateur League and Richard Thomas & Baldwins and Wolverhampton Wanderers "B" also joined.

Midland Combination 1950-1956

1950-51

Jack Moulds Athletic	32	24	3	5	96	30	51
Smethwick Highfield	32	21	6	5	133	58	48
Halesowen Town Reserves	32	21	3	8	86	43	45
Bournville Athletic	32	17	8	7	87	57	42
Wolverhampton Wanderers "B"	32	17	5	10	116	54	39
Brierley Hill Alliance Reserves	32	18	2	12	109	82	38
Paget Rangers	32	17	4	11	72	60	38
Richard Thomas & Baldwins	32	14	5	13	55	71	33
Moor Green Reserves	32	14	4	14	71	60	32
Boldmere St. Michaels Reserves	32	13	5	14	53	66	31
Bromsgrove Rovers Reserves	32	9	8	15	76	82	26
Lye Town Reserves	32	11	3	18	68	91	25
Kingswinford Wanderers	32	10	5	17	55	92	25
Handsworth Wood	32	8	6	18	44	88	22
Stourbridge Reserves	32	10	0	22	51	87	20
British Legion (Austin)	32	9	2	21	49	117	20
Herman Smith	32	3	3	26	29	112	9

Herman Smith left the league.
Evesham United joined from the Worcester & DL, Lower Gornal Athletic joined from the Wolverhampton Amateur League and Walsall Wood joined from the SCL(S).

1951-52

Walsall Wood	36	31	2	3	129	37	64
Smethwick Highfield	36	30	2	4	140	48	62
Evesham United	36	23	6	7	108	65	52
Wolverhampton Wanderers "B"	36	19	7	10	113	71	45
Paget Rangers	36	18	5	13	88	68	41
Halesowen Town Reserves	36	19	3	14	74	64	41
Brierley Hill Alliance Reserves	36	18	4	14	99	103	40
Jack Moulds Athletic	36	16	6	14	86	66	38
Lower Gornal Athletic	36	14	7	15	102	89	35
Moor Green Reserves	36	13	9	14	82	78	35
Bromsgrove Rovers Reserves	36	15	3	18	94	99	33
Stourbridge Reserves	36	13	7	16	72	84	33
Richard Thomas & Baldwins	36	13	6	17	63	81	32
Bournville Athletic	36	12	4	20	68	82	28
Lye Town Reserves	36	9	8	19	67	87	26
Kingswinford Wanderers	36	12	1	23	61	101	25
British Legion (Austin)	36	8	7	21	59	119	23
Boldmere St. Michaels Reserves	36	9	3	24	48	80	21
Handsworth Wood	36	3	4	29	54	185	10

Smethwick Highfield changed their name to Smethwick Town.
Handsworth Wood left and joined the Birmingham AFA.

1952-53

Evesham United	34	28	3	3	147	41	59
Smethwick Town	34	26	3	5	130	44	55
Walsall Wood	34	23	6	5	97	38	52
Wolverhampton Wanderers "B"	34	22	2	10	109	61	46
Paget Rangers	34	19	3	12	73	69	41
Jack Moulds Athletic	34	18	4	12	96	80	40
Bournville Athletic	34	17	4	13	108	76	38
Stourbridge Reserves	34	14	9	11	66	66	37
Boldmere St. Michaels Reserves	34	15	7	12	70	80	37
Moor Green Reserves	34	15	5	14	82	69	35
Lower Gornal Athletic	34	15	3	16	106	102	33
Bromsgrove Rovers Reserves	34	10	7	17	69	113	27
Halesowen Town Reserves	34	11	4	19	63	86	26
Richard Thomas & Baldwins	34	9	4	21	42	77	22
Brierley Hill Alliance Reserves	34	9	3	22	45	92	21
Kingswinford Wanderers	34	6	6	22	63	117	18
Lye Town Reserves	34	6	3	25	55	109	15
British Legion (Austin)	34	4	2	28	45	146	10

Kingswinford Wanderers were replaced by Kingswinford & Wallheath and British Legion (Austin) also left the league.
Quarry Bank Celtic joined from the WWMA.

1953-54

Brierley Hill Alliance Reserves	34	26	3	5	100	52	55
Walsall Wood	34	25	2	7	102	53	52
Evesham United	34	24	4	6	84	45	52
Wolverhampton Wanderers "B"	34	19	4	11	83	50	42
Smethwick Town	34	19	3	12	92	61	41
Paget Rangers	34	17	7	10	75	60	41
Jack Moulds Athletic	34	18	4	12	81	59	40
Lower Gornal Athletic	34	16	6	12	76	74	38
Bournville Athletic	34	15	5	14	101	73	35
Halesowen Town Reserves	34	14	6	14	77	73	34
Stourbridge Reserves	34	15	3	16	81	69	33
Lye Town Reserves	34	13	5	16	88	75	31
Quarry Bank Celtic	34	10	7	17	61	85	27
Bromsgrove Rovers Reserves	34	9	4	21	66	114	22
Moor Green Reserves	34	7	7	20	38	71	21
Boldmere St. Michaels Reserves	34	7	3	24	48	113	17
Richard Thomas & Baldwins	34	7	2	25	47	113	16
Kingswinford & Wallheath	34	4	7	23	48	108	15

Kingswinford & Wallheath left the league.
Stratford Town joined from the WWMA.

1954-55

Evesham United	34	26	4	4	120	40	56
Walsall Wood	34	24	3	7	99	52	51
Jack Moulds Athletic	34	18	8	8	76	55	44
Stratford Town	34	19	5	10	120	61	43
Bromsgrove Rovers Reserves	34	19	4	11	89	60	42
Bournville Athletic	34	18	5	11	91	79	41
Stourbridge Reserves	34	17	2	15	70	71	36
Quarry Bank Celtic	34	14	7	13	83	82	35
Smethwick Town	34	14	5	15	80	79	33
Halesowen Town Reserves	34	13	7	14	71	78	33
Paget Rangers	34	13	7	14	62	72	33
Wolverhampton Wanderers "B"	34	11	10	13	82	74	32
Brierley Hill Alliance Reserves	34	14	3	17	69	75	31
Moor Green Reserves	34	11	4	19	59	86	26
Lye Town Reserves	34	9	4	21	51	117	22
Boldmere St. Michaels Reserves	34	8	5	21	56	89	21
Richard Thomas & Baldwins	34	7	5	22	57	109	19
Lower Gornal Athletic	34	4	6	24	55	111	14

Evesham United moved to the Birmingham League.
Malvern Town joined from the Worcester & DL.

1955-56

Malvern Town	34	20	9	5	96	41	49
Stratford Town	34	21	6	7	95	42	48
Halesowen Town Reserves	34	20	8	6	97	55	48
Jack Moulds Athletic	34	20	4	10	84	52	44
Wolverhampton Wanderers "B"	34	17	9	8	92	60	43
Lower Gornal Athletic	34	16	8	10	74	54	40
Bromsgrove Rovers Reserves	34	17	4	13	82	69	38
Smethwick Town	34	15	7	12	71	64	37
Walsall Wood	34	12	11	11	77	73	35
Quarry Bank Celtic	34	15	4	15	95	89	34
Lye Town Reserves	34	13	7	14	75	90	33
Moor Green Reserves	34	11	9	14	55	62	31
Paget Rangers	34	13	5	16	58	68	31
Bournville Athletic	34	11	5	18	69	81	27
Brierley Hill Alliance Reserves	34	9	8	17	74	93	26
Stourbridge Reserves	34	7	9	18	54	82	23
Boldmere St. Michaels Reserves	34	7	5	22	46	90	19
Richard Thomas & Baldwins	34	1	4	29	31	160	6

Richard Thomas & Baldwins moved to the Wolverhampton Works League. Allens Cross joined from the WWMA.

1956-57

Team	P	W	D	L	F	A	Pts
Stratford Town	34	25	5	4	98	35	55
Wolverhampton Wanderers "B"	34	23	3	8	110	57	49
Malvern Town	34	21	6	7	102	58	48
Allens Cross	34	20	5	9	89	54	45
Jack Moulds Athletic	34	19	5	10	92	54	43
Walsall Wood	34	19	3	12	94	61	41
Bournville Athletic	34	17	7	10	87	64	41
Smethwick Town	34	14	5	15	76	80	33
Lower Gornal Athletic	34	12	8	14	86	86	32
Bromsgrove Rovers Reserves	34	12	7	15	68	72	31
Paget Rangers	34	15	1	18	63	75	31
Moor Green Reserves	34	12	6	16	53	66	30
Stourbridge Reserves	34	10	6	18	64	83	26
Quarry Bank Celtic	34	12	2	20	72	96	26
Halesowen Town Reserves	34	12	1	21	79	120	25
Lye Town Reserves	34	11	2	21	72	93	24
Brierley Hill Alliance Reserves	34	10	3	21	54	100	23
Boldmere St. Michaels Reserves	34	3	3	28	48	143	9
					1407	1397	

Stratford Town moved to the Birmingham League.
Worcester City "A" joined from the Warwickshire Combination.

1957-58

Team	P	W	D	L	F	A	Pts
Wolverhampton Wanderers "B"	34	26	3	5	125	36	55
Walsall Wood	34	25	4	5	122	49	54
Jack Moulds Athletic	34	19	5	10	89	54	43
Malvern Town	34	17	8	9	80	63	42
Lower Gornal Athletic	34	19	2	13	101	63	40
Bromsgrove Rovers Reserves	34	18	4	12	75	59	40
Allens Cross	34	17	4	13	68	58	38
Smethwick Town	34	15	4	15	77	75	34
Paget Rangers	34	13	7	14	73	65	33
Bournville Athletic	34	15	3	16	80	88	33
Lye Town Reserves	34	14	5	15	72	80	33
Quarry Bank Celtic	34	14	4	16	64	77	32
Brierley Hill Alliance Reserves	34	13	4	17	82	69	30
Halesowen Town Reserves	34	12	6	16	70	86	30
Boldmere St. Michaels Reserves	34	10	5	19	63	98	25
Moor Green Reserves	34	9	5	20	59	88	23
Stourbridge Reserves	34	9	4	21	49	97	22
Worcester City "A"	34	1	3	30	32	176	5

Worcester City "A" left the league.
Shelfield Athletic joined from the Staffordshire County League (South).

1958-59

Team	P	W	D	L	F	A	Pts
Shelfield Athletic	34	25	4	5	115	43	54
Walsall Wood	34	24	5	5	108	40	53
Wolverhampton Wanderers "B"	34	24	4	6	110	44	52
Halesowen Town Reserves	34	21	3	10	93	70	45
Lower Gornal Athletic	34	19	4	11	88	73	42
Paget Rangers	34	15	6	13	75	64	36
Quarry Bank Celtic	34	17	0	17	73	70	34
Malvern Town	34	15	4	15	80	84	34
Brierley Hill Alliance Reserves	34	13	8	13	54	61	34
Stourbridge Reserves	34	13	7	14	87	85	33
Bromsgrove Rovers Reserves	34	12	9	13	70	82	33
Moor Green Reserves	34	12	6	16	55	70	30
Allens Cross	34	12	4	18	73	78	28
Bournville Athletic	34	10	5	19	73	109	25
Jack Moulds Athletic	34	8	7	19	56	81	23
Boldmere St. Michaels Reserves	34	9	4	21	60	107	22
Smethwick Town	34	7	6	21	39	84	20
Lye Town Reserves	34	4	6	24	43	107	14

1959-60

Team	P	W	D	L	F	A	Pts
Paget Rangers	34	25	7	2	100	31	57
Shelfield Athletic	34	25	1	8	99	43	51
Wolverhampton Wanderers "B"	34	21	5	8	104	47	47
Malvern Town	34	18	7	9	124	71	43
Lower Gornal Athletic	34	20	3	11	93	57	43
Allens Cross	34	17	6	11	73	51	40
Walsall Wood	34	14	11	9	62	47	39
Halesowen Town Reserves	34	16	5	13	77	65	37
Bromsgrove Rovers Reserves	34	17	3	14	86	83	37
Quarry Bank Celtic	34	12	6	16	72	89	30
Smethwick Town	34	12	6	16	63	87	30
Brierley Hill Alliance Reserves	34	12	6	16	63	94	30
Bournville Athletic	34	10	5	19	80	106	25
Moor Green Reserves	34	7	11	16	48	80	25
Boldmere St. Michaels Reserves	34	10	4	20	55	104	24
Jack Moulds Athletic	34	10	3	21	68	86	23
Stourbridge Reserves	34	6	6	22	47	99	18
Lye Town Reserves	34	4	5	25	45	119	13

Lye Town Reserves left the league.
Blakenall joined from the Staffordshire County League (South).

1960-61

Team	P	W	D	L	F	A	Pts
Paget Rangers	34	26	4	4	136	45	56
Walsall Wood	34	24	4	6	110	48	52
Blakenall	34	23	4	7	110	50	50
Allens Cross	34	23	4	7	101	51	50
Smethwick Town	34	19	6	9	70	65	44
Malvern Town	34	19	5	10	104	62	43
Bromsgrove Rovers Reserves	34	20	3	11	96	82	43
Wolverhampton Wanderers "B"	34	19	4	11	101	68	42
Stourbridge Reserves	34	13	6	15	69	63	32
Halesowen Town Reserves	34	13	5	16	86	78	31
Lower Gornal Athletic	34	10	10	14	72	81	30
Quarry Bank Celtic	34	9	7	18	76	88	25
Jack Moulds Athletic	34	11	2	21	62	83	24
Bournville Athletic	34	9	3	22	65	118	21
Brierley Hill Alliance Reserves	34	7	6	21	84	110	20
Boldmere St. Michaels Reserves	34	9	2	23	50	127	20
Moor Green Reserves	34	6	6	22	54	118	18
Shelfield Athletic	34	3	5	26	41	150	11

Shelfield Athletic left the league.
Alvechurch joined from the West Midland Alliance, Premier Division.

A new Second Division was formed by the following clubs:
Castle Rovers and Yardley Wood Social (both ex-West Midland Alliance), British Legion (Austin) (ex-Kings Norton League), Olton (ex-BYOB), Crabbs Cross and Lye Town Reserves, plus 11 Division One Reserve sides: Allens Cross, Bournville Athletic and Paget Rangers (all ex-BYOB), Alvechurch (ex-West Midland Alliance Division One), Jack Moulds Athletic and Smethwick Town (both ex-West Midland Alliance), Blakenall and Walsall Wood (both ex-SCL(S)), Malvern Town (ex-Worcester League), Lower Gornal Athletic and Quarry Bank Celtic.

Midland Combination 1961-1964

1961-62

Promoted clubs are shown in bold, relegated clubs in bold-italics.

Division One

Allens Cross	34	22	7	5	92	33	51
Jack Moulds Athletic	34	22	7	5	90	37	51
Walsall Wood	34	23	5	6	99	42	51
Malvern Town	34	18	8	8	113	68	44
Blakenall	34	16	8	10	87	53	40
Paget Rangers	34	16	7	11	88	69	39
Alvechurch	34	15	8	11	81	62	38
Bromsgrove Rovers Reserves	34	15	5	14	63	71	35
Halesowen Town Reserves	34	12	8	14	80	75	32
Wolverhampton Wanderers "B"	34	13	5	16	60	78	31
Quarry Bank Celtic	34	12	6	16	75	76	30
Smethwick Town	34	13	4	17	64	67	30
Lower Gornal Athletic	34	12	6	16	62	98	30
Brierley Hill Alliance Reserves	34	13	2	19	59	90	28
Stourbridge Reserves	34	12	3	19	54	76	27
Moor Green Reserves	34	7	7	20	49	103	21
Bournville Athletic	34	6	8	20	46	83	20
Boldmere St. Michaels Reserves	34	3	8	23	30	111	14

Division Two

Allens Cross Reserves	32	24	4	4	101	44	52
Yardley Wood Social	32	22	4	6	85	35	48
Castle Rovers	32	22	2	8	83	50	46
Paget Rangers Reserves	32	20	5	7	87	48	45
Lye Town Reserves	32	17	5	10	83	52	39
Walsall Wood Reserves	32	17	4	11	77	55	38
Blakenall Reserves	32	15	4	13	66	74	34
Malvern Town Reserves	32	14	5	13	74	70	33
Alvechurch Reserves	32	13	5	14	71	56	31
British Legion (Austin)	32	14	2	16	90	85	30
Olton	32	14	2	16	66	69	30
Jack Moulds Athletic Reserves	32	13	2	17	60	64	28
Smethwick Town Reserves	32	9	5	18	69	92	23
Bournville Athletic Reserves	32	10	2	20	59	99	22
Lower Gornal Athletic Reserves	32	7	6	19	51	104	20
Crabbs Cross	32	5	5	22	44	104	15
Quarry Bank Celtic Reserves	32	2	6	24	55	120	10

Quarry Bank Celtic Reserves left the league. Hall Green Amateurs joined from the West Midland Alliance and Shirley Town also joined.

1962-63

Division One

Alvechurch	34	27	3	4	117	46	57
Wolverhampton Wanderers "B"	34	23	4	7	127	37	50
Paget Rangers	34	21	3	10	77	59	45
Blakenall	34	18	7	9	84	56	43
Malvern Town	34	20	3	11	97	65	43
Allens Cross	34	18	4	12	75	46	40
Jack Moulds Athletic	34	18	4	12	75	64	40
Walsall Wood	34	15	6	13	64	76	36
Halesowen Town Reserves	34	14	7	13	75	65	35
Stourbridge Reserves	34	15	4	15	73	77	34
Lower Gornal Athletic	34	12	8	14	58	96	32
Smethwick Town	34	13	2	19	67	75	28
Brierley Hill Alliance Reserves	34	11	6	17	59	71	28
Bromsgrove Rovers Reserves	34	10	7	17	59	77	27
Quarry Bank Celtic	34	10	6	18	46	72	26
Bournville Athletic	34	8	1	25	45	99	17
Boldmere St. Michaels Reserves	**34**	**7**	**2**	**25**	**48**	**119**	**16**
Moor Green Reserves	34	6	3	25	46	92	15

Smethwick Town changed their name to Smethwick Highfield. Lower Gornal Athletic moved to the WMRL and Boldmere St. Michaels joined from the WMRL.

Division Two

Hall Green Amateurs	**34**	**28**	**2**	**4**	**93**	**28**	**58**
Yardley Wood Social	34	25	3	6	122	34	53
Allens Cross Reserves	34	24	4	6	91	37	52
Shirley Town	34	20	7	7	76	43	47
Castle Rovers	34	20	6	8	83	44	46
Paget Rangers Reserves	34	16	8	10	95	59	40
Blakenall Reserves	34	18	4	12	74	55	40
Alvechurch Reserves	34	18	4	12	87	85	40
Lye Town Reserves	34	18	2	14	93	67	38
Malvern Town Reserves	34	13	5	16	97	98	31
Jack Moulds Athletic Reserves	34	14	3	17	64	74	31
Walsall Wood Reserves	34	12	5	17	72	77	29
Olton	34	11	5	18	66	88	27
Smethwick Town Reserves	34	8	7	19	46	85	23
British Legion (Austin)	34	6	5	23	45	133	17
Lower Gornal Athletic Reserves	34	6	4	24	54	94	16
Bournville Athletic Reserves	34	6	2	26	63	125	14
Crabbs Cross	34	4	2	28	45	140	10

Crabbs Cross left the league.
Coleshill Hall Hospital joined from the BYOB as Coleshill Hall.

1963-64

Division One

Hall Green Amateurs	34	28	4	2	85	28	60
Alvechurch	34	23	5	6	102	40	51
Walsall Wood	34	19	5	10	67	49	43
Halesowen Town Reserves	34	19	5	10	75	60	43
Wolverhampton Wanderers "B"	34	15	10	9	69	46	40
Quarry Bank Celtic	34	16	8	10	72	65	40
Moor Green Reserves	34	14	5	15	60	67	33
Boldmere St. Michaels	34	11	10	13	46	55	32
Allens Cross	34	12	7	15	56	63	31
Smethwick Highfield	34	12	7	15	64	76	31
Blakenall	34	10	10	14	61	63	30
Stourbridge Reserves	34	12	6	16	65	74	30
Paget Rangers	34	11	8	15	59	73	30
Jack Moulds Athletic	34	12	5	17	66	82	29
Brierley Hill Alliance Reserves	34	10	8	16	59	69	28
Malvern Town	34	11	5	18	69	81	27
Bromsgrove Rovers Reserves	34	9	4	21	48	68	22
Bournville Athletic	**34**	**4**	**4**	**26**	**47**	**111**	**12**

Kidderminster Harriers Reserves joined from the Warwickshire Combination.

Division Two

Castle Rovers	33	27	3	3	115	27	57
Coleshill Hall	34	26	2	6	143	61	54
Lower Gornal Athletic Reserves	33	25	2	6	99	34	52
Lye Town Reserves	34	20	6	8	102	55	46
Paget Rangers Reserves	33	21	2	10	87	39	44
Boldmere St. Michaels Reserves	33	17	6	10	76	61	40
Walsall Wood Reserves	33	16	5	12	66	63	37
Allens Cross Reserves	34	16	3	15	80	85	35
Shirley Town	27	11	3	13	57	57	25
Blakenall Reserves	34	13	4	17	75	95	30
Yardley Wood Social	34	10	8	16	66	68	28
Olton	34	10	4	20	53	86	24
Jack Moulds Athletic Reserves	34	9	6	19	46	90	24
Alvechurch Reserves	34	10	3	21	67	117	23
Smethwick Highfield Reserves	33	7	8	18	34	69	22
Malvern Town Reserves	34	10	1	23	61	97	21
British Legion (Austin)	34	9	3	22	73	134	21
Bournville Athletic Reserves	33	5	5	23	47	109	15

Shirley Town resigned in mid-season. Their position was decided on points average. British Legion (Austin) moved to the Kings Norton League and Yardley Wood Social moved to the WWMA. Bournville Athletic Reserves also left. Highgate United joined from the WWMA and Alkamatic joined from the Redditch League. Hall Green Amateurs Reserves also joined.

1964-65
Division One

Alvechurch	34	26	2	6	112	43	54
Hall Green Amateurs	34	24	4	6	73	32	52
Boldmere St. Michaels	34	18	7	9	75	53	43
Blakenall	34	19	4	11	75	57	42
Kidderminster Harriers Reserves	34	18	4	12	71	63	40
Allens Cross	34	15	8	11	74	65	38
Halesowen Town Reserves	34	16	4	14	63	56	36
Walsall Wood	34	16	4	14	59	64	36
Stourbridge Reserves	34	15	5	14	67	64	35
Bromsgrove Rovers Reserves	34	14	5	15	72	72	33
Jack Moulds Athletic	34	14	5	15	57	70	33
Wolverhampton Wanderers "B"	34	11	9	14	72	71	31
Paget Rangers	34	12	7	15	53	61	31
Malvern Town	34	11	6	17	62	77	28
Brierley Hill Alliance Reserves	34	11	3	20	56	74	25
Smethwick Highfield	34	8	7	19	49	81	23
Quarry Bank Celtic	**34**	**7**	**5**	**22**	**54**	**86**	**19**
Moor Green Reserves	**34**	**4**	**5**	**25**	**31**	**86**	**13**

Stourbridge Reserves and Kidderminster Harriers Reserves moved to the WMRL and Hall Green Amateurs also left the league.
Evesham United joined from the Warwickshire Combination and Moor Green and Sutton Coldfield Town joined from the WMRL.

Division Two

Hall Green Amateurs Reserves	34	24	5	5	89	44	53
Lower Gornal Athletic Reserves	34	22	7	5	100	39	51
Coleshill Hall	34	22	7	5	101	52	51
Highgate United	**34**	**20**	**5**	**9**	**94**	**58**	**45**
Alvechurch Reserves	34	20	5	9	98	62	45
Lye Town Reserves	34	20	3	11	87	53	43
Paget Rangers Reserves	34	18	4	12	104	80	40
Bournville Athletic	34	14	5	15	83	72	33
Castle Rovers	**34**	**14**	**4**	**16**	**58**	**77**	**32**
Walsall Wood Reserves	34	9	10	15	69	96	28
Malvern Town Reserves	34	10	7	17	78	87	27
Allens Cross Reserves	34	12	3	19	69	86	27
Alkamatic	34	10	6	18	74	109	26
Olton	34	11	3	20	74	99	25
Boldmere St. Michaels Reserves	34	10	4	20	76	105	24
Blakenall Reserves	34	9	4	21	62	110	22
Jack Moulds Athletic Reserves	34	9	3	22	54	96	21
Smethwick Highfield Reserves	34	8	3	23	57	102	19

Olton changed their name to Olton F.C. (Holdings) Ltd.
Lower Gornal Athletic Reserves moved to the WMRL and Blakenall Reserves, Walsall Wood Reserves and Hall Green Amateurs Reserves also left. Alcester Town and Castle Rovers Reserves joined from the Warwickshire Combination, Highgate United Reserves joined from the Birmingham AFA and Sutton Coldfield Town Reserves also joined.

1965-66
Division One

Evesham United	34	27	4	3	142	45	58
Alvechurch	34	23	5	6	101	27	51
Moor Green	34	23	4	7	87	42	50
Blakenall	34	16	10	8	80	53	42
Castle Rovers	34	17	8	9	56	43	42
Paget Rangers	34	13	9	12	51	47	35
Jack Moulds Athletic	34	14	5	15	59	65	33
Smethwick Highfield	34	14	5	15	59	74	33
Walsall Wood	34	9	12	13	58	71	30
Malvern Town	34	12	6	16	76	95	30
Boldmere St. Michaels	34	12	5	17	68	76	29
Bromsgrove Rovers Reserves	34	10	7	17	57	59	27
Halesowen Town Reserves	34	12	3	19	55	76	27
Sutton Coldfield Town	34	11	5	18	59	100	27
Brierley Hill Alliance Reserves	34	9	8	17	49	95	26
Highgate United	34	10	5	19	47	64	25
Allens Cross	34	11	3	20	53	95	25
Wolverhampton Wanderers "B"	34	8	6	20	49	79	22

Allens Cross and Castle Rovers merged to form Cross Castle United.
Oldbury United joined from the WWMA.

Division Two

Alvechurch Reserves	34	27	2	5	111	32	56
Coleshill Hall	34	26	1	7	116	53	53
Alkamatic	34	25	2	7	101	54	52
Moor Green Reserves	34	19	4	11	85	62	42
Alcester Town	34	17	6	11	77	58	40
Quarry Bank Celtic	34	14	10	10	85	75	38
Jack Moulds Athletic Reserves	34	15	3	16	59	70	33
Bournville Athletic	34	13	6	15	64	68	32
Boldmere St. Michaels Reserves	34	13	6	15	68	95	32
Paget Rangers Reserves	34	13	4	17	67	62	30
Malvern Town Reserves	34	12	6	16	72	83	30
Castle Rovers Reserves	34	9	9	16	57	74	27
Allens Cross Reserves	34	9	9	16	54	83	27
Sutton Coldfield Town Reserves	34	10	6	18	70	75	26
Lye Town Reserves	34	9	8	17	63	82	26
Olton F.C. (Holdings) Ltd.	34	8	10	16	53	74	26
Smethwick Highfield Reserves	34	10	5	19	58	97	25
Highgate United Reserves	34	6	5	23	38	101	17

Coleshill Hall disbanded and Olton F.C. (Holdings) Ltd. also left the league.
Knowle joined from the WWMA and Evesham United Reserves also joined.

1966-67
Division One

Alvechurch	34	26	5	3	94	20	57
Evesham United	34	25	5	4	115	39	55
Boldmere St. Michaels	34	23	4	7	75	44	50
Highgate United	34	21	7	6	79	37	49
Moor Green	34	18	6	10	87	54	42
Malvern Town	34	15	7	12	57	44	37
Jack Moulds Athletic	34	14	8	12	55	57	36
Paget Rangers	34	12	11	11	69	65	35
Walsall Wood	34	14	7	13	65	74	35
Oldbury United	34	12	10	12	80	67	34
Cross Castle United	34	14	4	16	42	46	32
Sutton Coldfield Town	34	12	6	16	63	61	30
Bromsgrove Rovers Reserves	34	7	10	17	51	92	24
Halesowen Town Reserves	34	9	4	21	53	89	22
Brierley Hill Alliance Reserves	34	9	4	21	50	90	22
Smethwick Highfield	34	8	4	22	51	90	20
Blakenall	34	8	3	23	62	103	19
Wolverhampton Wanderers "B"	34	3	7	24	33	109	13

Division Two

Highgate United Reserves	32	22	3	7	84	48	47
Alkamatic	32	17	9	6	65	41	43
Lye Town Reserves	32	16	7	9	79	57	39
Alcester Town	32	15	8	9	69	61	38
Knowle	32	16	5	11	74	61	37
Boldmere St. Michaels Reserves	32	15	6	11	80	69	36
Bournville Athletic	32	15	5	12	75	60	35
Alvechurch Reserves	32	13	8	11	73	57	34
Moor Green Reserves	32	14	6	12	63	59	34
Jack Moulds Athletic Reserves	32	14	5	13	59	78	33
Malvern Town Reserves	32	15	2	15	71	72	32
Paget Rangers Reserves	32	12	7	13	70	71	31
Cross Castle United Reserves	32	12	7	13	46	51	31
Quarry Bank Celtic	32	11	6	15	78	79	28
Sutton Coldfield Town Reserves	32	11	3	18	59	69	25
Smethwick Highfield Reserves	32	6	3	23	49	89	15
Evesham United Reserves	32	2	2	28	39	147	6

Alkamatic and Evesham United Reserves left the league.
Coleshill Town joined from the BYOB Mercian League, Whitmore Old Boys joined from the Wolverhampton Amateur League and Oldbury United Reserves also joined.

MIDLAND COMBINATION

1967-68

Division One

	P	W	D	L	F	A	Pts
Evesham United	34	27	2	5	90	43	56
Alvechurch	34	26	1	7	98	30	53
Moor Green	34	19	9	6	76	44	47
Malvern Town	34	18	9	7	63	40	45
Highgate United	34	19	6	9	82	40	44
Oldbury United	34	16	9	9	63	41	41
Paget Rangers	34	14	10	10	60	47	38
Jack Moulds Athletic	34	15	7	12	59	45	37
Boldmere St. Michaels	34	16	3	15	52	45	35
Bromsgrove Rovers Reserves	34	11	9	14	56	67	31
Cross Castle United	34	9	11	14	54	65	29
Blakenall	34	11	7	16	55	74	29
Walsall Wood	34	10	8	16	51	70	28
Sutton Coldfield Town	34	8	11	15	51	64	27
Brierley Hill Alliance Reserves	34	10	4	20	53	89	24
Smethwick Highfield	34	8	5	21	47	77	21
Halesowen Town Reserves	34	8	5	21	32	72	21
Wolverhampton Wanderers "B"	34	2	2	30	25	114	6

Jack Moulds Athletic changed their name to Solihull Amateurs. Halesowen Town Reserves and Brierley Hill Alliance Reserves moved to the WMRL and Bromsgrove Rovers Reserves also left the league.
Lydbrook Athletic and Warwickshire Constabulary joined from the Warwickshire Combination and Bridgnorth Town joined from the Kidderminster League.

Division Two

	P	W	D	L	F	A	Pts
Whitmore Old Boys	34	25	3	6	92	38	53
Coleshill Town	34	18	11	5	84	51	47
Bournville Athletic	34	19	7	8	71	48	45
Boldmere St. Michaels Reserves	34	18	8	8	67	43	44
Sutton Coldfield Town Reserves	34	18	4	12	71	65	40
Smethwick Highfield Reserves	34	17	4	13	72	68	38
Paget Rangers Reserves	34	14	8	12	63	55	36
Alcester Town	34	14	7	13	54	47	35
Moor Green Reserves	34	13	9	12	66	68	35
Quarry Bank Celtic	34	15	4	15	66	77	34
Lye Town Reserves	34	12	7	15	52	73	31
Highgate United Reserves	34	11	8	15	68	71	30
Malvern Town Reserves	34	10	8	16	56	74	28
Cross Castle United Reserves	34	9	7	18	57	82	25
Alvechurch Reserves	34	9	6	19	51	60	24
Jack Moulds Athletic Reserves	34	8	8	18	53	68	24
Knowle	34	7	8	19	46	76	22
Oldbury United Reserves	34	7	7	20	51	76	21

Lye Town Reserves moved to the WMRL.
Blakenall Reserves joined from the Bloxwich Combination.

1968-69

Division One

	P	W	D	L	F	A	Pts
Evesham United	34	23	8	3	107	39	54
Alvechurch	34	24	3	7	81	31	51
Oldbury United	34	21	8	5	67	29	50
Paget Rangers	34	23	3	8	69	34	49
Malvern Town	34	21	5	8	101	45	47
Sutton Coldfield Town	34	21	3	10	75	48	45
Moor Green	34	16	7	11	76	61	39
Highgate United	34	16	7	11	79	64	39
Boldmere St. Michaels	34	13	11	10	59	49	37
Solihull Amateurs	34	14	6	14	53	53	34
Cross Castle United	34	11	7	16	57	61	29
Whitmore Old Boys	34	10	8	16	48	69	28
Lydbrook Athletic	34	10	6	18	48	73	26
Blakenall	34	9	6	19	46	90	24
Bridgnorth Town	34	9	5	20	56	85	23
Smethwick Highfield	34	7	5	22	46	79	19
Walsall Wood	34	6	2	26	38	90	14
Warwickshire Constabulary	34	0	4	30	49	155	4

Warwickshire Constabulary changed name to Birmingham City Police.
Cross Castle United changed their name to Northfield Amateurs.

Division Two

	P	W	D	L	F	A	Pts
Highgate United Reserves	34	25	6	3	94	42	56
Knowle	34	22	7	5	88	42	51
Moor Green Reserves	34	20	7	7	85	44	47
Malvern Town Reserves	34	20	6	8	85	57	46
Coleshill Town	34	20	5	9	97	60	45
Alcester Town	34	17	5	12	82	68	39
Bournville Athletic	34	17	5	12	66	66	39
Paget Rangers Reserves	34	14	7	13	64	58	35
Oldbury United Reserves	34	14	6	14	59	58	34
Alvechurch Reserves	34	13	6	15	76	66	32
Cross Castle United Reserves	34	13	5	16	65	68	31
Solihull Amateurs Reserves	34	11	8	15	59	66	30
Sutton Coldfield Town Reserves	34	10	8	16	52	66	28
Quarry Bank Celtic	34	8	9	17	59	87	25
Wolverhampton Wanderers "B"	34	10	4	20	57	82	24
Smethwick Highfield Reserves	34	8	5	21	50	82	21
Blakenall Reserves	34	5	5	24	45	115	15
Boldmere St. Michaels Reserves	34	5	4	25	36	92	14

Blakenall Reserves and Cross Castle United Reserves both left the league.
Solihull Borough joined from the BYOB Mercian League and Northfield Amateurs Reserves also joined..

1969-70

Division One

Paget Rangers	34	23	7	4	97	31	53
Sutton Coldfield Town	34	21	6	7	75	31	48
Alvechurch	34	18	11	5	72	35	47
Evesham United	34	18	9	7	75	43	45
Malvern Town	34	18	6	10	75	53	42
Bridgnorth Town	34	17	4	13	78	66	38
Moor Green	34	11	14	9	57	48	36
Oldbury United	34	12	11	11	70	48	35
Solihull Amateurs	34	12	10	12	57	56	34
Blakenall	34	13	8	13	46	58	34
Birmingham City Police	34	13	7	14	51	55	33
Highgate United	34	12	6	16	58	72	30
Smethwick Highfield	34	9	8	17	52	66	26
Northfield Amateurs	34	9	8	17	47	72	26
Whitmore Old Boys	**34**	**10**	**6**	**18**	**43**	**79**	**26**
Boldmere St. Michaels	34	7	9	18	43	72	23
Walsall Wood	34	7	9	18	33	76	23
Lydbrook Athletic	34	5	3	26	33	101	13

Northfield Amateurs changed their name to Northfield.
Solihull Amateurs moved to the WMRL and Lydbrook Athletic moved to the Gloucestershire County League.
Stratford Town joined from the WMRL.

Division Two

Coleshill Town	34	27	4	3	99	30	58
Bournville Athletic	34	19	8	7	86	59	46
Moor Green Reserves	34	17	10	7	74	44	44
Alcester Town	34	17	8	9	56	41	42
Knowle	34	17	4	13	77	61	38
Solihull Borough	**34**	**14**	**9**	**11**	**66**	**56**	**37**
Highgate United Reserves	34	12	13	9	63	58	37
Wolverhampton Wanderers "B"	34	16	4	14	63	54	36
Malvern Town Reserves	34	14	6	14	78	80	34
Smethwick Highfield Reserves	34	10	12	12	55	71	32
Paget Rangers Reserves	34	10	11	13	39	41	31
Alvechurch Reserves	34	12	7	15	66	74	31
Sutton Coldfield Town Reserves	34	13	2	19	52	62	28
Northfield Amateurs Reserves	34	12	3	19	60	68	27
Oldbury United Reserves	34	9	7	18	62	80	25
Boldmere St. Michaels Reserves	34	11	3	20	55	94	25
Quarry Bank Celtic	34	7	7	20	52	84	21
Solihull Amateurs Reserves	34	5	10	19	36	82	20

Solihull Amateurs Reserves and Wolverhampton Wanderers "B" left the league. Mile Oak Rovers joined from the BYOB Mercian League and Solihull Town and Astwood Bank Rovers joined from the Worcester & DL.

1970-71

Division One

Paget Rangers	34	25	5	4	81	32	55
Sutton Coldfield Town	34	22	8	4	75	32	52
Evesham United	34	19	8	7	78	45	46
Moor Green	34	17	9	8	63	33	43
Alvechurch	34	17	7	10	67	47	41
Boldmere St. Michaels	34	16	9	9	62	52	41
Malvern Town	34	15	8	11	60	59	38
Blakenall	34	16	5	13	65	56	37
Oldbury United	34	14	8	12	64	40	36
Highgate United	34	13	8	13	58	52	34
Bridgnorth Town	34	12	5	17	70	83	29
Smethwick Highfield	34	10	8	16	45	70	28
Walsall Wood	34	10	7	17	49	71	27
Knowle	34	8	10	16	57	70	26
Birmingham City Police	34	9	5	20	39	76	23
Northfield	34	8	6	20	41	68	22
Stratford Town	34	6	6	22	27	70	18
Whitmore Old Boys	34	5	6	23	45	90	16

Division Two

Solihull Town	34	22	8	4	80	33	52
Solihull Borough	34	22	8	4	77	35	52
Highgate United Reserves	34	21	5	8	89	56	47
Oldbury United Reserves	34	18	9	7	62	36	45
Astwood Bank Rovers	34	19	4	11	58	48	42
Moor Green Reserves	34	12	16	6	65	32	40
Coleshill Town	34	17	5	12	67	47	39
Mile Oak Rovers	34	14	8	12	64	67	36
Bournville Athletic	34	10	11	13	50	61	31
Sutton Coldfield Town Reserves	34	11	8	15	59	61	30
Alvechurch Reserves	34	13	4	17	61	70	30
Paget Rangers Reserves	34	11	7	16	49	51	29
Northfield Reserves	34	11	7	16	40	59	29
Malvern Town Reserves	34	9	9	16	47	60	27
Alcester Town	34	10	5	19	37	75	25
Quarry Bank Celtic	34	10	3	21	59	88	23
Boldmere St. Michaels Reserves	34	6	7	21	30	71	19
Smethwick Highfield Reserves	34	4	8	22	33	77	16

Smethwick Highfield Reserves, Paget Rangers Reserves and Alvechurch Reserves all left the league.
Albion Haden United joined from the West Midland Metropolitan League and Bridgnorth Town Reserves and Westphalians also joined.

1971-72

Division One

Alvechurch	34	27	1	6	111	27	55
Oldbury United	34	23	6	5	68	35	52
Sutton Coldfield Town	34	17	11	6	65	44	45
Highgate United	34	18	8	8	63	31	44
Evesham United	34	18	7	9	62	44	43
Moor Green	34	13	12	9	55	44	38
Malvern Town	34	13	10	11	50	44	36
Bridgnorth Town	34	13	7	14	48	50	33
Walsall Wood	34	14	4	16	48	54	32
Knowle	34	12	7	15	50	54	31
Solihull Borough	34	11	9	14	52	59	31
Blakenall	34	10	7	17	46	62	27
Boldmere St. Michaels	34	9	9	16	38	54	27
Birmingham City Police	34	10	7	17	42	73	27
Paget Rangers	34	8	10	16	35	52	26
Stratford Town	34	7	11	16	46	66	25
Northfield	34	10	4	20	46	70	24
Smethwick Highfield	**34**	**4**	**8**	**22**	**30**	**87**	**16**

Racing F.C. (Warwick) joined from the West Midlands Regional League.

Division Two

Highgate United Reserves	34	21	10	3	83	31	52
Alcester Town	34	19	12	3	77	43	50
Moor Green Reserves	34	21	6	7	79	46	48
Coleshill Town	34	18	10	6	67	30	46
Albion Haden United	34	21	4	9	93	50	46
Bridgnorth Town Reserves	34	17	6	11	80	64	40
Astwood Bank Rovers	34	17	4	13	62	43	38
Solihull Town	34	13	8	13	45	52	34
Whitmore Old Boys	34	12	7	15	55	62	31
Oldbury United Reserves	34	14	2	18	40	50	30
Mile Oak Rovers	34	10	8	16	51	56	28
Northfield Reserves	34	12	4	18	52	71	28
Boldmere St. Michaels Reserves	34	9	10	15	47	65	28
Bournville Athletic	34	11	6	17	45	71	28
Sutton Coldfield Town Reserves	34	9	9	16	49	56	27
Malvern Town Reserves	34	8	6	20	42	72	22
Westphalians	34	6	9	19	37	78	21
Quarry Bank Celtic	34	5	5	24	28	92	15

Westphalians and Quarry Bank Celtic left the league.
Chelmsley Town joined from the BYOB Mercian League.

Midland Combination 1972-1975

1972-73

Division One

Highgate United	34	28	5	1	85	21	61
Alvechurch	34	27	4	3	104	23	58
Sutton Coldfield Town	34	23	5	6	75	31	51
Evesham United	34	20	8	6	70	35	48
Malvern Town	34	17	8	9	64	53	42
Oldbury United	34	16	8	10	50	39	40
Racing Club (Warwick)	34	14	8	12	50	45	36
Paget Rangers	34	14	7	13	45	52	35
Moor Green	34	12	10	12	45	43	34
Birmingham City Police	34	10	10	14	46	61	30
Bridgnorth Town	34	10	8	16	44	66	28
Stratford Town	34	9	9	16	35	38	27
Walsall Wood	34	9	6	19	36	71	24
Solihull Borough	34	7	9	18	42	57	23
Northfield	34	6	10	18	33	60	22
Boldmere St. Michaels	34	6	8	20	41	71	20
Knowle	34	8	4	22	36	70	20
Blakenall	34	4	5	25	17	82	13

Alvechurch moved to the West Midlands Regional League.

Division Two

Albion Haden United	34	21	9	4	80	40	51
Whitmore Old Boys	34	20	10	4	68	32	50
Solihull Town	34	20	8	6	72	26	48
Astwood Bank Rovers	34	19	5	10	57	33	43
Alcester Town	34	14	12	8	50	37	40
Sutton Coldfield Town Reserves	34	16	5	13	56	46	37
Oldbury United Reserves	34	11	14	9	45	39	36
Smethwick Highfield	34	13	8	13	47	57	34
Northfield Reserves	34	14	6	14	44	55	34
Chelmsley Town	34	12	9	13	57	54	33
Coleshill Town	34	12	9	13	47	52	33
Boldmere St. Michaels Reserves	34	12	4	18	52	71	28
Highgate United Reserves	34	9	8	17	44	58	26
Bournville Athletic	34	8	10	16	46	65	26
Moor Green Reserves	34	10	5	19	59	80	25
Mile Oak Rovers	34	8	9	17	46	63	25
Malvern Town Reserves	34	7	11	16	37	57	25
Bridgnorth Town Reserves	34	6	6	22	28	70	18

Solihull Town and Highgate United Reserves left the league.
Rowley Regis joined from the Staffordshire County League (South),
Wolverhampton Wanderers "A" joined from the WMRL and Racing Club
(Warwick) Reserves and Coventry Amateurs Reserves also joined.

1973-74

Division One

Highgate United	32	27	3	2	95	16	57
Malvern Town	32	19	7	6	69	34	45
Solihull Borough	32	17	8	7	58	31	42
Sutton Coldfield Town	32	14	10	8	52	35	38
Blakenall	32	12	14	6	47	32	38
Northfield	32	14	8	10	52	49	36
Bridgnorth Town	32	13	9	10	43	35	35
Evesham United	32	13	9	10	54	46	35
Moor Green	32	13	9	10	51	48	35
Racing Club (Warwick)	32	11	10	11	41	39	32
Paget Rangers	32	13	5	14	48	49	31
Oldbury United	32	11	5	16	40	46	27
Birmingham City Police	32	9	5	18	45	53	23
Stratford Town	32	7	7	18	38	66	21
Boldmere St. Michaels	32	7	5	20	31	72	19
Knowle	32	5	5	22	26	85	15
Walsall Wood	32	4	7	21	23	77	15

Birmingham City Police merged with West Midlands Constabulary of the SCL(S), and continued in the Midland Combination as West Midlands Police. Northfield changed their name to Northfield Town.
Cinderford Town joined from the Gloucestershire County League.

Division Two

Astwood Bank Rovers	38	26	6	6	88	31	58
Moor Green Reserves	38	27	4	7	84	39	58
Wolverhampton Wanderers "B"	38	20	7	11	88	50	47
Albion Haden United	38	17	13	8	71	49	47
Coleshill Town	38	18	7	13	85	60	43
Chelmsley Town	38	15	11	12	75	65	41
Whitmore Old Boys	38	16	8	14	78	62	40
Bridgnorth Town Reserves	38	11	16	11	54	59	38
Smethwick Highfield	38	12	14	12	54	62	38
Malvern Town Reserves	38	15	7	16	67	69	37
Northfield Reserves	38	13	11	14	55	67	37
Oldbury United Reserves	38	14	8	16	68	61	36
Sutton Coldfield Town Reserves	38	14	8	16	61	70	36
Mile Oak Rovers	38	12	9	17	69	66	33
Racing Club (Warwick) Reserves	38	12	9	17	65	68	33
Bournville Athletic	38	15	3	20	75	107	33
Rowley Regis	38	12	5	21	56	81	29
Coventry Amateurs Reserves	38	10	8	20	49	66	28
Alcester Town	38	11	6	21	45	74	28
Boldmere St. Michaels Reserves	38	7	6	25	46	127	20

Coventry Amateurs changed their name to Coventry Sporting.
Racing Club (Warwick) Reserves and Bridgnorth Town Reserves both left the league. Walsall Sportsco joined from the Birmingham Works League and Hurley Daw Mill Welfare joined from the BYOB Mercian League.

1974-75

Division One

Highgate United	34	22	10	2	71	20	54
Moor Green	34	22	6	6	67	38	50
Solihull Borough	34	17	10	7	49	40	44
Blakenall	34	16	11	7	53	32	43
Sutton Coldfield Town	34	16	8	10	59	40	40
Cinderford Town	34	15	8	11	64	44	38
West Midlands Police	34	15	8	11	42	39	38
Malvern Town	34	15	7	12	55	39	37
Northfield Town	34	13	11	10	55	45	37
Bridgnorth Town	34	12	10	12	43	50	34
Evesham United	34	13	7	14	54	47	33
Paget Rangers	34	11	10	13	45	44	32
Oldbury United	34	12	8	14	45	46	32
Stratford Town	34	10	7	17	45	64	27
Racing Club (Warwick)	34	7	8	19	26	59	22
Knowle	34	7	6	21	42	62	20
Boldmere St. Michaels	34	6	6	22	30	72	18
Walsall Wood	**34**	**3**	**7**	**24**	**23**	**87**	**13**

Stratford Town moved to the Hellenic League.
Cadbury Heath joined from the Gloucestershire County League.

Division Two

Whitmore Old Boys	38	27	7	4	94	32	61
Coleshill Town	**38**	**26**	**5**	**7**	**80**	**36**	**57**
Alcester Town	38	20	11	7	78	41	51
Smethwick Highfield	38	21	8	9	86	49	50
Walsall Sportsco	38	19	9	10	69	35	47
Albion Haden United	38	18	9	11	72	50	45
Astwood Bank Rovers	38	17	10	11	71	60	44
Wolverhampton Wanderers "A"	38	16	9	13	74	56	41
Malvern Town Reserves	38	14	12	12	66	50	40
Mile Oak Rovers	38	16	7	15	65	39	39
Hurley Daw Mill Welfare	38	17	3	18	77	88	37
Moor Green Reserves	38	10	14	14	45	52	34
Chelmsley Town	38	15	4	19	57	71	34
Rowley Regis	38	10	11	17	41	77	31
Northfield Town Reserves	38	12	6	20	60	72	30
Sutton Coldfield Town Reserves	38	12	5	21	60	78	29
Coventry Sporting Reserves	38	11	7	20	51	68	29
Oldbury United Reserves	38	10	7	21	42	79	27
Bournville Athletic	38	7	6	25	45	106	20
Boldmere St. Michaels Reserves	38	4	6	28	36	104	14

Albion Haden United changed their name to Cradley Town.
Northfield Town Reserves left the league.
Studley Sporting joined from the BYOB Mercian League.

Midland Combination 1975-1978

1975-76 Division One

Northfield Town	34	23	5	6	63	30	51
Moor Green	34	20	10	4	72	39	50
Malvern Town	34	20	9	5	66	30	49
Paget Rangers	34	19	7	8	50	39	45
Racing Club (Warwick)	34	17	8	9	42	29	42
Sutton Coldfield Town	34	16	9	9	57	33	41
West Midlands Police	34	14	10	10	46	40	38
Blakenall	34	12	13	9	54	33	37
Bridgnorth Town	34	9	18	7	48	45	36
Evesham United	34	12	11	11	51	40	35
Solihull Borough	34	9	15	10	41	43	33
Cadbury Heath	34	11	8	15	47	47	30
Highgate United	34	11	8	15	46	53	30
Cinderford Town	34	8	8	18	40	60	24
Oldbury United	34	6	10	18	35	57	22
Boldmere St. Michaels	34	5	12	17	23	49	22
Coleshill Town	34	2	11	21	26	72	15
Knowle	34	2	8	24	21	89	12

Division Two

Whitmore Old Boys	38	27	4	7	79	35	58
Cradley Town	38	25	7	6	112	42	57
Alcester Town	38	24	8	6	90	41	56
Hurley Daw Mill Welfare	38	24	7	7	79	35	55
Astwood Bank Rovers	38	21	11	6	101	53	53
Walsall Sportsco	38	18	11	9	59	41	47
Studley Sporting	38	20	6	12	81	54	46
Walsall Wood	38	18	9	11	61	46	45
Moor Green Reserves	38	16	6	16	70	66	38
Chelmsley Town	38	13	10	15	53	65	36
Smethwick Highfield	38	12	11	15	61	60	35
Malvern Town Reserves	38	12	10	16	55	66	34
Mile Oak Rovers	38	9	12	17	45	70	30
Oldbury United Reserves	38	11	7	20	53	71	29
Coventry Sporting Reserves	38	8	11	19	44	67	27
Boldmere St. Michaels Reserves	38	12	3	23	42	81	27
Wolverhampton Wanderers "A"	38	10	7	21	44	87	27
Rowley Regis	38	6	9	23	44	94	21
Bournville Athletic	38	5	10	23	46	94	20
Sutton Coldfield Town Reserves	38	7	5	26	33	84	19

Astwood Bank Rovers changed their name to Astwood Bank.
Whitmore Old Boys merged with Oxley of the WMRL where they played as Wolverhampton United. Coventry Sporting Reserves moved to the WMRL and Oldbury United Reserves also left the league.
Polesworth joined from the BYOB Mercian League, Rockwood Albion joined from the West Midland Metropolitan League and West Midlands Police Reserves joined from the SCL(S).

1976-77 Division One

Blakenall	34	19	10	5	52	24	48
Bridgnorth Town	34	22	4	8	77	36	48
West Midlands Police	34	19	8	7	47	26	46
Cinderford Town	34	16	9	9	59	46	41
Malvern Town	34	16	8	10	44	35	40
Evesham United	34	17	5	12	52	41	39
Sutton Coldfield Town	34	15	8	11	46	35	38
Highgate United	34	13	9	12	44	36	35
Paget Rangers	34	14	7	13	45	45	35
Knowle	34	11	10	13	50	52	32
Moor Green	34	13	4	17	46	54	30
Coleshill Town	34	12	6	16	39	54	30
Oldbury United	34	12	5	17	41	49	29
Boldmere St. Michaels	34	12	5	17	38	49	29
Racing Club (Warwick)	34	8	12	14	33	46	28
Solihull Borough	34	11	4	19	42	65	26
Northfield Town	34	9	7	18	40	58	25
Cadbury Heath	34	2	9	23	18	62	13

Cadbury Heath moved to the Avon Premier Combination.
Stratford Town joined from the Hellenic League.

Division Two

Astwood Bank	38	27	3	8	93	44	57
Walsall Sportsco	**38**	**22**	**9**	**7**	**68**	**33**	**53**
Polesworth	38	23	5	10	68	41	51
Moor Green Reserves	38	18	13	7	87	49	49
Cradley Town	38	22	4	12	82	53	48
Hurley Daw Mill Welfare	38	16	13	9	54	41	45
Mile Oak Rovers	**38**	**18**	**8**	**12**	**58**	**48**	**44**
Rowley Regis	38	18	6	14	62	41	42
Sutton Coldfield Town Reserves	38	14	11	13	47	51	39
Studley Sporting	38	14	11	13	58	70	39
Alcester Town	38	14	10	14	70	63	38
Walsall Wood	38	15	7	16	64	58	37
Wolverhampton Wanderers "A"	38	11	10	17	51	56	32
Malvern Town Reserves	38	10	11	17	49	80	31
Chelmsley Town	38	11	8	19	41	56	30
West Midlands Police Reserves	38	6	15	17	42	56	27
Rockwood Albion	38	10	7	21	53	86	27
Smethwick Highfield	38	7	11	20	49	89	25
Bournville Athletic	38	7	9	22	56	100	23
Boldmere St. Michaels Reserves	38	6	11	21	36	73	23

Polesworth changed their name to Polesworth North Warwick.
Wolverhampton Wanderers "A" left the league. Stafford F.C. joined from the SCL(S), Kings Heath joined from the BYOB Mercian League and Tamworth Reserves also joined.

1977-78 Division One

Sutton Coldfield Town	38	20	12	6	77	34	52
Paget Rangers	38	21	9	8	74	36	51
Blakenall	38	19	13	6	57	24	51
Walsall Sportsco	38	20	10	8	62	32	50
Cinderford Town	38	18	10	10	73	39	46
Bridgnorth Town	38	16	14	8	60	28	46
Moor Green	38	16	14	8	66	41	46
Malvern Town	38	16	13	9	59	41	45
Racing Club (Warwick)	38	16	10	12	51	44	42
Evesham United	38	15	12	11	49	46	42
Solihull Borough	38	10	17	11	45	48	37
Highgate United	38	14	7	17	56	62	35
Mile Oak Rovers	38	9	17	12	35	47	35
Northfield Town	38	11	12	15	55	60	34
Boldmere St. Michaels	38	11	10	17	35	48	32
Oldbury United	38	10	12	16	51	65	32
Coleshill Town	38	8	10	20	38	79	26
West Midlands Police	38	4	17	17	32	61	25
Knowle	38	7	6	25	38	80	20
Stratford Town	**38**	**4**	**5**	**29**	**29**	**127**	**13**

Division Two

Hurley Daw Mill Welfare	38	27	8	3	69	19	62
Cradley Town	38	24	9	5	76	35	57
Walsall Wood	**38**	**19**	**13**	**6**	**72**	**49**	**51**
Sutton Coldfield Town Reserves	38	20	9	9	85	50	49
Rowley Regis	38	19	9	10	58	39	47
Astwood Bank	38	18	8	12	61	43	44
Studley Sporting	38	16	10	12	70	53	42
Stafford F.C.	38	15	11	12	62	60	41
Tamworth Reserves	38	15	9	14	53	61	39
Rockwood Albion	38	13	12	13	55	48	38
Boldmere St. Michaels Reserves	38	15	8	15	52	47	38
Moor Green Reserves	38	6	6	16	71	70	38
Kings Heath	38	13	7	18	45	53	33
Chelmsley Town	38	10	13	15	39	49	33
Smethwick Highfield	38	10	11	17	46	52	31
West Midlands Police Reserves	38	13	5	20	52	75	31
Bournville Athletic	38	10	9	19	58	76	29
Polesworth North Warwick	38	10	8	20	45	67	28
Alcester Town	38	6	5	27	32	91	17
Malvern Town Reserves	38	3	6	29	30	100	12

Malvern Town Reserves left and Witton Social joined.

Midland Combination 1978-1980

1978-79

Division One

Team	P	W	D	L	F	A	Pts
Sutton Coldfield Town	38	26	9	3	104	30	61
Oldbury United	38	20	11	7	49	29	51
Bridgnorth Town	38	19	11	8	54	31	49
Boldmere St. Michaels	38	20	9	9	44	35	49
Walsall Sportsco	38	18	11	9	58	41	47
Blakenall	38	17	10	11	57	38	44
Solihull Borough	38	18	8	12	59	46	44
Paget Rangers	38	16	10	12	50	41	42
Knowle	38	17	7	14	51	44	41
Mile Oak Rovers	38	15	10	13	42	37	40
Moor Green	38	16	7	15	70	55	39
Highgate United	38	13	7	18	46	54	33
Malvern Town	38	9	15	14	39	51	33
West Midlands Police	38	11	11	16	32	46	33
Racing Club (Warwick)	38	11	10	17	41	46	32
Walsall Wood	38	10	11	17	43	65	31
Cinderford Town	38	10	10	18	36	64	30
Northfield Town	38	12	5	21	41	62	29
Evesham United	38	7	5	26	29	80	19
Coleshill Town	38	1	11	26	22	72	13

Malvern Town, Blakenall & Sutton Coldfield Town moved to the WMRL.
Chipping Norton Town joined from the Hellenic League.

Division Two

Team	P	W	D	L	F	A	Pts
Stafford F.C.	38	27	6	5	82	29	60
Studley Sporting	**38**	**25**	**6**	**7**	**105**	**46**	**56**
Stratford Town	38	21	12	5	69	32	54
Cradley Town	**38**	**21**	**7**	**10**	**73**	**44**	**49**
Rowley Regis	38	19	10	9	76	39	48
Astwood Bank	38	18	11	9	74	52	47
Hurley Daw Mill Welfare	38	18	10	10	70	40	46
Chelmsley Town	38	17	8	13	61	44	42
Kings Heath	38	14	12	12	51	49	40
Moor Green Reserves	38	16	6	16	63	56	38
Witton Social	38	12	12	14	40	44	36
Polesworth North Warwick	38	12	10	16	51	59	34
Alcester Town	38	12	10	16	48	67	34
Sutton Coldfield Town Reserves	38	13	7	18	69	83	33
Smethwick Highfield	38	11	9	18	56	80	31
Rockwood Albion	38	8	14	16	55	71	30
Boldmere St. Michaels Reserves	38	8	7	23	46	79	23
West Midlands Police Reserves	38	7	8	23	47	90	22
Tamworth Reserves	38	9	4	25	46	97	22
Bournville Athletic	38	4	7	27	32	113	15

Witton Social changed their name to GEC Witton Social.
Boldmere St. Michaels Reserves and West Midlands Police Reserves left the league. Ludlow Colts, Bedworth United Reserves, Mile Oak Rovers Reserves and Highgate United Reserves all joined.

A new Third Division was formed with 18 founder members:
Bartley Green, Bilston United, Darlaston Old Boys, Hay Green, Kingsbury United, Littleton, Sheldon Promovere, Solihull Social, Stone Town, Wythall, Yardley Wood United and the Reserves of:
Boldmere St. Michaels, Bridgnorth Town, Bromsgrove Brookfield, Cradley Town, GEC Witton Social, Studley Sporting and Walsall Wood.

1979-80

Division One

Team	P	W	D	L	F	A	Pts
Bridgnorth Town	38	26	7	5	78	20	59
Moor Green	38	24	8	6	83	39	56
Oldbury United	38	21	8	9	71	41	50
Walsall Sportsco	38	18	13	7	55	36	49
Highgate United	38	18	8	12	65	56	44
Chipping Norton Town	38	16	11	11	56	41	43
Mile Oak Rovers	38	13	16	9	46	42	42
Boldmere St. Michaels	38	14	13	11	51	34	41
Evesham United	38	16	9	13	58	42	41
West Midlands Police	38	16	8	14	52	56	40
Cinderford Town	38	12	15	11	41	41	39
Solihull Borough	38	13	10	15	53	63	36
Knowle	38	11	11	16	36	43	33
Coleshill Town	38	12	9	17	42	54	33
Racing Club (Warwick)	38	8	15	15	31	54	31
Walsall Wood	38	7	15	16	36	57	29
Paget Rangers	38	9	9	20	41	64	27
Cradley Town	38	9	8	21	34	57	26
Studley Sporting	**38**	**6**	**9**	**23**	**40**	**97**	**21**
Northfield Town	**38**	**5**	**10**	**23**	**31**	**63**	**20**

Division Two

Team	P	W	D	L	F	A	Pts
Hurley Daw Mill Welfare	**38**	**26**	**7**	**5**	**77**	**32**	**59**
Smethwick Highfield	**38**	**26**	**5**	**7**	**100**	**39**	**57**
GEC Witton Social	38	23	7	8	64	34	53
Bedworth United Reserves	38	20	12	6	76	45	52
Mile Oak Rovers Reserves	38	20	11	7	70	42	51
Chelmsley Town	38	20	7	11	61	44	47
Stratford Town	38	19	7	12	71	48	45
Stafford F.C.	38	19	7	12	59	46	45
Moor Green Reserves	38	15	13	10	78	56	43
Rockwood Albion	38	15	6	17	55	63	36
Kings Heath	38	11	13	14	47	49	35
Polesworth North Warwick	38	12	10	16	49	49	34
Alcester Town	38	12	10	16	38	51	34
Sutton Coldfield Town Reserves	38	12	8	18	58	59	32
Astwood Bank	38	11	9	18	29	54	31
Tamworth Reserves	38	10	6	22	37	76	26
Ludlow Colts	38	7	10	21	42	79	24
Bournville Athletic	38	5	10	23	37	82	20
Rowley Regis	38	5	9	24	37	77	19
Highgate United Reserves	**38**	**5**	**7**	**26**	**41**	**101**	**17**

Tamworth Reserves moved to the WMRL and Rowley Regis also left.
Banbury United Reserves joined.

Division Three

Team	P	W	D	L	F	A	Pts
Sheldon Promovere	**34**	**30**	**3**	**1**	**140**	**30**	**63**
Wythall	34	21	5	8	83	40	47
Yardley Wood United	**34**	**21**	**4**	**9**	**66**	**44**	**46**
Stone Town	34	19	4	11	83	58	42
Kingsbury United	34	17	7	10	56	41	41
Bartley Green	34	15	8	11	55	54	38
Bromsgrove Brookfield	34	15	6	13	57	52	36
Darlaston Old Boys	34	11	12	11	50	60	34
Bridgnorth Town Reserves	34	14	5	15	49	57	33
Littleton	34	13	4	17	44	50	30
Hay Green	34	10	9	15	50	72	29
Studley Sporting Reserves	34	8	11	15	44	55	27
Solihull Social	34	11	5	18	46	68	27
Walsall Wood Reserves	34	10	6	18	49	58	26
Boldmere St. Michaels Reserves	34	8	10	16	45	64	26
GEC Witton Social Reserves	34	8	9	17	52	81	25
Cradley Town Reserves	34	9	6	19	41	73	24
Bilston United	34	6	6	22	43	90	18
					1053	1047	

Bilston United, Stone Town, Studley Sporting Reserves and Solihull Social left the league. Bolehall Swifts joined from the SCL(S), Southam United joined from the Coventry & North Warwickshire League and Polesworth North Warwick Reserves also joined.

1980-81
Division One

Moor Green	38	28	7	3	109	30	63
Bridgnorth Town	38	22	7	9	76	38	51
Mile Oak Rovers	38	21	8	9	63	43	50
Cinderford Town	38	22	5	11	68	30	49
Boldmere St. Michaels	38	18	11	9	50	39	47
Oldbury United	38	18	10	10	65	47	46
Chipping Norton Town	38	16	11	11	58	45	43
Racing Club (Warwick)	38	16	10	12	66	46	42
Knowle	38	16	10	12	50	42	42
Hurley Daw Mill Welfare	38	14	11	13	54	56	39
Highgate United	38	16	6	16	79	61	38
West Midlands Police	38	11	15	12	62	58	37
Paget Rangers	38	13	11	14	42	41	37
Solihull Borough	38	13	10	15	58	69	36
Evesham United	38	10	10	18	57	81	30
Walsall Sportsco	38	8	12	18	49	69	28
Walsall Wood	38	10	8	20	42	71	28
Smethwick Highfield	38	8	10	20	37	74	26
Cradley Town	38	5	4	29	33	100	14
Coleshill Town	38	5	4	29	27	104	14

Division Two

Sheldon Promovere	38	27	11	0	123	41	65
Bedworth United Reserves	38	22	7	9	73	37	51
Kings Heath	38	21	8	9	79	52	50
Stratford Town	**38**	**21**	**8**	**9**	**59**	**47**	**50**
Moor Green Reserves	38	17	9	12	78	56	43
Astwood Bank	38	17	9	12	63	53	43
GEC Witton Social	38	17	8	13	74	58	42
Northfield Town	**38**	**16**	**9**	**13**	**78**	**58**	**41**
Studley Sporting	38	17	7	14	66	61	41
Sutton Coldfield Town Reserves	38	17	6	15	67	60	40
Yardley Wood United	38	16	6	16	74	63	38
Banbury United Reserves	38	13	9	16	46	59	35
Chelmsley Town	38	11	12	15	52	75	34
Mile Oak Rovers Reserves	38	13	7	18	48	72	33
Alcester Town	38	12	8	18	62	69	32
Bournville Athletic	38	9	10	19	51	78	28
Polesworth North Warwick	38	11	5	22	55	90	27
Stafford F.C.	38	9	8	21	42	74	26
Ludlow Colts	*38*	*8*	*5*	*25*	*34*	*78*	*21*
Rockwood Albion	*38*	*7*	*6*	*25*	*34*	*77*	*20*

Stafford F.C. changed their name to Stafford Town.
Sheldon Promovere left the league.
Alvechurch Reserves joined from the WMRL and Knowle Reserves also joined.

Division Three

Southam United	**30**	**26**	**3**	**1**	**103**	**28**	**55**
Walsall Wood Reserves	**30**	**19**	**5**	**6**	**68**	**34**	**43**
Kingsbury United	**30**	**15**	**6**	**9**	**59**	**37**	**36**
Boldmere St. Michaels Reserves	30	14	6	10	47	47	34
Littleton	30	14	6	10	40	40	34
Bromsgrove Brookfield	30	14	5	11	50	35	33
Bolehall Swifts	30	12	8	10	50	46	32
Bartley Green	30	12	6	12	48	43	30
Hay Green	30	12	5	13	51	47	29
Wythall	30	11	6	13	61	62	28
Darlaston Old Boys	30	8	8	14	48	63	24
Bridgnorth Town Reserves	30	7	8	15	33	50	22
Polesworth North Warwick Res.	30	9	4	17	34	70	22
GEC Witton Social Reserves	30	9	2	19	33	62	20
Cradley Town Reserves	30	8	4	18	32	70	20
Highgate United Reserves	30	6	6	18	43	66	18

Darlaston Old Boys and Bartley Green left the league.
Ashted Rovers, Enville Athletic and the Reserves of Paget Rangers, Coleshill Town, Smethwick Highfield, Stratford Town and Solihull Borough all joined.

Goal difference replaced goal average from the next season onwards.

1981-82
Division One

Chipping Norton Town	42	27	9	6	106	43	63
Highgate United	42	27	6	9	85	46	60
Mile Oak Rovers	42	24	10	8	78	49	58
Cinderford Town	42	19	16	7	71	40	54
Oldbury United	42	22	8	12	67	44	52
Bridgnorth Town	42	20	12	10	65	47	52
Moor Green	42	22	7	13	84	59	51
Knowle	42	16	16	10	64	50	48
Walsall Sportsco	42	18	10	14	68	54	46
Racing Club (Warwick)	42	16	13	13	68	64	45
West Midlands Police	42	14	14	14	70	70	42
Boldmere St. Michaels	42	14	14	14	59	60	42
Coleshill Town	42	16	8	18	57	68	40
Stratford Town	42	12	12	18	37	49	36
Smethwick Highfield	42	13	10	19	49	64	36
Northfield Town	42	15	6	21	56	76	36
Solihull Borough	42	11	13	18	46	68	35
Cradley Town	42	12	10	20	60	80	34
Paget Rangers	42	10	14	18	43	63	34
Walsall Wood	42	9	8	25	40	82	26
Evesham United	42	6	9	27	40	83	21
Hurley Daw Mill Welfare	42	3	7	32	42	96	13

Walsall Sportsco and Walsall Wood merged to form Walsall Borough.
Oldbury United moved to the Southern League.

Division Two

Bedworth United Reserves	38	29	3	6	93	37	61
Southam United	38	24	11	3	82	40	59
Studley Sporting	38	24	9	5	87	50	57
Kings Heath	38	23	7	8	86	45	53
GEC Witton Social	38	21	7	10	65	40	49
Knowle Reserves	38	19	8	11	66	56	46
Mile Oak Rovers Reserves	38	19	4	15	85	73	42
Alvechurch Reserves	38	13	12	13	65	64	38
Moor Green Reserves	38	16	4	18	66	66	36
Sutton Coldfield Town Reserves	38	11	13	14	56	68	35
Chelmsley Town	38	11	12	15	52	55	34
Yardley Wood United	38	14	6	18	63	77	34
Astwood Bank	38	10	13	15	53	52	33
Kingsbury United	38	12	9	17	64	71	33
Alcester Town	38	11	9	18	51	67	31
Bournville Athletic	38	12	7	19	51	70	31
Polesworth North Warwick	38	9	7	22	51	75	25
Stafford Town	38	9	7	22	49	92	25
Walsall Wood Reserves	38	8	6	24	42	82	22
Banbury United Reserves	38	4	8	26	40	87	16

GEC Witton Social changed their name to Witton Social.
Stafford Town moved to the Staffordshire Senior League and Yardley Wood United, Knowle Reserves and Banbury United Reserves also left the league.
Redditch United Reserves joined.

Midland Combination 1982-1983

Division Three

	P	W	D	L	F	A	Pts
Paget Rangers Reserves	38	25	7	6	93	60	57
Boldmere St. Michaels Reserves	38	26	2	10	99	46	54
Hay Green	38	21	9	8	93	52	51
Wythall	38	23	5	10	94	62	51
Littleton	38	17	12	9	54	37	46
Rockwood Albion	38	15	12	11	63	57	42
Ludlow Colts	38	16	9	13	50	52	41
Coleshill Town Reserves	38	13	13	12	60	57	39
Bridgnorth Town Reserves	38	14	10	14	62	54	38
Smethwick Highfield Reserves	38	14	8	16	46	51	36
Enville Athletic	38	14	8	16	46	51	36
GEC Witton Social Reserves	38	14	7	17	51	53	35
Stratford Town Reserves	38	11	12	15	58	68	34
Bromsgrove Brookfield	38	12	10	16	47	66	34
Highgate United Reserves	38	12	9	17	47	57	33
Bolehall Swifts	38	13	5	20	62	69	31
Cradley Town Reserves	38	11	7	20	61	72	29
Ashted Rovers	38	9	10	19	55	84	28
Solihull Borough Reserves	38	11	6	21	52	81	28
Polesworth North Warwick Res.	38	5	7	26	28	92	17

Littleton, Ashted Rovers, Solihull Borough Reserves and Polesworth North Warwick Reserves all left the league. Earlswood Town joined from the BYOB Mercian League, Oldbury United Reserves joined from the SCL(S) and Whitmore Old Boys, Racing Club (Warwick) and Hurley Daw Mill Welfare also joined.

1982-83

Division One

	P	W	D	L	F	A	Pts
Bridgnorth Town	38	29	6	3	102	30	64
Moor Green	38	27	6	5	106	44	60
Boldmere St. Michaels	38	25	7	6	60	36	57
Highgate United	38	20	12	6	74	38	52
Cinderford Town	38	21	7	10	76	51	49
Paget Rangers	38	17	9	12	63	40	43
Stratford Town	38	15	11	12	59	62	41
Mile Oak Rovers	38	15	10	13	58	50	40
Hurley Daw Mill Welfare	38	13	10	15	60	62	36
Evesham United	38	13	10	15	52	58	36
Cradley Town	38	14	7	17	62	74	35
West Midlands Police	38	10	13	15	66	73	33
Racing Club (Warwick)	38	12	9	17	52	65	33
Coleshill Town	38	13	7	18	45	58	33
Walsall Borough	38	10	9	19	34	67	29
Smethwick Highfield	38	8	12	18	38	58	28
Northfield Town	38	10	6	22	53	81	26
Chipping Norton Town	38	7	11	20	32	59	25
Solihull Borough	38	6	8	24	43	83	20
Knowle	38	6	8	24	43	89	20

Knowle changed their name to Knowle North Star and Hurley Daw Mill Welfare changed their name to Hurley Daw Mill.
Bridgnorth Town and Moor Green moved to the Southern League and Cradley Town moved to the WMRL.

Division Two

	P	W	D	L	F	A	Pts
Studley Sporting	36	25	5	6	88	37	55
Kings Heath	36	22	9	5	76	38	53
Southam United	36	19	7	10	71	51	45
Astwood Bank	36	18	8	10	69	48	44
Paget Rangers Reserves	36	17	7	12	76	61	41
Sutton Coldfield Town Reserves	36	17	7	12	62	51	41
Moor Green Reserves	36	15	8	13	80	61	38
Polesworth North Warwick	36	16	5	15	56	57	37
Bournville Athletic	36	12	12	12	56	53	36
Bedworth United Reserves	36	13	10	13	63	72	36
Alvechurch Reserves	36	13	7	16	54	60	33
Boldmere St. Michaels Reserves	36	13	6	17	51	57	32
Mile Oak Rovers Reserves	36	11	10	15	45	73	32
Kingsbury United	36	13	5	18	58	66	31
Witton Social	*36*	*12*	*7*	*17*	*53*	*68*	*31*
Alcester Town	36	10	9	17	51	59	29
Chelmsley Town	36	9	8	19	46	73	26
Redditch United Reserves	*36*	*8*	*6*	*22*	*47*	*81*	*22*
Walsall Borough Reserves	36	8	6	22	42	79	22
					1144	1145	

Banbury United Reserves withdrew when their record was

	17	5	2	10	20	39	12

Astwood Bank, Walsall Borough Reserves and Bedworth United Reserves left the league. Bloxwich AFC and New World both joined from the SCL(S).

Division Three

	P	W	D	L	F	A	Pts
Bridgnorth Town Reserves	36	26	4	6	88	36	56
Oldbury United Reserves	36	25	3	8	92	46	53
Bromsgrove Brookfield	36	23	5	8	75	44	51
Earlswood Town	36	20	9	7	92	50	49
Wythall	36	17	10	9	75	41	44
Highgate United Reserves	36	18	8	10	63	41	44
Whitmore Old Boys	36	18	6	12	69	55	42
Enville Athletic	36	18	5	13	60	42	41
Bolehall Swifts	36	13	10	13	67	63	36
Ludlow Colts	36	14	6	16	45	53	34
Racing Club (Warwick) Reserves	36	14	6	16	58	69	34
Witton Social Reserves	36	13	5	18	50	58	31
Coleshill Town Reserves	36	14	1	21	50	71	29
Hay Green	36	11	6	19	64	89	28
Rockwood Albion	36	9	8	19	35	64	26
Smethwick Highfield Reserves	36	9	7	20	30	46	25
Hurley Daw Mill Welfare Reserves	36	9	6	21	39	81	24
Cradley Town Reserves	36	8	3	25	51	100	19
Stratford Town Reserves	36	6	6	24	30	84	18

Hay Green and the Reserves of Hurley Daw Mill Welfare, Cradley Town and Witton Social left the league.
Kingswinford Town joined from the SCL(S) and Princes End United, Sedgley Rovers, Henley Forest of Arden, Colinthians '83, Kings Norton Old Boys and Northfield Town Reserves also joined.

The Divisions were renamed Premier, One and Two from next season.

1983-84
Premier Division

Studley Sporting	38	22	8	8	83	49	52
Coleshill Town	38	22	7	9	77	43	51
West Midlands Police	38	20	10	8	82	52	50
Highgate United	38	17	14	7	70	41	48
Racing Club (Warwick)	38	21	4	13	79	66	46
Paget Rangers	38	15	15	8	55	35	45
Hurley Daw Mill	38	16	11	11	68	55	43
Evesham United	38	16	10	12	55	49	42
Stratford Town	38	16	6	16	58	71	38
Boldmere St. Michaels	38	14	9	15	46	37	37
Northfield Town	38	14	9	15	63	56	37
Mile Oak Rovers	38	15	7	16	58	53	37
Solihull Borough	38	15	7	16	54	57	37
Chipping Norton Town	38	13	10	15	49	51	36
Kings Heath	38	11	14	13	50	59	36
Cinderford Town	38	12	9	17	51	63	33
Walsall Borough	38	13	6	19	54	58	32
Smethwick Highfield	38	7	13	18	45	66	27
Southam United	38	7	8	23	35	76	22
Knowle North Star	38	3	5	30	34	129	11

Cinderford Town moved to the Gloucestershire County League and Chipping Norton Town moved to the Oxfordshire Senior League.

Division One

New World	34	25	6	3	94	25	56
Polesworth North Warwick	34	21	7	6	70	27	49
Bromsgrove Brookfield	34	17	6	11	51	42	40
Bridgnorth Town Reserves	34	15	9	10	60	42	39
Kingsbury United	34	17	4	13	59	55	38
Moor Green Reserves	34	16	6	12	50	51	38
Bloxwich AFC	34	14	8	12	54	58	36
Sutton Coldfield Town Reserves	34	14	7	13	81	59	35
Oldbury United Reserves	34	12	9	13	55	48	33
Chelmsley Town	34	13	7	14	54	63	33
Alcester Town	34	14	3	17	52	62	31
Alvechurch Reserves	34	9	12	13	42	52	30
Bournville Athletic	34	9	11	14	49	55	29
Wythall	34	12	5	17	44	61	29
Boldmere St. Michaels Reserves	34	10	7	17	29	51	27
Mile Oak Rovers Reserves	34	8	9	17	39	64	25
Paget Rangers Reserves	34	8	8	18	31	59	24
Highgate United Reserves	34	7	6	21	47	87	20

Alvechurch Reserves left and Cheltenham Town Reserves joined.

Division Two

Kingswinford Town	36	23	7	6	89	38	53
Princes End United	36	23	5	8	91	43	51
Sedgley Rovers	36	22	7	7	82	47	51
Enville Athletic	36	21	6	9	63	29	48
Henley Forest of Arden	36	19	9	8	74	39	47
Whitmore Old Boys	36	20	7	9	73	46	47
Northfield Town Reserves	36	18	6	12	82	54	42
Smethwick Highfield Reserves	36	16	9	11	45	36	41
Coleshill Town Reserves	36	17	6	13	62	56	40
Colinthians '83	36	16	7	13	70	57	39
Racing Club (Warwick) Reserves	36	16	5	15	62	59	37
Bolehall Swifts	36	15	3	18	57	69	33
Kings Norton Old Boys	36	11	10	15	52	55	32
Redditch United Reserves	36	12	6	18	55	76	30
Earlswood Town	36	9	6	21	49	62	24
Ludlow Colts	36	6	9	21	42	98	21
Rockwood Albion	36	7	6	23	30	94	20
Witton Social	36	4	8	24	37	79	16
Stratford Town Reserves	36	3	6	27	31	109	12

Witton Social changed their name to Witton.
Ludlow Colts and Redditch United Reserves left the league.
Wilmcote joined from the Stratford Alliance and Priors Sports, Triplex, West Heath United and the Reserves of Bedworth United, Bournville Athletic, Kings Heath and Solihull Borough all joined.

1984-85
Premier Division

Mile Oak Rovers	38	27	6	5	91	28	60
Solihull Borough	38	22	10	6	68	36	54
Paget Rangers	38	21	10	7	60	35	52
Boldmere St. Michaels	38	21	8	9	67	40	50
New World	38	21	6	11	71	41	48
Highgate United	38	20	8	10	73	47	48
Polesworth North Warwick	38	20	8	10	58	34	48
West Midlands Police	38	17	9	12	80	56	43
Stratford Town	38	15	13	10	53	40	43
Racing Club (Warwick)	38	13	12	13	69	67	38
Walsall Borough	38	13	10	15	47	44	36
Smethwick Highfield	38	10	13	15	50	58	33
Evesham United	38	13	7	18	57	81	33
Hurley Daw Mill	38	11	9	18	43	56	31
Studley Sporting	38	8	14	16	50	69	30
Northfield Town	38	11	7	20	63	76	29
Coleshill Town	38	10	8	20	44	60	28
Kings Heath	38	7	11	20	31	61	25
Southam United	38	6	5	27	45	102	17
Knowle North Star	38	4	6	28	40	129	14

Mile Oak Rovers moved to the Southern League.

Division One

Cheltenham Town Reserves	40	24	10	6	106	40	58
Sutton Coldfield Town Reserves	40	23	8	9	99	50	54
Paget Rangers Reserves	40	19	14	7	63	35	52
Bridgnorth Town Reserves	40	21	9	10	86	59	51
Princes End United	40	19	9	12	98	59	47
Sedgley Rovers	40	19	9	12	77	57	47
Bromsgrove Brookfield	40	18	11	11	78	67	47
Chelmsley Town	40	20	6	14	78	60	46
Kingsbury United	40	18	9	13	84	67	45
Enville Athletic	40	14	12	14	62	54	40
Bloxwich AFC	**40**	**15**	**10**	**15**	**58**	**64**	**40**
Moor Green Reserves	40	17	6	17	67	74	40
Mile Oak Rovers Reserves	40	14	9	17	57	80	37
Boldmere St. Michaels Reserves	40	12	11	17	61	58	35
Henley Forest of Arden	40	16	3	21	62	68	35
Alcester Town	40	12	10	18	56	73	34
Highgate United Reserves	40	12	9	19	65	67	33
Wythall	40	11	10	19	55	76	32
Oldbury United Reserves	40	9	8	23	47	121	26
Kingswinford Town	40	7	10	23	50	90	24
Bournville Athletic	40	5	7	28	39	129	17

Bournville Athletic changed their name to Bournville.
Bromsgrove Brookfield, Kingswinford Town and Oldbury United Reserves left the league.

Division Two

Bolehall Swifts	38	27	7	4	80	32	61
West Heath United	38	26	6	6	105	43	58
Racing Club (Warwick) Res.	38	21	6	11	80	52	48
Smethwick Highfield Reserves	38	21	5	12	63	41	47
Rockwood Albion	38	17	11	10	77	54	45
Northfield Town Reserves	38	18	9	11	72	56	45
Colinthians '83	38	19	6	13	84	63	44
Bedworth United Reserves	38	18	8	12	75	58	44
Stratford Town Reserves	38	17	9	12	68	54	43
Kings Norton Old Boys	38	15	10	13	58	57	40
Triplex	38	16	8	14	50	51	40
Kings Heath Reserves	38	13	11	14	47	46	37
Wilmcote	38	15	6	17	64	70	36
Coleshill Town Reserves	38	12	8	18	53	58	32
Solihull Borough Reserves	38	11	9	18	51	68	31
Whitmore Old Boys	38	11	6	21	72	84	28
Earlswood Town	38	9	8	21	58	93	26
Witton	38	7	9	22	35	68	23
Bournville Athletic Reserves	38	8	7	23	51	106	23
Priors Sports	38	1	7	30	30	119	9

Midland Combination 1985-1987

Colinthians '83 and Bournville Athletic Reserves left the league.
Dudley Sports joined from the Birmingham Works League, Fairfield Villa joined from the Kidderminster League and Alvechurch Reserves, Bromsgrove Rovers Reserves, Enville Athletic Reserves, Little Bloxwich Strollers, Shelfield United and Wellesbourne also joined.

1985-86

Premier Division

Boldmere St. Michaels	38	25	10	3	72	24	60
Paget Rangers	38	24	9	5	94	31	57
West Midlands Police	38	23	8	7	65	41	54
Northfield Town	38	18	12	8	74	50	48
Bloxwich AFC	38	18	11	9	77	50	47
Stratford Town	38	17	12	9	53	32	46
Solihull Borough	38	18	7	13	62	45	43
Walsall Borough	38	15	13	10	52	37	43
Polesworth North Warwick	38	16	10	12	52	46	42
Racing Club (Warwick)	38	13	15	10	52	50	41
Coleshill Town	38	14	13	11	54	54	41
Highgate United	38	16	8	14	56	55	40
Evesham United	38	12	9	17	62	80	33
Hurley Daw Mill	38	12	8	18	44	59	32
New World	38	9	7	22	46	73	25
Knowle North Star	38	8	9	21	35	63	25
Southam United	38	6	12	20	52	90	24
Studley Sporting	38	7	8	23	43	75	22
Smethwick Highfield	38	5	11	22	31	75	21
Kings Heath	38	5	6	27	24	70	16

Walsall Borough changed their name to Walsall Wood and Smethwick Highfield changed their name to Ashtree Highfield.
Hurley Daw Mill and New World left the league.

Division One

Moor Green Reserves	40	28	6	6	90	45	62
Boldmere St. Michaels Reserves	40	24	9	7	95	42	57
Paget Rangers Reserves	40	25	7	8	76	30	57
Princes End United	40	23	10	7	68	36	56
Bolehall Swifts	40	19	16	5	71	36	54
Cheltenham Town Reserves	40	21	7	12	83	52	49
West Heath United	40	20	5	15	80	56	45
Sutton Coldfield Town Reserves	40	17	8	15	72	61	42
Alcester Town	40	15	11	14	48	48	41
Mile Oak Rovers Reserves	40	16	8	16	49	44	40
Highgate United Reserves	40	15	9	16	76	75	39
Chelmsley Town	40	14	11	15	58	72	39
Racing Club (Warwick) Reserves	40	12	11	17	54	69	35
Kingsbury United	40	10	12	18	46	62	32
Wythall	40	11	10	19	42	64	32
Bridgnorth Town Reserves	40	12	8	20	59	82	32
Sedgley Rovers	40	13	5	22	56	81	31
Enville Athletic	40	11	7	22	58	67	29
Northfield Town Reserves	40	8	10	22	38	84	26
Smethwick Highfield Reserves	40	7	7	26	24	80	21
Henley Forest of Arden	40	7	7	26	36	93	21

Henley Forest of Arden, Sedgley Rovers and the Reserves of Northfield Town, Smethwick Highfield, Bridgnorth Town, Racing Club (Warwick), Moor Green, Boldmere St. Michaels, Paget Rangers, Cheltenham Town, Sutton Coldfield Town and Mile Oak Rovers all left and a new, separate Reserve Section was formed.
Shirley Town and Shifnal Wanderers United joined.

Division Two

Stratford Town Reserves	42	28	7	7	73	32	63
Kings Norton Old Boys	42	26	8	8	99	43	60
Bromsgrove Rovers Reserves	42	23	12	7	103	59	58
Wilmcote	42	23	9	10	82	54	55
Little Bloxwich Strollers	42	23	8	11	88	61	54
Triplex	42	22	10	10	88	62	54
Rockwood Albion	42	19	11	12	68	55	49
Shelfield United	42	18	9	15	78	58	45
Dudley Sports	42	15	12	15	81	72	42
Earlswood Town	42	16	9	17	68	67	41
Solihull Borough Reserves	42	16	8	18	64	57	40
Wellesbourne	42	15	9	18	68	85	39
Witton	42	15	9	18	66	86	39
Coleshill Town Reserves	42	16	6	20	67	70	38
Whitmore Old Boys	42	15	8	19	82	98	38
Fairfield Villa	42	13	10	19	67	72	36
Alvechurch Reserves	42	12	12	18	69	77	36
Kings Heath Reserves	42	14	7	21	76	91	35
Bedworth United Reserves	42	11	10	21	66	91	32
Enville Athletic Reserves	42	8	8	26	45	91	24
Bournville	42	6	12	24	54	101	24
Priors Sports	42	8	6	28	56	126	22

Kings Norton Old Boys changed their name to Kings Norton ex-Servicemen's Club and Little Bloxwich Strollers changed their name to Bloxwich Strollers.
Rockwood Albion, Priors Sports and the Reserves of Stratford Town, Bromsgrove Rovers, Alvechurch and Bedworth United all left the league.
Handrahan Timbers joined from the SCL(S), West Midland Fire Service joined from the Birmingham AFA and Bromsgrove Athletic, College Celtic, C.P. Dunchurch and the Reserves of Knowle North Star, Southam United and Dudley Sports also joined.

1986-87

Premier Division

Stratford Town	38	23	13	2	81	29	59
Paget Rangers	38	24	9	5	98	30	57
Racing Club (Warwick)	38	24	8	6	93	29	56
Boldmere St. Michaels	38	22	11	5	73	32	55
West Midlands Police	38	14	16	8	65	51	44
Northfield Town	38	15	10	13	57	46	40
Solihull Borough	38	13	13	12	58	69	39
Walsall Wood	38	16	6	16	54	52	38
Highgate United	38	15	7	16	50	49	37
Ashtree Highfield	38	15	6	17	47	59	36
Polesworth North Warwick	38	13	10	15	51	64	36
Princes End United	38	14	8	16	51	69	36
Evesham United	38	10	11	17	62	75	31
Knowle North Star	38	11	8	19	51	66	30
Kings Heath	38	9	12	17	36	52	30
Bloxwich AFC	38	12	5	21	56	73	29
Southam United	**38**	**9**	**11**	**18**	**42**	**75**	**29**
Coleshill Town	38	11	5	22	49	81	27
Studley Sporting	38	9	8	21	43	78	26
Bolehall Swifts	38	7	11	20	46	84	25

Southam United were relegated two levels into Division Two.
Knowle North Star changed their name to Knowle.
Paget Rangers moved to the Southern League. Studley Sporting left the league and Leamington joined from the Southern League.

Division One

Wilmcote	32	19	6	7	73	41	44
Kings Norton ex-Servicemen's C.	32	22	3	7	78	39	47
Wythall	32	16	9	7	67	43	41
Kingsbury United	32	16	8	8	49	34	40
West Heath United	32	15	9	8	61	48	39
Chelmsley Town	32	13	11	8	59	36	37
Triplex	32	16	5	11	65	50	37
Shelfield United	32	12	10	10	38	39	34
Highgate United Reserves	32	11	8	13	53	53	30
Shirley Town	32	12	6	14	47	55	30
Bloxwich Strollers	32	12	5	15	39	53	29
Enville Athletic	32	10	9	13	31	48	29
Dudley Sports	32	9	9	14	38	42	27
Coleshill Town Reserves	32	9	7	16	54	68	25
Alcester Town	32	8	8	16	55	60	24
Solihull Borough Reserves	32	4	8	20	31	81	16
Shifnal Wanderers United	32	5	5	22	39	87	15

Kingsbury United, Shifnal Wanderers United and Highgate United Reserves left the league.

Division Two

Bromsgrove Athletic	30	17	9	4	71	28	43
College Celtic	30	17	9	4	64	30	43
West Midland Fire Service	30	17	6	7	64	44	40
Fairfield Villa	30	16	5	9	69	43	37
Whitmore Old Boys	30	15	4	11	72	56	34
Kings Heath Reserves	30	13	7	10	63	51	33
Witton	30	10	12	8	43	37	32
Handrahan Timbers	30	11	10	9	61	52	32
Bournville	30	10	11	9	42	43	31
Knowle North Star Reserves	30	10	9	11	50	61	29
Earlswood Town	30	11	5	14	47	43	27
Enville Athletic Reserves	30	8	7	15	34	69	23
C.P. Dunchurch	30	7	8	15	48	71	22
Southam United Reserves	30	7	6	17	41	62	20
Wellesbourne	30	6	7	17	51	96	19
Dudley Sports Reserves	30	5	5	20	40	74	15

Bournville, Whitmore Old Boys and Southam United Reserves left the league. Streetly Celtic joined from the BYOB Mercian League and Weston United also joined. Studley BKL joined from Sunday football.

Division One

Chelmsley Town	26	16	7	3	72	31	39
Shirley Town	26	16	6	4	51	30	38
Bloxwich Strollers	26	12	8	6	51	38	32
Kings Norton ex-Servicemen's C.	26	11	9	6	47	38	31
West Heath United	26	12	7	7	45	38	31
Bromsgrove Athletic	26	12	5	9	44	32	29
Dudley Sports	26	9	8	9	48	42	26
Alcester Town	26	9	7	10	33	34	25
Wythall	26	8	6	12	39	38	22
Shelfield United	26	9	4	13	32	43	22
Triplex	26	7	6	13	33	45	20
Solihull Borough Reserves	26	6	6	14	27	66	18
Coleshill Town Reserves	*26*	*5*	*6*	*15*	*34*	*55*	*16*
Enville Athletic	*26*	*3*	*9*	*14*	*28*	*54*	*15*

Division Two

West Midland Fire Service	30	22	3	5	70	25	47
Streetly Celtic	30	20	6	4	62	29	46
Weston United	30	18	5	7	71	36	41
Wellesbourne	30	17	4	9	64	36	38
Southam United	30	15	8	7	52	31	38
Studley BKL	30	15	5	10	60	39	35
College Celtic	30	14	7	9	42	42	35
Witton	30	12	6	12	45	48	30
Kings Heath Reserves	30	10	8	12	44	49	28
Earlswood Town	30	11	3	16	36	46	25
Fairfield Villa	30	7	10	13	40	57	24
Enville Athletic Reserves	30	7	9	14	25	49	23
Dudley Sports Reserves	30	10	3	17	30	55	23
Knowle North Star Reserves	30	9	3	18	40	54	21
Handrahan Timbers	30	7	2	21	25	54	16
C.P. Dunchurch	30	2	6	22	23	79	10

C.P. Dunchurch, College Celtic, Witton, Enville Athletic Reserves and Knowle North Star Reserves all left the league.
Upton Town joined from the Kidderminster League and Chelmsley Town Reserves and Shirley Town Reserves also joined.

1987-88

Premier Division

Racing Club (Warwick)	36	22	12	2	74	23	56
Boldmere St. Michaels	36	22	6	8	69	30	50
Ashtree Highfield	36	20	10	6	70	44	50
Stratford Town	36	20	8	8	65	40	48
Evesham United	36	20	6	10	81	47	46
West Midlands Police	36	20	3	13	77	57	43
Coleshill Town	36	16	10	10	61	41	42
Princes End United	36	16	9	11	55	55	41
Northfield Town	36	14	12	10	48	40	40
Kings Heath	36	12	12	12	45	50	36
Solihull Borough	36	14	6	16	62	65	34
Bolehall Swifts	36	11	8	17	40	53	30
Walsall Wood	36	10	9	17	51	61	29
Knowle	36	10	8	18	40	60	28
Leamington	36	8	11	17	37	59	27
Polesworth North Warwick	36	8	8	20	53	85	24
Highgate United	36	9	6	21	44	80	24
Wilmcote	*36*	*5*	*8*	*23*	*28*	*65*	*18*
Bloxwich AFC	*36*	*7*	*4*	*25*	*45*	*90*	*18*

Ashtree Highfield moved to the Southern League and Leamington ceased to run.
Hinckley FC joined from the Central Midlands League.

1988-89

Premier Division

Boldmere St. Michaels	34	23	9	2	76	22	55
Racing Club (Warwick)	34	22	8	4	77	31	52
Evesham United	34	21	7	6	82	30	49
Princes End United	34	17	9	8	58	37	43
West Midlands Police	34	18	6	10	66	41	42
Northfield Town	34	15	10	9	55	43	40
Stratford Town	34	14	10	10	60	44	38
Walsall Wood	34	13	10	11	49	52	36
Hinckley FC	34	12	11	11	49	55	35
Highgate United	34	9	15	10	60	61	33
Bolehall Swifts	34	12	8	14	44	55	32
Kings Heath	34	9	11	14	42	52	29
Chelmsley Town	34	10	7	17	37	65	27
Knowle	34	8	10	16	34	58	26
Polesworth North Warwick	34	4	14	16	37	62	22
Coleshill Town	34	8	6	20	46	73	22
Solihull Borough	34	7	6	21	41	72	20
Shirley Town	*34*	*4*	*3*	*27*	*20*	*80*	*11*

Racing Club (Warwick) moved to the Southern League.
Stapenhill joined from the Leicestershire Senior League and Mile Oak Rovers joined from the Southern League.

Midland Combination 1989-1991

Division One

Bloxwich AFC	26	18	4	4	78	28	40
Streetly Celtic	26	16	7	3	53	29	39
West Heath United	26	16	4	6	72	24	36
Dudley Sports	26	14	8	4	82	39	36
Bloxwich Strollers	26	13	9	4	51	29	35
Wythall	26	13	7	6	49	36	33
Kings Norton ex-Servicemen's C.	26	10	8	8	58	49	28
Wilmcote	26	7	9	10	45	39	23
Triplex	26	8	7	11	36	58	23
Bromsgrove Athletic	26	4	8	14	25	41	16
West Midland Fire Service	26	5	6	15	38	71	16
Alcester Town	*26*	*5*	*5*	*16*	*29*	*77*	*15*
Shelfield United	26	4	5	17	22	58	13
Solihull Borough Reserves	26	4	3	19	37	97	11

Bloxwich AFC changed their name to Bloxwich Town.
Shelfield United and Solihull Borough Reserves left the league.
Stapenhill Reserves joined.

Division Two

Upton Town	26	16	7	3	72	25	39
Wellesbourne	26	18	2	6	73	30	38
Studley BKL	26	15	4	7	73	47	34
Southam United	26	12	7	7	55	45	31
Weston United	26	11	6	9	54	55	28
Enville Athletic	26	12	4	10	38	39	28
Handrahan Timbers	26	12	3	11	54	37	27
Kings Heath Reserves	26	10	6	10	50	43	26
Coleshill Town Reserves	26	9	8	9	37	46	26
Fairfield Villa	26	8	8	10	41	41	24
Earlswood Town	26	6	8	12	34	48	20
Dudley Sports Reserves	26	5	8	13	44	64	18
Chelmsley Town Reserves	26	4	8	14	26	55	16
Shirley Town Reserves	26	3	3	20	24	100	9

Becketts Sporting and Hams Hall joined from the BYOB Mercian League
Archdale '73, Emerald Social, Greenway Sports, Kenilworth Rangers,
Pershore Town '88 (a newly reformed club) and also Thimblemill R.E.C.
joined.

Three points were awarded for a win from the next season onwards.

1989-90

Premier Division

Boldmere St. Michaels	38	24	9	5	72	24	81
Northfield Town	38	22	8	8	79	32	74
Evesham United	38	22	7	9	79	44	73
Stapenhill	38	21	7	10	77	35	70
Stratford Town	38	18	9	11	77	50	63
West Midlands Police	38	18	8	12	80	66	62
Bloxwich Town	38	17	9	12	65	62	60
Bolehall Swifts	38	16	6	16	70	58	54
Princes End United	38	14	11	13	68	55	53
Solihull Borough	38	16	3	19	53	52	51
Highgate United	38	12	13	13	46	50	49
Hinckley FC	38	13	9	16	39	69	48
Chelmsley Town	38	13	6	19	46	66	45
Polesworth North Warwick	38	11	10	17	51	72	43
Kings Heath	38	10	12	16	55	74	42
Coleshill Town	38	11	8	19	38	54	41
Walsall Wood	38	9	12	17	50	73	39
Knowle	38	10	9	19	50	81	39
Mile Oak Rovers	38	8	14	16	47	74	38
Streetly Celtic	*38*	*7*	*6*	*25*	*38*	*89*	*27*

Sandwell Borough joined from the Southern League.

Division One

Stapenhill Reserves	32	21	3	8	60	44	66
Kings Norton ex-Servicemen's	32	17	10	5	75	39	61
Studley BKL	32	18	6	8	57	42	60
Dudley Sports	32	16	7	9	67	38	55
West Heath United	32	13	12	7	50	36	51
Wythall	32	14	8	10	55	51	50
Southam United	32	14	5	13	56	44	47
Handrahan Timbers	32	13	7	12	52	41	46
Wellesbourne	32	13	7	12	63	56	46
Triplex	32	13	7	12	51	50	46
Upton Town	32	13	6	13	55	49	45
Bloxwich Strollers	32	12	9	11	60	58	45
West Midland Fire Service	32	9	8	15	49	55	35
Kings Heath Reserves	32	8	8	16	49	78	32
Wilmcote	32	9	5	18	39	73	32
Bromsgrove Athletic	32	6	5	21	35	67	23
Shirley Town	*32*	*5*	*3*	*24*	*29*	*81*	*18*

Bloxwich Strollers moved to the WMRL. Bromsgrove Athletic also left.

Division Two

Pershore Town '88	32	21	7	4	63	27	70
Alcester Town	32	16	11	5	66	35	59
Becketts Sporting	32	17	7	8	63	36	58
Earlswood Town	32	17	6	9	60	42	57
Hams Hall	32	16	8	8	72	37	56
Weston United	32	16	5	11	69	58	53
Kenilworth Rangers	32	13	10	9	65	59	49
Emerald Social	32	12	9	11	51	49	45
Archdale '73	'32	12	8	12	70	65	44
Thimblemill R.E.C.	32	11	9	12	54	57	42
Enville Athletic	32	9	9	14	48	55	36
Chelmsley Town Reserves	32	8	11	13	37	50	35
Fairfield Villa	32	9	7	16	35	54	34
Greenway Sports	32	9	6	17	45	65	33
Coleshill Town Reserves	32	8	7	17	45	64	31
Dudley Sports Reserves	32	7	6	19	33	69	27
Shirley Town Reserves	32	6	4	22	30	84	22

Greenway Sports and Shirley Town Reserves left the league.
Chelmsley Town Reserves disbanded and reformed as a separate club,
continuing in the league as Marston Green.
Badsey Rangers joined from the Worcester & DL and Monica Star,
Sherwood Celtic and Mile Oak Rovers Reserves also joined.

1990-91

Premier Division

West Midlands Police	40	22	14	4	84	41	80
Solihull Borough	40	24	6	10	74	35	78
Evesham United	40	21	11	8	83	46	74
Sandwell Borough	40	20	14	6	63	31	74
Stratford Town	40	19	12	9	81	43	69
Northfield Town	40	18	13	9	63	37	67
Stapenhill	40	18	12	10	60	50	66
Coleshill Town	40	18	11	11	57	42	65
Highgate United	40	18	11	11	48	35	65
Hinckley FC	40	18	9	13	56	47	63
Walsall Wood	40	17	8	15	53	48	59
Boldmere St. Michaels	40	14	11	15	51	56	53
Kings Heath	40	12	14	14	65	62	50
Knowle	40	14	7	19	47	66	49
Bloxwich Town	40	11	11	18	64	75	44
Bolehall Swifts	40	12	5	23	41	79	41
Mile Oak Rovers	40	9	10	21	40	73	37
Chelmsley Town	40	9	9	22	43	77	36
Princes End United	40	10	6	24	34	71	36
Polesworth North Warwick	*40*	*5*	*12*	*23*	*39*	*86*	*27*
Kings Norton ex-Servicemen's	*40*	*4*	*8*	*28*	*32*	*80*	*20*

Solihull Borough moved to the Southern League and Princes End United
disbanded.
Armitage '90 joined from the Staffordshire Senior League and Barlestone
St. Giles joined from the Leicestershire Senior League.

Midland Combination 1991-1993

Division One

Alcester Town	28	20	4	4	85	28	64
Wilmcote	28	19	3	6	47	20	60
Pershore Town '88	28	17	6	5	63	20	57
Studley BKL	28	16	8	4	56	27	56
Stapenhill Reserves	28	12	7	9	58	57	43
Wellesbourne	28	11	7	10	57	52	40
Dudley Sports	28	11	5	12	42	45	38
Handrahan Timbers	28	10	7	11	43	52	37
Triplex	28	9	8	11	33	41	35
Southam United	28	9	7	12	39	48	34
Kings Heath Reserves	28	7	7	14	41	54	28
West Midland Fire Service	28	8	4	16	37	63	28
West Heath United	28	6	5	17	39	65	23
Upton Town	28	5	7	16	31	57	22
Wythall	**28**	**5**	**5**	**18**	**28**	**70**	**20**

Streetly Celtic resigned during the season. Their record was expunged. Wigston Fields joined from the Leicestershire Senior League and Ledbury Town '84 and Solihull Borough Reserves also joined.

Division Two

Badsey Rangers	**34**	**25**	**6**	**3**	**78**	**29**	**81**
Becketts Sporting	**34**	**21**	**5**	**8**	**82**	**43**	**68**
Monica Star	34	18	8	8	64	39	62
Coleshill Town Reserves	34	18	7	9	73	45	61
Marston Green	34	18	6	10	55	34	60
Archdale '73	34	15	10	9	63	53	55
Thimblemill R.E.C.	34	16	5	13	67	62	53
Kenilworth Rangers	34	16	3	15	58	43	51
Emerald Social	34	14	8	12	61	57	50
Earlswood Town	34	13	9	12	52	58	48
Enville Athletic	34	11	8	15	57	66	41
Weston United	34	12	5	17	46	69	41
Hams Hall	34	10	10	14	61	60	40
Sherwood Celtic	34	11	7	16	47	57	40
Shirley Town	34	9	7	18	48	60	34
Dudley Sports Reserves	34	8	5	21	38	77	29
Mile Oak Rovers Reserves	34	6	7	21	39	75	25
Fairfield Villa	34	4	6	24	38	100	18

Weston United moved to the Shropshire County League and Mile Oak Rovers Reserves also left the league.
Swift Personalised Products joined from the Birmingham Works League as Swift PP, and the Reserves of Pershore Town '88, Wellesbourne, Wigston Fields and Barlestone St. Giles also joined.

1991-92

Premier Division

Evesham United	40	28	7	5	76	31	91
Armitage '90	40	27	7	6	84	28	88
West Midlands Police	40	24	8	8	86	44	80
Highgate United	40	22	11	7	71	34	77
Sandwell Borough	40	21	8	11	81	45	71
Pershore Town '88	40	19	11	10	76	41	68
Walsall Wood	40	18	13	9	66	42	67
Stapenhill	40	18	9	13	83	67	63
Boldmere St. Michaels	40	17	9	14	69	52	60
Bolehall Swifts	40	15	14	11	59	47	59
Northfield Town	40	14	15	11	48	54	57
Coleshill Town	40	12	15	13	46	48	51
Alcester Town	40	11	9	20	53	74	42
Stratford Town	40	11	8	21	47	64	41
Chelmsley Town	40	12	5	23	61	111	41
Knowle	40	10	9	21	59	77	39
Barlestone St. Giles	40	10	9	21	39	78	39
Kings Heath	**40**	**10**	**8**	**22**	**45**	**68**	**38**
Hinckley FC	40	10	8	22	49	79	38
Bloxwich Town	40	9	8	23	48	83	35
Mile Oak Rovers	40	3	7	30	35	114	16

Hinckley FC continued as Barwell after merging with Barwell Athletic of the Leicestershire Senior League. Evesham United moved to the Southern League and Walsall Wood moved to the Staffordshire Senior League. Meir KA joined from the Staffordshire Senior League.

Division One

Studley BKL	36	22	10	4	68	35	76
Badsey Rangers	36	22	7	7	78	37	73
Wellesbourne	36	21	8	7	76	41	71
West Heath United	36	21	7	8	77	37	70
Dudley Sports	36	18	8	10	57	46	62
Becketts Sporting	36	15	12	9	67	44	57
Southam United	36	13	12	11	52	50	51
Solihull Borough Reserves	36	14	7	15	65	66	49
Kings Norton ex-Servicemen's Cl.	36	13	9	14	55	56	48
Handrahan Timbers	36	11	14	11	45	38	47
Wigston Fields	36	12	10	14	47	45	46
Polesworth North Warwick	36	13	6	17	54	65	45
Triplex	36	11	10	15	50	59	43
Upton Town	36	12	6	18	49	51	42
Wilmcote	36	11	4	21	53	64	37
West Midland Fire Service	36	8	12	16	44	61	36
Ledbury Town '84	36	10	5	21	41	91	35
Stapenhill Reserves	36	7	8	21	60	106	29
Kings Heath Reserves	36	5	11	20	34	80	26

Kings Heath Reserves and Stapenhill Reserves left the league.

Division Two

Marston Green	**38**	**24**	**13**	**1**	**87**	**34**	**85**
Hams Hall	**38**	**24**	**7**	**7**	**96**	**42**	**79**
Kenilworth Rangers	**38**	**23**	**8**	**7**	**82**	**59**	**77**
Sherwood Celtic	**38**	**22**	**8**	**8**	**93**	**42**	**74**
Thimblemill R.E.C.	38	20	9	9	107	62	69
Monica Star	38	17	9	12	71	51	60
Pershore Town '88 Reserves	38	18	6	14	71	57	60
Enville Athletic	38	16	7	15	60	56	55
Emerald Social	38	14	10	14	76	83	52
Shirley Town	38	13	11	14	64	56	50
Wellesbourne Reserves	38	14	8	16	67	67	50
Swift PP	38	14	8	16	56	66	50
Coleshill Town Reserves	38	13	9	16	60	65	48
Earlswood Town	38	12	11	15	49	65	47
Wythall	38	10	11	17	60	75	41
Archdale '73	38	11	6	21	68	88	39
Wigston Fields Reserves	38	8	12	18	49	93	36
Barlestone St. Giles Reserves	38	8	6	24	50	91	30
Fairfield Villa	38	9	3	26	37	85	30
Dudley Sports Reserves	38	4	7	27	46	112	25

Kenilworth Rangers changed their name to Kenilworth Town. Wythall and Emerald Social left the league. Ansells joined from the Birmingham Works League, Colletts Green joined from Sunday football, Holly Lane joined as a new club and Burntwood Town and the Reserves of Meir KA, Kenilworth Town and Studley BKL Reserves also joined.

1992-93

Premier Division

Armitage '90	38	26	6	6	91	32	84
Stapenhill	38	25	4	9	105	45	79
Stratford Town	38	21	13	4	70	33	76
Sandwell Borough	38	21	9	8	89	47	72
Pershore Town '88	38	21	8	9	74	38	71
West Midlands Police	38	20	10	8	77	39	70
Coleshill Town	38	21	6	11	63	44	69
Boldmere St. Michaels	38	17	12	9	74	48	63
Bolehall Swifts	38	15	10	13	66	56	55
Knowle	38	15	10	13	70	71	55
Barwell	38	14	12	12	63	70	54
Northfield Town	38	13	12	13	58	59	51
Meir KA	38	9	12	17	47	60	39
Mile Oak Rovers	38	9	9	20	37	72	36
Studley BKL	38	7	14	17	39	71	35
Chelmsley Town	38	7	13	18	51	75	34
Highgate United	38	8	10	20	48	80	34
Bloxwich Town	38	5	11	22	28	74	26
Barlestone St. Giles	**38**	**5**	**5**	**28**	**40**	**104**	**20**
Alcester Town	38	3	10	25	30	102	19

Armitage '90 moved to the Southern League and Alcester Town disbanded. Shifnal Town joined from the Shropshire County League and Shepshed Albion joined from the Northern Premier League.

Midland Combination 1993-1994

Division One

Wellesbourne	40	27	8	5	89	41	89
Kings Heath	40	24	7	9	100	44	79
Kenilworth Town	40	23	7	10	86	49	76
West Heath United	40	23	4	13	92	64	73
Handrahan Timbers	40	19	10	11	66	52	67
Kings Norton ex-Servicemen's Cl.	40	20	6	14	71	54	66
Southam United	40	17	13	10	66	45	64
Becketts Sporting	40	17	13	10	69	61	64
Sherwood Celtic	40	19	6	15	76	63	63
West Midland Fire Service	40	18	7	15	71	58	61
Badsey Rangers	39	16	8	15	64	63	56
Hams Hall	40	15	11	14	68	68	56
Solihull Borough Reserves	40	15	10	15	65	64	55
Marston Green	40	14	8	18	69	75	50
Wilmcote	40	12	10	18	67	85	46
Polesworth North Warwick	40	12	8	20	68	95	44
Triplex	40	11	10	19	41	57	43
Dudley Sports	40	11	3	26	55	84	36
Wigston Fields	39	9	8	22	57	80	35
Upton Town	40	9	8	23	45	84	35
Ledbury Town '84	**40**	**5**	**1**	**34**	**31**	**130**	**16**

Badsey Rangers vs Wigston Fields was not played.
West Heath United changed their name to Olton Royale after being taken over by the Sunday League side of that name.
Wigston Fields moved to the Leicestershire Senior League, Marston Green moved into Sunday football and Triplex disbanded.

Division Two

Ansells	**40**	**32**	**4**	**4**	**137**	**41**	**100**
Shirley Town	**40**	**29**	**5**	**6**	**142**	**57**	**92**
Colletts Green	**40**	**27**	**5**	**8**	**122**	**52**	**86**
Monica Star	**40**	**26**	**5**	**9**	**104**	**41**	**83**
Coleshill Town Reserves	40	24	3	13	92	57	75
Fairfield Villa	40	22	8	10	96	60	74
Enville Athletic	40	20	9	11	88	67	69
Meir KA Reserves	40	20	9	11	75	57	69
Archdale '73	40	15	12	13	87	78	57
Holly Lane	40	16	9	15	90	82	57
Swift PP	40	17	5	18	78	67	56
Pershore Town '88 Reserves	40	15	10	15	76	59	55
Thimblemill R.E.C.	40	16	7	17	86	78	55
Burntwood Town	40	15	6	19	65	75	51
Kenilworth Town Reserves	**40**	**13**	**10**	**17**	**65**	**89**	**49**
Studley BKL Reserves	40	12	8	20	67	86	44
Earlswood Town	40	10	5	25	65	110	35
Wigston Fields Reserves	40	7	6	27	49	119	27
Barlestone St. Giles Reserves	**40**	**6**	**4**	**30**	**42**	**164**	**22**
Wellesbourne Reserves	**40**	**6**	**2**	**32**	**42**	**133**	**20**
Dudley Sports Reserves	**40**	**3**	**6**	**31**	**45**	**141**	**15**

Ansells were promoted to the Premier Division.
Wigston Fields Reserves and Pershore Town '88 Reserves left the league.
Massey Ferguson, Jaguar-Daimler, Sphinx, GPT (Coventry) and Alvis SGL joined from the Coventry Alliance, Rugby Town joined from the Coventry & North Warwickshire League and Sutton Coldfield Town Reserves also joined.

A new Third Division was formed by:
Albright & Wilson, Blackheath Electrodrives, Mitchells & Butlers and Park Rangers who all joined from the WMRL, Alveston from the Stratford Alliance, Bilston Community College from the SCL(S), Continental Star from the Birmingham Works League, the Reserves of West Midlands Police, Stapenhill, Ansells, Wilmcote and Enville Athletic plus the Reserves of Barlestone St. Giles, Wellesbourne, Dudley Sports and Kenilworth Town who were relegated from Division Two.

1993-94

Premier Division

Pershore Town '88	42	25	13	4	84	35	88
West Midlands Police	42	25	10	7	95	49	85
Shifnal Town	42	25	8	9	112	35	83
Shepshed Albion	42	23	10	9	87	47	79
Boldmere St. Michaels	42	22	7	13	74	54	73
Northfield Town	42	20	9	13	83	65	69
Studley BKL	42	19	11	12	91	76	68
Wellesbourne	42	18	11	13	78	60	65
Stratford Town	42	19	8	15	73	56	65
Meir KA	42	17	11	14	101	78	62
Stapenhill	42	17	11	14	77	55	62
Barwell	42	18	8	16	69	61	62
Sandwell Borough	42	15	14	13	82	71	59
Bolehall Swifts	42	17	7	18	61	77	58
Knowle	42	12	13	17	63	67	49
Bloxwich Town	42	14	6	22	65	108	48
Coleshill Town	42	10	15	17	53	72	45
Kings Heath	42	11	9	22	65	99	42
Highgate United	42	12	6	24	58	98	42
Chelmsley Town	42	8	9	25	55	94	33
Ansells	42	5	11	26	43	109	26
Mile Oak Rovers	42	2	9	31	32	135	15

The following left to become founder members of the Midland Alliance: Pershore Town '88, West Midlands Police, Shifnal Town, Shepshed Albion (as Shepshed Dynamo), Boldmere St. Michaels, Stratford Town, Stapenhill, Barwell, Sandwell Borough and Bolehall Swifts. Mile Oak Rovers moved to the Birmingham AFA and Alvechurch Villa joined as a new club.

Division One

West Midland Fire Service	36	25	5	6	86	35	80
Handrahan Timbers	36	22	9	5	72	44	75
Solihull Borough Reserves	36	21	5	10	95	55	68
Kenilworth Town	36	20	8	8	77	38	68
Colletts Green	36	19	8	9	76	46	65
Olton Royale	**36**	**19**	**6**	**11**	**64**	**43**	**63**
Sherwood Celtic	**36**	**16**	**12**	**8**	**68**	**41**	**60**
Shirley Town	**36**	**16**	**7**	**13**	**63**	**65**	**55**
Hams Hall	36	15	3	18	66	65	48
Kings Norton ex-Servicemen's Cl.	36	11	11	14	60	65	44
Southam United	36	11	11	14	45	54	44
Upton Town	**36**	**11**	**11**	**14**	**49**	**64**	**44**
Monica Star	36	13	2	21	52	74	41
Becketts Sporting	36	11	6	19	49	83	39
Badsey Rangers	36	10	7	19	43	61	37
Polesworth North Warwick	36	10	4	22	54	78	34
Barlestone St. Giles	36	10	3	23	58	84	33
Dudley Sports	36	7	11	18	53	84	32
Wilmcote	36	8	5	23	54	105	29

Becketts Sporting and Solihull Borough Reserves left the league.

Division Two

Massey Ferguson	36	30	5	1	137	27	95
Jaguar-Daimler	36	25	5	6	103	41	80
Thimblemill R.E.C.	36	24	5	7	79	31	77
Sphinx	36	23	7	6	96	49	76
GPT (Coventry)	36	21	7	8	75	49	70
Holly Lane	36	18	8	10	91	63	62
Fairfield Villa	36	16	7	13	61	38	55
Swift PP	36	14	7	15	64	54	49
Burntwood Town	36	13	7	16	61	84	46
Rugby Town	36	11	10	15	65	67	43
Archdale '73'	36	12	7	17	60	85	43
Studley BKL Reserves	36	12	5	19	57	73	41
Alvis SGL	36	10	10	16	36	56	40
Enville Athletic	36	11	5	20	59	81	38
Coleshill Town Reserves	36	9	7	20	41	81	34
Ledbury Town '84	36	8	7	21	66	100	31
Sutton Coldfield Town Reserves	36	7	10	19	53	87	31
Meir KA Reserves	36	9	2	25	46	117	29
Earlswood Town	36	5	7	24	29	96	22

Swift PP merged with Wythall Richmond of the Birmingham AFA and continued in the league as Richmond Swifts. Sutton Coldfield Town Reserves and Meir KA Reserves left the league.

Division Three

Albright & Wilson	30	22	4	4	91	30	70
Continental Star	30	22	2	6	99	35	68
Blackheath Electrodrives	30	21	2	7	86	38	65
Bilston Community College	30	19	5	6	96	40	62
West Midlands Police Reserves	30	18	5	7	84	48	59
Alveston	30	17	4	9	98	53	55
Mitchells & Butlers	30	16	6	8	102	57	54
Wellesbourne Reserves	30	15	7	8	86	47	52
Stapenhill Reserves	30	14	6	10	62	48	48
Ansells Reserves	30	12	5	13	58	61	41
Kenilworth Town Reserves	30	9	3	18	59	82	30
Wilmcote Reserves	30	7	7	16	34	84	28
Park Rangers	30	6	4	20	68	98	22
Enville Athletic Reserves	30	3	4	23	30	106	13
Dudley Sports Reserves	30	2	6	22	34	110	12
Barlestone St. Giles Reserves	30	1	2	27	16	166	5

Bilston Community College were promoted to Division One.
Kenilworth Town Reserves and Stapenhill Reserves left the league.
Cadbury Athletic joined as a new club, Cheslyn Hay and Wolverhampton Casuals Reserves joined from the WMRL, Brownhills Town joined from the Staffordshire County League (South), Studley United joined from the Stratford Alliance, Swan Sports joined from the Birmingham Works League as Birchfield Sports and Kings Heath Reserves and Moxley Rangers Reserves also joined.

1994-95

Premier Division

Northfield Town	34	27	3	4	96	38	84
Bloxwich Town	34	21	9	4	105	39	72
Wellesbourne	34	22	4	8	71	41	70
Olton Royale	34	18	5	11	74	72	59
Alvechurch Villa	34	15	11	8	66	41	56
Meir KA	34	15	8	11	73	63	53
Handrahan Timbers	34	14	9	11	62	48	51
Studley BKL	34	14	9	11	66	53	51
Shirley Town	34	13	6	15	56	68	45
West Midland Fire Service	34	11	11	12	39	45	44
Chelmsley Town	34	10	10	14	53	65	40
Kings Heath	34	10	7	17	51	69	37
Knowle	34	9	10	15	42	63	37
Coleshill Town	34	9	9	16	45	61	36
Ansells	34	10	5	19	42	64	35
Sherwood Celtic	34	9	5	20	55	81	32
Upton Town	34	7	7	20	45	68	28
Highgate United	34	6	4	24	35	97	22

Sherwood Celtic disbanded.

Division One

Massey Ferguson	32	20	10	2	73	27	70
Sphinx	32	21	5	6	72	27	68
Southam United	32	21	3	8	72	42	66
Bilston Community College	32	19	4	9	86	40	61
GPT (Coventry)	32	18	3	11	86	63	57
Jaguar-Daimler	32	16	6	10	57	43	54
Kenilworth Town	32	12	9	11	58	49	45
Hams Hall	32	13	6	13	45	51	45
Polesworth North Warwick	32	12	5	15	67	79	41
Dudley Sports	32	10	8	14	54	63	38
Colletts Green	32	10	7	15	54	65	37
Monica Star	32	8	12	12	40	51	36
Wilmcote	32	9	6	17	48	82	33
Badsey Rangers	32	8	7	17	43	64	31
Kings Norton ex-Servicemen's Cl.	32	8	7	17	50	73	31
Barlestone St. Giles	32	7	7	18	48	82	28
Thimblemill R.E.C.	32	6	3	23	40	92	21

Jaguar-Daimler moved to the Coventry Alliance and Wilmcote moved to the Stratford Alliance.
Newhall United joined from the Central Midlands League.

Division Two

Richmond Swifts	30	24	2	4	93	23	74
Alveston	30	18	5	7	58	30	59
Fairfield Villa	30	15	8	7	58	43	53
Holly Lane	30	16	4	10	81	47	52
Albright & Wilson	30	14	9	7	65	46	51
Alvis SGL	30	15	3	12	44	35	48
Rugby Town	30	14	6	10	61	57	48
Continental Star	30	14	4	12	57	47	46
Earlswood Town	30	11	10	9	54	40	43
Enville Athletic	30	12	6	12	53	56	42
Blackheath Electrodrives	30	10	8	12	43	49	38
Ledbury Town '84	30	9	3	18	54	73	30
Coleshill Town Reserves	30	8	6	16	38	85	30
Archdale '73'	30	8	4	18	42	66	28
Burntwood Town	30	6	3	21	28	80	21
Studley BKL Reserves	**30**	**2**	**7**	**21**	**27**	**79**	**13**

Bromsgrove Rangers joined from the Worcester & DL.

Division Three

West Midlands Police Reserves	32	24	4	4	99	35	76
Cheslyn Hay	32	23	3	6	106	48	72
Brownhills Town	32	22	6	4	86	34	72
Wolverhampton Casuals Res.	32	20	3	9	96	42	63
Mitchells & Butlers	32	17	7	8	72	48	58
Wellesbourne Reserves	**32**	**17**	**6**	**9**	**73**	**49**	**57**
Kings Heath Reserves	32	17	4	11	78	62	55
Studley United	32	14	8	10	72	58	50
Cadbury Athletic	**32**	**16**	**1**	**15**	**58**	**66**	**49**
Birchfield Sports	32	13	6	13	64	63	45
Dudley Sports Reserves	32	12	6	14	66	65	42
Ansells Reserves	32	10	6	16	58	82	36
Park Rangers	32	10	3	19	66	100	33
Enville Athletic Reserves	32	6	4	22	30	71	22
Barlestone St. Giles Reserves	32	7	0	25	50	107	21
Moxley Rangers	32	4	5	23	39	82	17
Wilmcote Reserves	32	2	4	26	32	133	10

Moxley Rangers Reserves, Wilmcote Reserves and Ansells Reserves left the league.
Feckenham joined from the Worcester & DL, Cradley Heath joined from the Kidderminster League, Alvechurch Villa Reserves joined from the Bromsgrove & DL. Tipton Rand Tipton Sports & Social both joined from the SCL(S) while Birmingham Vaults, Kenilworth Wardens, Swan Sports and Richmond Swifts Reserves also joined.

1995-96
Premier Division

Bloxwich Town	38	31	4	3	122	45	97
Sphinx	38	25	5	8	87	43	80
Massey Ferguson	38	23	8	7	77	36	77
Knowle	38	21	10	7	87	49	73
Studley BKL	38	17	11	10	93	64	62
Kings Heath	38	18	6	14	63	65	60
Meir KA	38	15	10	13	77	72	55
Wellesbourne	38	15	10	13	55	60	55
Southam United	38	13	14	11	69	63	53
Coleshill Town	38	14	9	15	76	66	51
Chelmsley Town	**38**	**14**	**8**	**16**	**65**	**62**	**50**
Upton Town	38	14	6	18	68	72	48
Ansells	38	12	10	16	64	81	46
Olton Royale	38	12	8	18	56	71	44
West Midland Fire Service	38	11	9	18	51	70	42
Alvechurch Villa	38	10	10	18	57	84	40
Highgate United	38	9	10	19	56	81	37
Handrahan Timbers	38	9	10	19	46	71	37
Shirley Town	38	8	8	22	51	74	32
Northfield Town	**38**	**3**	**6**	**29**	**33**	**124**	**15**

Upton Town moved to Worcester and changed their name to Worcester Athletico, Sphinx changed their name to Coventry Sphinx, Ansells changed their name to David Lloyd Sports and Alvechurch Villa changed their name to Alvechurch. Bloxwich Town moved to the Midland Alliance and Olton Royale disbanded. Bolehall Swifts joined from the Midland Alliance.

Division One

Richmond Swifts	**32**	**26**	**5**	**1**	**92**	**18**	**83**
Kenilworth Town	**32**	**17**	**10**	**5**	**75**	**31**	**61**
Bilston Community College	**32**	**18**	**7**	**7**	**78**	**41**	**61**
Colletts Green	32	18	7	7	76	54	61
GPT (Coventry)	32	19	3	10	84	47	60
Dudley Sports	32	16	8	8	63	39	56
Alveston	32	14	7	11	63	48	49
Polesworth North Warwick	32	12	9	11	60	69	45
Newhall United	32	11	10	11	68	63	43
Monica Star	32	11	8	13	55	56	41
Holly Lane	32	9	11	12	43	53	38
Hams Hall	32	11	4	17	55	68	37
Kings Norton ex-Servicemen's Cl.	32	12	1	19	49	82	37
Thimblemill R.E.C.	32	8	4	20	38	73	28
Barlestone St. Giles	32	8	3	21	44	91	27
Fairfield Villa	**32**	**6**	**4**	**22**	**27**	**75**	**22**
Badsey Rangers	**32**	**2**	**7**	**23**	**30**	**92**	**13**

Kings Norton ex-Servicemen's Club disbanded.
Yardley joined as a new club and Leicester YMCA also joined.

Division Two

Continental Star	**32**	**24**	**6**	**2**	**89**	**28**	**78**
Enville Athletic	32	21	5	6	71	31	68
Brownhills Town	**32**	**20**	**5**	**7**	**73**	**46**	**65**
Cheslyn Hay	**32**	**19**	**4**	**9**	**76**	**54**	**61**
Earlswood Town	32	16	9	7	56	30	57
West Midlands Police Reserves	32	13	8	11	47	41	47
Bromsgrove Rangers	32	12	8	12	63	59	44
Ledbury Town	32	11	9	12	71	50	42
Alvis SGL	32	10	12	10	52	41	42
Coleshill Town Reserves	32	12	6	14	49	61	42
Cadbury Athletic	32	11	6	15	36	49	39
Wolverhampton Casuals Reserves	32	11	4	17	46	79	37
Blackheath Electrodrives	32	8	8	16	40	49	32
Archdale '73'	32	7	8	17	46	60	29
Burntwood Town	32	7	7	18	41	64	28
Albright & Wilson	32	6	6	20	35	81	24
Wellesbourne Reserves	32	6	5	21	33	101	23

Rugby Town disbanded in October and their record was deleted.
Bromsgrove Rangers disbanded and the Reserves of Coleshill Town, Wellesbourne Reserves and Wolverhampton Casuals left the league.

Division Three

Feckenham	34	27	5	2	102	26	86
Richmond Swifts Reserves	34	25	4	5	89	29	79
Tipton Sports & Social	34	21	5	8	68	30	68
Birmingham Vaults	34	20	8	6	62	38	68
Mitchells & Butlers	34	16	9	9	74	44	57
Studley United	34	16	6	12	64	56	54
Cradley Heath	34	13	8	13	53	46	47
Kenilworth Wardens	34	13	7	14	51	56	46
Dudley Sports Reserves	34	14	3	17	48	55	45
Kings Heath Reserves	34	13	2	19	53	79	41
Enville Athletic Reserves	34	10	8	16	47	60	38
Birchfield Sports	34	10	8	16	46	71	38
Tipton Rovers	34	10	7	17	51	59	37
Swan Sports	34	10	6	18	76	85	36
Studley BKL Reserves	34	9	6	19	45	71	33
Alvechurch Villa Reserves	34	9	4	21	45	85	31
Barlestone St. Giles Reserves	34	8	7	19	35	81	31
Park Rangers	34	5	11	18	51	89	26

Park Rangers and Studley United disbanded.
Kings Heath Reserves and Tipton Rovers both left the league.
Tipton Town Reserves joined from the SCL(S) and Kenilworth Town Reserves also joined.

1996-97
Premier Division

Richmond Swifts	38	30	5	3	92	29	95
Meir KA	38	26	6	6	97	34	84
Coleshill Town	38	22	10	6	69	30	76
Studley BKL	38	22	6	10	100	49	72
Knowle	38	22	4	12	83	47	70
Worcester Athletico	38	20	7	11	85	60	67
Kings Heath	38	16	8	14	66	50	56
Massey Ferguson	38	15	11	12	62	61	56
David Lloyd Sports	38	14	11	13	54	57	53
Handrahan Timbers	38	15	6	17	46	54	51
Coventry Sphinx	38	14	8	16	51	74	50
Bilston Community College	38	14	7	17	83	71	49
Bolehall Swifts	38	11	14	13	62	59	47
Southam United	38	13	8	17	53	62	47
Wellesbourne	38	12	5	21	62	89	41
Kenilworth Town	38	11	8	19	49	80	41
Highgate United	38	11	3	24	55	77	36
Alvechurch	38	9	5	24	46	82	32
Shirley Town	**38**	**7**	**8**	**23**	**51**	**94**	**29**
West Midland Fire Service	**38**	**4**	**4**	**30**	**26**	**122**	**16**

Richmond Swifts moved to the Midland Alliance as Kings Norton Town.

Division One

GPT (Coventry)	34	26	3	5	91	16	81
Continental Star	34	21	8	5	91	37	71
Alveston	34	21	7	6	78	39	70
Cheslyn Hay	**34**	**20**	**4**	**10**	**89**	**59**	**64**
Northfield Town	34	18	7	9	68	41	61
Newhall United	34	16	10	8	82	52	58
Dudley Sports	**34**	**17**	**7**	**10**	**64**	**42**	**58**
Colletts Green	34	15	6	13	59	50	51
Yardley	34	16	3	15	63	55	51
Polesworth North Warwick	34	15	5	14	62	66	50
Holly Lane	34	13	9	12	50	50	48
Monica Star	34	12	8	14	59	50	44
Leicester YMCA	34	12	5	17	57	70	41
Chelmsley Town	34	10	6	18	51	66	36
Thimblemill R.E.C.	34	5	8	21	34	99	23
Barlestone St. Giles	34	5	6	23	27	98	21
Hams Hall	34	4	5	25	44	90	17
Brownhills Town	**34**	**4**	**5**	**25**	**29**	**118**	**17**

Yardley left the league.

Division Two

Feckenham	30	21	5	4	79	27	68
Fairfield Villa	30	19	5	6	72	37	62
Ledbury Town	30	17	7	6	77	42	58
Richmond Swifts Reserves	30	17	5	8	68	32	56
Tipton Sports & Social	30	14	7	9	50	35	49
Burntwood Town	30	15	4	11	47	41	49
Alvis SGL	30	13	8	9	46	37	47
Earlswood Town	30	13	6	11	58	40	45
Blackheath Electrodrives	30	12	6	12	35	38	42
Cadbury Athletic	30	11	8	11	48	39	41
West Midlands Police Reserves	30	10	8	12	42	49	38
Enville Athletic	30	10	5	15	36	48	35
Birmingham Vaults	30	7	6	17	28	68	27
Albright & Wilson	30	6	6	18	40	75	24
Badsey Rangers	30	5	5	20	22	65	20
Archdale '73'	30	2	5	23	29	104	11

Richmond Swifts Reserves changed their name to Kings Norton Town Reserves.
Badsey Rangers left and Stourbridge College & Community joined.

Division Three

Swan Sports	22	16	2	4	55	20	50
Studley BKL Reserves	22	14	5	3	40	16	47
Mitchells & Butlers	22	13	2	7	57	36	41
Cradley Heath	22	12	4	6	46	24	40
Kenilworth Wardens	22	12	3	7	50	26	39
Tipton Town Reserves	22	10	7	5	41	29	37
Alvechurch Reserves	22	9	3	10	42	42	30
Birchfield Sports	22	7	4	11	29	48	25
Enville Athletic Reserves	22	6	3	13	29	45	21
Kenilworth Town Reserves	22	6	1	15	29	53	19
Dudley Sports Reserves	22	5	3	14	30	52	18
Barlestone St. Giles Reserves	22	2	3	17	10	67	9

Cradley Heath, Barlestone St. Giles Reserves and Enville Athletic Reserves all left the league.
Wyre Forest joined from the Kidderminster League and Old Hill Town, Handsaker, Barnt Green Spartak, Knowle Reserves, Erdington, GNP Sports and Continental Star Reserves also joined.

1997-98

Premier Division

Worcester Athletico	40	26	12	2	111	41	90
Southam United	40	24	11	5	84	38	83
Bolehall Swifts	40	25	8	7	76	43	83
Studley BKL	40	24	4	12	79	36	76
Coleshill Town	40	21	9	10	78	38	72
GPT (Coventry)	40	20	8	12	71	46	68
Meir KA	40	20	7	13	81	58	67
David Lloyd Sports	40	19	7	14	80	66	64
Kings Heath	40	17	12	11	62	45	63
Continental Star	40	18	7	15	78	69	61
Knowle	40	14	12	14	81	72	54
Bilston Community College	40	15	9	16	69	76	54
Coventry Sphinx	40	15	9	16	72	78	54
Cheslyn Hay	40	14	9	17	66	86	51
Highgate United	40	12	14	14	59	54	50
Handrahan Timbers	40	11	10	19	52	53	43
Alvechurch	40	12	6	22	67	88	42
Massey Ferguson	40	12	5	23	49	73	41
Kenilworth Town	40	6	8	26	43	98	26
Dudley Sports	40	4	7	29	54	137	19
Wellesbourne	40	1	6	33	38	155	9

Worcester Athletico were merged into Pershore Town of the Midland Alliance.
David Lloyd Sports and Bilston Community College disbanded.

Division One

Alveston	30	23	5	2	82	24	74
Northfield Town	30	18	6	6	70	40	60
Feckenham	30	18	5	7	60	36	59
Fairfield Villa	30	17	6	7	85	38	57
Colletts Green	30	17	3	10	67	45	54
Polesworth North Warwick	30	15	4	11	86	62	49
Monica Star	30	12	8	10	70	53	44
Shirley Town	30	10	11	9	54	48	41
Leicester YMCA	30	11	7	12	52	60	40
Newhall United	30	11	5	14	52	51	38
Thimblemill R.E.C.	30	12	2	16	55	62	38
Chelmsley Town	30	11	3	16	50	68	36
Holly Lane	30	8	5	17	33	59	29
Barlestone St. Giles	30	7	5	18	45	74	26
Hams Hall	30	7	3	20	26	73	24
West Midland Fire Service	30	3	2	25	26	120	11

Monica Star moved to the Birmingham AFA, Leicester YMCA moved to the Leicestershire Senior League, Newhall United moved to the Burton & DL and Polesworth North Warwick disbanded.
Loughborough Athletic joined.

Division Two

Blackheath Electrodrives	32	18	8	6	66	28	62
Kings Norton Town Reserves	32	18	8	6	79	45	62
Alvis SGL	32	16	11	5	70	35	59
Stourbridge College & Community	32	18	5	9	70	50	59
Swan Sports	32	16	9	7	67	53	57
Burntwood Town	32	15	8	9	83	45	53
Studley BKL Reserves	32	16	4	12	52	37	52
Mitchells & Butlers	32	13	6	13	59	56	45
Cadbury Athletic	32	13	5	14	45	50	44
Brownhills Town	32	12	5	15	65	66	41
Ledbury Town	32	11	6	15	53	61	39
Albright & Wilson	32	9	6	17	52	64	33
Tipton Sports & Social	32	9	9	14	56	74	36
Birmingham Vaults	32	9	6	17	46	72	33
Earlswood Town	32	7	11	14	46	69	32
Enville Athletic	32	8	2	22	29	96	26
West Midlands Police Reserves	32	6	7	19	32	69	25

Albright & Wilson, Tipton Sports & Social and Swan Sports disbanded.
Birmingham Vaults changed their name to Wonder Vaults.
Mitchells & Butlers and Stourbridge College & Community left the league.
Mile Oak Rovers joined from the Birmingham AFA and County Sports also joined.

Division Three

Old Hill Town	28	20	4	4	88	40	64
Handsaker	28	19	2	7	81	27	59
Wyre Forest	28	18	5	5	84	35	59
GNP Sports	28	16	4	8	44	31	52
Kenilworth Wardens	28	15	4	9	61	49	49
Continental Star Reserves	28	15	1	12	52	49	46
Barnt Green Spartak	28	12	7	9	71	70	43
Birchfield Sports	28	12	6	10	60	69	42
Knowle Reserves	28	9	10	9	64	50	37
Erdington	28	9	6	13	62	71	33
Archdale '73'	28	9	3	16	50	69	30
Tipton Town Reserves	28	7	7	14	65	78	28
Dudley Sports Reserves	28	7	3	18	41	75	24
Alvechurch Reserves	28	5	5	18	54	95	20
Kenilworth Town Reserves	28	1	5	22	31	100	8

Alvechurch Reserves, Erdington and Birchfield Sports left the league.
Wilmcote Sports & Social joined from the Stratford Alliance after merging with Stratford Froth & Elbow and MCL Claines, Burman Hi-Ton, Lichfield Enots, Leamington Hibernian and the Reserves of Bustleholme, Northfield Town, Chelmsley Town and Massey Ferguson also joined.

Midland Combination 1998-2000

1998-99

Premier Division

Team	P	W	D	L	F	A	Pts
Alveston	34	21	8	5	74	32	71
Cheslyn Hay	34	18	10	6	61	42	64
Southam United	34	16	10	8	70	49	58
Kings Heath	34	17	6	11	66	51	57
Massey Ferguson	34	15	10	9	57	51	55
Meir KA	34	15	9	10	69	47	54
Studley BKL	34	14	11	9	67	43	53
GPT (Coventry)	34	15	8	11	67	65	53
Handrahan Timbers	34	14	10	10	56	47	52
Bolehall Swifts	34	13	8	13	58	48	47
Highgate United	34	13	7	14	69	59	46
Feckenham	34	10	14	10	45	42	44
Coventry Sphinx	34	12	7	15	53	64	43
Alvechurch	34	12	4	18	61	77	40
Continental Star	34	11	7	16	57	69	40
Kenilworth Town	34	8	8	18	37	67	32
Coleshill Town	34	6	6	22	46	78	24
Dudley Sports	**34**	**2**	**5**	**27**	**27**	**109**	**11**

GPT (Coventry) changed their name to Marconi (Coventry).
Nuneaton Griff joined from the Coventry Alliance.

Division One

Team	P	W	D	L	F	A	Pts
Northfield Town	**30**	**22**	**2**	**6**	**95**	**32**	**68**
Knowle	30	20	4	6	78	33	64
Blackheath Electrodrives	**30**	**19**	**7**	**4**	**83**	**45**	**64**
Alvis SGL	30	16	3	11	69	66	51
Thimblemill R.E.C.	30	14	5	11	67	43	47
Chelmsley Town	30	15	2	13	61	58	47
Holly Lane	30	13	6	11	59	51	45
Wellesbourne	30	14	2	14	57	55	44
Shirley Town	30	12	4	14	50	74	40
Burntwood Town	30	10	6	14	70	71	36
Hams Hall	30	9	9	12	52	54	36
Studley BKL Reserves	30	10	5	15	49	58	35
Kings Norton Town Reserves	30	9	3	18	52	82	30
Loughborough Athletic	30	10	0	20	38	84	30
West Midland Fire Service	30	8	5	17	40	68	29
Colletts Green	30	5	5	20	40	86	20

Alvis SGL changed name to Alvis Oakwood Coventry and Colletts Green changed their name to Malvern Athletic.
Studley BKL Reserves left the league. Brookvale Athletic and Romulus joined from the Birmingham Festival Sunday League.

Division Two

Team	P	W	D	L	F	A	Pts
Fairfield Villa	**30**	**22**	**4**	**4**	**91**	**28**	**70**
Brownhills Town	**30**	**22**	**2**	**6**	**99**	**43**	**68**
Wyre Forest	30	18	6	6	79	36	60
County Sports	**30**	**18**	**6**	**6**	**75**	**34**	**60**
Mile Oak Rovers	**30**	**19**	**3**	**8**	**75**	**45**	**60**
Old Hill Town	30	17	3	10	61	44	54
Handsaker	30	15	6	9	68	39	51
Earlswood Town	30	15	4	11	56	47	49
GNP Sports	30	13	2	15	59	73	41
West Midlands Police Reserves	30	8	12	10	48	50	36
Barlestone St. Giles	30	10	5	15	53	75	35
Cadbury Athletic	30	9	7	14	50	71	34
Kenilworth Wardens	30	8	5	17	40	69	29
Ledbury Town	30	4	2	24	42	100	14
Enville Athletic	30	3	5	22	37	101	14
Wonder Vaults	30	2	2	26	30	108	8

Ledbury Town moved to the WMRL and Wonder Vaults also left the league. Polesworth North Warwick joined after re-forming.

Division Three

Team	P	W	D	L	F	A	Pts
MCL Claines	30	22	6	2	86	30	72
Burman Hi-Ton	30	19	3	8	67	47	60
Archdale '73'	30	14	7	9	57	36	49
Bustleholme Reserves	30	13	7	10	59	58	46
Lichfield Enots	**30**	**16**	**5**	**9**	**77**	**57**	**53**
Leamington Hibernian	30	12	8	10	54	47	44
Continental Star Reserves	30	12	6	12	66	73	42
Knowle Reserves	30	12	5	13	55	62	41
Chelmsley Town Reserves	30	11	7	12	55	58	40
Wilmcote Sports & Social	30	11	3	16	54	54	36
Northfield Town Reserves	30	10	6	14	45	52	36
Tipton Town Reserves	30	10	6	14	56	64	36
Kenilworth Town Reserves	30	10	5	15	46	68	35
Barnt Green Spartak	30	8	10	12	57	57	34
Massey Ferguson Reserves	30	9	7	14	60	66	34
Dudley Sports Reserves	30	3	5	22	38	103	14

Dudley Sports Reserves left the league.
County Sports Reserves, Droitwich St. Peters, Blackheath Electrodrive Reserves, Central Ajax and West Hagley joined.

1999-2000

Premier Division

Team	P	W	D	L	F	A	Pts
Nuneaton Griff	38	25	10	3	118	41	85
Kings Heath	38	22	10	6	79	42	76
Studley BKL	38	21	7	10	85	50	70
Marconi (Coventry)	38	20	9	9	81	51	69
Meir KA	38	18	10	10	81	48	64
Coventry Sphinx	38	18	7	13	69	47	61
Massey Ferguson	38	17	10	11	75	59	61
Cheslyn Hay	38	17	9	12	82	60	60
Feckenham	38	16	11	11	60	47	59
Alvechurch	38	17	8	13	74	77	59
Continental Star	38	14	11	13	62	75	53
Handrahan Timbers	38	15	7	16	51	61	52
Northfield Town	38	15	6	17	57	57	51
Bolehall Swifts	38	14	8	16	90	63	50
Blackheath Electrodrives	38	13	9	16	54	73	48
Southam United	38	11	8	19	58	78	41
Alveston	38	11	5	22	52	93	38
Highgate United	38	8	7	23	53	88	31
Coleshill Town	**38**	**5**	**5**	**28**	**52**	**124**	**17**
Kenilworth Town	**38**	**3**	**3**	**32**	**34**	**139**	**12**

Coleshill Town had 3 points deducted.
Marconi (Coventry) changed their name to Coventry Marconi and Blackheath Electrodrives changed their name to Blackheath Invensys.
Pershore Town joined from the Midland Alliance.

Division One

Team	P	W	D	L	F	A	Pts
Brookvale Athletic	38	31	3	4	145	29	93
Romulus	38	28	6	4	121	44	90
Fairfield Villa	38	25	6	7	121	46	81
Mile Oak Rovers	38	23	7	8	95	60	76
County Sports	38	21	3	14	105	61	66
Brownhills Town	38	21	3	14	91	47	66
Holly Lane	38	17	10	11	79	67	61
Thimblemill R.E.C.	38	18	6	14	100	82	60
Burntwood Town	38	17	8	13	78	59	59
Shirley Town	38	17	8	13	84	90	59
Alvis Oakwood Coventry	38	15	5	18	76	78	50
Knowle	38	13	10	15	83	74	49
Hams Hall	38	13	10	15	76	79	49
Kings Norton Town Reserves	38	13	7	18	66	91	46
Loughborough Athletic	38	13	4	21	60	90	43
West Midland Fire Service	38	10	6	22	65	101	36
Dudley Sports	38	9	8	21	54	86	35
Wellesbourne	38	12	2	24	65	109	35
Malvern Athletic	**38**	**2**	**4**	**32**	**35**	**166**	**4**
Chelmsley Town	**38**	**2**	**4**	**32**	**31**	**171**	**4**

Brookvale Athletic, Shirley Town and Wellesbourne each had 3 points deducted.

Chelmsley Town and Malvern Athletic each had 6 points deducted.
Brookvale Athletic changed their name to Sutton Town.
Kings Norton Town disbanded and their Reserves resigned.
West Midland Fire Service also resigned.

2000-01

Premier Division

Nuneaton Griff	40	31	4	5	93	34	97
Studley BKL	40	30	6	4	98	32	96
Romulus	40	27	7	6	79	34	88
Pershore Town	40	22	8	10	82	62	74
Coventry Sphinx	40	20	7	13	63	38	67
Meir KA	40	20	7	13	67	53	67
Alvechurch	40	21	3	16	77	64	66
Coventry Marconi	40	19	8	13	87	61	65
Kings Heath	40	15	12	13	61	53	57
Sutton Town	40	16	7	17	67	57	55
Bolehall Swifts	40	15	9	16	77	76	54
Massey Ferguson	40	15	8	17	81	81	53
Handrahan Timbers	40	12	7	21	51	69	43
Cheslyn Hay	40	11	9	20	53	71	42
Alveston	40	11	9	20	53	87	42
Feckenham	40	9	11	20	49	80	38
Blackheath Invensys	**40**	**10**	**7**	**23**	**51**	**91**	**37**
Highgate United	40	11	4	25	49	96	37
Northfield Town	**40**	**8**	**12**	**20**	**44**	**83**	**36**
Southam United	40	10	5	25	53	79	32
Continental Star	40	10	4	26	64	98	31

Southam United and Continental Star each had 3 points deducted. Sutton Town changed their name to Grosvenor Park and Continental Star changed their name to Handsworth Continental Star.
Studley BKL moved to the Midland Alliance and West Midlands Police joined from the Midland Alliance.

Division Two

Wyre Forest	28	18	6	4	82	27	60
Polesworth North Warwick	**28**	**17**	**5**	**6**	**69**	**35**	**56**
Old Hill Town	**28**	**17**	**4**	**7**	**72**	**47**	**55**
Handsaker	**28**	**14**	**8**	**6**	**70**	**38**	**50**
MCL Claines	28	14	6	8	50	31	48
Kenilworth Wardens	28	12	6	10	66	51	42
Lichfield Enots	28	12	5	11	60	58	41
Barlestone St. Giles	28	11	7	10	49	52	40
West Midlands Police Reserves	28	11	6	11	53	50	39
Cadbury Athletic	28	10	7	11	53	53	37
Archdale '73'	28	9	6	13	37	58	33
Earlswood Town	28	9	6	13	36	64	33
Enville Athletic	28	6	4	18	33	62	22
Burman Hi-Ton	28	4	5	19	32	69	17
GNP Sports	28	4	3	21	24	91	15

MCL Claines, Barlestone St. Giles and GNP Sports left the league.
Leamington, Rugby Town and Rugby AFC joined.

Division One

Shirley Town	**36**	**23**	**5**	**8**	**104**	**47**	**74**
County Sports	**36**	**23**	**5**	**8**	**108**	**61**	**74**
Knowle	36	22	8	6	78	33	74
Coleshill Town	**36**	**20**	**5**	**11**	**72**	**56**	**65**
Brownhills Town	36	19	6	11	76	48	63
Handsaker	36	19	9	8	63	35	63
Alvis Oakwood Coventry	36	17	9	10	80	59	60
Old Hill Town	36	19	3	14	86	73	60
Thimblemill R.E.C.	36	17	7	12	88	63	58
Fairfield Villa	36	17	7	12	81	57	58
Dudley Sports	36	14	8	14	52	63	50
Polesworth North Warwick	36	11	6	19	64	74	39
Holly Lane	36	8	13	15	62	76	37
Mile Oak Rovers	36	10	7	19	59	90	37
Burntwood Town	36	9	8	19	45	81	35
Loughborough Athletic	36	10	4	22	47	85	34
Hams Hall	36	10	3	23	51	85	33
Kenilworth Town	36	10	2	24	72	121	32
Wellesbourne	**36**	**6**	**1**	**29**	**38**	**119**	**10**

Wellesbourne were relegated two levels into Division Three.
Handsaker had 3 points deducted.
Loughborough Athletic changed their name to Loughborough.
Alvis Oakwood Coventry and Hams Hall left the league.

Division Three

Wilmcote Sports & Social	**32**	**27**	**2**	**3**	**104**	**27**	**83**
County Sports Reserves	**32**	**21**	**5**	**6**	**98**	**40**	**68**
Bustleholme Reserves	32	16	7	9	61	52	55
Droitwich St. Peters	**32**	**16**	**6**	**10**	**58**	**41**	**54**
Leamington Hibernian	**32**	**16**	**6**	**10**	**73**	**66**	**54**
Chelmsley Town Reserves	32	16	3	13	68	48	51
Tipton Town Reserves	32	14	6	12	53	60	48
Barnt Green Spartak	**32**	**13**	**8**	**11**	**84**	**59**	**47**
Northfield Town Reserves	32	12	6	14	70	67	42
Blackheath Electrodrive Reserves	32	13	3	16	56	54	42
Central Ajax	32	12	6	14	66	69	42
West Hagley	32	11	8	13	57	52	41
Continental Star Reserves	32	10	7	15	72	80	37
Massey Ferguson Reserves	32	11	4	17	64	80	34
Birchfield Oaklands	32	9	7	16	51	85	34
Knowle Reserves	32	9	4	19	42	74	31
Kenilworth Town Reserves	32	1	2	29	27	150	2

Massey Ferguson Reserves and Kenilworth Town Reserves each had 3 points deducted.
Droitwich St. Peters changed their name to Droitwich Spa.
Birchfield Oaklands and the Reserves of Bustleholme, Tipton Town and Kenilworth Town left the league. Wilncote Sports, Fernhill Heath Old Boys and the Reserves of Alvechurch, Cadbury Athletic, Enville Athletic, Brownhills Town, Wellesbourne, Wilmcote Sports & Social and Loughborough Athletic joined.

Midland Combination 2001-2002

2001-02

Premier Division

Grosvenor Park	42	31	4	7	111	39	97
Coventry Sphinx	42	27	13	2	91	41	94
Nuneaton Griff	42	26	6	10	98	54	84
Romulus	42	22	7	13	88	59	73
Feckenham	42	20	11	11	78	64	71
Pershore Town	42	20	7	15	86	68	67
West Midlands Police	42	18	7	17	69	75	61
Coventry Marconi	42	16	12	14	74	66	60
Massey Ferguson	42	17	9	16	82	81	60
Coleshill Town	42	18	5	19	76	68	59
Shirley Town	42	18	5	19	97	102	59
Handsworth Continental Star	42	16	9	17	76	75	57
Highgate United	42	13	12	17	70	74	51
Kings Heath	42	14	9	19	61	71	51
Meir KA	42	13	11	18	64	71	50
Handrahan Timbers	42	12	13	17	49	66	49
Cheslyn Hay	42	14	6	22	51	83	48
County Sports	42	11	13	18	64	108	46
Bolehall Swifts	42	11	11	20	68	84	44
Alvechurch	42	10	10	22	58	79	40
Alveston	42	11	5	26	56	89	38
Southam United	42	8	7	27	52	102	31

County Sports merged with Fernhill Heath Old Boys (from Division Two) to form Fernhill County Sports.
Handsworth Continental Star changed name back to Continental Star.
Grosvenor Park moved to the Midland Alliance and Shirley Town left the league.

Division One

Rugby Town	36	30	3	3	100	25	93
Leamington	36	28	6	2	107	30	90
Knowle	36	23	8	5	91	41	77
Loughborough	36	18	8	10	77	45	62
Fairfield Villa	36	15	6	15	70	87	51
Thimblemill R.E.C.	36	15	5	16	72	69	50
Brownhills Town	36	15	5	16	70	70	50
Dudley Sports	36	14	7	15	66	55	49
Polesworth North Warwick	36	13	9	14	72	57	48
Wilmcote Sports & Social	36	13	7	16	64	68	46
Mile Oak Rovers	36	14	2	20	59	67	44
Handsaker	36	11	10	15	39	66	43
Old Hill Town	36	13	3	20	51	70	42
Blackheath Invensys	36	11	6	19	43	77	39
Northfield Town	36	9	11	16	44	64	38
Burntwood Town	36	11	4	21	45	85	37
Cadbury Athletic	36	11	3	22	47	77	36
Holly Lane	36	10	8	18	52	76	35
Kenilworth Town	36	10	5	21	56	96	35

Holly Lane had 3 points deducted.
Blackheath Invensys changed their name to Blackheath, Mile Oak Rovers left the league and Bloxwich Town joined as a newly re-formed club.

Division Two

Leamington	34	28	4	2	96	31	88
Rugby Town	34	25	6	3	106	24	81
Wilmcote Sports & Social	34	22	8	4	87	28	74
Cadbury Athletic	34	21	6	7	71	34	69
Archdale '73'	34	19	8	7	82	43	65
Leamington Hibernian	34	18	7	9	102	76	61
Droitwich Spa	34	17	3	14	64	55	54
Enville Athletic	34	16	6	12	53	49	54
Burman Hi-Ton	34	13	6	15	59	61	45
Earlswood Town	34	11	7	16	58	73	40
Chelmsley Town	34	11	5	18	43	72	38
West Midlands Police Reserves	34	9	8	17	50	77	35
Barnt Green Spartak	34	10	5	19	46	75	35
Lichfield Enots	34	9	7	18	43	72	34
Rugby AFC	34	7	10	17	55	81	31
Kenilworth Wardens	34	7	3	24	48	94	24
Malvern Athletic	34	6	3	25	50	112	21
County Sports Reserves	34	4	4	26	61	117	16
Wyre Forest resigned when their record was:		7	4	0	3	18	17	12

They joined the WMRL in 2001-02.
Lichfield Enots, Rugby AFC, County Sports Reserves and Malvern Athletic left the league. Stockingford AA joined from the Coventry Alliance.

Division Three

West Hagley	30	25	5	0	99	20	80
Alvechurch Reserves	30	20	4	6	85	35	64
Wilmcote Sports	30	17	5	8	75	47	56
Central Ajax	30	17	4	9	76	43	55
Fernhill Heath Old Boys	30	15	8	7	61	32	53
Cadbury Athletic Reserves	30	13	4	13	47	43	43
Northfield Town Reserves	30	12	7	11	56	53	43
Enville Athletic Reserves	30	12	6	12	55	51	42
Knowle Reserves	30	11	5	14	61	68	38
Brownhills Town Reserves	30	12	3	15	48	65	36
Wellesbourne Reserves	30	10	4	16	44	77	34
Massey Ferguson Reserves	30	8	9	13	59	72	30
Chelmsley Town Reserves	30	8	6	16	38	78	30
Blackheath Invensys Reserves	30	8	4	18	57	78	28
Continental Star Reserves	30	8	2	20	50	72	26
Wilmcote Sports & Social Reserves	30	4	4	22	31	108	16
Loughborough Athletic Reserves resigned when their record was:		5	0	0	5	0	21	0

Brownhills Town Reserves and Massey Ferguson Reserves each had 3 points deducted. Wellesbourne Reserves were replaced by their first XI who were relegated from Division One. The Reserves of Alvechurch, Enville Athletic and Blackheath Invensys left the league.
Halfords joined from the Stratford Alliance, Handsworth Wesleyan Youth joined from the Birmingham A.F.A. and Littleton, Birmingham United, Droitwich Sports and the Reserves of Coleshill Town, Chasetown and Rugby Town also joined.

Division Two

Burman Hi-Ton	30	26	1	3	96	26	79
Stockingford AA	30	23	3	4	77	28	72
Enville Athletic	30	20	8	2	91	33	68
Barnt Green Spartak	30	19	4	7	64	42	61
Central Ajax	30	15	3	12	46	40	48
Leamington Hibernian	30	13	5	12	58	51	44
Wilnecote Sports	30	12	7	11	55	55	43
West Midlands Police Reserves	30	12	5	13	55	51	41
Earlswood Town	30	9	9	12	42	43	36
Droitwich Spa	30	10	3	17	46	58	33
Fernhill Heath Old Boys	30	9	5	16	50	59	32
West Hagley	30	8	8	14	40	61	32
Cadbury Athletic Reserves	30	8	4	18	46	71	28
Chelmsley Town	30	7	9	14	33	63	27
Archdale '73	30	7	6	17	50	81	27
Kenilworth Wardens	30	1	2	27	22	109	5

Chelmsley Town had 3 points deducted.
Burman Hi-Ton changed their name to Pilkington XXX.
Fernhill Heath Old Boys merged with County Sports (from the Premier Division) and became Fernhill County Sports Reserves.
Wilnecote Sports left the league.

Division Three

Littleton	30	26	4	0	107	24	82
Halfords	30	21	7	2	72	23	70
Handsworth Wesleyan Youth	30	17	5	8	85	62	56
Droitwich Sports	30	16	5	9	100	54	53
Coleshill Town Reserves	30	14	8	8	68	47	50
Knowle Reserves	30	15	3	12	48	50	48
Massey Ferguson Reserves	30	13	7	10	76	59	46
Chasetown Reserves	30	13	5	12	62	47	44
Northfield Town Reserves	30	12	6	12	63	56	42
Handsworth Continental Star Res.	30	11	8	11	63	55	41
Wellesbourne	30	11	5	14	58	58	38
Rugby Town Reserves	30	11	3	16	59	82	36
Brownhills Town Reserves	30	9	5	16	47	65	32
Wilmcote Sports & Social Reserves	30	7	2	21	42	88	23
Chelmsley Town Reserves	30	3	5	22	29	82	14
Birmingham United	30	1	2	27	30	157	5

Handsworth Wesleyan Youth changed name to Handsworth United.
Chasetown replaced their Reserves with their "A" team and Droitwich Sports, Brownhills Town Reserves and Chelmsley Town Reserves all left the league. Newhall United joined from the Burton & District League, Inkberrow joined from the Worcester & District League, Birchfield Oaklands joined after re-forming and the Reserves of Romulus, Tipton Town and Kenilworth Town joined.

2002-03 Premier Division

Alvechurch	42	30	7	5	126	48	97
Coventry Marconi	42	29	5	8	94	37	92
Leamington	42	27	9	6	92	48	90
Bolehall Swifts	42	27	5	10	82	53	86
Romulus	42	24	5	13	107	58	77
Rugby Town	42	22	10	10	90	52	76
Coventry Sphinx	42	23	6	13	95	72	75
Fernhill County Sports	42	21	8	13	74	59	71
Highgate United	42	23	3	16	95	67	69
Meir KA	42	21	6	15	94	75	69
Castle Vale Kings Heath	42	19	6	17	86	66	63
Nuneaton Griff	42	17	3	22	66	80	54
Continental Star	42	14	9	19	86	88	51
Coleshill Town	42	13	9	20	54	68	48
Pershore Town	42	13	7	22	74	86	46
Massey Ferguson	42	13	7	22	85	112	46
Feckenham	42	12	6	24	66	85	42
West Midlands Police	42	11	9	22	56	87	42
Handrahan Timbers	42	11	8	23	57	73	41
Alveston	42	9	7	26	66	114	34
Southam United	42	7	2	33	43	162	23
Cheslyn Hay	42	4	7	31	47	145	19

Highgate United had 3 points deducted.
Kings Heath changed their name to Castle Vale Kings Heath during the season. Alvechurch moved to the Midland Alliance and Fernhill County Sports, Handrahan Timbers and Cheslyn Hay also left the league.
Brocton joined from the Midland League and Shifnal Town joined from the Midland Alliance.

Division One

Knowle	36	27	3	6	104	40	84
Stockingford AA	36	26	4	6	100	45	82
Pilkington XXX	36	23	5	8	92	48	74
Dudley Sports	36	24	1	11	78	47	73
Polesworth North Warwick	36	20	3	13	66	46	63
Fairfield Villa	36	18	7	11	61	53	61
Wilmcote Sports & Social	36	16	5	15	65	63	53
Northfield Town	36	15	4	17	72	71	49
Kenilworth Town	36	14	6	16	69	82	48
Blackheath	36	12	10	14	69	73	46
Loughborough	36	11	11	14	59	57	44
Thimblemill R.E.C.	36	11	10	15	69	67	43
Burntwood Town	36	11	9	16	49	69	42
Cadbury Athletic	36	11	6	19	55	72	39
Handsaker	36	11	6	19	39	64	39
Old Hill Town	36	10	8	18	70	83	38
Bloxwich Town	36	11	3	22	59	82	36
Holly Lane	36	10	4	22	54	101	34
Brownhills Town	36	5	7	24	31	98	22

Holly Lane left the league.

Division Two

Barnt Green Spartak	28	20	4	4	85	31	64
Littleton	28	20	1	7	78	32	61
Droitwich Spa	28	14	7	7	65	47	49
Halfords	28	14	6	8	47	36	48
Fernhill County Sports Reserves	28	11	6	11	49	44	39
Enville Athletic	28	11	9	8	34	39	39
Cadbury Athletic Reserves	28	10	8	10	54	56	38
West Midlands Police Reserves	28	10	7	11	51	58	37
Earlswood Town	28	9	8	11	38	39	35
West Hagley	28	9	8	11	37	50	35
Leamington Hibernian	28	8	8	12	45	57	32
Archdale '73	28	9	5	14	48	70	32
Central Ajax	28	9	3	16	55	56	27
Handsworth United	28	9	4	15	43	72	22
Chelmsley Town	28	2	6	20	38	80	12

Kenilworth Wardens resigned when their record was:
16 1 3 12 24 52 6
Central Ajax and Enville Athletic each had 3 points deducted.
Handsworth United had 9 points deducted.
Fernhill County Sports Reserves became Fernhill Heath Sports.
Halfords left and joined the Stratford Alliance.
Heather St. Johns joined from the Leicester & District League and changed their name to Heather Athletic.

Division Three

Wellesbourne	30	24	4	2	129	43	76
Newhall United	30	22	3	5	107	48	69
Tipton Town Reserves	30	19	5	6	82	52	62
Continental Star Reserves	30	17	5	8	102	53	56
Chasetown "A"	30	17	3	10	88	62	54
Massey Ferguson Reserves	30	15	3	12	95	64	48
Inkberrow	30	14	4	12	54	50	46
Romulus Reserves	30	14	2	14	58	73	44
Knowle Reserves	30	12	5	13	82	73	41
Birchfield Oaklands	30	13	1	16	81	85	40
Coleshill Town Reserves	30	12	3	15	63	67	39
Northfield Town Reserves	30	10	3	17	41	73	33
Wilmcote Sports & Social Reserves	30	7	4	19	43	104	25
Kenilworth Town Reserves	30	7	3	20	51	108	24
Birmingham United	30	5	4	21	56	105	19
Rugby Town Reserves	30	5	2	23	50	122	17

Birchfield Oaklands, Coleshill Town Reserves and Rugby Town Reserves each had 3 points deducted.

Midland Combination 2003-2004

Birchfield Oaklands, Chasetown "A" and the Reserves of Romulus, Coleshill Town and Rugby Town Reserves left the league.
Attleborough Village joined from the Coventry Alliance, Blackheath Reserves joined from the Kidderminster League and University of Birmingham, Mile Oak Rovers, Himley Athletic and the Reserves of Feckenham, Castle Vale Kings Heath, Bolehall Swifts and Heather Athletic also joined.

2003-04

Premier Division

Romulus	40	31	2	7	128	44	95
Leamington	40	30	4	6	101	36	94
Rugby Town	40	25	5	10	80	55	80
Coventry Sphinx	40	23	8	9	74	55	77
Feckenham	40	21	8	11	79	63	71
Coventry Marconi	40	22	4	14	84	53	70
Meir KA	40	18	11	11	89	68	65
Nuneaton Griff	40	15	15	10	74	62	60
Castle Vale Kings Heath	40	17	8	15	76	72	59
Dudley Sports	40	16	9	15	84	64	57
West Midlands Police	40	16	9	15	67	78	57
Highgate United	40	15	11	14	62	52	56
Bolehall Swifts	40	16	8	16	67	78	56
Brocton	40	15	10	15	53	59	55
Pershore Town	40	10	15	15	65	83	45
Shifnal Town	40	11	10	19	44	52	43
Massey Ferguson	40	12	5	23	65	93	41
Coleshill Town	40	11	5	24	49	83	38
Continental Star	40	6	9	25	53	88	27
Southam United	40	3	6	31	33	115	15
Alveston	40	2	8	30	29	103	14

Castle Vale Kings Heath became Castle Vale KH.
Romulus moved to the Midland Alliance and Rugby Town disbanded.

Division One

Barnt Green Spartak	**34**	**25**	**2**	**7**	**90**	**41**	**77**
Pilkington XXX	**34**	**21**	**3**	**10**	**84**	**52**	**66**
Littleton	33	18	7	8	64	41	61
Polesworth North Warwick	33	17	8	8	75	46	59
Old Hill Town	34	16	7	11	69	59	55
Cadbury Athletic	34	16	5	13	70	57	53
Bloxwich Town	**34**	**14**	**10**	**10**	**53**	**43**	**52**
Northfield Town	33	14	8	11	79	61	50
# Knowle	33	13	9	11	56	39	48
# Wilmcote Sports & Social	34	15	4	15	49	61	49
Thimblemill R.E.C.	34	14	4	16	64	74	46
Burntwood Town	33	13	4	16	59	66	43
Fairfield Villa	34	11	6	17	44	64	39
# Stockingford AA	33	10	7	16	61	82	34
# Blackheath	34	9	7	18	40	59	34
Kenilworth Town	34	6	5	23	34	90	23
Loughborough	33	4	8	21	30	74	20

Stockingford AA had 3 points deducted.
Handsaker resigned when their record was:
27 9 4 14 34 46 31
It was decided that other clubs' results against them would stand and that final positions would be decided on average points per game. Clubs affected are denoted with "#".
Blackheath left and Atherstone Town joined as a re-formed club.

Division Two

Wellesbourne	32	23	5	4	94	31	74
Enville Athletic	32	20	6	6	84	45	66
Newhall United	**32**	**17**	**7**	**8**	**89**	**43**	**58**
Earlswood Town	32	15	11	6	67	36	56
Heather Athletic	**32**	**17**	**5**	**10**	**68**	**44**	**56**
Archdale '73'	32	17	8	7	49	25	56
Tipton Town Reserves	**32**	**15**	**9**	**8**	**71**	**40**	**54**
West Hagley	32	15	8	9	44	37	53
Leamington Hibernian	**32**	**11**	**6**	**15**	**63**	**67**	**39**
Droitwich Spa	32	10	8	14	59	63	38
Continental Star Reserves	32	10	5	17	44	65	35
West Midlands Police Reserves	32	8	9	15	45	64	33
Handsworth United	32	9	6	17	43	74	33
Fernhill Heath Sports	32	8	9	15	48	75	30
Cadbury Athletic Reserves	32	5	10	17	42	77	25
Central Ajax	32	6	5	21	37	94	23
Chelmsley Town	32	4	7	21	38	105	19

Brownhills Town resigned when their record was:
9 4 2 3 15 18 14
Archdale '73' and Fernhill Heath Sports each had 3 points deducted.
Fernhill Heath Sports changed their name to Nunnery Wood Sports and Central Ajax changed their name to Warwick Town.
Wellesbourne left the league.

Division Three

University of Birmingham	**28**	**20**	**6**	**2**	**88**	**27**	**66**
Castle Vale Kings Heath Res.	**28**	**17**	**7**	**4**	**54**	**16**	**58**
Feckenham Reserves	**28**	**17**	**3**	**8**	**55**	**33**	**54**
Attleborough Village	**28**	**14**	**5**	**9**	**53**	**37**	**47**
Mile Oak Rovers	**28**	**13**	**6**	**9**	**66**	**43**	**45**
Wilmcote Sports & Social Reserves	28	12	7	9	67	45	43
Inkberrow	28	10	9	9	59	59	39
Himley Athletic	**28**	**11**	**8**	**9**	**69**	**47**	**38**
Blackheath Reserves	28	10	5	13	37	40	35
Knowle Reserves	28	9	8	11	43	51	35
Northfield Town Reserves	28	10	3	15	44	50	33
Birmingham United	28	11	2	15	68	75	32
Bolehall Swifts Reserves	28	8	7	13	40	58	31
Heather Athletic Reserves	28	6	4	18	32	68	22
Kenilworth Town Reserves	28	2	0	26	18	144	6

Massey Ferguson Reserves resigned when their record was:
9 1 1 7 12 40 4
Himley Athletic and Birmingham United each had 3 points deducted.
Blackheath Reserves left the league. Coton Green joined from the Birmingham A.F.A., Droitwich Spa Reserves joined from the Worcester & District League, Shipston Excelsior joined from the Stratford-upon-Avon Alliance, Greenhill and Atherstone Town Reserves joined as new clubs and Himley Athletic Reserves also joined.

2004-05

Premier Division

	P	W	D	L	F	A	Pts
Leamington	42	35	4	3	132	40	109
Coventry Sphinx	42	28	6	8	137	73	90
Coventry Marconi	42	28	4	10	111	55	88
Bloxwich Town	42	26	7	9	91	55	85
Barnt Green Spartak	42	22	11	9	93	60	77
Southam United	42	23	5	14	84	68	74
Brocton	42	18	11	13	89	61	65
Feckenham	42	19	10	13	85	78	61
Coleshill Town	42	19	4	19	80	78	61
Castle Vale KH	42	19	4	19	79	77	61
Bolehall Swifts	42	16	9	17	67	75	57
Nuneaton Griff	42	17	4	21	75	79	55
Dudley Sports	42	15	10	17	64	71	55
Meir KA	42	15	6	21	88	91	51
Pilkington XXX	42	12	11	19	75	89	47
Pershore Town	42	13	6	23	75	95	45
Shifnal Town	42	12	9	21	55	82	45
Highgate United	42	12	8	22	50	94	44
Massey Ferguson	42	13	2	27	57	88	38
Continental Star	42	10	6	26	56	108	36
Alveston	42	9	5	28	59	122	32
West Midlands Police	42	8	4	30	47	110	28

Massey Ferguson had 3 points deducted. Feckenham had 6 points deducted. Castle Vale KH changed their name to Castle Vale and Coventry Marconi changed their name to Coventry Copsewood.
Leamington moved to the Midland Alliance. Bloxwich Town also left the league.
Bridgnorth Town joined from the Midland Alliance.

Division One

	P	W	D	L	F	A	Pts
Atherstone Town	34	27	5	2	108	25	86
Cadbury Athletic	34	27	2	5	103	45	83
Polesworth North Warwick	34	19	6	9	77	48	63
Littleton	34	18	7	9	64	40	61
Knowle	34	16	10	8	70	51	58
Old Hill Town	34	16	7	11	79	56	55
Northfield Town	34	16	5	13	63	62	53
Stockingford AA	34	14	6	14	66	65	48
Wilmcote Sports & Social	34	14	4	16	67	60	43
Tipton Town Reserves	34	13	7	14	65	50	43
Loughborough	34	11	8	15	41	60	41
Thimblemill R.E.C.	34	12	6	16	61	78	39
Heather Athletic	34	11	6	17	53	73	39
Newhall United	34	10	5	19	61	90	35
Burntwood Town	34	8	8	18	58	84	32
Leamington Hibernian	34	8	8	18	59	76	29
Fairfield Villa	34	8	4	22	37	82	28
Kenilworth Town	34	5	2	27	31	116	17

Wilmcote Sports & Social, Tipton Town Reserves, Thimblemill R.E.C. and Leamington Hibernian each had 3 points deducted.
Wilmcote Sports & Social changed their name to Ettington and Kenilworth Town changed their name to Kenilworth Town KH.
Old Hill Town and Tipton Town Reserves both left the league.

Division Two

	P	W	D	L	F	A	Pts
Archdale '73'	34	24	4	6	98	35	76
Handsworth United	34	23	3	8	86	33	72
University of Birmingham	34	21	6	7	79	34	69
Mile Oak Rovers	34	20	5	9	77	44	65
West Midlands Police Reserves	34	19	6	9	62	40	63
Droitwich Spa	34	17	10	7	85	45	61
West Hagley	34	18	6	10	61	44	60
Earlswood Town	34	18	3	13	48	50	57
Castle Vale KH Reserves	34	15	7	12	79	58	52
Himley Athletic	34	13	8	13	72	63	47
Chelmsley Town	34	13	6	15	56	67	45
Feckenham Reserves	34	12	7	15	61	57	43
Cadbury Athletic Reserves	34	10	5	19	51	77	35
Nunnery Wood Sports	34	9	5	20	46	61	32
Enville Athletic	34	9	4	21	61	105	31
Continental Star Reserves	34	7	4	23	47	110	25
Warwick Town	34	7	2	25	47	98	23
Attleborough Village	34	4	3	27	27	122	15

Castle Vale KH Reserves, Feckenham Reserves, Enville Athletic and Warwick Town each had 3 points deducted.
Bartley Green joined from the Birmingham A.F.A.
West Midlands Police Reserves and Attleborough Village left the league.

Division Three

	P	W	D	L	F	A	Pts
Coton Green	25	18	5	2	56	14	59
Kenilworth Town Reserves	26	18	3	5	96	39	57
Atherstone Town Reserves	25	17	2	6	53	32	53
Knowle Reserves	25	12	7	6	59	42	43
Bolehall Swifts Reserves	26	11	6	9	55	40	39
Greenhill	26	9	8	9	39	39	35
Studley Entaco	23	10	8	5	46	46	32
Wilmcote Sports & Social Reserves	26	9	5	12	47	55	32
Droitwich Spa Reserves	26	8	5	13	37	51	29
Heather Athletic Reserves	26	7	7	12	34	50	28
Inkberrow	26	8	6	12	45	45	27
Shipston Excelsior	26	5	8	13	34	60	23
Northfield Town Reserves	26	5	4	17	27	49	19
Himley Athletic Reserves	26	3	4	19	25	91	12

Birmingham United resigned when their record was:

	10	4	1	5	17	28	13

Three of Studley Entaco's games were not played.
Studley Entaco had 6 points deducted. Inkberrow had 3 points deducted. Himley Athletic Reserves had 1 point deducted.
Studley Entaco, Inkberrow, and the Reserves of Kenilworth Town, Atherstone Town and Himley Athletic left the league. Perrywood joined from the Worcester & District League and Wellesbourne and the Reserves of Halesowen Town, Coventry Sphinx, Barnt Green Spartak, Worcester City, Coleshill Town and Chelmsley Town also joined.

Midland Combination 2005-2007

2005-06
Premier Division

Atherstone Town	42	32	7	3	131	27	103
Coventry Sphinx	42	33	4	5	150	61	103
Barnt Green Spartak	42	28	3	11	82	51	87
Feckenham	42	25	6	11	107	64	81
Bridgnorth Town	42	24	7	11	75	48	79
Bolehall Swifts	42	24	6	12	90	59	78
Shifnal Town	42	23	8	11	86	44	77
Nuneaton Griff	42	19	6	17	73	72	63
Castle Vale	42	18	8	16	73	76	62
Alveston	42	18	4	20	65	61	58
Coleshill Town	42	14	9	19	79	93	51
Brocton	42	13	10	19	56	70	49
Southam United	42	13	9	20	56	65	48
Highgate United	42	13	8	21	51	86	47
Coventry Copsewood	42	14	7	21	56	79	46
Pershore Town	42	14	3	25	63	88	45
Meir KA	42	12	9	21	55	92	45
Dudley Sports	42	11	11	20	51	71	44
Pilkington XXX	42	11	8	23	62	108	41
Massey Ferguson	42	11	5	26	46	91	38
Cadbury Athletic	42	11	8	23	68	92	37
Continental Star	42	5	6	31	51	128	21

Coventry Copsewood had 3 points deducted.
Cadbury Athletic had 4 points deducted.
Bridgnorth Town, Shifnal Town and Dudley Sports moved to the WMRL and Atherstone Town moved to the Midland Alliance.
Heath Hayes, Walsall Wood and Brereton Social joined from the WMRL.

Division One

Knowle	34	21	8	5	62	22	71
Northfield Town	34	20	9	5	84	30	69
Ettington	34	19	4	11	62	50	61
Fairfield Villa	34	18	5	11	59	43	59
Burntwood Town	34	15	6	13	57	58	51
Thimblemill R.E.C.	34	15	6	13	59	66	51
Stockingford AA	34	14	8	12	75	54	50
Polesworth North Warwick	34	14	8	12	64	49	50
Mile Oak Rovers	34	14	6	14	49	43	48
Archdale '73'	34	13	7	14	48	60	46
Handsworth United	34	14	5	15	81	77	44
Heather Athletic	34	12	8	14	45	49	44
Littleton	34	12	3	19	61	70	39
Loughborough	34	11	6	17	42	70	39
West Midlands Police	34	11	4	19	49	59	37
Leamington Hibernian	34	10	5	19	42	61	35
Newhall United	34	8	11	15	46	74	32
Kenilworth Town KH	34	8	5	21	38	88	29

Handsworth United and Newhall United each had 3 points deducted.
Handsworth United changed their name to Birmingham Academy but then left the league. Loughborough moved to the North Leicestershire League and Polesworth North Warwick disbanded.

Division Two

Bartley Green	**26**	**17**	**7**	**2**	**67**	**26**	**58**
University of Birmingham	**25**	**16**	**5**	**4**	**69**	**24**	**53**
Earlswood Town	26	14	7	5	47	27	49
Coton Green	26	11	9	6	47	42	42
Enville Athletic	26	11	5	10	58	54	38
Feckenham Reserves	26	12	2	12	41	43	38
Droitwich Spa	25	10	5	10	31	30	35
Cadbury Athletic Reserves	25	10	3	12	39	42	33
West Hagley	26	9	6	11	51	50	30
Continental Star Reserves	25	7	6	12	42	58	27
Castle Vale Reserves	**25**	**7**	**5**	**13**	**34**	**60**	**26**
Chelmsley Town	25	6	5	14	45	64	23
Warwick Town	25	5	7	13	35	45	22
Himley Athletic	19	3	2	14	22	63	11

West Hagley had 3 points deducted.

Himley Athletic resigned during the season but their record was allowed to stand.
Nunnery Wood Sports also resigned but their record was deleted:
5   1   0   4   8   14   3
Castle Vale Reserves became Castle Vale JKS and West Hagley left the league. Wernley Athletic joined as a new club.

Division Three

Halesowen Town Reserves	28	18	6	4	84	25	60
Coventry Sphinx Reserves	**28**	**18**	**6**	**4**	**79**	**22**	**60**
Perrywood	**28**	**18**	**5**	**5**	**66**	**36**	**59**
Barnt Green Spartak Reserves	28	17	4	7	58	41	55
Worcester City "A"	**28**	**16**	**5**	**7**	**54**	**36**	**53**
Greenhill	28	16	2	10	49	42	50
Coleshill Town Reserves	28	14	7	7	53	34	49
Droitwich Spa Reserves	28	11	6	11	52	62	39
Knowle Reserves	28	11	5	12	50	57	38
Shipston Excelsior	28	10	5	13	47	65	35
Heather Athletic Reserves	28	7	8	13	25	43	29
Northfield Town Reserves	28	7	4	17	43	64	25
Wellesbourne	28	3	3	22	35	88	12
Chelmsley Town Reserves	28	2	5	21	27	71	11
Ettington Reserves	28	2	9	17	38	74	15

Ettington Reserves had 6 points deducted.
Bolehall Swifts Reserves resigned when their record was:
4   0   0   4   3   28   0
Wellesbourne and the Reserves of Halesowen Town, Barnt Green Spartak and Coleshill Town all left the league.
BNJS Mann & Co., Studley Athletic and Dosthill Colts joined as new clubs. Kenilworth Town KH and Burntwood Town Reserves also joined.

2006-07
Premier Division

Coventry Sphinx	40	29	7	4	110	40	94
Castle Vale	40	26	7	7	103	47	85
Highgate United	40	25	9	6	90	38	81
Coleshill Town	40	23	7	10	85	43	76
Pilkington XXX	40	21	11	8	65	53	74
Southam United	40	19	7	14	64	67	64
Bolehall Swifts	40	16	12	12	81	67	60
Heath Hayes	40	17	8	15	74	70	56
Barnt Green Spartak	40	16	9	15	72	57	54
Meir KA	40	15	9	16	65	62	54
Nuneaton Griff	40	15	8	17	85	71	53
Walsall Wood	40	14	11	15	50	60	53
Massey Ferguson	40	14	6	20	56	65	48
Pershore Town	40	14	6	20	66	86	48
Brocton	40	12	9	19	51	70	45
Brereton Social	40	11	9	20	49	80	42
Cadbury Athletic	40	11	9	20	48	85	42
Feckenham	40	9	10	21	50	75	37
Continental Star	40	10	7	23	59	89	36
Coventry Copsewood	40	8	11	21	39	78	35
Alveston	40	4	10	26	37	96	22

Continental Star had 1 point deducted. Barnt Green Spartak, Heath Hayes and Highgate United each had 3 points deducted.
Heather Athletic changed their name to Heather St. Johns. Coventry Sphinx moved to the Midland Alliance and Loughborough University joined as a newly-formed club.

Division One

Bartley Green	30	20	1	9	70	31	61
Northfield Town	30	19	3	8	60	34	60
Stockingford AA	30	17	5	8	57	36	56
Fairfield Villa	30	16	4	10	61	53	52
University of Birmingham	30	13	8	9	65	36	47
Heather Athletic	30	13	7	10	53	36	46
Mile Oak Rovers	30	13	6	11	56	45	45
Knowle	30	13	6	11	50	39	45
Littleton	30	13	6	11	55	45	45
Thimblemill R.E.C.	30	12	9	9	43	39	41
Archdale '73'	30	11	6	13	53	61	39
Newhall United	30	11	6	13	49	58	36
Leamington Hibernian	30	7	9	14	31	51	30
West Midlands Police	30	7	7	16	36	58	28
Ettington	30	7	3	20	32	82	24
Burntwood Town	30	4	2	24	22	89	14
Kenilworth Town KH resigned from the league and their record at the time was deleted:		6	0	1	5	7	21	1

Thimblemill R.E.C. had 4 points deducted.
Newhall United had 3 points deducted.
University of Birmingham and Ettingham both left the league.
Wernley Athletic changed their name to Oldbury Athletic.

Division Two

Wernley Athletic	24	19	2	3	98	30	59
Coton Green	24	17	4	3	62	26	55
Droitwich Spa	24	15	2	7	39	26	47
Earlswood Town	24	13	4	7	49	33	43
Coventry Sphinx Reserves	24	13	3	8	61	43	42
Chelmsley Town	24	10	4	10	49	54	34
Warwick Town	24	9	3	12	39	61	30
Continental Star Reserves	24	8	5	11	31	44	29
Cadbury Athletic Reserves	24	6	6	12	39	57	24
Feckenham Reserves	24	6	6	12	24	44	24
Worcester City "A"	24	7	2	15	43	50	23
Enville Athletic	24	6	3	15	41	60	21
Perrywood	24	3	4	17	26	73	10

Perrywood had 3 points deducted.
Worcester City "A" changed their name to Worcester City Academy and Coventry Sphinx Reserves left the league.

Division Three

Castle Vale JKS	26	17	7	2	70	28	58
Ettington Reserves	26	17	4	5	76	50	55
BNJS Mann & Co.	26	16	3	7	69	33	51
Greenhill	26	15	2	9	45	36	47
Dosthill Colts	26	12	7	7	63	46	43
Chelmsley Town Reserves	26	10	8	8	35	39	38
Droitwich Spa Reserves	26	8	12	6	28	27	36
Burntwood Town Reserves	26	9	6	11	39	41	33
Northfield Town Reserves	26	8	7	11	37	38	31
Knowle Reserves	26	8	7	11	49	55	31
Heather Athletic Reserves	26	7	6	13	36	51	24
Shipston Excelsior	26	4	8	14	36	67	20
Studley Athletic	26	5	3	18	36	76	18
Kenilworth Town KH	26	3	6	17	21	53	15

Heather Athletic Reserves had 3 points deducted.
Studley Athletic and Ettington Reserves both left the league.
Austin Sports & Social joined from the Stratford-on-Avon Alliance having changed their name from Austin Social Select. Henley Forest, Littleton Reserves and Earlswood Town Reserves also joined from the Stratford-on-Avon Alliance. GSA & Smethwick Town joined as a new club while Castle Vale Reserves, Evesham United "A" and Racing Club Warwick Reserves all joined as newly-formed teams. Heather Athletic Reserves changed their name to Heather St. Johns Reserves.

2007-08 Premier Division

Coleshill Town	42	30	5	7	124	47	95
Highgate United	42	29	8	5	95	49	95
Southam United	42	22	9	11	83	63	75
Loughborough University	42	21	10	11	78	55	73
Castle Vale	42	20	11	11	85	62	70
Pilkington XXX	42	19	11	12	83	75	68
Heather St. Johns	42	19	10	13	80	64	67
Pershore Town	42	21	7	14	77	61	67
Brocton	42	18	12	12	77	65	66
Heath Hayes	42	18	10	14	99	80	64
Walsall Wood	42	17	11	14	62	53	62
Cadbury Athletic	42	16	11	15	80	72	59
Nuneaton Griff	42	16	11	15	69	66	59
Bartley Green	42	14	6	22	70	83	48
Massey Ferguson	42	14	6	22	65	94	48
Barnt Green Spartak	42	13	7	22	67	75	46
Bolehall Swifts	42	11	11	20	57	77	44
Continental Star	42	11	9	22	79	99	42
Feckenham	**42**	**11**	**9**	**22**	**52**	**96**	**42**
Meir KA	42	11	9	22	51	73	39
Coventry Copsewood	42	9	11	22	57	84	38
Brereton Social	**42**	**2**	**6**	**34**	**25**	**122**	**12**

Castle Vale had 1 point deducted.
Meir KA and Pershore Town each had 3 points deducted.
Feckenham were relegated to Division Two where they replaced their reserves. Coleshill Town and Highgate United both moved to the Midland Alliance. Barnt Green Spartak changed their name to GSA Sports.

Division One

Knowle	**32**	**23**	**7**	**2**	**82**	**21**	**76**
Coton Green	**32**	**21**	**5**	**6**	**75**	**40**	**68**
Oldbury Athletic	**32**	**20**	**6**	**6**	**98**	**48**	**66**
Northfield Town	32	19	8	5	71	31	65
Stockingford AA	32	20	5	7	74	42	65
Mile Oak Rovers	32	17	6	9	73	49	57
Fairfield Villa	32	16	3	13	77	67	51
West Midlands Police	32	13	9	10	66	48	48
Littleton	32	12	3	17	58	60	39
Earlswood Town	32	11	4	17	57	60	37
Droitwich Spa	32	9	8	15	43	66	35
Archdale	32	8	7	17	59	69	31
Newhall United	32	8	6	18	49	74	30
Thimblemill R.E.C.	32	10	2	20	49	84	29
Leamington Hibernian	**32**	**6**	**6**	**20**	**39**	**86**	**24**
Burntwood Town	32	5	7	20	41	95	22
Alveston	32	6	4	22	23	94	22

Thimblemill R.E.C. had 3 points deducted.

Division Two

Castle Vale JKS	**26**	**20**	**4**	**2**	**78**	**19**	**64**
Dosthill Colts	**26**	**18**	**6**	**2**	**68**	**23**	**60**
Worcester City Academy	26	16	4	6	81	34	52
Cadbury Athletic Reserves	26	14	3	9	62	46	42
Enville Athletic	26	12	6	8	50	46	42
Chelmsley Town	26	13	3	10	43	48	42
BNJS Mann & Co.	26	11	4	11	41	49	37
Continental Star Reserves	26	9	6	11	39	42	33
Feckenham Reserves	26	9	6	11	44	53	33
Greenhill	26	7	7	12	39	40	28
Droitwich Spa Reserves	26	6	6	14	28	52	24
Northfield Town Reserves	26	6	3	17	18	54	21
Perrywood	26	6	3	17	44	51	18
Burntwood Town Reserves	26	2	5	19	30	110	11

Cadbury Athletic Reserves and Perrywood each had 3 points deducted.
Warwick Town resigned after just one game (a 1-1 draw) and their record was deleted.
BNJS Mann & Co., Burntwood Town Reserves, Feckenham Reserves and Northfield Town Reserves all left the league. Austin Sports & Social changed their name to Shirley Town and GSA & Smethwick Town changed their name to AFC Internazionale.

Midland Combination 2008-2010

Division Three

GSA & Smethwick Town	24	17	4	3	67	26	55
Austin Sports & Social	24	18	1	5	76	40	55
Castle Vale Reserves	24	15	6	3	77	25	51
Racing Club Warwick Reserves	24	15	1	8	52	30	43
Henley Forest	24	12	5	7	50	32	41
Shipston Excelsior	24	12	3	9	49	53	39
Knowle Reserves	24	10	2	12	54	55	32
Heather St. Johns Reserves	24	9	5	10	30	42	32
Kenilworth Town KH	24	10	1	13	55	45	31
Chelmsley Town Reserves	24	6	6	12	45	55	24
Littleton Reserves	24	4	5	15	26	77	17
Earlswood Town Reserves	24	5	1	18	24	69	16
Evesham United "A"	24	2	2	20	23	79	8

Racing Club Warwick Reserves had 3 points deducted.
Heather St. Johns Reserves moved to the reserve division and Earlswood Town Reserves left the league. Lichfield City joined from the Burton & District F.A. and Coton Green Reserves joined from the Birmingham AFA. Hampton, Clements 83 and Coventry Amateurs joined as a newly formed clubs and Dosthills Colts Reserves joined as a newly formed team.

2008-09

Premier Division

Loughborough University	40	31	3	6	96	34	96
Castle Vale	40	27	8	5	84	42	89
Southam United	40	24	10	6	83	36	82
Oldbury Athletic	40	26	4	10	101	55	82
Heather St. Johns	40	18	12	10	68	45	66
Nuneaton Griff	40	18	10	12	64	51	64
Walsall Wood	40	18	9	13	59	50	63
Pilkington XXX	40	17	6	17	79	83	57
Coventry Copsewood	40	16	8	16	75	66	56
Heath Hayes	40	17	5	18	56	79	56
Cadbury Athletic	40	16	7	17	62	57	55
Knowle	40	13	11	16	50	64	50
Pershore Town	40	13	10	17	59	81	46
GSA Sports	40	13	6	21	64	84	45
Massey Ferguson	40	11	11	18	61	72	44
Brocton	40	11	8	21	60	71	41
Continental Star	40	11	7	22	70	84	40
Bartley Green	40	11	8	21	58	81	38
Bolehall Swifts	40	10	7	23	43	71	37
Meir KA	40	9	8	23	52	87	35
Coton Green	*40*	*5*	*12*	*23*	*59*	*110*	*27*

Pershore Town and Bartley Green each had 3 points deducted
Oldbury Athletic and Pelsall Villa both joined from the WMRL and Loughborough University moved to the Midland Alliance.
Racing Club Warwick joined from the Midland Alliance.

Division One

Castle Vale JKS	30	21	4	5	82	29	67
Dosthill Colts	30	18	4	8	68	38	58
Stockingford AA	30	18	3	9	77	39	57
Fairfield Villa	30	17	5	8	76	31	56
Littleton	30	16	8	6	64	36	56
Earlswood Town	30	15	7	8	55	32	52
Archdale	30	16	4	10	66	51	52
Alveston	30	16	2	12	51	46	50
Brereton Social	30	14	6	10	60	49	48
West Midlands Police	30	12	5	13	55	55	41
Northfield Town	30	12	3	15	47	59	39
Droitwich Spa	30	9	8	13	43	59	35
Mile Oak Rovers	30	7	6	17	52	74	27
Thimblemill R.E.C.	30	6	2	22	41	91	20
Newhall United	30	3	7	20	33	85	16
Burntwood Town	30	1	4	25	25	121	4

Burntwood Town had 3 points deducted.
Thimblemill R.E.C. changed their name to Phoenix United.

Division Two

Shirley Town	26	20	3	3	82	28	63
Castle Vale Reserves	26	16	5	5	68	35	53
Continental Star Reserves	26	13	7	6	61	48	46
Worcester City Academy	26	14	3	9	60	44	45
Racing Club Warwick Reserves	26	12	7	7	68	52	43
AFC Internazionale	26	12	6	8	41	30	42
Feckenham	26	13	2	11	51	42	41
Chelmsley Town	26	10	4	12	44	48	34
Greenhill	26	9	6	11	26	40	33
Droitwich Spa Reserves	26	9	4	13	37	49	31
Enville Athletic	26	7	3	16	60	86	24
Perrywood	26	6	5	15	44	60	23
Leamington Hibernian	26	7	0	19	31	78	21
Cadbury Athletic Reserves	26	6	1	19	50	83	19

Worcester City Academy left the league.
AFC Internazionale changed their name to AFC Smethwick.

Division Three

Hampton	24	20	3	1	76	19	63
Henley Forest	24	16	3	5	79	28	51
Knowle Reserves	24	12	9	3	46	25	45
Kenilworth Town KH	24	13	5	6	53	30	44
Lichfield City	24	13	4	7	64	36	43
Dosthill Colts Reserves	24	12	3	9	53	51	39
Clements 83	24	7	8	9	30	32	29
Coton Green Reserves	24	8	3	13	27	75	27
Chelmsley Town Reserves	24	5	8	11	35	53	23
Coventry Amateurs	24	6	5	13	40	66	23
Shipston Excelsior	24	5	3	16	23	43	18
Littleton Reserves	24	4	5	15	40	64	17
Evesham United "A"	24	3	5	16	21	65	14

Inkberrow joined from the Stratford-on-Avon Alliance, Blackwood joined from Sunday football and Young Warriors joined from youth football.
Polesworth joined as a newly formed club while Archdale Reserves, Earlswood Town Reserves, Stratford Town "A", Northfield Town Reserves and Pershore Town Reserves all joined as new teams.
Evesham United "A" left the league.

2009-10

Premier Division

Heath Hayes	42	29	4	9	128	60	91
Heather St. Johns	42	26	10	6	119	42	88
Pilkington XXX	42	26	5	11	95	73	80
Castle Vale	42	23	10	9	98	55	79
Coventry Copsewood	42	22	11	9	81	55	77
Walsall Wood	42	21	8	13	79	76	71
Brocton	42	20	6	16	94	65	66
Dosthill Colts	42	17	13	12	77	62	64
GSA Sports	42	18	9	15	97	80	63
Bartley Green	42	19	5	18	99	63	62
Knowle	*42*	*18*	*6*	*18*	*59*	*57*	*60*
Nuneaton Griff	42	15	12	15	74	64	57
Massey Ferguson	42	16	8	18	72	88	56
Continental Star	42	15	9	18	81	84	54
Southam United	42	13	14	15	77	82	53
Castle Vale JKS	42	13	10	19	83	82	49
Pelsall Villa	42	14	7	21	70	97	49
Bolehall Swifts	42	12	8	22	65	91	44
Cadbury Athletic	42	10	11	21	63	109	41
Pershore Town	42	9	8	25	45	98	35
Meir KA	42	9	5	28	46	105	32
Racing Club Warwick	42	7	1	34	44	158	22

Pilkington XXX had 3 points deducted.
Heath Hayes moved to the Midland Alliance and GSA Sports disbanded.
Meir KA also left the league.

Division One

Stockingford AA	32	22	7	3	104	38	73
Earlswood Town	32	21	6	5	95	37	69
Alveston	**32**	**21**	**5**	**6**	**80**	**43**	**68**
Fairfield Villa	32	20	7	5	74	37	67
Archdale	32	20	4	8	81	42	64
Northfield Town	32	17	10	5	69	31	61
West Midlands Police	32	16	4	12	73	59	52
Littleton	32	15	6	11	51	37	51
Castle Vale Reserves	32	14	8	10	56	50	50
Shirley Town	32	14	2	16	77	69	44
Phoenix United	32	11	7	14	67	74	40
Brereton Social	32	11	5	16	53	74	38
Coton Green	32	8	4	20	53	71	28
Droitwich Spa	32	7	5	20	44	77	26
Burntwood Town	32	5	2	25	28	115	17
Newhall United	32	4	3	25	47	116	12
Mile Oak Rovers	32	2	3	27	19	101	9

Newhall United had 3 points deducted.
Newhall United moved to the Leicestershire Senior League, Mile Oak Rovers disbanded and Stockingford AA also left the league.
Stretton Eagles joined from the Staffordshire County Premier League and Castle Vale Reserves changed their name to FC Glades Sporting.

Division Two

Hampton	**28**	**22**	**2**	**4**	**68**	**23**	**68**
Kenilworth Town KH	**28**	**20**	**5**	**3**	**82**	**35**	**65**
Lichfield City	28	18	5	5	80	37	59
Feckenham	28	16	1	11	51	38	49
Knowle Reserves	28	13	4	11	43	48	43
Perrywood	28	11	6	11	60	62	39
Cadbury Athletic Reserves	28	11	6	11	52	67	39
Continental Star Reserves	28	12	2	14	56	51	38
Henley Forest	28	11	4	13	60	59	37
AFC Smethwick	28	12	3	13	52	52	36
Leamington Hibernian	28	10	3	15	46	52	33
Enville Athletic	28	8	4	16	39	61	28
Chelmsley Town	28	6	4	18	34	58	22
Droitwich Spa Reserves	28	5	7	16	30	65	22
Greenhill	28	8	2	20	26	71	20

AFC Smethwick had 3 points deducted.
Racing Club Warwick Reserves left the league during the season and their record was deleted: 15 2 1 12 23 62 7
AFC Smethwick moved to the West Midlands Regional League and Bromsgrove Sporting joined as a newly formed club.

Division Three

Blackwood	**30**	**26**	**2**	**2**	**94**	**24**	**80**
Clements 83	**30**	**20**	**6**	**4**	**82**	**28**	**66**
Young Warriors	**30**	**18**	**6**	**6**	**96**	**59**	**60**
Earlswood Town Reserves	30	16	4	10	85	55	52
Stratford Town "A"	30	16	4	10	91	64	52
Dosthill Colts Reserves	30	16	3	11	75	56	51
Archdale Reserves	30	13	5	12	73	68	44
Inkberrow	30	14	4	12	75	68	43
Northfield Town Reserves	30	12	6	12	52	57	42
Shipston Excelsior	30	8	11	11	44	55	35
Polesworth	30	10	2	18	54	65	32
Littleton Reserves	30	9	3	18	56	84	30
Pershore Town Reserves	30	8	6	16	45	77	30
Coton Green Reserves	30	6	6	18	41	87	24
Coventry Amateurs	30	5	4	21	42	91	19
Chelmsley Town Reserves	30	5	4	21	58	125	19

Inkberrow had 3 points deducted.
Shipston Excelsior moved to the Stratford Alliance and Chelmsley Town Reserves, Archdale Reserves, Pershore Town Reserves and Earlswood Town Reserves all also left the league. Aston joined from the Birmingham AFA., Lichfield City Reserves joined from the Burton & District League and Walsall Wood Reserves joined from the Reserve Division. Future Legends joined from youth football, JDG Alliance joined as a newly formed club and Alveston Reserves joined as a newly formed team.

2010-11

Premier Division

Heather St. Johns	36	25	6	5	112	34	81
Nuneaton Griff	36	22	7	7	93	50	70
Castle Vale	36	19	10	7	67	38	67
Coventry Copsewood	36	21	4	11	75	49	67
Dosthill Colts	36	19	6	11	63	52	63
Cadbury Athletic	36	17	9	10	61	40	60
Bolehall Swifts	36	18	5	13	56	43	59
Brocton	36	18	4	14	80	53	58
Walsall Wood	36	16	10	10	42	33	58
Southam United	36	14	10	12	43	33	52
Continental Star	36	14	8	14	58	52	50
Bartley Green	36	12	10	14	66	76	46
Pershore Town	36	10	9	17	47	64	39
Castle Vale JKS	36	11	5	20	62	86	38
Pilkington XXX	36	7	12	17	53	80	33
Massey Ferguson	36	8	9	19	51	93	33
Pelsall Villa	36	10	1	25	34	80	31
Alveston	36	8	3	25	41	110	27
Racing Club Warwick	36	4	10	22	45	83	21

Nuneaton Griff had 3 points deducted.
Racing Club Warwick had 1 point deducted.
Alveston moved to the Stratford Alliance and Heather St. Johns moved to the Midland Alliance. Dosthill Colts were absorbed into Coleshill Town of the Midland Alliance. Massey Ferguson changed their name to Massey Ferguson Athletic and moved to the Coventry Alliance. Bloxwich United joined from the WMRL.

Division One

Earlswood Town	**30**	**23**	**5**	**2**	**112**	**25**	**74**
Knowle	30	21	4	5	82	30	67
Stretton Eagles	30	19	3	8	82	40	60
Fairfield Villa	30	19	1	10	59	42	58
Littleton	30	16	5	9	74	44	53
Shirley Town	30	14	6	10	71	58	48
FC Glades Sporting	30	15	3	12	64	66	48
Droitwich Spa	30	12	7	11	59	53	43
Kenilworth Town KH	30	13	4	13	67	62	43
Hampton	30	11	5	14	54	52	38
Northfield Town	30	10	7	13	52	60	37
West Midlands Police	30	8	8	14	56	80	32
Archdale	30	8	6	16	52	77	30
Coton Green	30	4	12	14	46	58	24
Phoenix United	30	5	5	20	40	78	20
Burntwood Town	*30*	*0*	*3*	*27*	*19*	*164*	*3*

Brereton Social resigned during the season and their record was deleted.
Kenilworth Town KH moved to the Stratford Alliance and Alvis Sporting Club joined from the Coventry Alliance.

Division Two

Blackwood	**30**	**23**	**4**	**3**	**81**	**21**	**73**
Feckenham	**30**	**21**	**2**	**7**	**73**	**36**	**65**
Bromsgrove Sporting	**30**	**20**	**4**	**6**	**82**	**27**	**64**
Lichfield City	**30**	**19**	**6**	**5**	**85**	**33**	**63**
Henley Forest	30	17	5	8	75	44	55
Continental Star Reserves	30	13	8	9	59	47	47
Young Warriors	30	15	5	10	81	62	41
Perrywood	30	11	6	13	39	58	39
Cadbury Athletic Reserves	30	10	4	16	37	66	34
Leamington Hibernian	30	9	6	15	53	82	33
Chelmsley Town	30	9	4	17	42	61	31
Droitwich Spa Reserves	30	6	9	15	46	68	27
Greenhill	30	7	6	17	29	72	27
Clements 83	30	8	2	20	36	60	26
Enville Athletic	30	7	5	18	51	80	26
Knowle Reserves	30	4	6	20	24	76	18

Henley Forest had 1 point deducted.
Young Warriors had 9 points deducted.
Continental Star Reserves, Cadbury Athletic Reserves, Droitwich Spa Reserves and Knowle Reserves all moved to the Reserve Division.

Midland Combination 2011-2013

Barton United joined from the Staffordshire County Senior League. Coventry Amateurs changed their name to Coventry Spartans and Stratford Town "A" changed their name to FC Stratford.

Division Three

Polesworth	26	21	4	1	87	27	67
Aston	26	19	3	4	77	22	60
Littleton Reserves	26	18	4	4	69	34	58
Inkberrow	26	13	5	8	56	41	44
Walsall Wood Reserves	26	13	4	9	53	40	43
Northfield Town Reserves	26	13	3	10	43	42	42
Lichfield City Reserves	26	13	3	10	43	51	42
Dosthill Colts Reserves	26	10	3	13	35	38	33
Future Legends	26	10	3	13	52	57	33
Stratford Town "A"	26	10	2	14	50	65	32
Coton Green Reserves	26	7	4	15	37	46	25
JDG Alliance	26	7	0	19	53	96	21
Coventry Amateurs	26	5	1	20	34	74	16
Alveston Reserves	26	3	1	22	22	78	10

Coton Green Reserves, Lichfield City Reserves, Northfield Town Reserves and Walsall Wood Reserves all moved to the Reserve Division while Future Legends, JDG Alliance, Dosthill Colts Reserves, Littleton Reserves and Alveston Reserves all also left the league. Division Three was disbanded and the reserve section of the league was expanded to two divisions.

2011-12

Premier Division

Continental Star	32	21	7	4	72	39	70
Southam United	32	21	3	8	87	48	66
Coventry Copsewood	32	18	6	8	58	30	60
Bolehall Swifts	32	17	7	8	73	44	58
Castle Vale	32	17	6	9	56	34	57
Brocton	32	17	4	11	67	45	55
Bloxwich United	32	16	6	10	68	62	54
Earlswood Town	32	12	6	14	52	54	42
Bartley Green	32	11	6	15	39	53	39
Pilkington XXX	32	11	5	16	41	68	38
Nuneaton Griff	32	9	10	13	56	64	37
Cadbury Athletic	*32*	*9*	*8*	*15*	*46*	*56*	*35*
Racing Club Warwick	32	10	5	17	46	57	35
Walsall Wood	32	9	6	17	45	50	33
Pelsall Villa	32	9	5	18	33	58	32
Pershore Town	32	8	7	17	43	72	31
Castle Vale JKS	32	6	5	21	57	105	23

Continental Star moved to the Midland Alliance, Bartley Green moved to the WMRL and Castle Vale also left the league. Atherstone Town joined from the Midland Alliance and Stafford Town joined from the WMRL.

Division One

Blackwood	34	24	2	8	72	46	74
Littleton	34	22	2	10	82	52	68
Bromsgrove Sporting	**34**	**19**	**8**	**7**	**94**	**44**	**65**
Lichfield City	**34**	**19**	**6**	**9**	**72**	**44**	**63**
Alvis Sporting Club	34	18	6	10	67	46	60
Shirley Town	34	18	3	13	67	46	57
Knowle	34	14	14	6	56	35	56
Archdale	34	15	7	12	81	62	52
Hampton	34	15	6	13	57	71	51
West Midlands Police	34	14	6	14	75	80	48
Stretton Eagles	34	13	8	13	68	61	47
Feckenham	34	12	7	15	62	62	43
Fairfield Villa	34	11	9	14	67	65	42
Coton Green	34	7	10	17	39	74	31
FC Glades Sporting	34	7	9	18	42	74	30
Northfield Town	34	8	5	21	39	73	29
Droitwich Spa	34	6	4	24	38	76	22
Phoenix United	34	6	4	24	34	101	22

Division Two

Greenhill	26	18	6	2	59	22	60
Aston	26	17	4	5	66	28	55
Chelmsley Town	26	16	7	3	64	31	55
Henley Forest	26	16	4	6	73	40	52
Barton United	26	13	8	5	59	37	47
Perrywood	26	11	3	12	58	60	36
FC Stratford	26	10	5	11	53	57	35
Polesworth	26	10	1	15	42	52	31
Enville Athletic	26	7	5	14	36	56	26
Coventry Spartans	26	5	9	12	33	59	24
Leamington Hibernian	26	6	5	15	30	59	23
Clements 83	26	6	7	13	40	51	22
Inkberrow	26	5	7	14	34	49	22
Burntwood Town	26	4	5	17	31	77	17

Clements 83 had 3 points deducted.
Young Warriors left during the season and their record was deleted.
Alcester Town, Coventry Spires and Kenilworth Town KH all joined from the Stratford Alliance, Sutton United joined from the Birmingham AFA while Barnt Green Spartak and Rugeley Rangers also joined.

2012-13

Premier Division

Walsall Wood	34	25	5	4	75	31	80
Littleton	34	19	8	7	75	39	65
Earlswood Town	34	18	9	7	86	47	63
Nuneaton Griff	34	19	4	11	71	53	61
Brocton	34	17	7	10	76	51	58
Bromsgrove Sporting	34	18	6	10	73	54	57
Southam United	34	16	6	12	69	59	54
Bolehall Swifts	34	16	6	12	56	49	54
Atherstone Town	34	17	5	12	63	52	53
Lichfield City	34	16	5	13	68	62	53
Stafford Town	34	15	7	12	73	52	52
Coventry Copsewood	34	13	10	11	58	55	49
Pershore Town	34	9	12	13	56	69	39
Pelsall Villa	34	8	4	22	39	75	28
Blackwood	34	6	9	19	47	83	27
Pilkington XXX	34	6	5	23	46	102	23
Racing Club Warwick	34	5	4	25	42	92	19
Castle Vale JKS	34	4	6	24	46	94	18

Bromsgrove Sporting and Atherstone Town each had 3 points deducted.
Bloxwich United resigned during the season and their record was deleted.
Walsall Wood moved to the Midland Alliance and Studley joined from the Midland Alliance.

Division One

Alvis Sporting Club	34	29	2	3	122	32	89
Hampton	34	25	4	5	99	38	79
Cadbury Athletic	34	23	5	6	105	33	74
Archdale	34	23	2	9	94	58	71
Stretton Eagles	34	21	3	10	86	52	66
Phoenix United	34	22	2	10	100	51	65
Fairfield Villa	34	19	2	13	84	56	59
Knowle	34	18	2	14	73	48	56
West Midlands Police	34	17	3	14	71	69	54
Aston	34	17	2	15	72	81	53
FC Glades Sporting	34	16	4	14	60	54	52
Feckenham	34	12	6	16	59	77	42
Chelmsley Town	34	9	5	20	48	78	32
Greenhill	34	7	6	21	39	86	27
Shirley Town	34	5	6	23	34	83	21
Droitwich Spa	34	6	3	25	36	91	21
Coton Green	34	3	3	28	28	116	12
Northfield Town	**34**	**3**	**2**	**29**	**28**	**135**	**11**

Phoenix United had 3 points deducted.
Archdale, Stretton Eagles and Greenhill all left the league.

Division Two

Barnt Green Spartak	32	23	6	3	93	49	75
Sutton United	32	22	6	4	103	32	71
Perrywood	32	22	5	5	78	42	71
Polesworth	32	20	5	7	105	69	65
Alcester Town	32	18	6	8	90	49	60
Barton United	32	18	4	10	69	49	58
Henley Forest	32	13	8	11	69	58	47
Coventry Spires	32	12	6	14	62	69	42
Enville Athletic	32	13	3	16	56	82	42
FC Stratford	32	12	5	15	58	61	41
Leamington Hibernian	32	10	8	14	46	47	38
Clements 83	32	10	3	19	54	82	33
Kenilworth Town KH	32	8	8	16	47	69	32
Burntwood Town	32	9	5	18	53	85	32
Coventry Spartans	32	8	3	21	52	78	27
Inkberrow	32	6	1	25	37	79	19
Rugeley Rangers	32	3	8	21	38	110	17

Sutton United had 1 point deducted.
Clements 83, Coventry Spires, Coventry Spartans and Henley Forest all left the league. Paget Rangers joined from the Birmingham AFA, Badsey Rangers joined from the Stratford Alliance and Rostance Edwards joined from the Wolverhampton Combination. Coventry United and Austrey Rangers joined as newly formed clubs.

2013-14
Premier Division

Brocton	34	25	6	3	100	49	81
Bromsgrove Sporting	34	23	3	8	92	35	72
Nuneaton Griff	34	20	4	10	96	75	64
Bolehall Swifts	34	18	6	10	73	50	60
Atherstone Town	34	18	6	10	75	55	60
Studley	34	16	8	10	64	54	56
Lichfield City	34	13	11	10	52	50	50
Stafford Town	34	14	8	12	56	57	50
Alvis Sporting Club	34	14	8	12	69	79	50
Southam United	34	14	5	15	62	80	47
Littleton	34	14	4	16	74	60	46
Racing Club Warwick	34	11	7	16	60	63	40
Earlswood Town	*34*	*11*	*4*	*19*	*47*	*66*	*37*
Blackwood	34	11	4	19	49	74	37
Pershore Town	34	10	3	21	57	80	33
Coventry Copsewood	34	8	10	16	54	77	33
Pilkington XXX	34	6	8	20	53	77	26
Pelsall Villa	34	5	5	24	41	93	20

Coventry Copsewood had 1 point deducted.
Castle Vale JKS resigned in February 2014 and their record was deleted.

Division One

Cadbury Athletic	**28**	**21**	**4**	**3**	**93**	**26**	**67**
Fairfield Villa	28	17	5	6	67	33	56
Sutton United	28	16	7	5	68	32	55
Aston	28	18	1	9	62	43	55
Phoenix United	28	17	5	6	73	44	53
Chelmsley Town	28	13	5	10	45	48	44
Hampton	28	12	7	9	53	49	43
Feckenham	28	11	6	11	49	50	39
West Midlands Police	28	8	8	12	46	59	32
Shirley Town	28	10	2	16	36	59	32
Knowle	28	8	6	14	29	47	30
Barnt Green Spartak	28	7	6	15	43	53	27
Droitwich Spa	28	7	4	17	46	71	25
FC Glades Sporting	28	4	4	19	35	73	16
Coton Green	28	2	6	20	22	80	12

Phoenix United and FC Glades Sporting each had 3 points deducted.

Division Two

Kenilworth Town KH	**30**	**22**	**3**	**5**	**90**	**48**	**69**
Coventry United	**30**	**22**	**2**	**6**	**105**	**33**	**68**
Paget Rangers	**30**	**20**	**6**	**4**	**98**	**33**	**66**
Badsey Rangers	30	16	7	7	69	39	55
Rostance Edwards	30	15	6	9	72	59	51
Leamington Hibernian	30	14	7	9	48	40	49
Alcester Town	30	15	4	11	79	71	46
Barton United	30	13	4	13	48	65	43
Polesworth	30	12	6	12	59	90	42
Perrywood	30	12	4	14	58	50	40
Enville Athletic	30	10	3	17	59	62	33
Austrey Rangers	30	10	3	17	55	64	33
Northfield Town	30	9	6	15	45	63	33
FC Stratford	30	6	3	21	43	92	21
Burntwood Town	30	5	4	21	54	102	16
Inkberrow	30	2	6	22	39	110	12

Alcester Town and Burntwood Town each had 3 points deducted.
Rugeley Rangers resigned during the season and their record was deleted.

At the end of the season, the Midland Combination merged with the Midland Alliance to form the Midland League.

Members of the Midland Combination Premier Division were placed in Division One of the Midland League, members of the Midland Combination Division One were placed in Division Two of the Midland League and members of the Midland Combination Division Two were placed in Division Three of the Midland League apart from the following exceptions.

Premier Division: Brocton were placed in the Premier Division of the Midland League and Blackwood disbanded.

Division One: Phoenix United, West Midlands Police and Shirley Town all left the league.

Division Two: Polesworth left the league.

WARWICKSHIRE COMBINATION

Background and Summary

The massive influence of the city of Birmingham and its leagues meant that for many years Warwickshire had no county league of its own. Just after the war, there was a Warwickshire and West Midland Alliance but the very name gives away the fact that most of its members were based in the Birmingham conurbation and this league did not always keep the Warwickshire part of its title. In the 1952-53 season it had a 15 club Southern Section but more than half of that section's members were based in Birmingham or even to the north of the city and some of the remainder wanted a more local fixture list. As a result, the South Warwickshire League came into being in 1953. In its first season it had only nine members and so the fixture list was supplemented by a cup competition in which the clubs played each other again in a league format. However the popularity of the new league allowed it to expand its membership to 19 clubs in 1954-55, when it adopted the name "Warwickshire Combination".

The nine founder members of the South Warwickshire League were Cubbington Albion, Flavels, Saltisford Rovers, Warwick Town, Warwickshire Constabulary and the reserve sides of Banbury Spencer, Bedworth Town, Cheltenham Town and Lockheed (Leamington). Of these Lockheed Reserves, Saltisford Rovers and Warwick Town had played in the Warwickshire and West Midland Alliance in 1952-53.

The league contained several junior clubs, some of whom - Evesham United, Cinderford Town, Coventry Amateurs (later Coventry Sporting) and Saltisford Rovers (as R.C. Warwick) - later grew and joined the Southern League. Other members included the third or fourth sides of Football League clubs and some reserve sides of Southern and Birmingham League clubs. This last category expanded in 1960 when the Birmingham League adopted a policy of including first teams only and so the Warwickshire Combination expanded to two regional divisions. However after a few years, the reserve sides formed their own league while the neighbouring Worcestershire Combination continued to expand. Squeezed by these two factors, the Warwickshire Combination closed in 1967.

Several of the published tables contained errors. Additional research has succeeded in correcting some of these. Those totals that still do not balance are shown below the relevant columns in italics.

SOUTH WARWICKSHIRE LEAGUE

1953-54

League championship

Cheltenham Town Reserves	16	11	3	2	61	21	25
Cubbington Albion	16	11	1	4	45	33	23
Lockheed (Leamington) Reserves	16	9	3	4	51	25	21
Saltisford Rovers	16	6	4	6	39	40	16
Bedworth Town Reserves	16	7	0	9	40	54	14
Banbury Spencer Reserves	16	6	1	9	42	49	13
Warwick Town	16	5	2	9	44	58	12
Flavels	16	3	4	9	36	51	10
Warwickshire Constabulary	16	4	2	10	33	55	10
					391	*386*	

Cup competition

Cheltenham Town Reserves	16	13	1	2	56	18	27
Lockheed (Leamington) Reserves	16	8	2	6	37	23	18
Saltisford Rovers	16	7	4	5	45	28	18
Cubbington Albion	16	5	8	3	32	23	18
Flavels	16	8	1	7	30	31	17
Warwick Town	16	6	3	7	35	44	15
Banbury Spencer Reserves	16	4	5	7	29	51	13
Warwickshire Constabulary	16	3	4	9	29	45	10
Bedworth Town Reserves	16	3	2	11	20	49	8
					313	*312*	

Cheltenham Town Reserves left. West Bromwich Albion "A" joined from the Birmingham Combination, Nuneaton Borough Reserves joined from the Staffordshire County League (South), Stratford Town Reserves joined from the Warwickshire & West Midlands Alliance, Birch Coppice Colliery Reserves joined from the Tamworth & Trent Valley League and Ansley Hall Colliery, Aston Villa "B", Birmingham City "A", Coventry City "A", Rootes Athletic, Rugby Town Reserves and Worcester City "A" also joined.

After abortive discussions concerning a merger with the Birmingham Combination, the league changed its name to Warwickshire Combination during the 1954-55 season.

WARWICKSHIRE COMBINATION

1954-55

West Bromwich Albion "A"	36	30	2	4	166	41	62
Birmingham City "A"	36	27	5	4	163	39	59
Warwick Town	36	21	7	8	114	73	49
Rugby Town Reserves	36	18	12	6	87	64	48
Worcester City "A"	36	19	6	11	88	67	44
Nuneaton Borough Reserves	36	17	9	10	78	69	43
Banbury Spencer Reserves	36	16	7	13	86	81	39
Aston Villa "B"	36	12	13	11	56	51	37
Coventry City "A"	36	15	6	15	74	79	36
Lockheed (Leamington) Reserves	36	15	6	15	101	72	34
Rootes Athletic	36	14	6	16	91	82	34
Bedworth Town Reserves	36	14	6	16	61	60	34
Cubbington Albion	36	12	7	17	59	96	31
Flavels	36	12	5	19	80	90	29
Stratford Town Reserves	36	9	6	21	46	74	24
Warwickshire Constabulary	36	10	3	23	79	119	23
Ansley Hall Colliery	36	8	5	23	40	77	21
Saltisford Rovers	36	7	5	24	57	131	19
Birch Coppice Colliery Reserves	36	6	6	24	40	136	18
		684	282	122	280	1566	1501	684

Lockheed (Leamington) Reserves had 2 points deducted for fielding an ineligible player.
West Bromwich Albion's "B" side joined the league instead of the "A" side who moved to the Birmingham League. Birch Coppice Colliery Reserves left and were replaced by their first team who moved from the Birmingham League. Coventry Amateurs joined from the Warwickshire & West Midlands Alliance.

1955-56

Lockheed (Leamington) Reserves	38	29	3	6	137	49	61
Birmingham City "A"	38	26	7	5	125	44	59
Banbury Spencer Reserves	38	27	2	9	140	57	56
Bedworth Town Reserves	38	25	4	9	116	39	54
Rugby Town Reserves	38	25	3	10	100	54	53
Aston Villa "B"	38	18	10	10	97	79	46
West Bromwich Albion "B"	38	17	7	14	85	65	41
Coventry City "A"	38	17	7	14	72	67	41
Saltisford Rovers	38	14	12	12	87	90	40
Rootes Athletic	38	14	11	13	74	76	39
Nuneaton Borough Reserves	38	16	4	18	64	80	36
Warwick Town	38	15	5	18	83	80	35
Flavels	38	15	5	18	66	75	35
Birch Coppice Colliery	38	13	8	17	80	100	34
Worcester City "A"	38	13	5	20	65	94	31
Cubbington Albion	38	10	8	20	62	90	28
Stratford Town Reserves	38	11	5	22	64	117	27
Coventry Amateurs	38	7	5	26	46	108	19
Ansley Hall Colliery	38	6	5	27	54	114	17
Warwickshire Constabulary	38	3	6	29	61	188	12
		760	321	122	317	1678	1666	764

Flavels moved to the Coventry Works League and Stratford Town Reserves also left, replacing their "A" team in the Warwickshire & West Midlands Alliance. Kenilworth Rangers joined from the Warwickshire and West Midlands Alliance.

1956-57

Birmingham City "A"	36	29	2	5	133	45	60
Kenilworth Rangers	36	28	3	5	134	34	59
Coventry City "A"	36	19	12	5	98	53	50
Lockheed (Leamington) Reserves	36	20	7	9	91	56	47
Rugby Town Reserves	36	20	6	10	115	69	46
Warwick Town	36	20	5	11	105	73	45
West Bromwich Albion "B"	36	19	3	14	89	65	41
Saltisford Rovers	36	16	8	12	110	98	40
Bedworth Town Reserves	36	15	8	13	81	72	38
Nuneaton Borough Reserves	36	16	6	14	92	65	38
Cubbington Albion	36	16	5	15	68	69	37
Aston Villa "B"	36	15	6	15	91	73	36
Rootes Athletic	36	12	10	14	89	74	34
Banbury Spencer Reserves	36	13	1	22	82	93	27
Coventry Amateurs	36	8	6	22	49	73	22
Ansley Hall Colliery	36	9	3	24	79	121	21
Birch Coppice Colliery	36	7	7	22	68	124	21
Worcester City "A"	36	6	3	27	71	178	15
Warwickshire Constabulary	36	3	1	32	51	221	7
						1696	1656	

Worcester City "A" moved to the Worcestershire Combination and Birch Coppice Colliery also left. Birmingham City and Coventry City placed their "B" sides in the league instead of their "A" sides, who moved to the Birmingham League. Smethwick Town joined from the Birmingham Youths and Old Boys League and Hinckley Athletic Reserves joined from the Leicestershire Senior League.

1957-58

Warwick Town	36	29	3	4	151	52	61
Banbury Spencer Reserves	36	22	7	7	105	52	51
Birmingham City "B"	36	21	9	6	99	53	51
Kenilworth Rangers	36	22	6	8	127	58	50
Lockheed (Leamington) Reserves	36	21	1	14	114	69	43
West Bromwich Albion "B"	36	17	9	10	98	73	43
Rugby Town Reserves	36	18	5	13	87	62	41
Smethwick Town	36	18	5	13	116	80	41
Hinckley Athletic Reserves	36	17	6	13	103	66	40
Cubbington Albion	36	15	6	15	84	98	36
Saltisford Rovers	36	14	7	15	85	96	35
Rootes Athletic	36	15	4	17	77	92	34
Nuneaton Borough Reserves	36	14	5	17	88	97	33
Bedworth Town Reserves	36	11	9	16	59	114	31
Aston Villa "B"	36	13	4	19	82	89	30
Coventry City "B"	36	10	4	22	71	113	24
Coventry Amateurs	36	9	5	22	63	88	23
Warwickshire Constabulary	36	3	3	30	54	184	9
Ansley Hall Colliery	36	3	2	31	42	177	8
						1705	1713	

Ansley Hall Colliery moved to the West Midland Alliance and Coventry City "B", Nuneaton Borough Reserves and Warwickshire Constabulary also left. Stratford Town Reserves joined from the Warwickshire and West Midlands Alliance and Sterling Metals also joined.

Warwickshire Combination 1958-1963

1958-59

Birmingham City "B"	32	22	4	6	122	55	48
Lockheed (Leamington) Reserves	32	23	1	8	109	48	47
Warwick Town	32	19	7	6	99	50	45
Aston Villa "B"	32	21	3	8	95	48	45
Banbury Spencer Reserves	32	19	7	6	81	56	45
Cubbington Albion	32	18	5	9	85	65	41
Smethwick Town	32	17	5	10	76	69	39
West Bromwich Albion "B"	32	18	2	12	91	50	38
Hinckley Athletic Reserves	32	17	4	11	85	62	38
Rugby Town Reserves	32	16	5	11	94	61	37
Kenilworth Rangers	32	14	3	15	78	87	31
Rootes Athletic	32	10	4	18	57	81	24
Coventry Amateurs	32	6	9	17	58	83	21
Saltisford Rovers	32	7	6	19	73	115	20
Bedworth Town Reserves	32	4	4	24	51	108	12
Stratford Town Reserves	32	4	1	27	47	111	9
Sterling Metals	32	0	4	28	23	166	4
					1324	1315	

Rugby Town Reserves left and Easington Sports joined.

1959-60

Aston Villa "B"	32	26	3	3	122	43	55
Lockheed (Leamington) Reserves	32	21	4	7	95	37	46
Banbury Spencer Reserves	32	20	5	7	85	51	45
Hinckley Athletic Reserves	32	21	2	9	92	45	44
Birmingham City "B"	32	17	7	8	92	53	41
Warwick Town	32	17	4	11	84	67	38
Rootes Athletic	32	15	5	12	64	56	35
Easington Sports	32	14	6	12	85	65	34
West Bromwich Albion "B"	32	14	2	16	68	61	30
Stratford Town Reserves	32	12	6	14	69	78	30
Cubbington Albion	32	12	5	15	91	89	29
Coventry Amateurs	32	14	1	17	54	66	29
Kenilworth Rangers	32	11	5	16	60	90	27
Saltisford Rovers	32	10	5	17	67	88	25
Smethwick Town	32	8	2	22	54	115	18
Bedworth Town Reserves	32	6	3	23	55	107	15
Sterling Metals	32	0	3	29	32	151	3
					1269	1262	

Smethwick Town moved to the West Midlands Alliance and Sterling Metals also left but nine new clubs joined increasing membership to 24. The league was split into two 12 club divisions, Eastern and Western, with Baddesley Liberals from the West Midlands Alliance and West Bromwich Albion "C" joining the Eastern Division while Netherton Town from the West Midlands Alliance and the reserves of Cheltenham Town, Hereford United, Wellington Town and Worcester City moved to the Western Division from the Birmingham League. Gloucester City Reserves and Rugby Town Reserves also joined the Western Division.

1960-61

Eastern Division

Rootes Athletic	22	16	4	2	83	33	36
Banbury Spencer Reserves	22	14	2	6	48	29	30
Cubbington Albion	22	12	4	6	63	41	28
Coventry Amateurs	22	11	4	7	39	34	26
Stratford Town Reserves	22	8	7	7	50	52	23
West Bromwich Albion "C"	22	10	2	10	50	46	22
Baddesley Liberals	22	8	3	11	63	54	19
Saltisford Rovers	22	7	5	10	41	54	19
Warwick Town	22	7	5	10	31	57	19
Easington Sports	22	6	3	13	45	60	15
Bedworth Town Reserves	22	6	2	14	27	58	14
Kenilworth Rangers	22	5	3	14	34	56	13

Baddesley Liberals, Bedworth Town Reserves, Kenilworth Rangers and West Bromwich Albion "C" left. Lockheed (Leamington) Reserves transferred from the Western Division. Forest of Arden joined from the Leamington League.

Western Division

Wellington Town Reserves	22	14	3	5	55	26	31
Hereford United Reserves	22	13	4	5	65	37	30
Birmingham City "B"	22	13	3	6	71	40	29
Cheltenham Town Reserves	22	13	2	7	59	40	28
Worcester City Reserves	22	13	1	8	51	37	27
Rugby Town Reserves	22	10	5	7	62	39	25
Hinckley Athletic Reserves	22	9	4	9	34	40	22
West Bromwich Albion "B"	22	9	3	10	70	61	21
Netherton Town	22	7	6	9	31	46	20
Aston Villa "B"	22	7	3	12	31	40	17
Lockheed (Leamington) Reserves	22	4	2	16	25	49	10
Gloucester City Reserves	22	2	0	20	17	116	4

Birmingham City "B" and Gloucester City Reserves left. Kidderminster Harriers Reserves joined from the West Midlands Alliance and Nuneaton Borough Reserves and Sankeys (Wellington) Reserves also joined.

1961-62

Eastern Division

Rootes Athletic	18	13	3	2	54	25	29
Cubbington Albion	18	13	1	4	63	29	27
Coventry Amateurs	18	11	2	5	50	32	24
Stratford Town Reserves	18	9	3	6	45	42	21
Lockheed (Leamington) Reserves	18	9	1	8	38	32	19
Saltisford Rovers	18	7	4	7	42	44	18
Banbury Spencer Reserves	18	8	1	9	41	34	17
Easington Sports	18	4	3	11	30	52	11
Forest of Arden	18	2	5	11	33	60	9
Warwick Town	18	2	1	15	24	70	5

Forest of Arden moved to the Stratford League. Evesham United joined from the Birmingham League, Alcester Town joined from the Redditch League and Bedworth Town Reserves also joined.

Western Division

Worcester City Reserves	22	15	3	4	39	18	33
Hereford United Reserves	22	14	3	5	61	29	31
Nuneaton Borough Reserves	22	11	6	5	45	31	28
Sankeys (Wellington) Reserves	22	12	3	7	47	43	27
Wellington Town Reserves	22	12	1	9	46	30	25
Rugby Town Reserves	22	10	3	9	35	30	23
Cheltenham Town Reserves	22	11	0	11	60	53	22
Kidderminster Harriers Reserves	22	8	4	10	37	47	20
Aston Villa "B"	22	8	3	11	43	50	19
Hinckley Athletic Reserves	22	8	1	13	51	61	17
Netherton Town	22	3	5	14	22	50	11
West Bromwich Albion "B"	22	2	4	16	27	71	8

Stafford Rangers Reserves joined from the Staffordshire County League (South) and Lydbrook Athletic also joined.

1962-63

Eastern Division

Evesham United	22	19	3	0	111	24	41
Rootes Athletic	22	19	1	2	99	26	39
Lockheed (Leamington) Reserves	22	10	8	4	45	22	28
Cubbington Albion	22	12	2	8	55	47	26
Coventry Amateurs	22	10	2	10	47	49	22
Banbury Spencer Reserves	22	8	3	11	49	55	19
Alcester Town	22	8	3	11	48	73	19
Stratford Town Reserves	22	8	2	12	39	55	18
Bedworth Town Reserves	22	6	5	11	44	66	17
Warwick Town	22	7	1	14	33	71	15
Easington Sports	22	5	4	13	44	56	14
Saltisford Rovers	22	2	2	18	29	99	6

Warwickshire Combination 1963-1967

Western Division

Cheltenham Town Reserves	26	18	4	4	71	35	40
Worcester City Reserves	26	16	6	4	63	31	38
Wellington Town Reserves	26	15	2	9	61	41	32
Rugby Town Reserves	26	14	4	8	54	46	32
Nuneaton Borough Reserves	26	13	4	9	53	35	30
Lydbrook Athletic	26	13	4	9	54	45	30
Stafford Rangers Reserves	26	15	0	11	51	45	30
Hereford United Reserves	26	11	6	9	53	37	28
West Bromwich Albion "B"	26	11	2	13	42	54	24
Hinckley Athletic Reserves	26	9	6	11	31	50	24
Kidderminster Harriers Reserves	26	9	2	15	52	61	20
Sankeys (Wellington) Reserves	26	6	4	16	48	61	16
Aston Villa "B"	26	5	6	15	33	64	16
Netherton Town	26	1	2	23	21	82	4

Netherton Town left and Cinderford Town joined.

1963-64

Eastern Division

Evesham United	22	17	3	2	97	22	37
Lockheed (Leamington) Reserves	22	15	7	0	62	25	37
Banbury Spencer Reserves	22	14	3	5	65	30	31
Cubbington Albion	22	11	4	7	59	49	26
Coventry Amateurs	22	10	3	9	46	36	23
Warwick Town	22	10	3	9	37	62	23
Saltisford Rovers	22	10	2	10	48	45	22
Rootes Athletic	22	9	2	11	49	49	20
Stratford Town Reserves	22	7	4	11	59	67	18
Easington Sports	22	5	2	15	44	76	12
Alcester Town	22	4	2	16	29	72	10
Bedworth Town Reserves	22	1	3	18	21	83	5

Rootes Athletic moved to the Coventry Works League and Easington Sports also left. Castle Rovers joined from the Kings Norton League and Feckenham United joined from the Redditch League. Evesham United and Lockheed (Leamington) Reserves transferred to the Western Division.

Western Division

Worcester City Reserves	26	20	4	2	80	25	44
Hereford United Reserves	26	17	3	6	71	36	37
Nuneaton Borough Reserves	26	14	6	6	59	33	34
Cheltenham Town Reserves	26	16	2	8	52	36	34
Cinderford Town	26	14	5	7	88	44	33
Lydbrook Athletic	26	10	8	8	36	39	28
Wellington Town Reserves	26	12	3	11	51	52	27
Aston Villa "B"	26	12	3	11	49	53	27
Kidderminster Harriers Reserves	26	11	2	13	55	62	24
Stafford Rangers Reserves	26	9	4	13	48	61	22
West Bromwich Albion "B"	26	4	7	15	39	70	15
Sankeys (Wellington) Reserves	26	5	5	16	33	71	15
Rugby Town Reserves	26	4	5	17	29	57	13
Hinckley Athletic Reserves	26	4	3	19	37	88	11

Kidderminster Harriers Reserves moved to the Warwickshire Combination while Aston Villa "B", West Bromwich Albion "B" and the reserves of Rugby Town, Sankeys (Wellington) and Stafford Rangers also left the league.

1964-65

Eastern Division

Castle Rovers	18	14	3	1	67	22	31
Saltisford Rovers	18	12	4	2	49	21	28
Banbury Spencer Reserves	18	10	4	4	59	28	24
Stratford Town Reserves	18	6	4	8	33	43	16
Coventry Amateurs	18	6	4	8	29	39	16
Feckenham United	18	7	1	10	40	48	15
Cubbington Albion	18	6	3	9	32	51	15
Alcester Town	18	6	2	10	44	47	14
Warwick Town	18	4	5	9	21	40	13
Bedworth Town Reserves	18	3	2	13	20	55	8

Western Division

Cinderford Town	18	11	5	2	42	19	27
Worcester City Reserves	18	10	3	5	66	34	23
Evesham United	18	10	2	6	46	30	22
Wellington Town Reserves	18	9	1	8	55	45	19
Hereford United Reserves	18	9	1	8	48	46	19
Nuneaton Borough Reserves	18	7	4	7	34	38	18
Lockheed (Leamington) Reserves	18	6	4	8	27	33	16
Lydbrook Athletic	18	7	2	9	24	36	16
Hinckley Athletic Reserves	18	2	6	10	22	40	10
Cheltenham Town Reserves	18	4	2	12	34	77	10

Banbury Spencer changed their name to Banbury United. Cinderford Town moved to the West Midlands Regional League. Alcester Town, Castle Rovers and Evesham United moved to the Worcestershire Combination. Feckenham United and the Reserves of Cheltenham Town, Hinckley Athletic, Lockheed (Leamington), Nuneaton Borough and Wellington Town also left. Walsgrave Lodge and Warwickshire Constabulary joined. The League consolidated into a single 12 club division.

Alcester Town, Castle Rovers and Evesham United all moved to the Worcestershire Combination. Cinderford Town, Nuneaton Borough Reserves and Wellington Town Reserves all moved to the West Midlands Regional League while Feckenham United and the Reserves of Cheltenham Town, Hinckley Athletic and Lockheed (Leamington) also left the league. Walsgrave Lodge and Warwickshire Constabulary both joined. Banbury Spencer changed their name to Banbury United.

The League was consolidated into a single 12 club division.

1965-66

Saltisford Rovers	22	16	5	1	71	13	37
Banbury United Reserves	22	15	3	4	63	28	33
Lydbrook Athletic	22	15	3	4	49	27	33
Hereford United Reserves	22	13	6	3	54	25	32
Coventry Amateurs	22	10	5	7	45	29	25
Worcester City Reserves	22	10	3	9	71	42	23
Warwick Town	22	10	2	10	48	47	22
Walsgrave Lodge	22	8	3	11	42	54	19
Bedworth Town Reserves	22	3	6	13	24	54	12
Warwickshire Constabulary	22	5	2	15	28	86	12
Stratford Town Reserves	22	4	1	17	37	66	9
Cubbington Albion	22	3	1	18	27	88	7

Stratford Town Reserves moved to the Warwickshire and West Midlands Alliance, Banbury United Reserves moved to the Hellenic League and Worcester City Reserves also left. Fisher & Ludlow joined from the Birmingham Works League and Aston Villa "B" and Redditch B.A. also joined.

1966-67

Hereford United Reserves	22	19	2	1	92	17	40
Saltisford Rovers	22	18	3	1	76	21	39
Warwickshire Constabulary	22	12	3	7	77	53	27
Walsgrave Lodge	22	12	2	8	62	43	26
Lydbrook Athletic	22	11	2	9	60	48	24
Aston Villa "B"	22	9	5	8	62	42	23
Fisher & Ludlow	22	10	3	9	43	41	23
Coventry Amateurs	22	8	4	10	43	50	20
Bedworth Town Reserves	22	7	5	10	37	52	19
Warwick Town	22	4	4	14	26	72	12
Redditch B.A.	22	3	0	19	30	82	6
Cubbington Albion	22	2	1	19	18	105	5

Saltisford Rovers and Warwick Town merged as Warwick Saltisford Rovers and resigned to join the West Midlands Regional League. Bedworth Town Reserves also resigned to join the West Midlands Regional League and Aston Villa "B", Cubbington Albion and Redditch B.A. also resigned leaving 6 existing members.

Applications were received from 5 new clubs – Redditch Transport, Ross All Whites, Rugby St. Johns, Saunders Hall and Warley Reserves who were a new club. However at the A.G.M. in June 1967 it was revealed that Fisher & Ludlow and Walsgrave Lodge had also resigned and that Redditch Transport had withdrawn their application, reducing membership for 1967-68 to 8 clubs. Several clubs were unhappy with this and Coventry Amateurs and Hereford United Reserves were successful with late applications to the West Midlands Regional League.

Of the remaining 6 clubs, only Saunders Hall and Warwickshire Constabulary remained committed to the Warwickshire Combination and so the league was officially wound up at a special meeting on Thursday 6th July, 1967.

MIDLAND FOOTBALL ALLIANCE 1994-2014

Although their roots were very different, the West Midlands Regional League (WMRL) and the Midland Combination had for many years been gradually converging. By the early 1990s, their catchment areas and the standard of clubs competing were almost identical and both leagues were at the same level in the non-League pyramid. It made sense for the best clubs in the two competitions to play each other in a stronger league and so, in 1994, the Midland Football Alliance was formed. Ten of the top clubs were selected from each of the two older leagues both of which then became feeders to the new competition.

The clubs from the Midland Combination were: Barwell, Boldmere St. Michaels, Bolehall Swifts, Pershore Town, Sandwell Borough, Shifnal Town, Stapenhill, Stratford Town and West Midlands Police. The tenth club were Shepshed Dynamo who were a quickly formed replacement for Shepshed Albion who had folded with financial difficulties in May 1994.

The ten from the West Midlands Regional League were: Brierley Hill Town, Chasetown, Halesowen Harriers, Hinckley Athletic, Knypersley Victoria, Oldbury United, Paget Rangers, Rocester, Rushall Olympic and Willenhall Town. The Midland Football Alliance itself then became a feeder to the Southern League.

1994-95

Paget Rangers	38	24	9	5	65	32	81
Hinckley Athletic	38	20	9	9	76	49	69
Stratford Town	38	19	9	10	69	46	66
Shepshed Dynamo	38	18	10	10	63	51	64
Halesowen Harriers	38	19	6	13	87	55	63
Shifnal Town	38	16	14	8	65	45	62
Boldmere St. Michaels	38	18	8	12	65	48	62
Oldbury United	38	18	8	12	58	47	62
Knypersley Victoria	38	15	12	11	82	54	57
Willenhall Town	38	15	7	16	55	58	52
West Midlands Police	38	14	8	16	53	51	50
Stapenhill	38	15	5	18	60	80	50
Rocester	38	12	12	14	48	50	48
Sandwell Borough	38	12	12	14	62	69	48
Barwell	38	12	9	17	58	69	45
Pershore Town	38	12	9	17	49	71	45
Chasetown	38	8	13	17	52	72	37
Rushall Olympic	38	9	10	19	60	85	37
Bolehall Swifts	38	9	9	20	45	60	36
Brierley Hill Town	**38**	**3**	**5**	**30**	**27**	**107**	**14**

Paget Rangers were promoted to the Southern League being replaced by relegated Armitage 90. Brierley Hill Town were relegated to the WMRL being replaced by promoted Blakenall.

1995-96

Shepshed Dynamo	36	22	10	4	90	37	76
Blakenall	36	19	11	6	60	36	68
Hinckley Athletic	36	21	4	11	78	54	67
Rocester	36	19	9	8	55	50	66
Knypersley Victoria	36	18	8	10	73	43	62
Boldmere St. Michaels	36	18	5	13	73	51	59
Sandwell Borough	36	17	5	14	56	50	56
Willenhall Town	36	16	7	13	52	62	55
Barwell	36	15	6	15	57	53	51
Oldbury United	36	14	8	14	49	41	50
Rushall Olympic	36	15	5	16	57	65	50
Halesowen Harriers	36	13	7	16	54	62	46
Stratford Town	36	12	9	15	56	54	45
Pershore Town	36	12	9	15	58	73	45
West Midlands Police	36	11	11	14	49	55	44
Chasetown	36	10	10	16	44	52	40
Shifnal Town	36	8	9	19	38	60	33
Stapenhill	36	5	6	25	38	87	21
Bolehall Swifts	**36**	**5**	**5**	**26**	**30**	**82**	**20**

Armitage resigned on 13th December 1995 while leading the league and their record was expunged.
Shepshed Dynamo were promoted to the Southern League being replaced by relegated Bridgnorth Town. Bolehall Swifts were relegated to the Midland Combination being replaced by promoted Bloxwich Town. Pelsall Villa were promoted from the WMRL.

1996-97

Blakenall	38	23	11	4	85	39	80
Hinckley Athletic	38	22	10	6	77	44	76
Boldmere St. Michaels	38	22	7	9	69	41	73
Willenhall Town	38	20	9	9	77	45	69
Barwell	38	17	10	11	65	51	61
Bridgnorth Town	38	18	4	16	76	67	58
Rocester	38	16	9	13	62	53	57
Stratford Town	38	15	10	13	53	48	55
Bloxwich Town	38	16	6	16	63	53	54
Oldbury United	38	14	11	13	50	43	53
Pelsall Villa	38	13	9	16	52	70	48
Knypersley Victoria	38	11	12	15	42	53	45
Stapenhill	38	10	14	14	45	58	44
Shifnal Town	38	11	10	17	45	50	43
West Midlands Police	38	10	11	17	37	60	41
Rushall Olympic	38	10	10	18	40	59	40
Sandwell Borough	38	9	13	16	48	69	40
Chasetown	38	9	12	17	44	65	39
Halesowen Harriers	38	8	12	18	44	67	36
Pershore Town	38	8	6	24	41	80	30

Hinckley Athletic merged with Hinckley Town of the Southern League and the merged club continued playing in the Southern League as Hinckley United. Blakenall were promoted to the Southern League. Wednesfield were promoted from the WMRL and Kings Norton Town were promoted from the Midland Combination, having changed their name from Richmond Swifts.

1997-98

Bloxwich Town	38	28	4	6	77	31	88
Rocester	38	23	7	8	74	36	76
Oldbury United	38	20	11	7	73	43	71
Boldmere St. Michaels	38	19	11	8	54	38	68
Kings Norton Town	38	18	13	7	57	37	67
Barwell	38	16	12	10	68	55	60
Bridgnorth Town	38	15	13	10	64	47	58
West Midlands Police	38	15	12	11	58	42	57
Halesowen Harriers	38	17	5	16	53	63	56
Chasetown	38	14	11	13	57	43	53
Wednesfield	38	14	11	13	56	49	53
Knypersley Victoria	38	11	17	10	52	53	50
Willenhall Town	38	12	13	13	45	44	49
Pelsall Villa	38	10	15	13	66	66	45
Sandwell Borough	38	10	15	13	57	63	45
Rushall Olympic	38	12	8	18	51	57	44
Stapenhill	38	7	12	19	39	74	33
Stratford Town	38	8	7	23	39	70	31
Pershore Town	38	4	6	28	36	97	18
Shifnal Town	38	3	5	30	35	103	14

Bloxwich Town were promoted to the Southern League.
Stourport Swifts joined following promotion from the WMRL.

1998-99

Rocester	38	25	7	6	80	36	82
Kings Norton Town	38	25	5	8	65	29	80
Oldbury United	38	19	9	10	67	42	66
Boldmere St. Michaels	38	19	8	11	56	49	65
Barwell	38	17	10	11	69	54	61
Halesowen Harriers	38	17	8	13	65	63	59
Rushall Olympic	38	16	10	12	57	44	58
Shifnal Town	38	16	8	14	59	60	56
West Midlands Police	38	15	10	13	50	52	55
Chasetown	38	12	17	9	48	38	53
Bridgnorth Town	38	14	11	13	44	40	53
Stourport Swifts	38	13	11	14	56	50	50
Knypersley Victoria	38	13	8	17	59	61	47
Willenhall Town	38	13	8	17	51	53	47
Wednesfield	38	12	6	20	63	72	42
Pelsall Villa	38	11	7	20	41	67	40
Stapenhill	38	11	5	22	51	82	38
Sandwell Borough	38	10	7	21	37	65	37
Pershore Town	38	8	11	19	47	64	35
Stratford Town	38	7	8	23	39	83	29

Rocester were promoted to the Southern League, being replaced by relegated Bloxwich Town. Cradley Town were promoted from the WMRL and Oadby Town were promoted from the Leicestershire Senior League.

The League was increased to 22 clubs.

1999-2000

Oadby Town	42	27	7	8	107	48	88
Stratford Town	42	22	12	8	73	47	78
Willenhall Town	42	20	13	9	77	42	73
Wednesfield	42	21	9	12	71	56	72
Boldmere St. Michaels	42	20	12	10	61	48	72
Stourport Swifts	42	19	13	10	73	57	70
Rushall Olympic	42	20	9	13	75	65	69
Shifnal Town	42	17	16	9	66	50	67
Barwell	42	18	12	12	85	57	66
Oldbury United	42	17	13	12	62	45	64
Chasetown	42	18	7	17	61	62	61
Knypersley Victoria	42	17	10	15	75	71	61
West Midlands Police	42	15	8	19	62	71	53
Bridgnorth Town	42	15	7	20	70	72	52
Halesowen Harriers	42	14	8	20	63	71	50
Sandwell Borough	42	12	13	17	53	69	49
Bloxwich Town	42	11	13	18	57	84	46
Kings Norton Town	42	9	16	17	60	68	43
Cradley Town	42	10	12	20	56	87	42
Pelsall Villa	42	9	10	23	57	88	37
Stapenhill	42	8	6	28	42	91	30
Pershore Town	*42*	*7*	*6*	*29*	*46*	*103*	*27*

Kings Norton Town disbanded and Pershore Town were relegated to the Midland Combination. These two were replaced by Stourbridge who were relegated from the Southern League and Stafford Town who were promoted from the WMRL.

Midland Football Alliance 2000-2004

2000-01

Team	P	W	D	L	F	A	Pts
Stourport Swifts	42	28	9	5	109	38	93
Rushall Olympic	42	28	9	5	98	28	93
Barwell	42	26	11	5	74	35	89
Oadby Town	42	26	7	9	89	45	82
Stourbridge	42	23	10	9	93	52	79
Stratford Town	42	20	10	12	96	58	70
Boldmere St. Michaels	42	19	13	10	73	49	70
Willenhall Town	42	19	8	15	76	62	65
Bridgnorth Town	42	17	8	17	79	66	59
Chasetown	42	15	10	17	55	78	55
Oldbury United	42	14	11	17	70	71	53
Cradley Town	42	15	4	23	52	80	49
Stafford Town	42	12	12	18	68	83	48
Bloxwich Town	42	14	6	22	54	80	48
Wednesfield	42	14	6	22	60	91	48
Shifnal Town	42	12	11	19	56	75	47
Halesowen Harriers	42	13	7	22	55	73	46
Stapenhill	42	12	8	22	58	91	44
Pelsall Villa	42	12	6	24	60	90	42
Knypersley Victoria	42	10	10	22	64	100	37
West Midlands Police	42	9	7	26	67	112	34
Sandwell Borough	42	9	7	26	62	111	34

Knypersley Victoria and Oadby Town each had 3 points deducted. Bloxwich Town merged with Blakenall of the Southern League and the merged club continued playing in the Southern League as Bloxwich United. Sandwell Borough disbanded. Stourport Swifts were promoted to the Southern League being replaced by two relegated clubs, Bromsgrove Rovers and Paget Rangers. West Midlands Police were relegated to the Midland Combination being replaced by promoted Studley BKL. Ludlow Town were promoted from the WMRL and Quorn were promoted from the Leicestershire Senior League.

The League was increased to 23 clubs.

2001-02

Team	P	W	D	L	F	A	Pts
Stourbridge	42	27	7	8	82	39	88
Bromsgrove Rovers	42	26	9	7	94	41	87
Wednesfield	42	24	9	9	73	39	81
Stratford Town	42	24	7	11	81	49	79
Rushall Olympic	42	22	11	9	81	50	77
Oadby Town	42	21	12	9	78	62	75
Quorn	42	20	10	12	76	55	70
Barwell	42	15	17	10	67	44	62
Studley BKL	42	16	12	14	76	57	60
Ludlow Town	42	15	14	13	58	53	59
Bridgnorth Town	42	18	5	19	74	73	59
Willenhall Town	42	16	9	17	65	62	57
Boldmere St. Michaels	42	15	11	16	43	51	56
Halesowen Harriers	42	16	8	18	56	69	56
Paget Rangers	42	10	19	13	58	55	49
Stafford Town	42	13	6	23	59	88	45
Pelsall Villa	42	10	12	20	39	70	42
Chasetown	42	9	13	20	43	74	40
Shifnal Town	42	9	10	23	36	77	37
Knypersley Victoria	42	10	5	27	51	82	35
Oldbury United	42	7	11	24	39	77	32
Cradley Town	42	5	11	26	36	98	26

Stapenhill withdrew during the season and their record was expunged. Bromsgrove Rovers were promoted to the Southern League and Paget Rangers disbanded. Causeway United were promoted from the WMRL and Grosvenor Park were promoted from the Midland Combination. Knypersley Victoria changed their name to Biddulph Victoria. Studley BKL changed their name to Studley.

The League was reduced to 22 clubs.

2002-03

Team	P	W	D	L	F	A	Pts
Stourbridge	42	31	8	3	96	27	101
Rushall Olympic	42	31	6	5	94	37	99
Stratford Town	42	29	6	7	105	38	93
Oadby Town	42	26	7	9	87	52	85
Quorn	42	25	9	8	115	55	84
Willenhall Town	42	23	10	9	91	47	79
Studley	42	24	6	12	97	58	78
Oldbury United	42	22	7	13	88	58	73
Chasetown	42	20	8	14	79	64	68
Grosvenor Park	42	19	10	13	81	58	67
Causeway United	42	18	5	19	70	73	59
Barwell	42	17	7	18	70	68	58
Biddulph Victoria	42	17	6	19	51	69	57
Boldmere St. Michaels	42	16	5	21	59	63	53
Ludlow Town	42	12	8	22	63	76	44
Bridgnorth Town	42	11	9	22	48	79	42
Stafford Town	42	11	8	23	61	93	41
Pelsall Villa	42	10	11	21	64	97	41
Cradley Town	42	8	7	27	43	87	31
Shifnal Town	42	6	7	29	43	93	25
Halesowen Harriers	42	4	6	32	44	107	18
Wednesfield	42	4	0	38	19	169	12

Halesowen Harriers disbanded. Shifnal Town were relegated to the Midland Combination being replaced by promoted Alvechurch. Wednesfield were relegated to the WMRL being replaced by promoted Westfields. Racing Club Warwick and Rocester both joined after relegation from the Southern League and Coalville Town were promoted from the Leicestershire Senior League.

The League was increased to 24 clubs.

2003-04

Team	P	W	D	L	F	A	Pts
Rocester	46	28	12	6	96	45	96
Willenhall Town	46	27	13	6	114	49	94
Stratford Town	46	28	8	10	89	45	92
Quorn	46	26	12	8	84	47	90
Studley	46	26	7	13	96	52	85
Oadby Town	46	23	8	15	90	56	77
Chasetown	46	22	11	13	68	50	77
Coalville Town	46	20	12	14	87	61	72
Stourbridge	46	19	15	12	74	52	72
Bridgnorth Town	46	20	12	14	76	66	72
Oldbury United	46	19	14	13	72	55	71
Racing Club Warwick	46	20	9	17	64	63	69
Westfields	46	20	6	20	67	61	66
Rushall Olympic	46	15	16	15	58	55	61
Boldmere St. Michaels	46	17	9	20	76	73	60
Biddulph Victoria	46	16	12	18	66	74	60
Causeway United	46	15	11	20	66	82	56
Barwell	46	15	9	22	63	75	54
Alvechurch	46	12	14	20	67	87	50
Ludlow Town	46	12	11	23	56	84	47
Grosvenor Park	46	9	9	28	53	79	36
Cradley Town	46	8	12	26	60	92	36
Pelsall Villa	46	7	7	32	46	132	28
Stafford Town	46	1	5	40	27	176	8

Rocester and Willenhall Town were promoted to the Northern Premier League and Grosvenor Park moved to Sunday football. Pelsall Villa and Stafford Town were both relegated to the WMRL from where Malvern Town were promoted. Loughborough Dynamo were promoted from the Leicestershire Senior League and Romulus were promoted from the Midland Combination.

The League was reduced to 22 clubs.

2004-05

Rushall Olympic	42	27	7	8	88	44	88
Chasetown	42	25	6	11	78	45	81
Coalville Town	42	22	11	9	68	38	77
Quorn	42	21	11	10	78	52	74
Malvern Town	42	21	9	12	78	70	72
Westfields	42	18	13	11	61	48	67
Oadby Town	42	18	11	13	64	53	65
Stourbridge	42	19	7	16	85	65	64
Racing Club Warwick	42	19	7	16	79	68	64
Boldmere St. Michaels	42	19	7	16	79	70	64
Stratford Town	42	20	4	18	71	67	64
Romulus	42	17	11	14	74	66	62
Barwell	42	17	10	15	60	60	61
Loughborough Dynamo	42	16	6	20	69	83	54
Alvechurch	42	16	5	21	75	69	53
Causeway United	42	12	9	21	53	68	45
Oldbury United	42	13	8	21	70	90	44
Studley	42	11	11	20	55	76	44
Cradley Town	42	12	7	23	59	84	43
Biddulph Victoria	42	10	11	21	59	83	41
Ludlow Town	42	12	5	25	55	84	41
Bridgnorth Town	42	7	4	31	38	113	25

Oldbury United had 3 points deducted.

Rushall Olympic were promoted to the Southern League and Rocester joined after relegation from the Northern Premier League. Ludlow Town were relegated to the WMRL from where Tipton Town were promoted. Bridgnorth Town were relegated to the Midland Combination from where Leamington were promoted.

2005-06

Chasetown	42	29	7	6	74	32	94
Stourbridge	42	29	5	8	110	55	92
Malvern Town	42	27	4	11	95	56	85
Romulus	42	23	11	8	84	49	80
Leamington	42	21	11	10	79	44	74
Racing Club Warwick	42	22	7	13	72	55	73
Quorn	42	21	6	15	71	51	69
Coalville Town	42	21	6	15	63	60	69
Barwell	42	20	8	14	83	66	68
Boldmere St. Michaels	42	17	12	13	60	48	63
Tipton Town	42	15	13	14	74	69	58
Oldbury United	42	16	10	16	58	58	58
Loughborough Dynamo	42	16	8	18	53	53	56
Alvechurch	42	16	7	19	59	64	55
Stratford Town	42	15	6	21	49	55	51
Studley	42	14	7	21	54	81	49
Biddulph Victoria	42	12	9	21	55	83	45
Oadby Town	42	10	14	18	50	64	44
Causeway United	42	9	7	26	49	89	34
Westfields	42	8	9	25	48	88	33
Cradley Town	42	5	9	28	38	94	24
Rocester	42	4	8	30	36	100	20

Chasetown, Stourbridge and Malvern Town were all promoted to the Southern League. Market Drayton Town were promoted from the WMRL, Atherstone Town were promoted from the Midland Combination and Friar Lane & Epworth were promoted from the Leicestershire Senior League.

2006-07

Leamington	42	33	4	5	105	36	103
Romulus	42	25	11	6	102	47	86
Quorn	42	25	7	10	82	40	82
Stratford Town	42	25	7	10	81	47	82
Tipton Town	42	22	8	12	71	48	74
Barwell	42	22	5	15	88	68	71
Boldmere St. Michaels	42	20	6	16	73	56	66
Atherstone Town	42	16	16	10	71	50	64
Loughborough Dynamo	42	19	7	16	73	70	64
Alvechurch	42	17	12	13	66	57	63
Oadby Town	42	19	5	18	68	59	62
Rocester	42	16	7	19	45	66	55
Market Drayton Town	42	14	11	17	61	62	53
Oldbury United	42	13	13	16	48	57	51
Friar Lane & Epworth	42	12	12	18	66	86	48
Westfields	42	13	9	20	57	78	48
Causeway United	42	14	5	23	63	72	47
Coalville Town	42	15	2	25	51	83	47
Racing Club Warwick	42	10	8	24	57	88	38
Studley	42	11	5	26	55	86	38
Biddulph Victoria	42	10	8	24	51	84	38
Cradley Town	42	4	6	32	35	129	18

Oldbury United had 1 point deducted.

Leamington and Romulus were both promoted to the Southern League and Quorn were promoted to the Northern Premier League. Shifnal Town were promoted from the WMRL, Stapenhill were promoted from the Leicestershire Senior League and Coventry Sphinx were promoted from the Midland Combination.

2007-08

Atherstone Town	42	25	11	6	94	36	86
Loughborough Dynamo	42	25	10	7	90	47	85
Market Drayton Town	42	25	7	10	96	54	82
Boldmere St. Michaels	42	20	11	11	75	49	71
Rocester	42	18	13	11	77	72	67
Causeway United	42	18	12	12	59	42	66
Stratford Town	42	17	12	13	88	63	63
Coalville Town	42	18	7	17	64	56	61
Tipton Town	42	19	4	19	58	63	61
Barwell	42	16	12	14	61	60	60
Westfields	42	17	8	17	66	56	59
Biddulph Victoria	42	17	8	17	65	65	59
Studley	42	17	8	17	58	73	59
Alvechurch	42	17	7	18	68	68	58
Shifnal Town	42	15	11	16	64	64	56
Friar Lane & Epworth	42	15	11	16	72	77	56
Oadby Town	42	14	9	19	71	68	51
Racing Club Warwick	42	14	8	20	65	82	50
Coventry Sphinx	42	14	3	25	62	97	45
Stapenhill	42	8	11	23	53	97	35
Oldbury United	42	7	12	23	48	71	32
Cradley Town	42	6	5	31	31	125	23

Oldbury United had 1 point deducted.

Loughborough Dynamo were promoted to the Northern Premier League and Atherstone Town were promoted to the Southern League. Bridgnorth Town were promoted from the WMRL and Coleshill Town and Highgate United were both promoted from the Midland Combination. Stapenhill closed down after a fire destroyed their ground. They reformed and joined the Leicestershire Senior League in 2009.

Midland Football Alliance 2008-2012

2008-09

Team	P	W	D	L	F	A	Pts
Market Drayton Town	42	31	6	5	111	31	99
Barwell	42	27	10	5	91	36	91
Coalville Town	42	25	7	10	88	51	82
Boldmere St. Michaels	42	25	6	11	98	54	81
Tipton Town	42	23	9	10	82	44	78
Stratford Town	42	21	11	10	92	65	74
Coventry Sphinx	42	23	5	14	96	78	74
Shifnal Town	42	20	10	12	73	56	67
Causeway United	42	19	7	16	62	47	64
Alvechurch	42	16	15	11	73	55	63
Coleshill Town	42	18	9	15	70	59	63
Bridgnorth Town	42	17	8	17	76	85	59
Highgate United	42	15	9	18	67	75	54
Studley	42	15	6	21	55	77	51
Friar Lane & Epworth	42	14	9	19	70	96	51
Cradley Town	42	14	8	20	69	81	50
Westfields	42	13	10	19	75	79	49
Biddulph Victoria	42	12	8	22	57	102	44
Oadby Town	42	9	10	23	43	73	37
Rocester	42	8	9	25	49	88	33
Racing Club Warwick	42	4	6	32	31	131	18
Oldbury United	42	1	6	35	33	98	8

Oldbury United had 1 point deducted.
Shifnal Town had 3 points deducted.
Market Drayton Town were promoted to the Northern Premier League.
Racing Club Warwick were relegated to the Midland Combination and Oldbury United disbanded. Kirby Muxloe were promoted from the East Midlands Counties League and Loughborough University were promoted from the Midland Combination. Malvern Town joined following relegation from the Southern League.

2009-10

Team	P	W	D	L	F	A	Pts
Barwell	42	36	6	0	125	18	114
Coalville Town	42	31	3	8	106	43	96
Stratford Town	42	26	4	12	89	50	82
Tipton Town	42	23	13	6	65	28	82
Westfields	42	23	7	12	82	55	76
Boldmere St. Michaels	42	21	7	14	78	51	70
Alvechurch	42	19	9	14	86	64	66
Coleshill Town	41	18	9	14	77	55	63
Coventry Sphinx	42	18	8	16	89	69	62
Kirby Muxloe	42	17	11	14	81	62	62
Studley	42	18	8	16	63	62	62
Causeway United	42	17	8	17	61	54	59
Loughborough University	42	16	9	17	51	48	57
Oadby Town	42	16	7	19	70	77	55
Friar Lane & Epworth	41	15	5	21	75	90	50
Rocester	42	14	6	22	63	79	48
Biddulph Victoria	42	12	12	18	56	76	48
Highgate United	42	11	8	23	57	95	41
Malvern Town	42	9	8	25	64	96	35
Bridgnorth Town	42	9	7	26	42	93	34
Shifnal Town	42	7	8	27	39	105	29
Cradley Town	42	0	7	35	29	178	7

Friar Lane & Epworth vs Coleshill Town was not played.
Barwell were promoted to the Northern Premier League from where Willenhall Town were relegated. Cradley Town and Shifnal Town were both relegated to the WMRL from where Ellesmere Rangers were promoted. Heath Hayes were promoted from the Midland Combination and Dunkirk were promoted from the East Midlands Counties League.

2010-11

Team	P	W	D	L	F	A	Pts
Coalville Town	44	32	4	8	153	53	100
Tipton Town	44	31	7	6	101	32	100
Boldmere St. Michaels	44	26	10	8	86	33	88
Loughborough University	44	27	7	10	77	36	88
Stratford Town	44	26	8	10	92	48	86
Westfields	44	24	13	7	102	54	85
Studley	44	25	10	9	81	49	85
Dunkirk	44	25	9	10	104	67	84
Kirby Muxloe	44	25	7	12	89	58	82
Causeway United	44	26	2	16	85	59	80
Heath Hayes	44	20	11	13	84	83	71
Coleshill Town	44	18	11	15	67	55	65
Ellesmere Rangers	44	16	9	19	79	73	57
Rocester	44	16	5	23	57	73	53
Bridgnorth Town	44	14	6	24	61	84	48
Coventry Sphinx	44	12	9	23	66	75	45
Biddulph Victoria	44	12	6	26	63	81	42
Highgate United	44	10	9	25	59	104	39
Friar Lane & Epworth	44	10	3	31	69	117	33
Alvechurch	44	8	7	29	47	119	31
Willenhall Town	44	8	6	30	63	149	29
Oadby Town	44	5	7	32	55	129	22
Malvern Town	44	4	6	34	38	147	18

Willenhall Town had 1 point deducted.
Coalville Town were promoted to the Northern Premier League and Atherstone Town joined after relegation from the Southern League. Malvern Town were relegated to the WMRL from where Tividale were promoted. Oadby Town were relegated to the East Midlands Counties League from where Gresley were promoted while Heather St. Johns were promoted from the Midland Combination. Friar Lane & Epworth moved to the Leicestershire Senior League while Biddulph Victoria changed their name to Biddulph Town and moved to the Staffordshire County Senior League.

2011-12

Team	P	W	D	L	F	A	Pts
Gresley	42	27	8	7	96	56	89
Westfields	42	27	6	9	93	49	87
Coventry Sphinx	42	26	7	9	74	44	85
Tividale	42	21	9	12	81	56	72
Loughborough University	42	20	9	13	94	56	69
Rocester	42	20	7	15	77	58	67
Causeway United	42	17	15	10	74	56	66
Stratford Town	42	19	8	15	79	55	64
Tipton Town	42	18	10	14	73	63	64
Bridgnorth Town	42	17	11	14	59	56	62
Kirby Muxloe	42	16	12	14	75	68	60
Boldmere St. Michaels	42	14	12	16	58	61	54
Alvechurch	42	14	9	19	58	67	51
Heath Hayes	42	14	9	19	76	90	51
Ellesmere Rangers	42	13	11	18	49	65	50
Coleshill Town	42	14	8	20	55	73	50
Studley	42	16	6	20	78	82	48
Dunkirk	42	14	6	22	59	87	48
Heather St. Johns	42	13	8	21	56	73	47
Highgate United	42	12	8	22	60	77	44
Atherstone Town	42	11	9	22	48	78	42
Willenhall Town	42	3	4	35	43	145	13

Stratford Town had 1 point deducted.
Studley had 6 points deducted.
Gresley were promoted to the Northern Premier League and Stourport Swifts were relegated from the Southern League. Willenhall Town were relegated to the WMRL from where Gornal Athletic were promoted. Atherstone Town were relegated to the Midland Combination from where Continental Star were promoted.

2012-13

Team	P	W	D	L	F	A	Pts
Stratford Town	42	28	7	7	106	46	91
Westfields	42	28	6	8	103	52	90
Gornal Athletic	42	25	11	6	86	58	86
Loughborough University	42	23	6	13	89	39	75
Stourport Swifts	42	21	10	11	89	47	73
Tipton Town	42	21	9	12	91	65	72
Bridgnorth Town	42	19	10	13	62	54	67
Tividale	42	20	6	16	81	69	66
Boldmere St. Michaels	42	19	6	17	77	74	63
Dunkirk	42	18	8	16	69	69	62
Alvechurch	42	18	8	16	70	75	62
Kirby Muxloe	42	15	8	19	60	74	53
Rocester	42	13	13	16	66	66	52
Coventry Sphinx	42	15	5	22	47	68	50
Coleshill Town	42	13	8	21	52	69	47
Continental Star	42	13	7	22	57	78	46
Causeway United	42	11	11	20	52	67	44
Heath Hayes	42	12	7	23	64	111	43
Highgate United	42	11	9	22	65	100	42
Heather St. Johns	42	11	7	24	49	83	40
Studley	42	9	11	22	51	84	38
Ellesmere Rangers	42	8	9	25	52	90	33

Stratford Town were promoted to the Southern League. Studley were relegated to the Midland Combination from where Walsall Wood were promoted. Ellesmere Rangers were relegated to the WMRL from where AFC Wulfrunians were promoted. Quorn and Shepshed Dynamo both joined from the United Counties League and Bridgnorth Town disbanded.

2013-14

Team	P	W	D	L	F	A	Pts
Tividale	42	28	11	3	86	34	95
Boldmere St. Michaels	42	25	8	9	94	55	83
Highgate United	42	23	10	9	96	60	79
Coleshill Town	42	23	9	10	94	47	78
Quorn	42	23	8	11	91	48	77
Walsall Wood	42	20	11	11	70	43	71
Coventry Sphinx	42	19	10	13	77	73	67
AFC Wulfrunians	42	18	11	13	89	76	65
Causeway United	42	19	7	16	88	75	64
Stourport Swifts	42	18	9	15	72	61	63
Tipton Town	42	17	12	13	80	70	63
Westfields	42	17	10	15	84	70	61
Alvechurch	42	17	7	18	68	72	58
Kirby Muxloe	42	16	8	18	64	70	56
Loughborough University	42	14	10	18	82	86	52
Shepshed Dynamo	42	12	9	21	73	82	45
Continental Star	42	12	4	26	59	99	40
Heath Hayes	42	9	11	22	54	92	38
Dunkirk	42	9	9	24	56	99	36
Rocester	42	7	9	26	43	95	30
Heather St. Johns	42	7	9	26	56	116	30
Gornal Athletic	42	8	10	24	53	106	20

Gornal Athletic had 14 points deducted.

At the end of the season, the Midland Alliance merged with the Midland Combination to form the Midland League. Of the 22 clubs who were members of the Midland Alliance in 2013-14, 18 became founder members of the new Midland League – Premier Division. The 4 exceptions were Heather St. Johns and Highgate United who were both placed in Division One of the Midland League, Tividale who were promoted to the Northern Premier League and Gornal Athletic who were relegated to the WMRL. The Midland Alliance then closed down.

MIDLAND LEAGUE 2014-2019

The Midland League was formed in 2014 by a merger of the Midland Combination (founded 1927) and the Midland Alliance (founded 1994). In essence, Midland Alliance clubs formed the Premier Division of the Midland League while the Premier, Division One and Division Two clubs of the Midland Combination formed Divisions One, Two and Three respectively of the Midland League.

In the 2014-15 season, the 22-club Midland League Premier Division included 18 clubs from the Midland Alliance: AFC Wulfrunians, Alvechurch, Boldmere St. Michaels, Causeway United, Coleshill Town, Continental Star, Coventry Sphinx, Dunkirk, Heath Hayes, Kirby Muxloe, Loughborough University, Quorn, Rocester, Shepshed Dynamo, Stourport Swifts, Tipton Town, Walsall Wood and Westfields. The other 4 were Basford United and Long Eaton United (both from the Northern Counties East League – Premier Division), Brocton (from the Midland Combination – Premier Division) and Lye Town (from the West Midlands Regional League).

There were 20 clubs in Division One, 15 of which came from the Midland Combination – Premier Division: Alvis Sporting Club, Atherstone Town, Bolehall Swifts, Bromsgrove Sporting, Coventry Copsewood, Lichfield City, Littleton, Nuneaton Griff, Pelsall Villa, Pershore Town, Pilkington XXX, Racing Club Warwick, Southam United, Stafford Town and Studley. The other 5 were Heather St. Johns and Highgate United (both from the Midland Alliance), Cadbury Athletic (from the Midland Combination – Division One), Hinckley AFC (one of two newly formed clubs in Hinckley following the disbanding of Hinckley United of the Southern League) and Uttoxeter Town (from the Staffordshire County Senior League).

There were 16 clubs in Division Two, 11 of which came from the Midland Combination Division One: Aston, Barnt Green Spartak, Chelmsley Town, Coton Green, Droitwich Spa, Fairfield Villa, FC Glades Sporting, Feckenham, Hampton, Knowle and Sutton United. The other 5 were Coventry United, Kenilworth Town KH and Paget Rangers (all from the Midland Combination – Division Two), Earlswood

Midland League 2014-2015

Town (from the Midland Combination – Premier Division) and Leicester Road (the second of two newly formed clubs in Hinckley following the disbanding of Hinckley United of the Southern League).

There were 15 clubs in Division Three, 12 of which came from the Midland Combination – Division Two: Alcester Town, Austrey Rangers, Badsey Rangers, Barton United, Burntwood Town, Enville Athletic, FC Stratford, Inkberrow, Leamington Hibernian, Northfield Town, Perrywood and Rostance Edwards. The other 3 were Boldmere Sports & Social (from the Birmingham AFA), Smithswood Firs (also from the Birmingham AFA, having changed their name from Smithswood Colts) and Redditch Borough (previously playing in youth football).

MIDLAND LEAGUE
2014-15
Premier Division

Basford United	42	31	2	9	127	51	95
Coleshill Town	42	28	5	9	114	47	89
Long Eaton United	42	23	11	8	78	48	80
Walsall Wood	42	24	7	11	63	38	79
Kirby Muxloe	42	23	7	12	88	60	76
Lye Town	42	22	6	14	88	59	72
AFC Wulfrunians	42	21	6	15	70	57	69
Westfields	42	19	10	13	78	66	67
Boldmere St. Michaels	42	19	9	14	69	64	66
Stourport Swifts	42	17	11	14	60	50	62
Quorn	42	18	8	16	71	62	62
Rocester	42	17	4	21	59	93	55
Brocton	42	13	12	17	73	84	51
Causeway United	42	15	5	22	57	83	50
Alvechurch	42	12	12	18	52	63	48
Shepshed Dynamo	42	12	9	21	73	82	45
Continental Star	42	14	6	22	69	91	45
Coventry Sphinx	42	12	10	20	76	84	43
Dunkirk	42	12	6	24	52	90	42
Loughborough University	42	9	9	24	70	98	36
Tipton Town	42	9	7	26	55	103	34
Heath Hayes	**42**	**6**	**10**	**26**	**43**	**112**	**28**

Continental Star and Coventry Sphinx each had 3 points deducted.
Basford United moved to the Northern Premier League, Kirby Muxloe moved to the United Counties League, Tipton Town moved to the West Midlands Regional League and Causeway United disbanded. Sporting Khalsa joined from the West Midlands Regional League, Heanor Town joined from the Northern Counties East League, Bardon Hill joined from the East Midlands Counties League and Hereford joined as a newly formed club following the disbanding of Hereford United in December 2014.

Division One

Highgate United	**38**	**28**	**5**	**5**	**113**	**42**	**89**
Bromsgrove Sporting	38	27	5	6	121	41	86
Hinckley AFC	38	23	7	8	106	53	76
Bolehall Swifts	38	23	7	8	103	50	76
Uttoxeter Town	38	22	6	10	87	51	72
Cadbury Athletic	38	19	8	11	80	50	65
Southam United	38	20	3	15	71	69	63
Coventry Copsewood	38	17	10	11	83	55	60
Littleton	38	17	4	17	77	60	55
Studley	38	15	7	16	68	86	52
Pershore Town	38	15	6	17	51	61	51
Lichfield City	38	14	8	16	63	67	50
Atherstone Town	38	14	4	20	77	92	46
Stafford Town	38	13	7	18	74	93	46
Pilkington XXX	38	13	5	20	74	75	44
Heather St. Johns	38	12	7	19	63	85	43
Nuneaton Griff	38	11	8	19	66	79	41
Racing Club Warwick	38	10	4	24	52	102	34
Pelsall Villa	38	4	5	29	35	162	17
Alvis Sporting Club	**38**	**4**	**2**	**32**	**32**	**123**	**14**

Coventry Copsewood had 1 point deducted.
Uttoxeter Town moved to the Staffordshire County Senior League.

Division Two

Coventry United	**30**	**22**	**4**	**4**	**97**	**40**	**70**
Leicester Road	30	15	10	5	78	34	55
Fairfield Villa	30	17	4	9	83	61	55
Barnt Green Spartak	30	15	6	9	55	45	51
Sutton United	30	13	9	8	72	52	48
Chelmsley Town	30	13	7	10	60	54	46
Hampton	30	13	7	10	54	50	46
Droitwich Spa	30	15	1	14	64	66	46
Earlswood Town	30	12	9	9	49	57	45
Aston	30	12	8	10	59	47	44
Paget Rangers	30	12	6	12	52	38	42
Knowle	30	9	7	14	63	57	34
Feckenham	30	9	5	16	53	64	32
FC Glades Sporting	30	8	10	12	43	62	31
Kenilworth Town KH	30	5	4	21	39	114	16
Coton Green	30	1	1	28	24	104	4

FC Glades Sporting and Kenilworth Town KH each had 3 points deducted.
Aston moved to the Birmingham & District League (formerly called the Birmingham AFA) while FC Glades Sporting and Kenilworth Town KH also both left the league.

Division Three

Austrey Rangers	**28**	**21**	**4**	**3**	**76**	**27**	**67**
Rostance Edwards	28	18	6	4	73	38	60
Alcester Town	28	16	5	7	75	38	53
Redditch Borough	28	16	2	10	70	49	50
Smithswood Firs	28	13	7	8	75	50	46
Boldmere Sports & Social	28	11	9	8	60	51	42
Inkberrow	28	11	8	9	52	47	41
Enville Athletic	28	11	5	12	58	60	38
Badsey Rangers	28	9	7	12	55	57	34
Barton United	28	10	2	16	54	77	32
Perrywood	28	8	7	13	60	67	31
FC Stratford	28	8	4	16	44	72	28
Burntwood Town	28	8	3	17	38	78	27
Leamington Hibernian	28	7	2	19	38	86	23
Northfield Town	28	5	5	18	50	81	20

Badsey Rangers moved to the Stratford Alliance. Shipston Excelsior joined from the Stratford Alliance while AFC Solihull and Coventrians also both joined. Boldmere Sports & Social changed their name to Boldmere Sports & Social Falcons.

2015-16

Premier Division

Hereford	42	35	3	4	138	33	108
Alvechurch	42	32	5	5	99	30	101
Sporting Khalsa	42	25	8	9	90	49	83
Shepshed Dynamo	42	24	5	13	86	58	77
Coleshill Town	42	23	5	14	108	73	74
Heanor Town	42	22	7	13	99	77	73
Walsall Wood	42	21	7	14	76	66	70
Lye Town	42	22	3	17	86	58	69
Highgate United	42	19	10	13	75	60	64
Stourport Swifts	42	17	8	17	57	57	59
Boldmere St. Michaels	42	18	5	19	70	81	59
Rocester	42	17	7	18	67	82	58
AFC Wulfrunians	42	16	9	17	70	74	57
Loughborough University	42	16	6	20	79	83	54
Brocton	42	15	8	19	75	88	53
Westfields	42	13	12	17	69	68	51
Quorn	42	12	9	21	71	78	45
Long Eaton United	42	12	9	21	63	85	45
Coventry Sphinx	42	12	3	27	68	98	39
Dunkirk	42	8	6	28	49	121	30
Bardon Hill	42	7	9	26	56	120	27
Continental Star	**42**	**2**	**4**	**36**	**26**	**138**	**10**

Bardon Hill and Highgate United each had 3 points deducted.
Continental Star were relegated to Division Two. Hereford moved to the Southern League, Bardon Hill moved to the Leicestershire Senior League and Dunkirk moved to the East Midlands Regional League. St. Andrews joined from the East Midlands Regional League, Shawbury United joined from the West Midlands Regional League and Tividale joined from the Northern Premier League.

Division One

Coventry United	**38**	**33**	**1**	**4**	**123**	**33**	**100**
Bromsgrove Sporting	38	29	4	5	102	41	91
Nuneaton Griff	38	27	5	6	119	41	86
Leicester Road	38	23	8	7	98	41	77
Hinckley AFC	38	23	6	9	116	53	75
Pilkington XXX	38	20	7	11	73	57	67
Lichfield City	38	19	7	12	87	60	64
Heath Hayes	38	20	4	14	57	43	64
Littleton	38	19	4	15	61	58	61
Racing Club Warwick	38	16	7	15	71	76	55
Coventry Copsewood	38	15	9	14	75	78	54
Studley	38	13	7	18	67	89	46
Atherstone Town	38	11	8	19	55	71	41
Pershore Town	38	11	5	22	51	69	38
Cadbury Athletic	38	10	4	24	48	69	34
Heather St. Johns	38	10	3	25	56	115	33
Bolehall Swifts	38	9	3	26	65	103	30
Stafford Town	38	8	3	27	46	96	27
Pelsall Villa	38	7	6	25	46	122	27
Southam United	38	4	5	29	28	129	17

Pilkington XXX moved to the Bromsgrove & District Sunday League as Pilkington Sunday. Uttoxeter Town joined from the Staffordshire County Premier League.

Division Two

Alvis Sporting Club	26	23	3	0	93	21	72
Chelmsley Town	**26**	**20**	**3**	**3**	**71**	**27**	**63**
Droitwich Spa	26	16	5	5	65	23	53
Paget Rangers	26	16	4	6	64	33	52
Rostance Edwards	26	15	2	9	44	34	47
Sutton United	26	11	1	14	50	54	34
Coton Green	26	7	7	12	33	54	28
Hampton	26	8	4	14	37	63	28
Knowle	26	6	9	11	36	49	27
Barnt Green Spartak	26	7	4	15	35	49	25
Austrey Rangers	26	5	9	12	36	53	24
Feckenham	26	6	6	14	47	74	24
Fairfield Villa	26	6	5	15	40	64	23
Earlswood Town	26	3	4	19	19	72	13

Rostance Edwards changed their name to Bloxwich Town and Austrey Rangers disbanded.

Division Three

Leamington Hibernian	**28**	**21**	**3**	**4**	**88**	**38**	**66**
Redditch Borough	**28**	**20**	**2**	**6**	**90**	**34**	**62**
Smithswood Firs	**28**	**21**	**2**	**5**	**95**	**44**	**53**
FC Stratford	28	15	4	9	73	44	49
Alcester Town	28	16	0	12	74	53	48
Barton United	28	14	6	8	56	43	48
Shipston Excelsior	28	15	1	12	59	57	46
Northfield Town	28	14	4	10	62	61	46
Inkberrow	27	12	4	11	57	61	40
Coventrians	27	9	3	15	42	53	30
Burntwood Town	28	7	6	15	40	66	27
Boldmere Sports & Social Falcons	28	8	2	18	42	60	26
Enville Athletic	27	7	3	17	40	69	24
Perrywood	27	3	6	18	37	99	15
AFC Solihull	28	2	2	24	32	105	5

Smithswood Firs had 12 points deducted.
AFC Solihull had 3 points deducted.
Two games were unplayed.
Burntwood Town and Perrywood both left the league. NKF Burbage joined from the Leicestershire Senior League, Montpellier joined as a newly formed club and Moors Academy and Castle Vale Town both also joined.

2016-17

Premier Division

Alvechurch	42	28	8	6	91	33	92
Coleshill Town	42	27	5	10	109	59	86
Sporting Khalsa	42	24	10	8	92	50	82
Lye Town	42	22	10	10	73	45	76
Westfields	42	20	10	12	98	75	70
Heanor Town	42	20	9	13	87	65	69
Highgate United	42	18	9	15	84	71	63
Coventry United	42	18	8	16	63	57	62
St. Andrews	42	18	8	16	86	88	62
Coventry Sphinx	42	16	9	17	78	79	57
Quorn	42	16	9	17	58	74	57
Boldmere St. Michaels	42	15	10	17	73	63	55
Stourport Swifts	42	14	11	17	73	83	53
Long Eaton United	42	15	8	19	74	87	53
Shepshed Dynamo	42	14	10	18	65	68	52
Rocester	42	13	13	16	71	86	52
AFC Wulfrunians	42	14	8	20	55	72	50
Loughborough University	42	11	15	16	67	66	48
Shawbury United	42	14	5	23	69	91	47
Walsall Wood	**42**	**14**	**5**	**23**	**57**	**86**	**47**
Brocton	**42**	**10**	**4**	**28**	**50**	**112**	**34**
Tividale	42	6	6	30	48	111	24

Alvechurch moved to the Northern Premier League, St. Andrews moved to the United Counties League and Tividale moved to the West Midlands Regional League. Worcester City joined from the National League – North, Rugby Town joined from the Northern Premier League, South Normanton Athletic joined from the East Midlands Counties League and Haughmond joined from the West Midlands Regional League.

Midland League 2017-2018

Division One

Team	P	W	D	L	F	A	Pts
Bromsgrove Sporting	38	33	5	0	132	23	104
Hinckley AFC	38	27	4	7	133	47	85
Leicester Road	38	25	4	9	117	36	79
Atherstone Town	38	24	5	9	99	58	77
Cadbury Athletic	38	19	13	6	78	45	70
Racing Club Warwick	38	19	9	10	92	72	66
Lichfield City	38	17	7	14	66	61	58
Heather St. Johns	38	17	4	17	67	69	55
Littleton	38	16	4	18	64	64	52
Nuneaton Griff	38	15	6	17	71	76	51
Uttoxeter Town	38	14	7	17	68	82	49
Coventry Copsewood	38	14	5	19	74	90	47
Bolehall Swifts	38	15	1	22	80	97	46
Heath Hayes	38	12	8	18	67	69	44
Studley	38	12	5	21	69	97	41
Stafford Town	38	10	9	19	69	79	39
Chelmsley Town	38	10	8	20	62	81	38
Pershore Town	38	10	8	20	48	81	38
Pelsall Villa	**38**	**9**	**7**	**22**	**53**	**99**	**34**
Southam United	38	0	5	33	12	195	5

Southam United disbanded. Ilkeston Town joined as a newly formed club after Ilkeston F.C. of the Northern Premier League disbanded.
Alvis Sporting Club changed their name to Coventry Alvis following promotion from Division Two.

Division Two

Team	P	W	D	L	F	A	Pts
Droitwich Spa	30	20	5	5	80	31	65
Paget Rangers	**30**	**20**	**4**	**6**	**93**	**40**	**64**
Alvis Sporting Club	**30**	**19**	**6**	**5**	**59**	**29**	**63**
Redditch Borough	30	20	4	6	87	30	61
Fairfield Villa	30	17	4	9	75	51	55
Knowle	30	13	8	9	60	41	47
Coton Green	30	13	8	9	56	44	47
Sutton United	30	12	5	13	62	72	40
Earlswood Town	30	11	5	14	49	53	38
Feckenham	30	9	8	13	45	64	35
Smithwick Firs	30	8	9	13	63	70	33
Barnt Green Spartak	30	9	3	18	45	80	30
Bloxwich Town	30	8	6	16	32	67	30
Hampton	30	6	5	19	33	77	23
Leamington Hibernian	**30**	**6**	**4**	**20**	**38**	**79**	**22**
Continental Star	**30**	**3**	**8**	**19**	**32**	**81**	**17**

Redditch Borough had 3 points deducted.
Sutton United had 1 point deducted.
Sutton United left the league.

Division Three

Team	P	W	D	L	F	A	Pts
NKF Burbage	**26**	**22**	**4**	**0**	**76**	**14**	**70**
Montpellier	**26**	**19**	**4**	**3**	**88**	**34**	**61**
Moors Academy	**25**	**17**	**3**	**5**	**68**	**38**	**54**
Northfield Town	**26**	**17**	**3**	**6**	**69**	**36**	**54**
Shipston Excelsior	26	12	5	9	52	53	41
FC Stratford	26	11	3	12	64	47	36
Alcester Town	26	10	5	11	34	32	35
Inkberrow	26	9	5	12	45	57	32
Coventrians	26	9	3	14	50	72	30
Barton United	25	7	7	11	43	41	28
Enville Athletic	26	8	2	16	23	50	26
AFC Solihull	26	5	3	18	30	73	18
Boldmere Sports & Social Falcons	26	4	5	17	23	63	17
Castle Vale Town	26	3	4	19	34	89	13

Barton United left the league. Birmingham Tigers and CT Shush both joined from the Birmingham & District League, Bartestree joined from the Herefordshire County League. GNP Sports joined from the Coventry Alliance and Central Ajax joined from the Stratford Alliance.

2017-18

Premier Division

Team	P	W	D	L	F	A	Pts
Bromsgrove Sporting	42	31	5	6	110	50	98
Coleshill Town	42	28	8	6	106	47	92
Highgate United	42	28	6	8	92	47	90
Worcester City	42	24	11	7	94	41	83
Sporting Khalsa	42	20	11	11	83	58	71
Rugby Town	42	19	7	16	76	60	64
Shepshed Dynamo	42	18	9	15	95	76	63
Coventry United	42	18	7	17	80	77	61
Long Eaton United	42	18	7	17	65	86	61
Coventry Sphinx	42	16	12	14	73	65	60
Quorn	42	18	6	18	77	89	60
Westfields	42	17	8	17	86	83	59
Heanor Town	42	17	7	18	67	79	58
Boldmere St. Michaels	42	15	8	19	59	75	53
Stourport Swifts	42	13	10	19	65	88	49
Lye Town	42	13	8	21	62	79	47
AFC Wulfrunians	42	14	5	23	52	88	47
Loughborough University	42	12	7	23	57	82	43
South Normanton Athletic	42	12	7	23	59	91	43
Haughmond	42	9	11	22	58	80	38
Shawbury United	42	10	7	25	59	80	34
Rocester	**42**	**5**	**7**	**30**	**65**	**119**	**22**

Shawbury United had 3 points deducted.
Bromsgrove Sporting and Coleshill Town both moved to the Southern League, Shawbury United and Haughmond both moved to the West Midlands Regional League, Rugby Town moved to the United Counties League and Heanor Town moved to the East Midlands Counties League. Romulus joined from the Northern Premier League, Wolverhampton Sporting Community joined from the West Midlands Regional League and Dunkirk joined from the East Midlands Counties League.

Division One

Team	P	W	D	L	F	A	Pts
Walsall Wood	**42**	**36**	**2**	**4**	**173**	**36**	**110**
Ilkeston Town	**42**	**30**	**5**	**7**	**107**	**46**	**95**
Atherstone Town	42	29	5	8	128	50	92
Leicester Road	42	28	6	8	99	52	90
Racing Club Warwick	42	25	6	11	112	69	81
Hinckley AFC	42	25	5	12	136	76	80
Heather St. Johns	42	25	5	12	136	81	80
Littleton	42	24	1	17	88	53	73
Studley	42	21	8	13	84	77	71
Lichfield City	42	17	7	18	81	89	58
Uttoxeter Town	42	16	8	18	87	101	56
Paget Rangers	42	16	7	19	80	85	55
Coventry Copsewood	42	16	4	22	65	91	52
Heath Hayes	42	11	11	20	90	99	44
Cadbury Athletic	42	11	11	20	66	82	44
Chelmsley Town	42	12	8	22	55	89	44
Brocton	42	11	10	21	69	87	43
Pershore Town	42	11	8	23	64	95	41
Nuneaton Griff	42	10	8	24	52	102	38
Stafford Town	42	9	3	30	52	107	30
Bolehall Swifts	**42**	**7**	**4**	**31**	**34**	**143**	**25**
Coventry Alvis	**42**	**4**	**4**	**34**	**34**	**182**	**16**

Pershore Town moved to the West Midlands League and Stafford Town moved to the Staffordshire County Senior League. Stapenhill joined from the East Midlands Counties League.

Division Two

NKF Burbage	29	25	3	1	71	17	78
Smithswood Firs	27	22	2	3	74	32	68
Droitwich Spa	29	18		9	74	45	56
Feckenham	29	15	4	10	64	54	49
Hampton	30	15	4	11	57	63	49
Montpellier	30	12	5	13	59	69	41
Fairfield Villa	30	11	7	12	52	57	40
Moors Academy	30	11	6	13	60	52	39
Barnt Green Spartak	30	11	6	13	48	57	39
Northfield Town	29	11	5	13	41	51	38
Knowle	29	11	4	14	59	59	37
Coton Green	29	8	8	13	49	51	32
Earlswood Town	29	7	6	16	43	66	27
Redditch Borough	29	7	4	18	51	62	25
Bloxwich Town	30	7	4	19	39	70	25
Pelsall Villa	23	1	6	16	21	57	9

Bloxwich Town and Pelsall Villa each had a defeat added to their records. 9 games were not played.
Pelsall Villa were expelled for failing to complete their fixtures and moved into youth football and Bloxwich Town also moved into youth football. Droitwich Spa moved to the West Midlands Regional League, Smithswood Firs disbanded and Montpellier also left the league. Lane Head joined.

Division Three

GNP Sports	30	26	2	2	144	23	80
Boldmere Sports & Social Falcons	30	21	1	8	76	46	64
FC Stratford	30	18	5	7	98	36	59
Alcester Town	30	18	5	7	84	41	59
Bartestree	30	18	1	11	88	53	55
AFC Solihull	30	14	6	10	64	56	48
Coventrians	30	15	3	12	67	62	48
Central Ajax	30	13	7	10	74	78	46
Inkberrow	30	13	6	11	74	50	45
Shipston Excelsior	30	13	4	13	63	69	43
Birmingham Tigers	30	10	5	15	58	84	35
CT Shush	30	7	9	14	42	60	30
Continental Star	30	9	2	19	49	94	28
Enville Athletic	30	6	6	18	32	59	24
Castle Vale Town	30	4	3	23	33	117	15
Leamington Hibernian	30	1	3	26	26	144	6

Continental Star had 1 point deducted.
Coventry Plumbing joined from the Coventry Alliance while AFC Church and WLV Sport also joined. CT Shush changed their name to FC Shush.

2018-19

Premier Division

Ilkeston Town	38	25	4	9	93	50	79
Walsall Wood	38	24	7	7	67	32	79
Sporting Khalsa	38	20	7	11	61	44	67
Westfields	38	17	12	9	73	48	63
Boldmere St. Michaels	38	17	8	13	65	66	59
Quorn	38	16	10	12	74	61	58
Shepshed Dynamo	38	17	6	15	68	64	57
Coventry United	38	16	8	14	52	47	56
Coventry Sphinx	38	16	8	14	61	57	56
Lye Town	38	14	10	14	65	52	52
Worcester City	38	14	10	14	66	61	52
AFC Wulfrunians	38	14	9	15	53	54	51
Stourport Swifts	38	14	9	15	53	55	51
Highgate United	38	13	12	13	49	55	51
Long Eaton United	38	14	8	16	59	61	50
South Normanton Athletic	38	13	6	19	52	48	45
Romulus	38	12	8	18	53	68	44
Loughborough University	38	10	9	19	58	79	39
Dunkirk	38	6	7	25	40	102	25
Wolverhampton Sporting Comm.	38	5	8	25	52	110	23

Loughborough University, Quorn and Shepshed Dynamo all moved to the United Counties League, Ilkeston Town moved to the Northern Premier League, Westfields moved to the Hellenic League, Dunkirk moved to the East Midlands Counties League and Wolverhampton Sporting Community moved to the West Midlands Regional League. Tividale and Haughmond both joined from the West Midlands Regional League, Newark Flowserve and Selston both joined from the East Midlands Counties League and Gresley joined from the Northern Premier League.

Division One

Heather St. Johns	36	30	3	3	135	43	93
Racing Club Warwick	36	27	4	5	119	46	85
Atherstone Town	36	26	5	5	98	33	83
Lichfield City	36	24	2	10	107	59	74
Leicester Road	35	23	3	9	91	32	72
NKF Burbage	36	18	7	11	71	56	61
Uttoxeter Town	36	17	5	14	68	56	56
Cadbury Athletic	36	15	9	12	53	50	54
Studley	35	14	9	12	63	46	51
Paget Rangers	36	14	7	15	61	66	49
Brocton	36	14	6	16	73	79	48
Chelmsley Town	36	11	6	19	59	67	39
Stapenhill	36	10	7	19	49	96	37
Rocester	36	10	5	21	49	79	35
Coventry Copsewood	36	9	8	19	51	90	35
Hinckley AFC	36	8	10	18	46	69	34
Littleton	36	6	5	25	43	94	23
Heath Hayes	36	6	4	26	30	111	22
Nuneaton Griff	36	4	5	27	33	127	17

Ashby Ivanhoe joined from the East Midlands Counties League, Kirby Muxloe joined from the United Counties League, Littleton moved to the West Midlands Regional League and Stafford Town joined from the Staffordshire County Senior League.

Division Two

Northfield Town	30	23	4	3	80	30	73
GNP Sports	30	22	4	4	97	34	70
Boldmere Sports & Social Falcons	30	21	5	4	77	34	68
Moors Academy	30	20	5	5	105	40	65
Fairfield Villa	30	17	3	10	87	65	54
Coton Green	30	15	4	11	60	56	49
Coventry Alvis	30	13	6	11	68	68	45
Knowle	30	12	6	12	69	46	42
Barnt Green Spartak	30	11	3	16	52	89	36
Lane Head	30	10	5	15	52	64	35
Feckenham	30	9	5	16	54	69	32
Redditch Borough	30	10	2	18	52	78	32
Hampton	30	8	7	15	55	92	31
FC Stratford	30	7	1	22	50	93	22
Bolehall Swifts	30	5	2	23	32	88	17
Earlswood Town	30	4	4	22	36	80	16

Moors Academy changed their name to Moor Green AFC.

Division Three

Alcester Town	30	23	5	2	104	23	71
Continental Star	30	22	2	6	109	61	68
AFC Solihull	30	20	6	4	78	42	66
Coventry Plumbing	30	19	4	7	86	45	61
Inkberrow	30	19	4	7	64	35	61
Bartestree	30	15	7	8	76	32	52
Coventrians	30	14	5	11	70	65	47
Central Ajax	30	13	5	12	73	66	44
Enville Athletic	30	13	4	13	50	57	43
WLV Sport	30	8	8	14	50	66	32
FC Shush	30	8	4	18	66	91	26
AFC Church	30	7	6	17	49	70	27
Shipston Excelsior	30	5	6	19	41	89	21
Castle Vale Town	30	6	6	18	54	127	21
Leamington Hibernian	30	4	5	21	33	81	17
Birmingham Tigers	30	5	1	24	34	87	16

Alcester Town and Castle Vale Town each had 3 points deducted.
Bartestree moved to the Herefordshire County League and AFC Church also left the league. Upton Town joined from the Cheltenham League while Sutton United and Welland also joined.